HOME WORKS

HOME WORKS

A Book of Tennessee Writers

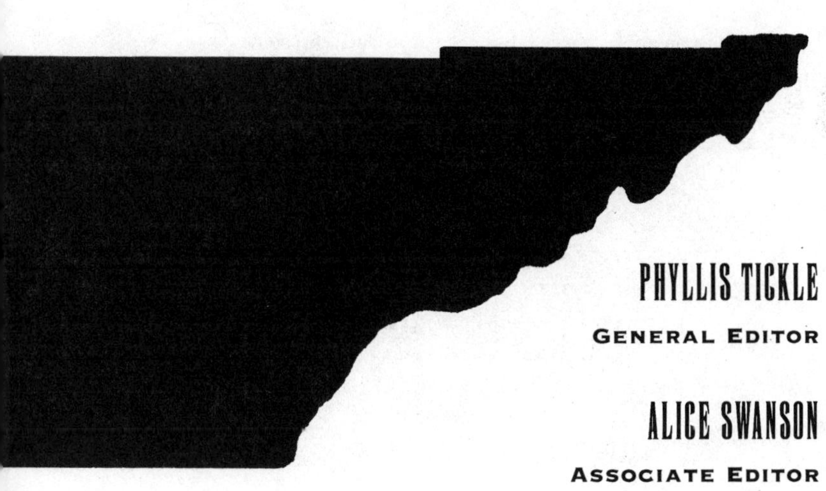

PHYLLIS TICKLE
General Editor

ALICE SWANSON
Associate Editor

Tennessee Arts Commission and
The University of Tennessee Press / Knoxville

Publication of this book was aided in part
by a grant from the Tennessee Arts Commission.

First Edition.

The paper in this book meets the minimum requirements of the
American National Standard for Permanence of Paper for Printed Library Materials.
♾ The binding materials have been chosen for strength and durability.

• • •

Library of Congress Cataloging-in-Publication Data

Homeworks : a book of Tennessee writers /
Phyllis Tickle, general editor;
Alice Swanson, associate editor. — 1st ed.
p. cm.
ISBN 0-87049-942-4 (cloth : alk. paper).
ISBN 0-87049-943-2 (pbk. : alk. paper)
1. American literature—Tennessee. 2. American literature—20th
century. 3. Tennessee—Literary collections. I. Tickle, Phyllis.
II. Swanson, Alice.
PS558.T2H65 1996
810.8'09768—dc20 95-50238
CIP

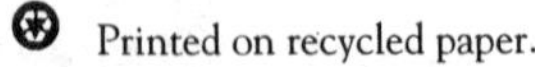
Printed on recycled paper.

CONTENTS

CONTENTS

ALPHABETICAL BY AUTHOR

EDITORS' PROLOGUE

Like surrogate mothers, we come to this completed volume aware that, while we have with affection and respect nurtured it, it is not bone of our bone or flesh of our flesh. *HomeWorks*, like its older sibling *HomeWords*, is the conceptual child of the late Douglas Paschall.

What Douglas left when he died during Christmas, 1994, was a beautifully realized *HomeWords* and an embryonic *HomeWorks*. If we—and there have been many of us not even acknowledged here—have not shaped as he would have shaped, have not tailored and disciplined according to his standards, have not envisioned and directed as his sights might have, then the fault lies not with our intent but with the impossibility of the task.

Doug Paschall's was a singularly inspired, exquisitely refined, and passionately marshaled expertise. His gifts to honest writing in Tennessee and in the wider South will be honored better by history than by us who, standing so close to him, always will lack the distance from which to comprehend the real breadth of his skills and influence. Suffice it to say here that all of us who are represented in this volume, and all of us who both overtly and covertly have shaped it, name it now as tribute to a strong, beloved, and deeply mourned leader.

Phyllis Tickle
Alice Swanson

EDITORIAL BOARD

EDITOR'S PREFACE

The people who, collectively, are this anthology have three things—perhaps only three—in common. They are all professional writers to some greater or lesser extent. That is, they all write for publication and have established audiences for their work. They all find in Tennessee and in their experiencing of Tennessee some informing constituency, some cordial context, for their work. And, thirdly, they are all still working.

The occasion for this gathering of poets, fiction writers, and essayists is twofold. It has been a decade since *HomeWords*, the last such anthologizing of Tennessee authors, was published. In the years since, that volume not only has received more than the usual amount of critical praise allotted to public projects, but also has been deeply enjoyed and broadly read. It has been and remains, in other words, a thing of pleasure as well as worth, and cordial reception always invites future visits.

Second and more immediately, Tennessee in 1996 observes its bicentennial. An event appropriately marked by bands and bright bumper stickers and flag-emblazoned coffee mugs, two hundred years of statehood want also some more studied, less transient celebration, some event that is as much predictive of the century to come as it is descriptive of the one just ending. For a state full of writers, editors, and readers, that challenge early translated into preparation for this collection.

There is no suggestion here that we who speak from these pages are the whole body of Tennessee's contemporary literature, of course. Many of our colleagues are absent for logistical reasons, some for reasons of editorial or thematic unity, and others, undoubtedly, more by accident than by design.

Unlike Lady Macbeth's guests, the writers who are collected here stand upon the order of their coming, our senior literati appearing first. In order to achieve a more euphonious balance of types and genres, however, I as editor have exercised some license in positioning our authors. While I have kept them all within the decade of their births and within the proximate company of their peers, I have not necessarily kept them always in absolute sequence within those ten-year spans. Since any discomfort occasioned by this arbitrary choosing is likely to be experienced more by the writers themselves than by our readers, it is of little concern here. What does matter, however, is a kind of overview of *HomeWorks* itself, as opposed to any extended overview of the processes by which it was generated.

It is my firm belief that most people read anthologies randomly, moving much as one does on an interactive disk, from option to option as the whim of the moment or the delights of an idle hour seduce time and the intelligence. Working from that premise, one assumes that only book critics and, presumably, the book's editors plus a very limited number of readers ever sit down to address an anthology from beginning to end, as if it were a novel or the telling of some entwining story.

An anthology is, obviously, neither sustained plot nor integrated experience; yet an anthology such as this one, based as it is upon a political and therefore by default upon a form of cultural unity, does have a threading consistency that becomes narrative. While the effect for most readers will indeed probably be achieved cumulatively rather than sequentially, there is a cascading of styles, concerns, and themes here that is a freestanding entity in and of itself and should be remarked upon.

Even the entry-surfing reader, dipping here and selecting there, will soon discover the pervasive presence of Native American influence and culture upon Tennessee's worldview. Not so much overt and politically correct as inherent and incorporated, a sense of communality with and indebtedness to the territory's first inhabitants and their living descendants runs like a river through these works.

The great war of secession that still informs so much of southern culture and so much of the literature of the Deep South is no more in these pages (perhaps for the first time in such a collection, in fact) than a leitmotif and a source for heroes. Dialect and the use of the colloquial in both structure and style are likewise most noticeable in their relative absence.

Replacing them as mode of choice is poetry—a strong, muscular, quotidian poetry that in the main has also found an audience in the world at large. Tennessee has, from the beginning, been host to and source of country music, America's most populist poetry, as well as to the more elaborated geniuses of an Allen Tate or a Robert Penn Warren. The resulting breadth of our received and acceptable tradition as poets and writers is an enrichment of opportunity and possibility that clearly is being exploited with zest in these pages.

More absent than the dialectic and colloquial, however, is the demigod of most southern literature, "a sense of place." Certainly, much of the work contained here remains rural or at least ruralized, but the shadow of the city falls closer than the shadow of any barn to the front porches and kitchens employed as backdrops and sets in these pages. Terrain and its distinguishing plant life, family possessions and community idiosyncrasies, history of house and blood-ownership of region, by and large, have given way to sly accommodation, to shared conversation as place, and to a kind of rugged but highly portable sufficiency that comes splendidly close to being hope made substantive. Put more humbly, the geography we receive as readers of this book is a temporal and an attitudinal one, full of raw-boned grace and credible expectations.

The shift in posture from regionalist to citizen of the moment is even more clearly exposed, of course, in the nonfiction writers included here; yet even in those essays and that reportage there resides the kind of dry, wise humor that is born of endurance and the secured perspective of those who know where and what home is . . . which is why, in the end, we settled upon our title, *HomeWorks*—that is, works of the heart and mind, done from and for home.

Throughout these paragraphs I have implied the presence of other editorial minds in addition to my own. It is time now in closing to render the implicit explicit. Five book professionals from across the state agreed to assume the herculean task of jurying the manuscripts for *HomeWorks*. In doing so, they gave up, among other things, the opportunity to have their own work considered for inclusion. There is not a doubt in my mind that, by their waiver, this collection was diminished in its contents just as surely as it was enriched in its concepts and integrity. To those men and women—Gary Cook, Reginald Martin, Nellie McNeil, Don Reynolds, and Maggi Vaughn—whose names will not appear again beyond this place, the thanks of all of us.

Phyllis Tickle
Lucy, Tennessee

ANDREW LYTLE

AT THE MOON'S INN

A silence came over the hall after the Marquesa was done, and Ysabel was crying. It seemed to her a pitiful thing for so great a queen to die in such a way, or die at all. She sought Hernan and their eyes met. His said: I would never leave you so. The fire had died, leaving them in shadow.

As the company rose to part for the night, he came and stood beside her. "Oh, never, never . . ." she whispered but could not finish.

She thought he had lost his voice, but at last he said, "I'll wait for you here, by the hearth." There was such a sweetness in his tones she could feel her stomach grow tight in its very well.

The duenna took her off to bed, babbling all the way to their chamber, "That poor queen, there's no pity in any man, king or varlet. His Christian wife dying and him off to the wars. They call it off to the wars. Off on three legs I call it. Even then, even while she was taking the last Sacrament, I've no doubt he was smelling around that eighteen-year-old Germaine de Foix. Well, God knows all. What's the matter with you, child? You're as white "

"Am I white?"

"As white as milk. It's your little heart grieving. Come, the Queen is done with hurting and you are in your days of grace. There's plenty of time for weeping and for rue."

The duenna talked on; she scarcely listened but made haste to get between the covers. She thought the duenna would never be done with her clothes. First she took her cap off and the skewers out of her hair. Then over her head she pulled her dress and petticoat. As she undid the band which held the hoops, rust showed upon the linen. From where Ysabel lay watching, she thought how it must always be moist under the fleshy folds about the duenna's waist. Next, she arranged her hair. The way the night cap went on displeased her. She took it off and did it over. She ate six oranges, one after the other, and threw sweet herbs on the fire. She scattered holy water about her bed. At last she said her prayers and, groaning, rose from her knees. Still she did not go to her bed. The girl despaired. Hernan would never wait, she knew. Or worse, he might come to seek her out.

The old woman walked idly about the room, opened a chest and went through the clothes. Ysabel could hear her yawn, and in a little move heavily to arrange bottles of elixirs on a table near the bed, take sips from three. Finally she blew the light, squatted on the jordan, and crawled into bed. She twisted about for a while and then grew still. She belched twice and afterwards it was everywhere quiet in the room. Very softly the duenna began to puff, then settled into loud and regular snoring.

At last she was free. She waited a little to make sure; then slipped to the floor and stood in the shivering air.

She had forgotten how long the corridor was and how dark. Through the bare glow from the hearth she saw him standing in the shadow of a tapestry. He had seen her first and whispered her name so as not to frighten her. She ran into his arms and they closed about her. If he had not held her against his leather shirt she must have fallen; and yet in their innocence they did not clasp like lovers. They held tightly together as frightened children do. She became aware of his warm breath travelling over her face. Once he called her name with his lips at her ear. He drew her behind the tapestry and threw his heavy cloak about them. As he drew its folds, everywhere that his lean fingers touched made her feel that much his. And they moved nervously along her throat, cold and moist. He lifted her face, and she looked up to take his kiss.

They sat together without words. They sat until it was very dark and the hearth a misty red. In his arms it was warm and dark. She could no more see his face, but their breaths met and crossed and his blew sweet about her face. "Tomorrow," he said, "I'll ask Don Pedro for your hand."

"Not tomorrow," she said, holding tight his hands. "Wait until he leaves. Then we'll find a way."

Hernan must have understood her fear but he replied a little coldly, "My four quarterings are noble. It is only fortune that I lack."

"Yes, I know, but wait a little."

The coat had fallen from their shoulders. Their hands were clasped so tight she could feel the bones rub together. "No," he said. "I want to hold you always mine." He was shaking her.

"You hurt," she said. Her mouth was dry and she began to tremble, for it was suddenly cold.

He pulled the cloak about her and brought her to her feet. "I want to hold you honourably," he said.

She must have understood it all, for her plea was desperate, sitting beside him in the black chill when the humours of the night are most hurtful. Naturally then she did not know what now she knew, but in the very fullness of innocent love she had glimpsed the crooked way, how beset it was. In those minutes there she might have turned him aside, but she had only her feeling to urge and it was not enough. A woman will go straight to her desire. It is the man who is devious in his house of pride.

She slept no more that night. Hollow-eyed and pale, her throat tight and dry, she presented herself before her father and mother after early morning Mass. The three of them were alone in the chapel, her father in his chair, her mother beside him. "Are you ill?' Her mother asked.

"No, Mother," she replied. "Father, Hernan has a suit to ask of you." Now that she had said it she felt more calm and assured.

"He's a worthy lad," Don Pedro answered in perplexity. "But why does he not come himself? I've always dealt generously with him."

An instant she hesitated and then spoke it out in a breath. "He is going to ask for my hand."

At first Don Pedro seemed not to understand; then his hands struck the arms of the chair. She saw the knuckles grow white. She could not bear to look at his face; it frightened her. But she knew she must say it out or do the damage she had tried to prevent.

"I love him," she said. The words seemed to go no further than her lips. She tried to concentrate and make them carry. "I will have no other for wedded lord. I will. . . ." Her throat closed in fright.

Don Pedro strained but could not rise from his seat. She felt her mother forcing her towards the door. "For God's sake, man," her mother said to the steward, "unlock the door and let us out."

Outside they stood an instant. From behind, muffled by the door, she heard the crash of the chair. They hurried away. She had scarcely reached her chamber when, below in the courtyard, there came the clatter of hoofs. She rushed to the window in time to see Don Pedro righting himself in the saddle. The horse leaped and he galloped through the open gates.

It was late when he returned. Hernan had been waiting in the yard. He ran forward and took the bridle and helped her father to dismount. The boy asked for an audience and it was granted at once. She had meant so well. She had thought if her father could see her desperation, it might soften his violence. She had no hope of his blessing. But all her fears were vague. She was as yet innocent of the cruel manner of his punishment. Don Pedro's ride seemed to have put him in fine humour. He made Hernan sit at table with him in his wardrobe, and with his most courteous and gentle manner told the boy it was not his blood—with that no house could be displeased; it was his lack of fortune, not entirely; it was rather his lack of spurs, of a bearded chin, and of a name for valour in his own right. He had a proposal: if only Hernan would follow him over the seas, the field was broad enough for fortune and for name; if he would prove himself a worthy and valiant man, then he, Pedrarias, could think of no reason to deny him. But naturally Hernan must understand that he should see no more of his daughter, just once to say farewell in the presence of the duenna; then he must be off to Seville and there take ship.

Hernan was taken so unawares that he agreed to every condition. At least so had she understood it then, but now she knew that Don Pedro had little to do to persuade him. He came to her grateful and enthusiastic. She had little heart to tell him her misgivings. Young as she was, she knew that few, through fair means or foul, ever returned from across the enchanted waters. She did what only a woman can do; she promised to wait. Half in love and half in despair she gave that promise. He vowed to return a conqueror rich in spoils before he would claim her. Both promises were kept. How well were they kept. She waited. He returned. Seventeen years of waiting for her. Seventeen years—of what for him? Sitting there before her embroidery frame in the convent, she felt the shadow of a presence, felt the needle tremble in her fingers, and looked up. There he stood with the insubstantial promise of the world upon his lips. He had not forgotten. In the moment of his triumph he had crossed the seas to lay the new world's treasure at her feet. He had made the promise to a girl of sixteen. The woman who rose to take his hand was thirty-three.

◆ ◆

ANDREW LYTLE is one of America's preeminent persons of letters. The editor of the *Sewanee Review* from 1961 to 1973, Lytle is the author of four novels, including *The Velvet Horn; The Long Night*, a biography of Nathan Bedford Forrest; and numerous essays and stories. He makes his home in Monteagle, Tennessee. [Andrew Lytle died in late 1995 while this manuscript was in process.]

SHELBY FOOTE

A Marriage Portion

This was in the middle Twenties, back before the flood. Snooky said he was coming by to pick me up a little after seven, but you know Snooky; he says one thing, then he does another. Only this time he came early. "Well, just tell him he can wait," I said, all soapy, and Buster went downstairs and told him. He told Buster, "Tell her if she's not down by seven, sharp, I'm long gone." So Buster came back up. Poor Buster: all those stairs. He was the houseboy, as you may have gathered, gray-haired, well past sixty, and though his bottom lip hung slack from feeble mindedness, he was very good at building fires, carrying messages, and such. He died two years later. I was just getting out of the tub; he had to talk through the door. "Tell him I'll do my level best," I said, and Buster went back down.

Snooky was sitting talking to Daddy; Daddy had just come in. Mother had been dead three years that month, October. He was still long-faced and of course he had those wisps of cotton all over his clothes, the way they always do that time of year. He's a cotton man. Buster stood there, dignified in his white jacket, till Daddy came to a pause in what he was saying. Then he delivered the message. "Looks like you've bout got her tamed," Daddy said, but Snooky didn't say anything; he just sat there looking determined, or anyhow his notion of determined. Buster waited to see was there any answer. When there wasn't, he went back to the kitchen with Louiza. She was his wife and she looked after him all those years until he died. You know how Negroes talk; "I slept true to that man," she used to say. All the same, she remarried within the month, a strange coal-black lantern-jawed man almost seven feet tall if he was an inch, and moved straight up to Memphis. After cooking for us for eighteen years, seven days a week, she barely took the time to say goodbye. That's how they are, that's typical; there's never been a one of them had ulcers.

When I got down at seven-twenty Snooky was downright purple in the face. He didn't say anything or even help me into my coat, just followed me out to the car. The porch light glistened on his hair, the part like a streak of white light down the middle. The car was a cut-down Essex with writing all over it, even under the fenders: *Chickens here's your coop. Fragile, handle with care. Shake well before using* - things like that. He had on his yellow slicker and there was writing on that as well: *Oh Min! This end up. Yes we have no bananas*, and so forth. I won't go into details except to say we drove up to Rosedale to a dance and didn't get home until almost four-thirty. By that time we weren't speaking. The last thing I said to him when he kissed me goodnight on the steps (he tried to put his tongue in my mouth, among other things) was, "I don't care if I never *see* you again!" I meant it, too. He left, racing the motor down the block the way he always did when he was mad.

It had happened before, more or less exactly, but this time he really scared me. He didn't call for nearly a week. Then he did and we were married in April, during a cold-snap. Our wedding night was in Jackson, at the Robert E. Lee Hotel. He had a bottle of real champagne; it was his daddy's, left over from before the war, but we couldn't get the bellboy to bring ice (there was some kind of convention going on, Baptists or something, all with their names on little squares of cardboard pinned to their lapels) so Snooky tried to cool it by holding it under the cold-water faucet in the bathroom. It fizzed all over the place when he popped the cork out. I drank almost half of it, luke warm like that, the first alcohol I ever really tasted except the sugary bottoms of Daddy's toddies when I was little, and next thing I knew I was standing under the shower, dripping wet, and all in the world I had on was a horrible nigger-pink bedspread wrapped around me and the wave had come out of my hair and I was bleeding. It was awful. What's more, Snooky didn't understand at all; he kept yelling for me to come back to bed. "Come on back to bed!" he kept yelling. He had been drinking whiskey too, and finally he stumbled into the bathroom (like a fool I was so flustered I forgot to lock the door) and tried to wrestle the spread away, the only stitch of covering I had. I was more than a match for him, though, even in my condition. He fell and bumped his head on a corner of the washstand, then sat on the cold tiles, rubbing his head and mumbling over and over, "Some wife. Some little wife. Some little wife *I* got." It was horrible, watching him squat there, naked like that, mumbling. His hair had always been smooth before, glossy as patent leather, but now it stuck out all around his head, like spikes. Then all of a sudden a solemn expression came over his face, as if he was about to pray or something, and he turned and threw up in the toilet with his chin hooked over the seat. Mind you, I had to stand there, watching, because I was afraid if I went back into the bedroom he'd recover and follow. He just kept on heaving, heaving, long after he was empty. It's no wonder I got disillusioned early.

I sometimes think I married him just to get him out of my system. Not that I didn't admire him; who wouldn't? He was so much older, twenty-four to eighteen, and such a sheik. He played the ukulele, wore wider-bottomed trousers than anyone, had a car and all those things. Also his folks had money, lots of it, and Daddy had lost our money on the market years ago. I knew if I didn't marry him I'd regret it all my life. Then too, everyone kept saying he could 'handle' me, get me 'tamed' as Daddy said. That was what I wanted, after what had happened between my parents; I wanted what my mother didn't have.

A while back I said she died but that's not true, or at least it's only true in a manner of speaking. What she did was she ran off with a man. It was an awful shock—I was terribly impressionable in my teens. It gave me an absolute horror of anything vulgar, and of course almost everything was vulgar in those days. I didn't understand at all but now I think I do. She wasn't bad. It was the times, the war being over, women doing the shimmy on dining-room tables, bobbed hair, short skirts, all that. And the truth was Daddy was lovable but dull, and not only dull but soft; he couldn't handle her at all. So I married Snooky and you know how that turned out, from the very first night in the Robert E. Lee Hotel.

He wasn't like they said. He was hard on the outside, all right, but soggy inside. I'd suspected it all along, but of course I had to find out for myself. Well, I found out soon enough. He turned to whiskey round the clock, what they call a night-drinker. His daddy sent him up to Keeley several times though it never really took. Then one afternoon I came home from playing bridge and found him in the living room with a hammer—killing flies, he said. You should have seen it, what he did to all my lovely things; the silver service from Aunt Agnes was mashed down to little wads of tin. So then I signed a paper and they put him in an institution. He didn't stay long, less than a year, but by that time I had the divorce. He soon married again; I heard she gave him a hard time, some Yankee who pronounced her final g's and all the r's. It served him right. Soon he left her and married another—a California one this time; I hear she's just as bad if not worse. Not that I care. I don't care. He can do whatever he likes, provided that check comes through on the first of every month. I gave him my youth; if we didn't have any children it wasn't my fault.

There now; I've talked about it and made myself all sad. Life *is* sad and there's no good men. Feel those tears. I guess you'd better get up now and go; I think that's daylight peeping through the shade.

◆ ◆

SHELBY FOOTE, who lives in Memphis, is the author of nine novels, including *Love in a Dry Season*, *September*, and *Jordan County*, from which our selection is taken. He is best known, however, as a historiographer of the Civil War; he was featured in Ken Burns' popular PBS series on that war.

WILL D. CAMPBELL

HERMAN'S PRESENT

Crossing the International Date Line is an exciting event. Or so we were told by an army captain who claimed to be heir to some vast New England fortune and had sailed, he said, across the Pacific Ocean on a luxury liner. But we were infantry combat replacements on a Liberty Ship—the USS MorMacwren I believe it was—bound for somewhere in the South Pacific. We weren't told where. It was December, 1943.

Most of us were still in our teens. We were seasick, homesick, a little afraid of what lay in store. And Christmas was a few days away.

"What are you going to send Sarah for Christmas?" I had asked my best pal, Herman Hyman, before we left Fort Ord, California. Herman was from the Bronx, a place as alien to me as where we were then, and to where we could soon be going.

"Nothing, " Herman replied. And that was all he replied. "Nothing?" I asked. "But you're going to marry her when the war is over. You write her every day and she writes you every day. Now you know you are going to send her something for Christmas. So what is it?"

"Nothing," Herman said again. And that was all he said.

I thought it was strange. I had already sent Brenda Fisher, my sweetheart, an eight by ten photograph of myself proudly wearing my marksman medal—the lowest M-1 rifle score one could make on the firing range and still finish the thirteen weeks of basic training, indicating that he was ready for battle. I had the picture made when Herman and I went to Monterey. Brenda had sent as my present a sterling silver bracelet engraved with Will D. Campbell, 38483013. I tried to pose for the picture so the bracelet would show but it didn't. At the PX I bought a picture frame with cardboard louvers arranged so that if you looked at the picture from an angle you saw an American flag. I had called Brenda before we shipped out and she said she liked it and it made her cry. I told Herman about that and he said that proved she loved me.

"Herman's Present," by Will D. Campbell, appeared in *The Tennessean*, Nashville, Tennessee, December 4, 1994. Reprinted with permission of *The Tennessean*.

That was when I protested again about no Christmas present for Sarah. That time he mumbled something about Hanukkah. I had no idea what he was talking about. Herman quickly changed the subject. Started talking about going overseas in a few days. I remember him joking about why it was that when a rich person, like Captain Blaine, sailed across an ocean on a luxury liner he was "going abroad," and when a poor foot soldier crossed the same ocean on a troop ship he was "going overseas." Things like that. Just evasive chat.

What had promised to be a bleak Christmas on a crowded troop ship in the middle of the Pacific Ocean turned even more dreary when the K.P. list was read from the Captain's deck on Christmas Eve.

"I'll do it for you," Herman said. He said it as soon as my name was called.

"Why?"

"Because I want to," he laughed, patting me on the head the way one might do a mascot. And in a way, that was sort of what I was, being such a runt and younger than most of the other soldiers and all. "And you can't stop me, little buddy," he went on, "because you weigh a hundred and nine pounds, and I weigh a hundred and seventy-eight, and not only that you're eighteen years old and I'm almost twenty-two."

I liked to listen to Herman talk. It wasn't the way we talked in Mississippi. I used to ask him questions I knew would take a long time to answer just to hear him.

"Now just hold on," I protested. "Man, you don't want to spend Christmas Day washing pots and pans and scrubbing decks. It's my name they called and I have to do it."

"Forget it, little buddy. Or I'll use your Rebel head for a scrub mop."

Christmas was the day we were crossing the International Date Line. That meant there would be two December twenty-fifths; two Christmases. The sergeant said that was just tough luck, that the duty roster had names for K.P. printed out before we left California and if a name was on it for December twenty-fifth and there were two December twenty-fifths there wasn't anything he could do about it.

It was late at night on the second December twenty-fifth when Herman found me standing alone on the ship's stern looking back at where we'd been. There wasn't anything else to see.

"Why'd you do that, Herman?" I asked as he handed me a can of ripe olives, my favorite delicacy, and leaned over the rail beside me. Herman had told me he would *lease* some olives from the officer's mess as my Christmas present. (Enlisted men didn't eat ripe olives on troop ships in World War II.)

"Why'd you do it?" I asked again.

He sighed deeply, shook his head in a sort of "you really don't know, do you?" fashion and said, "Because I'm a Jew, little buddy. And Jews don't celebrate Christmas."

Then he told me all about Hanukkah; about another war that had been fought almost two hundred years before my Jesus was even born; about the Maccabees whipping the Syrians, and how we were going to do the same thing when we got to wherever it was we were headed. He told me about the big celebration the Maccabees had and the rededication of the Temple of Jerusalem. Said we would have a celebration like that when we got back to the States. He said actually he had a better deal than I did because Hanukkah lasted eight days instead of one, like Christmas, and they got little presents for each day. Then I thought he was going to cry when he started talking about how his father would light a candle each night of Hanukkah. He described the dishes his mother prepared and recited the name of all his kinfolks that would gather, telling me something about each one. But he didn't cry. Just kept on telling me a lot of things I had not known before.

I was a naive eighteen year old Baptist lad from a rural community in Mississippi. There weren't any Jews there. No Catholics, Methodists or Presbyterians either. Just Baptists. But there was a Jew there when I got back. Herman died in the last days of the battle of Saipan. When the war was over and I went home to Amite County, Mississippi, Herman went with me.

Happy Hanukkah, Herman. You would be seventy-three now. I'll light the eighth candle and we'll be together still.

And tell Father Abraham it's my turn to do K.P.

• •

WILL D. CAMPBELL of Mt. Juliet—Brother Will, to most—is an ordained Southern Baptist preacher with a divinity degree from Yale and eleven books to his credit. Having served as minister and confidante to such a diverse group of friends as Waylon Jennings, Thomas Merton, and Martin Luther King, Jr., Brother Will has had a long career as an activist as well as an author. His *Brother to a Dragonfly* bears witness to both occupations, and *Forty Acres and a Goat* remains a classic of southern humor.

GEORGE SCARBROUGH

THE TRAIN

George Scarbrough

Tandem and straight we sat before
The washstand reading, my literate
Mother and I, while my unhappy father
Scoffed at us from his bed, restlessly
Turning in a room so small he could have
Reached out and torn the books from our
Hands. "A man can't sleep with the lamp
Lit," he said. "Douse it. It's late."
It was late. Eleven by the clock. We sat
On oblivious of time. "You make," he said,
"A short train with two cars," meaning
The local that ran past our house. "It'll
Get you nowhere," not knowing it had already
Carried us past all the houses he knew.

"The Train," by George Scarbrough, appeared in *The Southern Review* 28, no. 4 (Autumn 1992): 901. Reprinted by permission of the author.

Early Schooling

Retained for years,
Plagued by plagues,
I read the same book
Until I had it memorized.

My father raged at contagion,
Proclaiming his conviction
That schools were profligate places,
Disease the wage of sin.

It was the law, he declared,
That made his children sinners,
And took his gun to the truant officer,
Who left never to return.

Meanwhile, I chanted my book
Over again like a devotee
At text but failed the glory
Of office. My mind ached and dulled

And fell far behind,
Disenchanted with chanting.
Then immunity came to the hill.
Plagues were eradicated.

I could return to the cloakroom
Library with its spare shelves,
Wearing the great black blister
Of smallpox vaccination,

Indebted to modern medicine
For my first full term ever,
My father's near apoplexy,
And a new reader.

OLD TREES

Crouch in the purple grass
Of the cratered field
In the low mountaintop.
Under the misplaced willow,
By the gnarled apple,
Something will cough your name,
A whistle will come. You
Will know how familiar:
Gate twisted on its hinge,
Chain drawn through an eye.
You can hear them opening
And closing as they move,
Calling you out:
Woodnotes that impinge
On that still passionate place:
Syllables of mossy silence,
Lobe and larynx
Of once lingual ground.

GEORGE SCARBROUGH, a native of Patty Station in Polk County, Tennessee, taught school for a living and "wrote to please a need for expression." Published in the country's most prestigious journals, Scarbrough is also the author of five volumes of poetry and one novel. His most recent collection of poetry, *Invitation to Kin*, was nominated for the Pulitzer Prize in 1990.

WILMA DYKEMAN

RETURN THE INNOCENT EARTH

The day had started with a phone call from Stull.

"Jon." Not a question, not a greeting, a flat statement and assumption. He did not wait for me to answer. "Wanted you to fly down with Nat and me for the Jackson U. game tomorrow."

I resented that voice—especially at a quarter till seven on Friday morning—arranging my weekend. I did not want to traipse down south to watch the Jackson U. football squad grunt and crunch. I wanted to go to New York and be with Deborah Einemann.

Stull caught my hesitancy. He wasn't stupid. No one had ever accused Stull Clayburn of stupidity. "First game of the season. And Tech's rated the number two team in the country this year."

"Number one in the Southeast," I said, programmed to a right response.

"We'll pick you up at eight-thirty," he said.

"Hold on, Stull. I had other plans for tomorrow."

There was the briefest pause at the other end of the line. "There's something else, Jon—"

With Stull there was always something else. Most of us had learned that a long time ago—the hard way.

"What else, Stull?"

"A little problem at the Churchill plant."

"But tomorrow's Saturday. It'll be two-thirds shut down—"

"It's not that kind of a problem. You remember somebody named Burl Smelcer?"

Stull made him sound like an interchangeable part of one of the cabbage cutters. "Of course I remember Burl Smelcer," I said. "Foreman at the Riverbend Farm for twenty years. I used to pull beets and pick tomatoes on his crew when I was a boy. Two teeth,

"Return the Innocent Earth," from *Return the Innocent Earth*, by Wilma Dykeman (New York: Holt, Rinehart, and Winston, 1973; paperback reprint, Newport, Tenn.: Wakestone Books, 1994). Excerpt reprinted by permission of Wakestone Books.

eleven children, fourteen dogs."

"His wife's sick."

"Perlina." I could see Perlina Smelcer's great freckled arms bulging from the sleeves of her sweat-stained gingham dress whenever she drank from the dipper at the water bucket in the fields. In her greed for the water, rivulets ran from the sides of her mouth and fell on the red, heaving flesh of her neck, then disappeared in the depths of her bosom like a stream soaked up by desert sand dunes. Then she would grin with friendliness and satisfaction.

"Perlina her name?" Stull made it the most inconsequential knowledge since the date of invention of the yo-yo. "You haven't waked up yet have you, Jon? The Riverbend is the farm where we've been trying that new spray to delay vegetables ripening."

"Oh my god!" The chill reached up my back. "How sick is she?"

"Sick enough. Price Sims called last night. She's running a fever, vomiting, on the verge of convulsions."

"And why did Price Sims think that had anything to do with our spray?"

"Because Perlina had eaten herself a bait of greens the picking machine left behind."

"What about Burl and the children?"

"Price went into that, too. Burl was ailing and didn't eat. As for the others, none of them were home this week."

"So it's Perlina."

"Now we don't know that there's any connection at all between the new spray and her troubles," Stull said. "We don't know anything at all. You go down there just looking around, listening for a couple of days."

Why me? But I did not ask. Who else was there? Only Stull and Nat Lusk and I, of all the people who made up the midwestern home office of Clayburn-Durant, knew Churchill, had been born there, lived there, knew the way winter slipped in late or apple blooms broke through early or that a man would shoot his brother's son because of a rawboned black-and-tan foxhound.

"Jon?"

"Yes, Stull?"

"We can't mess this one up. This spray could mean the biggest break C-D has had in a long time. We can't let some old mountain woman who doesn't know a snuff stick from a chopstick ruin the whole ball game for us."

I didn't answer.

"You hear, Jon?"

"Sure, Stull. I hear."

Looking around, listening, I came to Churchill, to the offices, to the long lines of rattling cans and the noisy machinery that fed them, to the wake at Perlina Smelcer's crowded cabin, and to the farms.

In the falling part of the afternoon, as Cherokee–Ibo–Scotch Irish old Cebo used to say, I came out here to the fields. Alone. The gigantic bean pickers were just rolling out of the fields with the massive tread of dinosaurs. Where they passed the vines are strewn and crushed, the earth packed hard as asphalt.

I try to stir the dirt with the toe of my shoe. It is as unyielding as the concrete of streets I have just left. When we tended this land we were careful to keep it loose and loamy, never too wet for fear it would bake into clods, making sure it could breathe. I remember hearing about the day Elisha Clayburn, my grandfather, stood not far from where I am tonight and let the rich black dirt filter through his hands, saying, "The land outlives us all—" and within the month he was murdered. Once the Clayburns treated the land as if it were a deep, warm, fertile woman worthy of all the care they could lavish. Now the using is all.

Lightning scrawls across the sky like a match struck against the darkness. It has been a long day. The river below me is drowned in shadows. Trunks of the sycamores along the river shine like bleached skeletons in the moonlight. Starvation moon, the Cherokees who were once here called it.

I have been a company man for a long time but not so long, quite, that I have lost myself, although I learned yesterday that there is much I have buried and need to remember, for the company, for myself.

The river has made this earth I'm standing on, dragging topsoil and debris down from the uplands to enrich it for generations. And land such as this across America has made Clayburn-Durant Foods. But none of the Clayburns has been here in a long while.

My boyhood boots pulled against the suck of mud, my present British walkers have been jetted across continents. Down these muddy rows I used to drag battered crates and baskets; now my Gucci briefcase waits on the seat of the car at the edge of the field. Here the past, like all the data programmed into the company's computers, waits raw and formless. And no one remembers more of it than I do.

Blood soaked into the ground. Sweat mixed with mud and crates of tomatoes and machine grease. Tears and terror and waste, hurt too deep for scars, pure joy, gall of mistakes, the sweet balm of success, and the reach out. And out. And out.

I come from a line of remembering people. In generations past we built churches and ballads and a way of life out of our remembering, handing down words the way others pass along designs woven into coverlets, carved into wood, or worked into clay. But now that is going, too—the woven words and cloth and all.

Does anyone recall the face or form or all those anonymous figures—black and white—who gave strength and substance to the Clayburns and their dream through patient, wrenching years, lifetimes?

This is the memory I have come back to claim. My father. Shape of a world of love and honor, of word spoken as a bond given, of love-thy-neighbor-as-thyself, of something far and lost, abandoned.

I arrive at my car and climb in, turn the key with stiff fingers, turn toward town. The first drops of rain fall.

By the time I arrive at the motel the rain has settled to a steady downpour. I stop at the desk to pick up my room key and the clerk makes me welcome. Her formal greeting has been memorized from some innkeeper's manual but as I thank her she adds, "Turning cold yet? I heard thunder a little while ago. My grandpa always said autumn thunder meant a cold spell to come."

I smile at her and nod. All at once I see her. Her hair is set in beauty parlor majesty and her dress is a wholesale replica of some high-fashion design shown in a slick magazine. But the adaptation has not yet become total. It has not reached all the way inside. "My grandpa always said. . . ."

We can still remember.

And I need to remember because I must go on. Without yesterday Clayburn-Durant Foods would not be here. The question is, will any of us—on foot or hoof or wing or fin or root—be here tomorrow?

◆ ◆

WILMA DYKEMAN, one of Tennessee's preeminent writers and a professor of English at the University of Tennessee at Knoxville, is the author of seventeen books. She has been both a Guggenheim Fellow and a Senior Fellow of the National Endowment for the Humanities.

JACK FARRIS

SUMMER FLIES

"A silver dollar," papa said, "to whichever one
of you can kill more flies twixt now and summer's end."
(A stranger man I never knew, but what I wonder
still put that odd notion in his head.)

Two plaguey months to earn more wages than
eight of us had ever earned before. Odell
was six, I two years older.

Honor system, you understand. "Keep count," papa
said, as though any system so conceived could
overcome old Odell's lust for pelf.
"A dollar made dollar earned." 'Twas papa's
way to speak in platitudes; and call me "Boy,"
though he must have known my name, the same as his.

Leaving all haphazard games to Odell's hit-or-miss,
I bought on credit a swatter down at Tippin's store
and went in search of flies wherever they were apt
to congregate: to smoky compost heaps, holding my
breath against the stench—one swat, six flies,
counting them out at straw tip—the Honor System
don't you know.

At summer's end the count above five hundred, give
or take a wasp or two thrown in for measure.

By then Odell was gone, wasted away by summer sickness,
reed-thin, waving his spider arms against the heat,
mouth opening to a soundless cry.
On a day left sleeping in the cemetery down by
Keeland Creek, with Mrs. Hadlow's tuneless voice
above the grave to hallow both the ground and
grief of those who stood in rain to mourn the
passing of a cherished child.

I go there now and then, to weed the plot around
the stone, and sit and wait as dusk comes down.
And say aloud, against the ache of loss, "How many,
Odell? How many flies?"

For papa never spoke of it again.

Jack Farris

THE SALVATION OF LEANDER CATES

Leander Cates, the bluetick man, lived
　　on a farm at the edge of town,
Came one winter in a pickup truck with his
　　household goods and a bawl-voiced hound.
Still unsaved in the Autumn of his life, lived
　　with his sister and a prune-mouthed wife,
Pious women both good and true, cured the sick
　　with a pokeweed brew,
Spoke aloud in the Unknown Tongue, wept and
　　wailed when the choir sung JUST AS I AM.

So pious folk prayed against the day, Leander
　　would turn from his wicked way,
Asking the Lord to reach out his hand, but
　　the Lord stood aloof from the bluetick man,
　　　　　　　　WHAT A FRIEND WE HAVE IN JESUS

Three years passed, then one rainy night, when
　　the windswept willows seemed taking flight,
Leander's wife gave up the fight. Died of a
　　heartbreak some folks said, chilled and
Fevered she lay on her bed, babbling wildly,
　　half out of her head, then someone heard
a piteous cry, "Repent, Leander, before I die!"

So Leander Cates, the bluetick man, came
at last to the House of God,
Bowed him down at the mourner's bench,
chastised there by the Flaming Rod,
Took up the cross of a Christian Life, and kept
his promise to his prune-mouthed wife,
AMEN

♦ ♦

JACK FARRIS was, until his retirement, holder of the T. K. Young Chair in Literature at Rhodes College in Memphis. A versatile writer represented here by poetry, Farris perhaps is best known for his popular novels, such as *Me and Gallagher; The Abiding Gospel of Claude D. Moran, Jr.*; *Ramey*; and *The Family Holvak*, which became the basis for the CBS television series *Holvak*.

ELIZABETH SPENCER

Instrument of Destruction

I think that someday I am going to come home and not have to hear anything about the little boy next door. But that may be because he has killed my aunt or she has stopped being a lady long enough to kill him. Of course, what he's been doing in the yard is a shame. He's ruined all the flower beds with his tricycle and now he's starting on the shrubs, breaking the thinner fronds out of the center of the spirea to plait into whips and ropes, and removing blossoms from the crepe myrtle. Nobody can catch him. He waits till my aunt does her shopping, goes to the grocery, or uptown, or to a church meeting, or to the nursing home.

The reason my aunt doesn't like to make an issue about the boy next door is that she was so glad when he and his folks moved in. They have class and good taste and breeding; they come from an excellent family she has some connection with, down in Columbus, Mississippi, a very aristocratic town. Before they came she had nobody but the most ordinary neighbors, people of no interest to her. One woman—the one on the other side of her still—she really does not like and goes to some pains to avoid. The reason she gives is that the woman looks punished by life. True, the woman's husband is down-at-the-heels, has a low-paying job (night copy-desk editor at the newspaper), sleeps all day, looks unshaven, probably drinks too much, and never speaks. His wife's face reflects all this. Well, of course, it does, I tell her. But my aunt can't agree, can't see things this way.

She has terrible misfortunes about Uncle Paul's illness, being alone, no one to lean on, yet she keeps everything up to a certain mark. The yard is taken care of: a man comes once a week to clip, weed, and mow. Her dresses are always fresh-looking and smart, her gloves when she goes out are white as snow. Her table is set with the best linen and china, every meal. She feels that life has to reach a certain standard daily, has to be pretty and fresh, or it isn't worth calling life. She was beginning to get discouraged, to feel herself islanded in a world that didn't understand her feelings—I obviously do nothing to suit her, trailing out to class daily at the university in skirts and blouses she wouldn't be caught dead in, and going around with what she would call the dregs of humanity if she would come right out and say so.

Then the McAllisters moved in.

Her heart lifted—I could tell—even before she met them, because the painters came and took the horrible gray trim off the house next door with neat applications of white. The windows got removed and painted as well, and new screens installed. Suddenly there were no cobwebs and the panes were glossy clear. Next the porch got freshly done and touches of iron were covered in black enamel. It went on like that. One afternoon, vans arrived, and shining antiques were lifted out from dim, churchlike interiors padded with green quilted hangings, and were transferred smoothly within, not a scratch on the lot, so far as we could tell. Chests came passing after. It was late afternoon with my aunt in the rocker and me in the swing, out on the front porch. "Don't let's look," said my aunt and we both began to laugh, because we both were drinking it all in, from sheer curiosity. Those chests would have draperies in them, we agreed, and linens and silver. Then came packing boxes, lightly borne: china and ornaments, we bet. The rugs followed, bound with lengths of grass rope and bending supple and velvety in the middle. And last of all, on another day, the people came. We'd seen them before, as buyers and directors of workmen. But that day the car—a dark Buick—stopped in the drive with finality and out came the man, the woman, and the boy, and in they went, and the door closed fast.

I have to hand it to my aunt in a lot of ways. If her sort of standards interested me (they don't), I guess I would want to behave just the way she did. She did not, for one thing, try to talk to the new neighbors over the hedge or across the fence in the back yard. She did not send over a cake or some cookies, with a coy welcome-to-our-street note tucked inside. She did not—God forbid—go to "call." As a matter of fact, she did not seem to notice the new family at all. She came and went in her fresh summer outfits and her snow-white gloves. One day, up at the corner (our street slopes down hill) she ran into the woman next door and she was about to pass with a nod but the woman spoke to her and thus she—my aunt—found herself stopped, greeted, even welcomed, in a way, and asked about things. What did one do about cleaning women, gardeners, groceries, etc.? Wouldn't it be nice to break the ice and get better acquainted? The new family did not know Tennessee at all. They were from Columbus, Mississippi. My aunt let go the name of a family there, an exceptionally good family. Like a charming bird released from its cage, the name circled the heads of those two ladies twice and thrice before it shot singing into the bright blue sky. In a day or so my aunt was invited over for a drink.

That weekend she was happier, more content with life, than I had seen her in a long time. The difference was in her eyes and face, in her walk and her voice, everywhere. They had asked all about her. She had told them about Uncle Paul and about me, her niece at the university, and how she'd never had children. They had understood her, it seemed. They had liked her. The little boy was so sweet, she told me. He had got some paints as a present and had brought them to show her.

The next week she had a better chance than ever to see the paints—they were all over the sidewalk. I saw them myself. "Listen, Auntie," I said, "don't worry. It just means he subscribes to *Mad* magazine. That's where he's copied all that."

"I think he's an awful little midget," she said. "They're pretending he's a little boy."

But she kept on accepting when they asked her over for a drink and one warm lovely twilight, she had them, too, out in her garden. (They had got a sitter for the little boy.) Then, being so continually understood by them and so personally treated, she had them to a dinner with a couple of old friends. She loved to give small parties when Uncle Paul was there with her and now it all came back, the first she'd given since he went to the nursing home: she was both sad and excited. But being sociable at heart, her excitement won out and the dinner was a huge success. (The McAllisters, again, left the child with the baby-sitter.)

I myself am not interested in much social life; it seems to me a waste of time. I know when I graduate I will go on to graduate school in one of the sciences, that I will always know people in groups, we will always like music and books together, sex will be (already is) a pairing off among us, we will do cooking that is interesting and good. Married apartment living or small house living around campuses or research centers is what I see in my future. It is good enough. I don't care much where I live as long as it is humanly habitable. This is me. From about the time I got interested in high school chemistry and physics, I have been like this. I went to live with my aunt because my folks knew she needed money (she lives near the campus). But of course I haven't been any real help to her at all. We don't exchange confidences or ideas or anything. I have long dark hair and go around in sandals till my feet just about freeze. If she thinks I'm going to change, she is mistaken. This is me.

Little at a time, my aunt gave the McAllisters their whole social life in her city. She launched them. Otherwise they wouldn't have known the right people at all. This is what my aunt says, and she may be right. They had her to dinner soon with Mr. McAllister's boss (unimpressive, she said) and his wife (a bore, from a boring family she used to know in the church), and they also asked the couple she had introduced them to. Soon they were going to her church and she was leading them up to people there who had been friends of hers and Uncle Paul's and they were delighted with them all. She let them use her willingly because she had been longing for her own kind near her, people who understood her in a deep way. That was why she didn't raise too big a row when the little boy broke down the back fence. The McAllisters said he was an imaginative child and was always playing games in which something became something else. The fence was one wall of a fort, for instance, and was attacked and taken. Then the sidewalk was like a concrete tablet for drawing on and my aunt's flowers were enemy children from another planet and her crepe myrtle blossoms were a secret poison to be cooked in with Irish stew and fed to a visiting Indian chief who was treacherous and meant to attack in the night.

"Do you tell Uncle Paul all this?" I ask my aunt.

"Of course not," she says, "what can he do? I told him about the McAllisters, of course. He's glad I'm so happy with them."

I wonder if she really is. I think she worries. How can she end the trouble with that child? What can she do? I think the child is crazy. He doesn't bother any other house or property but hers. From her front gate he murmurs ugly words, conducts (as long as anybody will listen) a bad dialogue with passers-by. My aunt is afraid of making issues, of telling the whole truth. She is afraid not only of losing the McAllisters but also of losing something else which the McAllisters by recognizing have increased her faith in: that is, her own self-image, her own belief in her unfailing charm and courtesy. So she can't take any steps at all, or something terrible will happen.

Her new friendship, which had opened up so beautifully and which she had given her all to with such whole-hearted skill, is not what she had hoped for. I see she is looking strained again and lonelier than before. I could say I dreamed she was tied to a stake in an Indian village while a child raced round her on a tricycle with a feather stuck through a band around its brow, whooping. But I didn't dream that.

He has started cutting the bark off her trees. He has a knife and removes the bark skillfully, in long strips.

I come home unexpectedly. That day I have a headache from too much formaldehyde in the lab plus my worst day of the month. My aunt is away at the nursing home. The child is working away on her pretty young maple. I walk across the lawn.

"Listen, Buster," I say. "You can get away with that with everybody but me. Now you put up that knife and get the hell on home, *comprenez?*"

He goes into a rage, no kidding. The knife slashes me twice before I can knock him winding, which I do. I'm pretty strong, not bad at tennis, and angry. Shocked, too, from the blood actually starting up out of my arm. I just plain clobber him. Then (it's raining and cold) I am racing in for a tourniquet to save my own life and the child is yelling to wake the dead. I am tearing up a cup towel in my aunt's kitchen and calling a cab to get myself to the hospital outpatient emergency entrance. That little bastard nearly killed me. By the time they stitch me up I'm about passed out but faint thoughts murmur something about the mess in my aunt's kitchen, blood all over the floor and for all I know dripped through the hall, over rugs and tables, staining walk and doorway.

Once a month I make the effort to go out with my aunt to see Uncle Paul. A man with naturally dark skin, he has kept his color better than most people would with what he's got and though emaciated he still has his keen glance. He doesn't make you feel sorry for him. I never knew him very well. I don't know him now.

He sits and plays checkers with some of the patients in the sun parlor every day and sometimes bridge, which amuses him more. He reads. I guess he must have been fun to talk to once and in love with her and all that. She must have loved his wiriness, attractive in a man, and loved the thin blade of his cheekbone pressed to hers. Now they've had their love, at least, and they hold hands. When I'm not there they may cry a little, but with me present they make an occasion of the visit, something they charmingly measure up to. I'm not worth it, I want to say. No. No, not that. Nobody is worth it, I want to say. Yet they are going to do it. They go right ahead, light and conversational, pretending the abyss isn't there.

"What happened to your arm?" Uncle Paul asks me.

How far can I go? I don't want to worry him. "An accident," I say.

"She was cutting a cantaloupe," my aunt says, "with that knife—oh, you remember those knives I had to have, handmade with hickory handles, from way out in the country. You always warned me."

"Get those things too sharp, you've got more than a knife," Uncle Paul says. "You've got an instrument of destruction." He laughs. "Is it okay now?"

"Sure," I say.

"Mighty glad you're with Mary," he tells me. He always says that.

"She's great," I say. I like him.

"Sure she is."

He asks about the McAllisters and she says they're fine.

But relations have certainly cooled with the McAllisters since the day their little boy slashed into me. They don't telephone any more. I feel they're going to have to look back on knowing my aunt as an incident of their first year in the new town. Among the other families on the street, those people my aunt doesn't care to know, the word has got round that the boy has calmed down quite a bit since I knocked hell out of him. My aunt would have a great chance now, if she'd make the slightest effort, to make some real human relationships on that street. They all know all about her, and some are there, mysterious among them, like everywhere, who can hold things up—sustainers in time of need.

But she doesn't want them. She wants friends like the McAllisters are, or would have been, if they hadn't given birth to that awful child.

◆ ◆

ELIZABETH SPENCER, who studied under Donald Davidson at Vanderbilt before beginning her teaching career at Ward-Belmont University in Nashville, is a member of the American Institute of Arts and Letters. The author of a number of story collections and novels, including *Jack of Diamonds*, *The Voice at the Back Door*, and *The Light in the Piazza*, she has been the recipient of many awards and honors, including a Guggenheim Fellowship.

TOM T. HALL

The Last Fly of Summer

Jim Ridenour worked in a factory where he polished and inspected precision bearings for high technology industries. He saw the red light of the digital printer on his machine read 12,734 KIH. He checked his badge attachment that read 12,000 KIH. He had done 734 more pieces than his day's work required. Jim Ridenour reached for the red button on his machine and pushed it firmly. The tall, heavy gentleman waited for the whirring machine to stop. The digital printout read ENTER I.D.

He pulled a blue card from his pocket and dropped it into a lighted slot. The printout read HAVE A NICE DAY.

Jim Ridenour had finished more than a day's work in less than six hours. He nodded to his fellow workers as he passed them on his way to the locker room where he took off his goggles and his apron, changed shoes, and ran his fingers through his short hair. Washing his hands, he looked at his round, ruddy face in the mirror above the stainless steel sink. The locker room was metal-cool and clinical like the rest of the factory. The big man looked around him and seemed to nod his head in approval.

The parking lot was bathed in sunlight as he walked toward his car. He remembered that his wife and three children were at a Pee Wee League football game. *Nice weather for it*, he thought.

It was a warm day for late November. The first frost had arrived a few weeks earlier. The leaves had fallen. The nights had been cold enough for extra blankets on his bed. His wife had taken care of that.

Jim Ridenour's own contribution to the change of seasons had been the removal and storage of the window screens that kept out the flies.

He had carefully taken out all of the screws that held the screens, filled the holes with a mixture of steel wool and wood putty, stored the screens in the attic, and then sanded and retouched the holes where the screw holes had been. Jim Ridenour was a

"The Last Fly of Summer," from *Acts of Life: Tales by Tom T. Hall* (Fayetteville: University of Arkanas Press, 1986), 100–104. Reprinted by permission of the University of Arkansas Press.

kind, quiet man. Friends sometimes said that he would not hurt a fly.

When Jim Ridenour was six years old, his mother and father were killed in an oil refinery explosion in Gary, Indiana, just outside Chicago. Jim's mother had driven to the refinery to pick her husband up from work and was caught in the inferno. Jim was taken to his aunt's house to live.

It was while living with his aunt and uncle that Jim Ridenour was molded into the man he was. His uncle Fred had been a mentally sick man who drank too much and beat him. Jim had never forgotten the strange ritual of his beatings. As a seven-year-old child he would be made to sit in a chair in the corner of the room while his aunt and uncle argued. The uncle would say, "So this is what I get for marrying you, eh? This is it? A damned nephew to raise."

The uncle would then walk to the chair where Jim was sitting and slap him across the ears. This happened two or three times a week. The slap left a ringing hours after the sting had gone.

Jim searched for the source of his guilt. He was sorry for the circumstances, but could not find a way to make amends to his uncle. He considered his sins one by one.

In his junior year of high school, Jim dropped out and took a job with the Lupkin Manufacturing Company. He had worked there ever since.

Jim loved his job at the factory. The cold, impersonal machines gave him a sense of comfort throughout the day. He could get lost in his work.

Jim hauled his large, bulky frame from his small car and stood in front of the house he had bought fourteen years earlier. To the average person, it looked like the other houses on the street, but Jim could see how clearly it was different. He could see the patched screw holes where the screens had been taken down, he could see a small nick on the corner of the house where his son had run his tricycle into the molding, and he could see that his now dormant lawn was a little greener than his neighbor's. He entered the house, went to the refrigerator, opened a beer, went to the living room, and sat down in the chair he always sat in.

Now, he thought, *Here I am in my life. Here I sit in the house where I have never harmed my children. The house that I have bought and paid for with my hard work. The house where my children were conceived and born. The house that my uncle Fred has never entered.*

And then there was a ringing in Jim Ridenour's ears. A bright clear ringing, higher than the dial tone on a telephone.

Jim turned his chair toward the picture window that looked out to the street. A fly buzzed past his ear and settled on the glass of the window. It walked first one way and then the other, as if searching for something.

The huge man reached for the fly swatter that lay on the floor by his chair, one of the many he owned. It was a green plastic swatter molded to a wire frame. He had bought six of them from a rack at the supermarket, though his wife had protested that he already owned dozens of them.

Jim studied the swatter carefully. Sometimes, when he had not scrubbed them properly, the swatters would have specks of blood and guts on them. The one he held in his hand was clean. He laid it back on the floor.

The fly zoomed away from the window and disappeared in the poor light of the room. Jim studied the lamps and the tabletops, the favorite landing sites for flies. Except for an occasional automobile passing, the house was quiet. Jim listened. He sat silent and unmoving for five minutes before the fly returned to the window. *Ah*, he thought, *A very clever and resourceful creature, this last fly of summer.* Jim lifted his bulky frame. He padded barefoot to the kitchen. In the cupboard, to the left of the refrigerator, he found a can of fly spray stuck behind some rusty scouring pads.

The fly sat on the window, turning counterclockwise. Jim took this as a sign that it was suddenly aware of a human presence. He approached the window with slow, deliberate steps. The fly froze on the window. Jim aimed three feet above the target. He held the can of spray upright and touched the nozzle with his finger. A small mist of spray settled over the fly. Jim backed away and sat down in the chair.

The fly shook its head like an angry bull. It flew a short distance across the window to a dry, clean spot, and there shook its body and ruffled its wings. Then it began to beat its wings against the glass and moved frantically from spot to spot, as if it were in a panic trying to fly through the clear hardness out to the open air. Then the chemicals reached its tiny brain and as suddenly as its frantic movements had begun, they stopped and it sat silent and wobbly on the surface of the glass until once more it ruffled its wings and shook its head before it dropped to the window sill.

Jim sat watching the twitches until the fly lay silent. He spoke aloud. "Be still and know. Be still."

He got a soft, green tissue from the bathroom, held it below the window sill, and with a purse of his lips blew the fly onto it.

Gathering the tissue gently in his hands he went to the kitchen and opened the door into his garage that he had turned into a workshop. He folded the tissue gently and placed it in a small matchbox.

From a distance, it would have appeared that the man was crawling about on the grass looking for something he had lost. He used a trowel to remove a slab of sod, scooped out a small portion of dirt and scattered it aside, placed the match box in the little grave, and replaced the sod. He stood up clumsily and used his foot to tamp the sod back into place. The casual eye would not notice the slight disarray of the grass.

With trowel in hand, the sad-eyed man spoke aloud. "Lord, I ask you to receive this creature back into your kingdom. He was brave and resourceful. He made it along much better than the other flies who went with the frost. Ashes to ashes and dust to dust."

Jim Ridenour was sitting in his favorite chair when the family came home that afternoon. The children hugged and kissed him before rushing off to their rooms and turning on their record players and TV sets.

Mrs. Ridenour took the warm can of beer from him and replaced it with a cold one from the refrigerator. She spoke to him of social things. "We were invited to the Rotary dinner Thursday night, but I told them old Silent Jim would probably not want to come."

His reply was a small change of expression. The wife went off to the kitchen to prepare dinner.

The large man turned his chair toward the picture window. He had washed it clean and polished the sill with furniture polish. All traces of the afternoon were gone. *Amazing*, he thought, *All these years I have been able to fool my wife, my children, the people at work, and my friends. Everybody except my uncle Fred. He knew me from the very beginning.*

Tom T. Hall

TOM T. HALL, known to thousands of country music fans around the world as Mister Tom T. Hall, lives at Fox Hollow, his farm just outside Nashville. When he is not performing or farming, he is writing. With three novels, two children's books, and a short story collection already published, he is hard at work on another novel.

JESSE HILL FORD

Work

My Vanderbilt mentor, the late Donald Davidson, often spoke of the Southern Yeomanry, a tough, independent, self-sufficient class who owned no slaves, cultivated their lands with great skill, and were imbued with the virtues of Christian forbearance, being by and large a godly, righteous, and sober group. They outnumbered slave holders in the South and formed the gallant backbone of the forces of the Confederacy when war was forced upon them. They fought to the death to defend their land when the invasion from the north brought with it finally the twin devastations of defeat and bankruptcy.

From this breed, made up mostly of Scotch-Irish and English, but amply seasoned by Dutch, German, Spanish, and Italian migrants, came my attitudes toward work. As my late father told it: "Anything that is honest and productive is honorable."

My father had left home at age ten to work for an older cousin who owned a country store. He slept on the store counter and might never have gotten an education in that dark and distant outpost in Perry County, Alabama, had not a maiden lady witnessed his performance in a county declamation contest. His recitation, "The Dark Horse and His Rider," so enthralled the lady that she took him home with her where he earned his keep doing chores in her Marion, Alabama, household. Later, thanks to her influence, he won a full scholarship to Marion Institute, a prep military school, and from there went to Auburn University where he graduated with a degree in pharmacy. He meanwhile toiled in the steel mills at Birmingham, worked for the post office sorting mail on the railroad trains, and slaved summers in Omaha, Nebraska, with a tree surgery outfit. For want of inoculations he nearly died of smallpox. His other ailments included scarlet fever, typhoid fever, and every one of the childhood diseases such as mumps, measles, chickenpox, and so on.

When I came down with some of these he spent hours at my bedside patiently reading aloud from Mark Twain and James Fenimore Cooper. Never was there anyone who had more sympathy for the sick than my father.

He put me to work at age five watering a sprig of a pussy willow sapling in the backyard of our home on LaSalle Court in Nashville's Belle Meade district. From this I graduated to using a spading fork to break the clods in the quarter-acre plots he had plowed every year in a vacant field for his garden.

I was, when strong enough to push a hand mower, required to keep our lawn. The terraces in the front of the house were a terrible trial. Back then terraces were popular and almost all new houses had them. And power mowers were unknown. . . .

. . . I got a Social Security card at age fourteen when I went to work for Walgreen's Drug in downtown Nashville as stockboy. My reason for taking the job was founded in a determination, after graduation from grade school, to attend Montgomery Bell Academy, a private boys' school.

My father had forbidden me M.B.A. enrollment. He could not afford the tuition, he explained. When I said I would get a job and earn my tuition, he relented. So earn tuition I did, but it meant giving up football, and I had been Captain of the Parmer School team in eighth grade and had had ahead of me a career as a running back if only I could have continued football at M.B.A. But my sacrifice was worth it. I worked weekdays after school until after dark in the Walgreen's job, and from seven A.M. to eleven P.M. on weekends, when I was privileged to work as a sundries clerk.

My grades, for some reason, suffered, but I was able to make up Latin and Algebra in easy summer sessions at Peabody Demonstration School, the refuge of all the Nashville flunk bunnies, and so I made my way and managed to write for the M.B.A. school paper and to edit the M.B.A. annual my senior year—1947.

My last two years at M.B.A. were made easier when I won a half scholarship and my mother helped with the rest of my tuition, probably over my father's objections, for it had been his aim to put grit in my craw, as he termed it. He clung to this hope for many years afterward, but alas, he never succeeded.

I was ever the determined social butterfly. High school and college fraternities and formal dances and debut parties and even, just once, a football weekend in Mobile, where Vanderbilt whipped Alabama and where, next morning, I opened my first ever can of warm beer while my two college mates still lay sleeping off our wanton night before.

The final two years in Vanderbilt were as chaotic as the first two had been, but being past foreign languages and math requirements, I had smooth sailing. I graduated with a major in English and a minor in Classics.

My last months in Vanderbilt I worked full time for the *Tennessean*, a local daily, and earned my highest pay yet, forty dollars a week, and thus, at age twenty-one, bought my first ever automobile, a 1949 Ford.

Two summers, meanwhile, had been spent at Newport, Rhode Island, in Navy Officer Training, and my commission after graduation dovetailed nicely with the onset of the Korean War, to which I was sent for service with the Seventh Fleet as a 90-day-wonder ensign.

Woods Foster, the closest friend I ever had, died on the eve of his graduation from Air Force Cadet School. His oxygen supply failed on a night flight and his jet crashed and burned near Big Springs, Texas.

I was twenty-three and still in the Navy when I lost Woods, but I have the warmest memories of our growing up, of football at Parmer School, of fencing bouts with masks and foils at his pre-revolutionary childhood home on Old Hickory Boulevard, of our double dates with his sweetheart, Barbara Oman, and my heart throb, Dudley Brown, and of lazy mornings after the debut parties at the Belle Meade Country Club, when Woods and Richard Fletcher had come home with me for the night, and we would wake next morning with massive hangovers from all the champagne fountains, which were fortified, unfortunately, with an especially cheap sauterne. Fletcher would place a waste basket by the bed in which to throw up, which occasionally he did. My mother fixed breakfast for the three of us late the next morning.

Fletcher, too, is gone—from suicide of but a few years ago. We were in Navy training together at Newport, and, thanks to an aunt of his in New York City, we got invited to the Newport debut parties those two summers up there, when one threw the empty champagne glasses off the cliff into the cold New England sea.

Foskett and Frances Brown, both of whom took a hand in my early upbringing, when, as it happened, I was a prospective son-in-law, are gone with Woods and Fletcher to the hereafter.

But a word about Frances Brown is in order. She was president of the Junior League of America—national president. An only child, like her beautiful daughter, she graduated from Finch and made a first unhappy marriage to a dashing Easterner before returning to Nashville, divorced, to marry Foskett. She taught me so much I could never thank her enough. She related to me the history of Nashville society as only she knew it. One could not have asked for a more delightful mother-in-law, and I'm sorry even yet that Dudley and I somehow didn't make it as the married pair we might have been.

But our attitudes toward work and being responsible and being successful and useful were a real barrier. In love though we were, we had pledged not to marry until I had graduated from law school and she had received her diploma from Vanderbilt.

She got the diploma but I never made it to law school, for my war, the Korean War, intervened, and some men, somehow, have a hankering to mate and to have progeny when they see themselves soon going away to war. . . .

◆ ◆

JESSE HILL FORD's short stories have won many prizes, including the O. Henry, an Edgar, and inclusion in Martha Poley Prize collections. Two of his novels, *The Liberation of Lord Byron Jones* and *The Raider*, have been selections of the Book-of-the-Month Club. A Guggenheim Fellow, Fulbright Scholar, and Visiting Fellow at the Center for Advanced Study, he lives and works in the Nashville suburb of Bellevue.

JOAN WILLIAMS

VISTAS

The telephone had begun to ring almost daily at five. This afternoon, she decided abruptly, I just won't answer; then she put a hand to the receiver timidly. Amy stared at herself in a dressing-table mirror opposite, where she looked peculiarly elongated, as the mirror slanted. Why, she wondered, had she not been able long before middle age to cope with a telephone call from her mother?

Stretching the cord to its utmost, saying "Hello," she went over to peer more closely at her reflection. Had the apricot oil purchased in the health-food store made her look younger? In only ten days' time, the label had promised. She had questioned Andrew, her husband, explaining the situation; what did he think? This morning she had gazed at him speculatively, saying maybe she had rubbed a bit hard around the eyes and had reddish marks. Andrew, after cocking his head appraisingly, had said, "You look ten days younger." His lips barely twitched.

Now, touching one cheek, she thought, But hasn't it helped, maybe a fraction?

Meanwhile she had been answering the barrage of questions she dreaded. She took a deep breath and, hating to lie, said she had not gotten to the phone sooner because she was in the bathroom. "No, the dishwasher wasn't running. I heard. I was just in the bathroom." She went on wearily to answer that she had had enough dirty dishes to run it last night; and it did take a long time to fill the machine when there were only two people at home. "I will get used to it," she said defiantly, closing her eyes to gaze in inward darkness at fiery red stars bursting. She stood at a right angle between windows and looked out at their separate views. She prayed there might be something to talk about besides minutia. She burst out: "I did not say I was lonely." Even now, after so many years, she was bound by the conventions of her upbringing, her generation: not to talk back to your elders. Not to say what you thought, Amy added. Her mother was having more of an adjustment problem than she; Amy felt she had been preparing

"Vistas," from *Pariah and Other Stories*, by Joan Williams (New York: Little, Brown, 1983), 155–60. Reprinted by permission of the author.

herself for years for the time when her youngest would go off to college; preparations her mother could not fathom. She said evenly, "I know that you had to adjust, too, to my going away from home" She let out an exasperated breath, but away from the receiver.

Her ear ached, and she rubbed it while she went on listening. Far beyond the windows a mock-orange sunset was disappearing, and the ceiling was dabbled by lavender shadows as she stared across a hallway to two tidy, empty rooms that were side by side. She thought suddenly how much better they had looked messy. She wondered about the young mother who had stormed about them crying, "Clean up! Pick up!" Had it so mattered? If only the boys were here at that age, they could begin all over again. Twenty years there had been children in this house, and twenty years had been an instant. She wondered where she had been all that time.

She listened without comment to the latest developments in the various illnesses of her mother's friends. She heard which days her mother had been invited to play bridge. "Thank God," Mrs. Howard always said. But Amy was thinking about having two boys in diapers at the same time, a year and a half apart, and how that had equaled four girls, or four of anything else: chimpanzees even. Those early years she had thought that she would never be rested again, that never again would the hackles of her nerves lie flat, that never would she be unharried enough that she was not capable of tossing a tricycle in the general direction of a two-year-old, demanding one minute to herself: carefully avoiding him but putting a nasty hole in a plaster wall, over which she had put a Band-Aid; as she had not been able to explain to Andrew at the time, she had not come up with an answer yet, except that in that period of her life, the Band-Aid had seemed logical.

"Well," Mrs. Howard said, "I suppose we've said everything there is to say."

"I suppose so," Amy said.

"I thought I might drive over tomorrow afternoon." Then into the silence, she said, "Are you doing something then?"

Amy's mind fled this way and that, and settled on the fact that she might do no more than lie on the bed and revel in silence. "I'm working on a paper." Then she said in measured cadence, "I know you think taking a graduate course is silly." She could not say further, "But you see, the difference is that all these years I've been trying to use my brain." Therefore, she assured herself again, she was prepared for this new stage in her life. Why have her mother drive over from a neighboring town? Hadn't they just agreed that everything had been said? To meet, they would only say the same things again; sit avoiding one another's eyes in the silences that fell. Amy would stand at last to make tea, waiting with folded arms while the water boiled, her back carefully to the other room, and she would rattle the dishes to make noise, as she had as a child at meals to disrupt silence between three people at a table, bound by family ties but nothing more. "I have to get the paper done," she said. "Don't come too early. Maybe you had better come some other time, later." Having hung up and lying against the headboard, she could not remember an entire day to herself, without interruption.

The wind must have risen. A sycamore beside the house was scratching at a window, asking either to be listened to or let in. Its bending caused shadows in the hallway to rise and flee, or to shift and resettle; for an instant, she saw several as white mice.

The boys had of course that period of white mice; only, her boys set loose a cageful in the house. Where the mice had lived, week upon week, no one ever knew, nor where finally they all had gone; only at unsuspecting moments did they go scuttling across floors from one hiding place to another, escape artists all. One had come out of a closet in a room where she had been writing a novel; it could not be a simple mouse; this one circumvented her toes, with a homemade dart wobbling out of its side, made of a whittled matchstick with a needle imbedded in one end. She had not screeched about the mouse, nor even at acceptance of inherent male bestiality in her own sons; she had quietly rested her forehead on the typewriter keys, thinking about people all over America shut into rooms writing novels that wrenched their very entrails; she had asked them all a simple, heartfelt question: Is anyone else out there writing under these conditions? Once again she had thought about freedom.

Amy felt she had been quite a good mother about white mice; sitting in the dark and recalling, she began to have a great sense of warmth. As her thoughts lodged backwards with the children, she thought that consequently theirs might be lodging back toward home. All this time, in separate New England colleges, they might have been gazing at a similar sunset, then darkness, remembering that when the wind rose, the sycamore scratched at the window, how shortly car lights would come glancing round the school-bus corner and their father would be home, how she would begin to clatter about the kitchen, proclaiming darkly about the lot of women in life and endless meals to fix.

Amy settled upon the child with whom to mull all this over simply by deciding, first, upon the oldest. He spoke thickly but she only said, "How come a girl answered your dorm phone?"

"She lives here," he said.

"Oh," she said. "You sound funny."

"I was asleep," he said.

"Why are you asleep at this time of night!"

"I had a test and stayed up all last night to study."

"You shouldn't do that," she said. "It's not good for your health."

"Mom," he said.

"Are you taking the vitamins I sent you?"

"I'm taking the vitamins. I'm having a poo every day. I'm twenty-one years old. I can take care of myself. What's wrong?"

"Nothing's wrong," she said. "I was just looking at some shadows and they looked like white mice. I wondered if you remembered. . . ."

"Where's Dad?" he said.

"He's not home yet."

"You got to get yourself together," he said.

"I am together!" she said. "I just have memories."

"Mom," he said. "I got to run. Or I'll miss my ride to dinner."

"Oh. All right. Good-bye."

"Good-bye, Mom." he said.

"I love you," she said.

"Yeah," he said.

After a moment, Amy dialed with the eraser of a pencil. "Mother, come out tomorrow," she said. "Come for lunch."

◆ ◆

JOAN WILLIAMS, author of four novels and many stories, was a close friend and confidante of William Faulkner. Her first novel, *The Morning and the Evening*, published in 1961, won the John P. Marquand Award for the "most distinguished first novel" of the year. She now lives and works in Memphis.

ANN ALLEN SHOCKLEY

CRACK BABY

Bea laid very still on the narrow bed for fear of waking Kayota. The streetlight on the corner, where her bedroom was, made a ribbon's path glow through the darkness like a pencil flashlight. The streets had finally settled down somewhat. The Happy Day Club diagonal from her had closed, and the goodtimers, prostitutes, pimps, and drug dealers had vanished into the subterranean niches that harbored them. Only a few die-hard straggling night creatures continued to roam the main thoroughfare and the narrower streets dissecting the Harriet Tubman Project. Cars could be heard now and then, brakes squealing, doors slamming, voices calling, bottles meeting asphalt. A radio station playing rap music traveled into her window.

Whatever, Bea thought, just don't wake Kayota. It was too hard getting him to sleep at times, but, then, there were others when all he wanted to do *was* sleep. Kayota was different. Poor thing. Having to suffer for the sins of his mother. Her own daughter. Hooked on crack.

While Kayota was kept at the hospital in intensive care for six weeks after his birth, Mercedine just up and disappeared, leaving her with a grandson to look after. Sixty-six was too old to have to be fooling with a young baby, especially like him. She was half sick herself, high blood pressure, arthritis. Plus the cost. She depended on her social security check every month, and the weekend job as a part-time cook at Mo's Soul Food Heaven.

There were those—official and unofficial—always spouting out advice to her. Go to the Department of Human Services, Aid to Dependent Children, Welfare Office. Apply for this, and apply for that. She wasn't up to running all round town to fill out papers and answer questions. Later, no doubt, to be told that she couldn't get any of it. She had her pride.

Hadn't she taken care of Mercedine and Edward, Junior, without any government help by cleaning offices downtown and cooking after Edward, Senior, got killed unloading a moving van. The driver didn't know he was there and backed over him. They had to move to the projects, where there were too few who managed to live above it, and too many who didn't. Edward, Junior, didn't get a chance either way, stopping a bullet intended for someone else just walking down the street.

Was that Kayota whimpering? She eased out of the bed to go bend over the crib next to her. He was so tiny. She saw his arms and legs trembling like a drunk with the shakes. He required so much attention, wearing her out to the point where she would go to sleep over the Cosby Show.

And, Lordy, couldn't he cry! Yelling like pins and needles were sticking in him. She worried that it would disturb her neighbors through the tissue paper walls. But the project was full of hollering, yelling, screaming people. It was like they were all angry for being there together, blaming each other, hating, seeing themselves in one another.

Things sure happen in mysterious ways. Her last few years left taking care of a baby in a nickel-size one-bedroom apartment that she had changed to since she was by herself. Satisfied that Kayota was all right, she slumped back into bed, halfway sleeping, halfway listening.

At first, she thought that she was dreaming when the loud knocking came. Frowning, she squinted at the cheap small digital AM radio, one she had picked up at her church's rummage sale, on the bedstand. Its numbers were dim to her eyes. Five A.M. Somebody must have the wrong apartment. Probably wanted the one upstairs that had all the people coming and going and staying. The knock grew more persistent. Afraid that Kayota would awaken, she slipped out of bed into her houseshoes and robe.

"Who is it?" she asked, only partly unbolting the latch, letting the two chain locks and stick remain in place.

"Momma—it's me. Mercedine."

"Mercedine?" She fumbled with the locks, hands shaking, heart pounding.

"Hi, Momma—"

Bea turned on the lamp in the living room to look at her in disbelief. Her head exploded with questions. "Where you been?"

Mercedine's lips curved in a lopsided grin. "'Round—"

Bea's deep dark eyes swept over her. Mercedine used to be a real looker. Had all the men after her because of her honey-beige skin, sloe-eyes, and just right mouth. Her prettiness and outgoing personality drew males like flies to sticky paper. Besides having looks, she was smart too. She could have gone to college when finishing high school on a scholarship, but she got that waitress job at the Happy Day Club. Started joy-living, doing this and trying that. Having fun, she called it. She got carried away on fun. Fun's fun, *her* mother used to say, but there's all kinds, right kind and wrong kind.

Mercedine was thirty-one, but as Bea saw her now standing there, she looked ten years older. She was skinny as a toothpick, cheeks gaunt, skin blotched, and hair wild all over her head. She had on a pair of dirty jeans, a man's oversized torn denim jacket, and dirty sneakers with the shoestrings missing. A tote bag hung loosely over her shoulder. She smelled like she needed a bath.

"Well, Momma, aren't you glad to see me?"

"Sure—sure I'm glad to see you. To know that I got a daughter who's still living. Did you forgit you got a son?"

Mercedine playfully threw an arm about Bea that almost missed its mark. A cloud of alcohol brushed Bea's face. "Naw, Momma. That's why I'm here. To see him—and *you*! Where is he?"

Bea noticed that her eyes looked glassy, and the grin wouldn't stay still. "Sleep. Don't wake him up. Sometimes it's hard gittin' him to sleep." She paused to fidget with one of the two short white braids that she had put her hair in for sleeping. "Then, sometimes, he sleeps so long I have to wake him up."

The words were mere sounds in the air to Mercedine, who had dropped her bag on the floor and headed for the bedroom.

"Don't wake him!" Bea warned hushly, following.

"Just want to see my baby, Momma." The dawn was threading the sky, filtering through the window shade. "He's—he's so *little*!" she breathed, leaning over to inspect him. "He's got Duke's knotty curls. A flat nose like Jerry's—"

Bea closed her eyes, feeling the hurt cut through her. Her own daughter didn't even know who the father of the baby was. "One thing for sure, you the momma."

Mercedine turned away from the crib. "Can I sleep on the couch, Momma? I got no place to go right now." Yawning widely, she went back to the living room. "I'm beat."

"Wait a minute," Bea stopped her as she went for the couch. "Let me put some sheets on it." As soon as the couch was made up, Bea watched in amazement as Mercedine stretched out in her clothes and went promptly to sleep.

Bea shook her head. Mercedine was back. But for how long?

"Mercedine, hurry out of that bathroom!" Bea called, knocking on the door. "You been in there half the mornin'. I got to git myself straight 'fore I wake Kayota. He's sleepin' too long. Needs feedin'."

"Okay, Momma, hold your horses!"

Bea went into the kitchen to take stock of the milk, formula, and food supply. Her left leg was beginning to ache. Looking out the window, she saw that the day was cloudy. No wonder her leg was acting up. Rain was on the way. She hoped Mercedine wasn't in there getting her nose open. It was dangerous now. She could get put out.

Mercedine came out, smiling that loose-lipped grin. "Sure glad you hung on to a few of my things, Momma."

Things that she had left from time to time. At least she smelled better. Like soap and water. She looked better too, in a pair of black slacks, too large now, held up by a thick red leather belt, and a long-sleeved white blouse. She had combed her hair.

A loud cry sounded from the bedroom, and Bea went to it. Kayota was awake, brown face wrinkled, screaming fitfully.

"Hush—hush, now. Grandmom's here. Right here." Bea picked him up, rocking him gently.

Mercedine watched her. "Here, Momma, let me have him."

Hesitantly Bea placed him in Mercedine's arms. "Sweet—sweet baby," she crooned. Looking up at Bea, she asked: "Why are his eyes jerking like that? He can't seem to look at me?"

"You birthed him. You ought to know," Bea said, half angrily. "He's a crack baby."

Silently Mercedine handed Kayota back to her mother as a succession of cries belched forth. "I'm going to get off it, Momma. I promise. Get a job—take care of him."

"Yeah?" Bea narrowed her eyes. "When?"

Avoiding Bea's eyes, Mercedine looked away, changing the subject. "You got a new TV."

"Have to have somethin' for myself. Other one give out. Just pay five dollars a month for it." Kayota had stopped crying now as Bea rocked him rhythmically back and forth. "You hungry?"

"No. Think I'll walk around the old neighborhood. See how it is."

"Be mighty nice if you'd stay here today with your son. It's Friday. I work Fridays and Sat'days from 'leven to five cookin' for Mo. You here, I won't have to pay Hattie for keepin' him. Let's me have a bit more for us."

"Okay, Momma, I'll stay," Mercedine agreed. "Get to know my baby." Smiling, she ran a fingertip lightly across his face.

After Kayota was bathed and fed, Bea cooked a bowl of oatmeal and made toast for herself, while Mercedine idled over coffee. "If the buses ain't too crowded, I gits home 'bout five-thirty," Bea said. "Don't let him sleep over his feedin' time. You might have to wake him up."

"All right, Momma. Don't worry."

Bea's plum-colored face, still wrinkleless, gazed thoughtfully at Mercedine. "It takes a while to get food down him. When you feed him, sit him up in your arms and hold his chin down. Don't rush him. Let him rest while you doin' it. He might even throw up. When he's through, lay him down on his side or prone. That's what they told me at the hospital."

Mercedine looked abstractly out the window. "Got an extra key? I'll take him out to get some air."

Bea frowned. "Air? Can't you see it's goin' to rain?" She got up to prepare to leave. "His bottles and food's in the 'frigerator. Extra key's in my bedstand drawer." A bright smile lit up her face. "I'm glad to see you, Mercedine."

"I'm glad to see you too, Momma," Mercedine smiled back.

Five forty-five P.M., Bea came home in the rain, shaking out her worn black umbrella before going in. She opened the door to Kayota's wild screams from the bedroom. Mercedine was half slumped on the couch, eyes closed, nodding. Three empty cans of Budweiser were on the age-old scarred coffee table.

"I'm comin', little fella, I'm comin'." Bea hurried to Kayota, picking him up, rocking him to stop his cries. He smelled awful, diapers needing changing. He had had diarrhea again. She found a pacifier to quiet him. She would give him a warm bath.

After he was cleaned up, Bea looked into the refrigerator and saw that the bottles and baby food were all lined up like she had left them. He hadn't been fed since breakfast.

Mercedine didn't wake up until night ruled the sky and dinner was over. Bea sat in the lumpy chair with the broad worn flat arms, eyes on the television, but mind elsewhere. The room was half in darkness. She was tired, physically and mentally. She just wished that she could get one good night's uninterrupted sleep, have one day to herself.

When she saw Mercedine finally come awake, she said bluntly: "You can't stop. You need to go to one of those places that'll help you to stop. There's one over on—"

"Oh, Christ, Momma!"

"Your son needs *you* more'n his grandmomma. You *owe* him for what you done done to him. He's ruint pro'bly for the rest of his life."

Mercedine got up unsteadily from the couch. "I don't want to hear any of your lectures. Heard them all my life."

"Didn't seem to do much good, did they?"

"What time is it?"

"Eight."

"What'd you have for dinner?"

"What *you* like. Pork chops, rice, and sweet potatoes. Left some on the stove for you."

They heard Kayota. "Baby's cryin'." Bea said.

"Seems like that's all he does. He doesn't seem to smile or do what other babies do."

"What you 'xpect? I keep on tellin' you he ain't *like* other babies," Bea sighed, getting up wearily, careful not to put too much pressure on her left leg. "Got to go to him."

Saturday morning, Mercedine was gone before Bea and Kayota awakened. It didn't look as if she had slept there. Her pack, however, was on the floor by the couch. Bea shook her head sadly. Poor baby. Won't grow up to know its own momma.

Breakfast over, she gathered up diapers, bottles, and food to take Kayota to Hattie's. Hattie lived on social security like herself. This way, Hattie got helped too. And, Hattie liked babies, all kinds. Besides, Hattie was dependable.

That evening, Bea got off the bus in a light-hearted mood. The weather was good, springtime like. Being around other folks, young, middle-aged, and old, helped a lot. Talking to them, listening to their foolishness, getting away from the imprisonment of the routine, responsibilities, worries.

The days were getting longer, and the sidewalk was alive with children playing ball, running, jumping rope. Watching two little girls turn a rope for another, she wondered if Kayota would ever do that with such ease, abandonment, spirit. He wasn't even trying to pull himself up yet.

He was asleep when she got him from Hattie. That meant, if she was real careful, she could have a little time for herself. She carried him down the hall to her place, walking like on ice to keep from waking him.

Suddenly a strange feeling overcame her as she stepped inside. What was it? Frowning, she put Kayota on the couch. "Mercedine?" she called softly, sniffing the air. The place had *that* smell. What was it? Slowly she looked around the living room, her eyes a moving camera. Then she stopped at the empty corner where the television had been.

"Oh, my God!" Her comfort, relaxation, outside contact with the world—*Gone*!

She wanted to cry, shriek in frustration, flail her arms, beat on something. The last time she came home, it was the radio in the bedroom, a nice table model clock AM *and* FM with big digits she could read good in the dark.

Feeling faint, she sat down heavily on the couch. Her leg started hurting. The pain of it all was shooting straight through her, bothering all parts of her body. It wasn't right. You bring children into the world to go through this?

Kayota awakened and began to cry. She picked him up, hugging him close to her, tears flowing down her cheeks. Next time, she wouldn't let her in. She *wouldn't*. But, pressing Kayota tightly against her, she knew that she would. Just like she would take care of Kayota the best she could. They were both her own flesh and blood.

Tomorrow she would have to get the lock changed.

• •

ANN ALLEN SHOCKLEY, associate librarian in Special Collections at Fisk University, is the author of two published novels, *Loving Her* and *Say Jesus and Come to Me*, and a collection of short stories, *The Black and White of It*. She also is editor of the anthology, *Afro-American Women Writers, 1746–1933*.

JOHN FERGUS RYAN

ARTIST DRINKS PERFUME

"Look at that headline!" said the artist to the social worker who sat beside his bed in the Emergency Room. She was a thin young woman who lived on three jars of baby food a day and who weighed herself every two hours.

She took the newspaper from him and read the headline:

ARTIST HOSPITALIZED
AFTER DRINKING PERFUME

"What's wrong with it?" she asked.

"It was not perfume! It was a pine tar based grease solvent I found in a storeroom at the bus station!"

"In any case, I am here to help you" she said. "I will need to know everything you can tell me about yourself."

The artist's face brightened and he took off the artificial fur cap he was wearing because he could not afford a beret.

"I am a world figure," he began.

"Go on" said the social worker, entering that information on a blank form.

"I have always been a pioneer in the use of new mediums" said the artist. "For instance, I was the first man in history to sculpt a bust of William Jennings Bryan in frozen axle grease!"

"Indeed!" said the social worker. "What happened to it?"

"I sold it."

"How much did you get for it?"

"Eight cents a pound."

"I don't understand."

"Artist Drinks Perfume," from an unpublished novel, *Litmus Grogan*.

The artist stuffed the artificial fur cap into his mouth and bit it, trying to suppress a sob.

"It was bought by a farmer who melted it down and used it to lubricate the universal joint of a 1948 Packard."

The artist broke into tears.

"There, there" said the social worker, looking around the room to see if she could spot a scale.

"From the first, I scorned the traditional means of expression in art" he said. "I had a one man show six or eight years ago, but the police closed it because of the stench."

"How do you spell that?" asked the social worker.

"In an experimental study of shapes and moods, I spread slices of ripe cheese with colors worked into a garlic oil base, then I framed them with rolls of newspaper I had found behind the City Fish Market.

"Before the show was closed, I had actually sold one of them. For a while I was elated, but then I was almost destroyed when I learned it had been bought to feed to a cat.

"The story in the newspaper, and the pictures of police officers wearing gas masks as they smashed my work, was great publicity, and almost at once, I was commissioned to decorate the interior of a frozen meat locker.

"Another chance, it was, to restore my reputation as an innovator and one not tied to the past" continued the artist. "I had natural gas pipes installed along the walls of the locker, then punctured them at random along their length and set fire to the escaping gas.

"The resulting stream of flame along the walls produced an effect described as 'non static' by the critics, but unfortunately, the heat upset the thermostat in the locker and several thousands of dollars worth of refrigeration equipment, not to mention fifty cases of pork snouts, were destroyed and the store owners refused to pay my fee. In fact, they now have a judgement against me in the amount of three hundred and fifty eight thousand dollars."

"Were you a citizen of the United States at the time?" asked the social worker.

"I then abandoned art, gave it up entirely, and became a lounger in the waiting room of the Greyhound Bus Station, staying alive by stealing and eating the cheaper grades of imitation leather luggage.

"After what must have been months, I was found wandering in Soho, disoriented, disconsolate and all but starving, with nothing but two corners of a plasticene portmanteau to last me until better times.

"When the papers carried another story about me, me, once known the world over for fearless, non representational experimentation, now much reduced, it was seen by Diana Sweatgland, the heiress and art collector, and she sent her chauffer to find me, which he did."

"Has problems with his sweatglands," the social worker noted on her intake form.

"She has one of the most impressive collections of modern art in the country," said the artist. "As soon as I entered her apartment, I saw four priceless Picorellis on the wall. Picorelli, himself, lay under a crystal lid in the next room.

"Diana Sweatgland was touched by my plight and commissioned me to create a work of art for her collection.

"Here was a chance to re-establish myself with one Master Stroke! I locked myself in my apartment for a whole week, taking no nourishment, and at last, I fell into a swoon, where I conceived the design for the work.

"I finished my masterpiece in ten minutes and I was overawed by my achievement. Not simply because of the bright colors, but for the originality of my medium. I had spread one slice of day old white bread with molasses and cake decorator's colored sugar pastes and I called it MOODS: SOME SUBTLE, OTHERS NOT SO MUCH SO. A STUDY.

"I wanted to take it to Diana Sweatgland right then and there but I decided to let the colors set overnight."

"It was then you lost your job as a bus driver" stated the social worker.

"The next morning, after I had awakened and seen what had happened, I ran to the bus station, broke into a supply locker, picked up a can of floor cleaner and drank off two or three quarts of it!"

"But, WHY?" asked the social worker.

"WHY? I'll tell you WHY! There, in my very bedchamber, during the night before I was to be internationally acclaimed, and as my masterpiece lay on a chair beside my bed, it was eaten by roaches!"

"Roaches?"

"All right, then . . . RATS!"

"Rats in your apartment? You might be eligible for Rat Control Vouchers! Do you own the building?"

The artist started sobbing, the while chewing on his artificial fur hat.

"Cheer up!" said the social worker. "I am here to explain our agency's famous Two Part Rehab Program."

"Two part? Two part! It must be a grant! A grant AND a studio!"

"By Two Part, I mean you are to be trained to tend bar and hang wall paper. That way, you will always have something to fall back on."

"What?" asked the artist, in shock.

"We could also offer you Poultry Technician or Asphalt Specialist."

"What are you saying?" asked the artist, barely able to talk.

"We also offer Window Maintainance and China Mending."

"You have not been listening to me" said the artist. "I am a world figure!"

"If you refuse our help, I will have to close your case. Of course, if you request it, I can refer you for a DRAW A MAN test."

The artist buried his face in his pillow and pounded the mattress with his fists, but the social worker was unaware of his behavior.

She was in near panic, looking for a scale.

"Say something!" demanded the artist. "What's the matter? Is the cat got your tongue?"

THE END

JOHN FERGUS RYAN was born in Shanghai in 1931. A resident of Memphis since 1954 and a graduate of the University of Memphis, he is the author of seven novels, among them *The Redneck Bride* and *The Little Brothers of St. Mortimer*. His work has appeared in *Esquire*, *Atlantic*, *Penthouse* and the *New York Times*.

ELEANOR GLAZE

HUMMING SONG

"...Make my bed an' light my light . . . I'll be home . . . late to-night . . . bye . . . bye . . . black-bird. . . ."

—Home of the Blues

—And Guitar twanging hicks.

—Old country songs of every conceivable kind of messing around, wailed and warbled best by those with gravel in their voices.

—Home I am humming. Dixie.

—Songs of prison, songs of love, songs of the river, songs of the Blacks, songs of the Hebrew, songs of the wild poetic Irish. . . .

—All idiosyncrasy and eccentricity I sing.

—And those tall lanky slim-hipped Nashville stage cowboys getting on a plane at night in their white outfits, fringe at the elbows, Stetson hats and rhinestones. I've been to Paris, to Rome, Athens, Nadir, and elsewhere, and I'm here to argue that Southern men are much maligned.

". . . but oh, those hard luck stories they all hand me. . . ."

—Gifts. Excuses. Flowery flourishes of pure banality.

—And the austere and stately old maids; teachers, librarians, the gristle of every community.

—Old neon beer taverns. Stink of sweat and numbed bewilderment as they merge in the smoke-hazed dark stupor of an airless stagnant summer night. "Look away . . . look away. . . ."

". . . no one here can know or understand me. . . ."

—And here comes the King and Queen in a barge on the Mississippi to commence Cotton Carnival festivities. "Look away . . . look away, Dixieland. . . ."

—Dying off, are they? The feeble old bigots rocking on their front porches in mindless dedication to decay.

—Famous for barbecue. Notorious for violence.

—How should we endure this earthly vale without the solace of some shrimp creole, okra fried, or hush puppies? (The rest of the country eats so blandly.) Or some Red-Eye gravy, made with country ham grease, flour, salt, pepper, garlic, and strong black Cajun coffee. And where you can survive if you have to on turnip greens and peanuts is fairly common knowledge.

—Not much good walking weather here, so frequently does it rain. Winter wetness penetrates to the marrow of your bones. Summers are horrible. Blinded in the glare, crazy in the heat, we dash for necessities from one life support of air-conditioning to the next.

". . . Get up round-er . . . let a workin' man lay down. . . . O get up round-er . . . let a workin' man lay down. . . ."

—So Amen to every myopic fanatic who comes to my door with a message from Jesus. Or whoever. Every glazed-eyed idiot who pesters me with circulars at the bus stop, the stop light. It's hard to tolerate in the heat. Aggravation, aggravation, sizzling eyeballs I sing.

—But oh . . . how green. If you leave and come home you are dazzled, shocked by the abundance of green, a deep, primordial lushness. And the air is scented. People here will fight City Hall, go to war if they have to, over their trees. You will see a sidewalk, or an entire street made to defer, detour around an old sacred tree.

—Landmarks disfigured. So many old houses and their legends sacrificed to freeways. In Memphis we still have the depth and refuge of the primal forest in the center of the city. We defend our densities, and we gather in the shade.

—Home of a frail lady past seventy who spent thirty years of righteous zeal protecting the Zoo from an overpass which would tear it asunder, and with secret sources, hot lines to other little old lady secretaries in Washington, blocked every move of mere Governors and Senators to disturb the peacocks and bears in their peace.

—Lorraine Motel. A scarlet sin. The murder of Martin Luther King. The night before he was slain (these kinds of things don't get in the papers) there was a storm out of season . . . call it an Omen . . . one of the tallest trees in the forest in the middle of the city was lightning struck.

—Steaming fertile earth of Dixie. Humidity. Intensity. And no prejudice against adjectives.

—Land of death so sudden slow you sometimes hardly notice. Who are our notable heros, who comes to mind immediately? W. C. Handy. Elvis. Sad that Elvis died of junk. Squandered charisma is tragic. Yet sadder still (how desperate we are for heroes) . . . to see the starving multitudes lined up on the boulevard for miles to his mansion, as if on the banks of the Ganges.

—Antiques.

—Shanties.

—Squalor. Stupidity. Those little signs, I recall, in ragged front yards saying "Happiness is not Bussing." Where those who could barely afford a roof over their heads or shoes for their feet were sending their children to private schools to avoid integration. The inferno I sing.

—Poolside ceremonies. And the indolent rich dispatching themselves all over the world from one tennis court to the next.

—Another aimless lunch today? Praise God, I pass. I plead insanity.

—Honey

—Darlin'

—You all

—Endlessly, endlessly, what do we talk of here but the capricious weather, vengeful as senile, ignored old Gods. Yet out of a perfectly clear sky I have seen lightning strike. That helps me understand and appreciate the way Eudora Welty writes. That eerie iridescent light sometimes just before a storm reminds me of Eudora Welty.

—But even in this ferociously cruel and excruciating heat, most do remain harmless, relatively. That there are few mass slaughters in July and August I find encouraging. Relatively, a specialty.

—All those Court Squares . . . where you used to could count on a spontaneous creation or spiritual Black singing, or a crazy sermon to relieve the monotony.

—All those Saturday night Main Streets, blazing, gaudy, vital . . . now forlorn ghosts. Now, every time you turn around there is another insipid Mall.

—Yet in some places there is still the fountain, the pavilion. Beneath tall trees the squirrels still scamper; the pigeons are strutting and cooing and courting; old people sit on benches with folded hands, or hand on cane, as if patiently awaiting Gabriel, the good angel of death. By night no longer does anyone reasonable venture there as it is now full of drug addicts and dealers, prostitutes, and homeless derelicts.

—Beale Street, once authentic, once the Main Street of Black people ruined in the hope of white tourists, ruined by urban renewal.

—Do you remember Wallace in his prime, snorting, stomping, raising the dust like a barnyard stud? And that little bug-eyed Lester Maddox with his little hatchet, flapping his elbows like a scrawny chicken?

—Scars of an old war, a grotesque defeat. Which is the rage that all forms of communication became so damned-Yankee Wall Street dominated.

—On the bluff two impotent old cannons point out over the river, which makes some of us imagine that the entire Civil War was fought to defend our river from Yankee invaders. We lost the war. Yet still our river flows. So much for wars.

—And from whence with our immortality complexes there have emerged those geniuses of the word who created in travail, stalked in sullen pain. Flannery O'Conner. Faulkner. James Agee. Carson McCullers.

—So you Yankees make love on your own graves . . . and leave us be.

—Ole Dixie. With one and the same breath we damn and praise. Lascivious old dowager in Lavender, morbid and maudlin and weary and tipsy, maddened and tear-stained, yet still tenderly tending her lace.

—For you no doubt recall that ageless quotation of the will not only to endure but prevail, which we chose to interpret as the written word, the life-raft of humanity. That no mean triumph of giving earth flavor.

—Faulkner once said that Mississippi begins in the lobby of the Hotel Peabody and ends at Bourbon Street in New Orleans. Our boundaries are not sharply delineated. It's all South. All Dixie. All home. Encompassing those hoarse, indomitable, and rebellious portions which refuse to perish.

—Who, viewing the Derby, watching the stately procession of those magnificent thoroughbreds prance toward the gate, fighting the bit, eager to race, who can hold back a tear at the swelling drum roll of "My Old Kentucky Home"?

—Coming home from Europe late at night, exhausted from dancing and jet-lag dazed; having thought in Italy—Oh! Look at the Italian men! having thought in France and Greece—Dear Jesus, how gorgeous! I dozed on the plane and woke as we landed in Nashville. And getting on the plane there were those tall, lanky, slim-hipped Nashville cowboys all in white—which I have seen all my life, yet never really seen. How tall they were! Taller I believe than men anywhere the world over. How confident and easy and nonchalant and self-contained. Good Lord, I thought, would you look at the Southern men! Snuggling back down with that revelation I went back to sleep. . . .

—and dreamed of the river.

—That changeless river. Swift and choppy, perpetually gray, brackish, melancholy—our immortal mud river, the Mississippi, ever resounding if only in memory with the gruff moan of steamboats, tugboats, barges.

—At the river you remember old songs, you remember Black slaves, you remember Mark Twain. You listen to its mournful sucking, slapping, lapping. No telling how many un-exonerated bones of owners and slaves lie at the bottom of that mean old river. At the river you think of eternity. You think of the sea. You wonder if the river is ever seeking home.

". . . fish are jumpin' . . . an' the cotton is high. . . ."

—And it's fixin' to rain.

◆ ◆

Eleanor Glaze's work has appeared in the *New Yorker*, *Atlantic Monthly*, *Redbook*, *McCall's*, and various literary reviews. A Memphian, she has published three novels, *The Embrace*; *Stories*, *Fear and Tenderness*; and *Jalyavara*, and has been the recipient of a Bread Loaf Fellowship and of the Tennessee Arts Commission's Individual Artist Fellowship in Literature.

IRA E. HARRISON

Bush's Horse: Campaign '88

Willie Horton, a Black,
Was Bush's Horse—
Jumping on him;
Lashing his back and sides from coast to coast
Crime to crime, parole to parole;
White George
Rode Black Willie
RIGHT
Into the WHITE HOUSE.

My Mississippi Maiden

There lay my Mississippi maiden
All African, non cajun

II

Jet hair, soft and flowing
Ebony eyes, sloe and glowing

III

Hair, moist black—unlike cotton
Smile wide easy
Not soon forgotten.

IRA E. HARRISON, associate professor in the Department of Anthropology at the University of Tennessee at Knoxville, is a frequently published poet. His early works appeared in *The Phoenix* and *The Pegasus* while he was a student at Morehouse College. Currently on the staff of *Medical Anthropology Quarterly*, Harrison also has published two books of poetry, *They/m: Beautiful Black Women* and *Pop: Poems on Parenting*.

ROBERT DRAKE

ELLA BIGGS

Years later, long after Ann Louise Parker and her best friend Martha Alice Craig were grown and married, you could send them into a fit of the giggles any time you wanted, just by mentioning the name Ella Biggs. Actually, she had come into the world as Ella Biggs Scott and then gone on to marry Tom Hanks the lawyer; but everybody in town still naturally referred to her as Ella Biggs. For one thing, it wasn't the sort of name that could be confused with any other. And then there wasn't any danger that Ella Biggs herself might be taken for somebody else.

Because, when they made her, they threw the pattern away: everybody always said that. In the first place, she was a very pretty girl who grew up into a very handsome woman, for all that old Mrs. Scott, the grandmother for whom she was named, had been a Biggs and therefore one of the homeliest women you ever saw. In her teens, Ella Biggs was considered quite delicate, though, and at one point had even been put to bed, to take the rest cure—weak lungs, they said; a phrase which in those days could strike terror into the stoutest heart as a harbinger of consumption. But she had apparently recovered and ultimately gone off to school at the state university in Knoxville where she had then been supposed to cut quite a swath—or, as some less reverent spirits put it, was thought to have hoed a wide row.

Men, of course, they said—and a good many of them. And there was a time, apparently, when her reputation wasn't any too good, either in Knoxville or Woodville. Or so Ann Louise had gleaned from her mother's guarded remarks. There was even some kind of dim allusion occasionally to the quarter Ella Biggs had spent out of school, nobody knew where: Had she "gotten into trouble," Ann Louise wondered, maybe even gone away somewhere for what was then called an "illegal operation"? Nobody ever knew. But it wasn't long after that that Ella Biggs married Tom Hanks and came back

"Ella Biggs," from *My Sweetheart's House*, by Robert Drake (Macon, Ga.: Mercer University Press, 1993), 74–80. Used by permission of Mercer University Press. This work also appeared in *The Southern Review* 24 (Winter, 1988).

home to Woodville to live in that big old house with him and his widowed mother; and everybody thought whatever the case, she would now settle down and "start a family," and that would cure whatever was wrong with her.

But all this was background for Ann Louise: it was all "before her time," as people said. And she had mainly pieced it all together from her mother's elliptical comments and even from some things her mother *didn't* say. Because her mother and Ella Biggs had grown up together, even gone off to school together. And even at age eleven—right that minute in 1941—Ann Louise knew that this was one of those ties that *bind*. And she would have to be careful whatever she said or asked about Ella Biggs. Because even then Ella Biggs was a subject of fascination for her. For one thing, Ella Biggs was the first nice woman Ann Louise had ever seen who didn't wear stockings. No matter how dressed up she was, even when she was wearing her fur coat in the winter time, she still didn't wear hose. And once when she was even younger, Ann Louise had crawled under one of the tables when her mother had the bridge club and pinched Ella Biggs's leg, to make assurance double sure. And no, Ella Biggs wasn't wearing hose; and yes, Ann Louise had gotten a spanking for her pains.

But anyhow, Ann Louise always thought that was very peculiar of Ella Biggs—but somehow exotic and glamorous, maybe even a little wicked—not tacky like dyeing your hair (which no nice woman then would admit to doing) but rather what you might call *dashing*. And she wondered whether it might have anything to do with Ella Biggs's having taken the rest cure or maybe even having an illegal operation, if indeed she had had it. But of course she couldn't say anything to her mother about it, just mainly talk it over with Martha Alice and *wonder*.

As it turned out, Ella Biggs never had started a family, just gone on working downtown in her husband's law office and living in the house with old Mrs. Hanks. And Ann Louise thought that might be a trial. For one thing, Mrs. Hanks couldn't let there be a crack in the Baptist church door without her being there to see what it was all about; and she couldn't meet you on the street or even in the checkout line at Kroger's without asking you were you saved. Ella Biggs's own family, the Scotts, were all Methodists, though Ann Louise didn't think any of them had ever worked at it very hard; so she couldn't imagine living with old Mrs. Hanks was any kind of jollification for Ella Biggs.

But then Ella Biggs was different, and maybe none of it ever totally bothered her. The more Ann Louise thought about it, the less Ella Biggs seemed to fit into any of the Woodville molds anyhow. And more and more, she began to fascinate Ann Louise as a figure of romance, even drama—maybe something like those characters Bette Davis often played—women either doomed or damned, sometimes even both. And the mystery was further enhanced when Ann Louise stopped to reflect that she had hardly ever spoken to Ella Biggs in her life; she wasn't even sure what Ella Biggs's voice sounded like. It was almost as though she was one of those people (a symbol?) you talked about rather than talked to. But you couldn't ever ignore her; that much was certain. Whatever the case, she was a very attractive woman with an aura of mystery about her, and she might even have had a past. And her present life was probably none too pleasant.

Every time Ann Louise saw her coming down the stairs from her husband's law office up over the bank in the late afternoon, especially when it was cold weather, and Ella Biggs had her fur coat just lightly draped over her shoulders instead of securely and snugly worn and of course not a sign of a stocking anywhere in sight, she wondered whether Ella Biggs might not be preparing to rush off to meet her fate in the form of a dramatic car wreck (in a convertible of course) or else as the result of double pneumonia. (And when people went *into* pneumonia, as they were often said to do in those days, they rarely ever came *out*.) That's what would have happened to Bette Davis, Ann Louise knew; but of course she could tell right that minute that Ella Biggs was simply on her way to the post office with the day's outgoing mail and not about to wake up and find herself the heroine of a melodrama. Ann Louise had sense enough to know that. Real life was funny that way: it often seemed awfully shapeless and things didn't always add up—not like they would have in the picture show. But whom could you tell that sort of thing to? Most people would have thought you were crazy.

As it turned out, what actually happened was wilder than anything Ann Louise could ever have dreamed up; and she wondered, was it really true what people always said about truth being stranger than fiction. Because not long before Thanksgiving that year, Ella Biggs set out in her car late one afternoon, with a light snow falling, and headed down the Memphis highway. She was seen by all manner of people, of course, and was even said to have waved at a couple of them. But apparently she got no further than the bridge over the Obion River. Because that was where they found her car about an hour later—parked right beside the railing, the lights still on and her fur coat right where she had left it on the front seat. (They found out later she had taken the day's outgoing mail by the post office on her way out of town.) There was the footprint of a woman's shoe in the snow on the bridge railing, so of course they started dragging the river right away. But they never found Ella Biggs then or later; and for all anybody in Woodville knew, she had indeed vanished into thin air.

Well, or course, it was decidedly the most dramatic—and the most talked about—thing that had ever happened around Woodville in Ann Louise's memory; and her imagination had a field day. Some people who saw Ella Biggs driving down the highway that day said they had just assumed she was on her way to the early picture show over at Monroeville, but Ann Louise thought anybody ought to have better sense than that. Who on God's earth, she wondered, would want to leave home late in the afternoon of a snowy day and drive through the cold of the early dark just to see a picture show that would be playing right there in Woodville the very next week—and Jeannette MacDonald and Nelson Eddy at that, teeth and all? Later on, other people said they knew Ella Biggs must be in the river (and by this time Woodville was almost divided into two camps—those who did and those who did not believe Ella Biggs had committed suicide) because, they said, no woman, in her right mind or out of it, would ever have jumped in the water with a perfectly good fur coat on. But then Ann Louise thought you could have argued that either way: what woman anywhere would want to go off, to the grave or anywhere else, and leave a perfectly good fur coat behind? But then why did they never find Ella Biggs's body after days and days of dragging for it? And then why did nobody ever find a note or anything? There never was a funeral or anything like that either, so nobody even knew what to say to the family. And *they* certainly weren't talking.

A week later, Tom Hanks did put an "acknowledgment" in the weekly paper, to thank all those friends who had sent food and flowers and kind messages to him in what he called his "bereavement," but he never said a word of thanks to all the ones that had dragged the river. And some people thought that was strange, but then so was everything else about the whole business. And if Ella Biggs wasn't in the river, where on earth had she gone? It was the biggest mystery Ann Louise and Martha Alice and all their friends could ever have imagined; and they spent hours trying to "solve" it all, looking for clues, conjecturing motives, even acting out "The Disappearance of Ella Biggs," as they called it, like it was a picture show, with Ann Louise sometimes playing the lead and sometimes Martha Alice (depending on whose mother's fur coat they could get hold of).

But of course, they always had to steer clear of Ann Louise's mother, whatever they were doing. Because she was nothing if not *loyal,* and she always maintained that Ella Biggs *was* in the river. She told Ann Louise she thought maybe "poor Miss Ella Biggs" was afraid she might have to take the rest cure again and just couldn't face the prospect and that was why she had "done it." But Ann Louise noticed her mother was always looking out the window—or somewhere else—whenever she said that. And anyway, Ann Louise thought Ella Biggs must have had more sense—more to her—than that. There were other theories around town, of course: some people said Ella Biggs just couldn't stand living in the house with her Big Baptist mother-in-law any longer and it was her way of getting back at Tom Hanks, who had always been something of a mamma's boy anyway, and whom she never had really loved anyhow. But they didn't know where she was either. The wildest speculation of all had Ella Biggs's disappearance connected with the fairly sudden departure from Woodville a few weeks later of a very personable young man named Johnny Gitchell who worked up at the funeral home, a fairly new institution in Woodville back then. (The old families still patronized Waterfield and Hill, who operated their undertaking business on the second floor of their furniture store down on the Square; but everybody said they were on their way out because they weren't keeping up with the times.)

Ann Louise didn't remember that she had ever heard anything about Ella Biggs and Johnny Gitchell before all this happened; but then it just might be natural for two such people to be drawn to each other, she thought. There was Ella Biggs, who came of nice folks and had maybe had a past but, in any case, certainly didn't wear stockings, and Johnny Gitchell, whose history nobody knew except that the folks up at the funeral home said he could lay out the prettiest corpses you ever saw in your life—why shouldn't they be somehow connected? (It was the way Hollywood would have written it.) And why weren't Tom Hanks and Ella Biggs's own family more grieved than they apparently were? And what all did they know anyhow?

It was all the great mystery of Ann Louise's young life; there was simply no doubt about that. And even better than the picture show, in some ways. After all, it had really happened, right there in Woodville; and she herself had actually known Ella Biggs, even one time pinched her naked leg under the bridge table, to see for herself whether she was wearing hose. That was about as real as you could get. But why did they never find Ella Biggs, dead or alive, and nobody ever know for sure what had happened to her? The movies wouldn't have done it that way: they wouldn't have left you dangling like that. So the mystery went on and on and, in some ways, became more alluring still. After all, when you found out about Santa Claus and where babies came from and all that sort of thing—or even who had "done it" in a murder mystery, that was the end of it. But the mystery of Ella Biggs only deepened with time.

Over the years, while Ann Louise was growing up, there would be reports of people seeing Ella Biggs—usually "out" in Texas or somewhere west. (Places like that were always "out.") And every summer for years after that, Ella Biggs's mother, Mrs. Scott, would take a long trip somewhere by herself; and a lot of people assumed she was going to visit Ella Biggs, wherever she was—or perhaps they were just meeting somewhere, on "neutral ground." Ann Louise even heard of one man from Woodville who claimed to have spotted Ella Biggs and Johnny Gitchell operating a sideshow at an amusement park "out" in California; but she thought that was a little farfetched even for California. But even wilder was the report that came back from Texas that Ella Biggs—this time alone—had been seen on the streets of San Antonio dressed in a nun's habit! Tom Hanks finally remarried but had to get a divorce from Ella Biggs, *in absentia* as it were, because she hadn't been gone the seven years or whatever it took to be declared legally dead. And this time he built his wife a house of her own and didn't take her home to live with mamma. And this one was a real homebody—hardly ever went downtown, Ann Louise heard; and she wore stockings too. Ann Louise, who was off at school now, had asked about that right off.

But the riddle of Ella Biggs abided—for Ann Louise and, she suspected, for everybody else in town. The whole thing, of course, had long since made Ella Biggs community property; everybody could always put in his two cents' worth about what he thought had really happened—and why. And from then on, nobody ever had to ask *who* when you were driving over the Obion River bridge, usually on the way to Memphis, and somebody in the car would speak up and say, "Well, did she or didn't she?" Ann Louise herself could wake up in the night, all those years later, and think about the exciting time when Ella Biggs disappeared and ponder the mystery all over again and the revelation it had all become for her and Martha Alice in due course—what they had learned about folks and maybe even about themselves from it all. It had certainly been a kind of watershed in their lives, she knew. And she would think how funny, finally, it all was and wish Ella Biggs well, wherever she was, in this world or the next. And somehow it didn't seem to matter one way or the other.

So that was probably why when she and Martha Alice got together for the first time in a couple of years (Martha Alice lived in Memphis now and they hardly ever saw each other), they both practically had the hysterics when Martha Alice was telling her about her oldest daughter, who had just married and moved to Washington, being royally entertained up there by an elderly cousin who had left Woodville many years ago. And when the daughter had told her mother what a great time she had had, Martha Alice had been a little puzzled. "Really, I can't imagine what you two had in common," she had said. "She's been gone from Woodville so long, and she's so much older than you are anyway. What on earth did you have to talk about?"

"Why, Mother," the daughter had replied, "we talked about Ella Biggs."

Robert Drake

ROBERT DRAKE is professor of English at the University of Tennessee at Knoxville. Born and reared in Ripley, Tennessee, Drake was educated at Vanderbilt University and earned his Ph.D. at Yale. With five published collections of stories to his credit, he also has maintained an active career as an essayist and scholar.

COLEMAN BARKS

THESE THINGS, HEREAFTER

For James Augustus Pennington

I think the first poem I ever got was one by Edna St. Vincent Millay that Mr. Pennington read our 8th grade Latin class in (Good Lord!) 1951. It's called "Afternoon on a Hill."

I will be the gladdest thing
Under the sun!
I will touch a hundred flowers
And not pick one.

I will look at cliffs and clouds
With quiet eyes.
Watch the wind bow down the grass
And the grass rise.

And when lights begin to show
Up from the town,
I will mark which must be mine,
And then start down.

I was fourteen at the time and had grown up as a kind of joyful solitary wandering the Baylor hill. I knew those cliffs and clouds, and I had looked with quiet eyes. For the moment, *self* and *world* came together in *words*. I still like the poem, though the first stanza seems inflated. Too sticky-sweet for my taste now.

But O, I can still respond to the center of the poem, the grass and the wind part. There is a phenomenon in human experience that needs a name. Some have called it the *hieros gamos*, the sacred marriage, a kind of glistening in the consciousness. Calm,

"These Things, Hereafter," from *Gourd Seed*, by Coleman Barks (Athens, Ga.: Maypop Books, 1993), 97–100. Used by permission of the author.

trembling times when we feel a deep sense of harmony with the soul. It's part of the work of artists to find images and expressive form for that.

I'm happily snowbound in the north Georgia mountains as I write this (Sunday, April 5th, 1987), and hear suddenly the ten inches of snow slide off one whole side of the A-frame roof. A slow, undertowing sound, almost as though it's inside me, but the dog has her ears up. Each of us discovers different ways of welcoming the universe into us, of being less and less defended against the warmth of the sacred marriage. Poetry became one of my ways. My brother Herb has riding the whitewater of the Chattooga as one of his. That's what the Greek term means. It's something essential and exciting, what I felt in Pennington's class.

Ecstatic, pure-being moments are not, of course, the whole story. There's irony and wit. Reason and clear-eyed judgement, and the grounded ramble of an ornery human voice. There's Pennington's mighty opposite in those years, Jim Hitt. But what I, and others, learned from Pennington were *moments*, and the way sometimes words and the world can sing together.

Pennington could recognize those sacred-marriage, St. Vincent Millay grasses when he saw them shining in a Latin phrase, in the elegant condensation so possible in Latin. When Herb called and left the message on my machine that Mr. Pennington had died, I went to my old Virgil book and opened it at random. Now, there is some precedent for doing this. After Virgil's death it was a common practice, called the *Sortes Virgilianae*, to consult the works of Virgil to learn the future. On and off the practice continued, even into this century. The British High Command consulted Virgil for advice in World War I! (Pennington would love this scholarly aside.)

I open to page 474. It's Book VI of the *Aeneid*. Aeneas is getting a glimpse of the other world! The only phrase circled on the page, in my 1955 scrawly pencil script, is

Hac iter Elysium nobis,

which means, "This way (takes) us to the Elysian Fields (the sixth heaven)." How wonderful and incredible.

This is how it might have gone in the long ago classroom. "Which words did this guy Virgil choose to put next to each other?"

Silence.

"*Iter* and *Elysium*," he screams.

("Iter" is our word "itinerary.")

"What is he saying!" Pennington climbs up and is now standing on his desk.

More silence. Pennington descends and circles the room, prowling, pulling shirts up, untucking ties. "What is he saying?"

"The trip feels heavenly." Borisky feels brave.

"You would." Borisky's shirt gets unbuttoned two buttons.

"Go for the gold!"

"Hey, take a round off, Seessel, yehhhhhhhh."

"The journey is the kingdom." My try.

Long pause.

"You know, Coleman, I think so. I think soooooooooo."

(I was his favorite, some days.)
He sits back down in his tilt-back chair, relieved, and tilts way back.
"Oh young men, I love woids, woids, wooooiiiidddds."
Arms open, shivering upward, "Iter Elysium!"
Over his classroom door, as you went out, was the sign,

HAEC OLIM MEMINNISSE IUVABIT

Hereafter, it will have been pleasant to have remembered these things.
Haec olim. Yell it, HAEC OLIM!
These things hereafter, Mr. Pennnnnnyyyyyyyyyy.
As I look up the Millay poem to check how closely I remember it, close enough, here on the opposite page is another poem of hers that I remember Pennington loving.

Lord, I do fear
Thou'st made the world too beautiful this year;
My soul is all but out of me,—let fall
No burning leaf; prithee, let no bird call.

Such an extravagant heart, Edna Millay, and James Pennington, in his *moments*, was more than a match for her.

GAUZE

I played Joseph once in the Christmas tableau
at the First Presbyterian Church in Chattanooga.

Some girl, a beautiful madonna-hyphen-sexy
-older-than-me-ninth-grader was Mary, Amy,

Amy Somebody. We were lit by a baby-glow that
the congregation couldn't see what it was from out

in their lower dark. A light bulb covered
with gauze. There began my stagelife,

cuckolded by God, without a speaking part, standing
with fake wise men, in pure mystical solitude.

These Very Feet

A Spring stars-just-out nine-thirty when
I was five, or four, before school, that fear,
before clothes, I step out of my bath, am held in
the big towel, then out of that to the front porch
and out the screen door, along the curve of boxwoods
through the tower, down its flight of three stairs,
next flight, next and next, to the open
ocean of the quadrangle.

It doesn't seem like I am running,
rather more a thought sails into night,
an *idea* of nakedness and Blakean joy,
with, of course, my parents and older brother
close in pursuit laughing and reaching and finally
snaring the fleeing figure back to pajamas and bedroom,

but these fleet insouciant feet remember nothing
of that. They became evening air and a bit of sky
calmly taking another kind of bath, with no telling
how began their adoration of moss
in the cool brick wall.

The Look on the Dog's Face

How is it dogs know already the big
circling game they play with boys,

where the kid and the dog both get down
with forearms along the ground like sphinxes.

Then the boy runs at the dog and the dog
takes off in a circle that brings it back

close enough to be touched but not grabbed,
and changes tack to make a figure-eight out

the other way with the boy in the hourglass door.
The game needs a lot of space for the dog

to do right, a field, or a biggish backyard.
I've even seen it done on a steep hillside.

The look on the dog's face is
trickiness and barely embodiable joy.

COLEMAN BARKS, a native Tennessean who teaches English at the University of Georgia, published his first collection of poetry, *The Juice*, with Harper and Row in 1972. From the late seventies to the present he has been known as well for his translations of the thirteenth-century Sufi poet and mystic, Jelaluddin Rumi. His *The Essential Rumi* was published by HarperSanFrancisco in 1995.

JOHN EGERTON

SPEAKING THEIR MINDS

When I opened *The Mind of the South* for the first time, the book was almost two decades old and Jack Cash had been dead for nearly that long. The year was 1960. At the age of twenty-five, I was confined against my will in a hospital room in Tampa, Florida, having landed there for an extended stay after an automobile accident. I had plenty of time to read and reflect, to think about what I was missing outside. On a little black-and-white television set, I watched John F. Kennedy and Lyndon B. Johnson recapture the White House for the Democratic Party; a few weeks later, in his inaugural address, Kennedy would stir inside me (and millions of others) a deep sense of hope and expectation, a desire to *do* for my country. So much cried out to be done. In my homeland, my native South, the black minority was summoning the courage to challenge white supremacy with nonviolence, and the white majority was lashing back violently against adults trying to vote, college students at lunch counters, even little children at school and church.

The impact of Cash's book on me was about the same as if someone had rolled a hand grenade under my bed. In the very first pages, his voice seized my attention: ". . . the South is another land . . . there are many Souths . . . there is also one South . . . far from being modernized, in many ways it has actually always marched away, as to this day it continues to do, from the present toward the past. . . ." *The Mind of the South* echoed in my own mind like Jefferson's proverbial fire bell in the night. As a comatose person might emerge from deep unconsciousness, I slowly began to hear and see and understand. Cash's biographer Bruce Clayton said it well: "No one who reads Wilbur Joseph Cash is ever quite the same again."

Strange that a book of such perception and power should have come from the typewriter of a man like W. J. Cash. A giant in the minds of many who have read his book, he was actually an unimposing fellow who cut an unheroic, unromantic figure. Picture him in about 1938, before his book and his marriage gave him a brief period of happiness: He wore the melancholy expression of a misfit, a shy, withdrawn, moodily petulant bookworm with sad eyes blinking behind owlish, steel-rimmed glasses. Not yet forty, he was a rumpled bachelor lacking in style and social grace; he had lost his youthful slenderness and was losing his hair. He was a neurotic, a hypochondriac, a sickly man given to chronic bouts of depression, a lonely, tortured soul trapped between binding convention and a liberating imagination. One of seven children born to a fundamentalist yeoman couple in a Carolina mill village, he had somehow become an agnostic city dweller who drank and smoked too much, an intellectual without an academic base, an eccentric journalist yearning to write novels. For almost a decade he had been working on a big-idea book of Southern social analysis, but most of the time his friends on the staff of the Charlotte *News*—and he himself—seriously doubted that he would ever finish.

The Mind of the South was recognized early by H. L. Mencken as a potential book buried in Cash's disordered but penetrating thoughts (this after the young Carolina journalist had sold a freelance article by that title to Mencken's *American Mercury* in 1929). The Baltimore editor attracted Alfred and Blanche Knopf to Cash and his idea as a project for their New York publishing house, and for almost twelve years the Knopfs patiently endeavored to coax the book from him. The wait was certainly worth it. What they got was not journalism or scholarship or history, but a many-layered dissection and anatomy of the Southern white male rendered in a brilliantly original, provocative, judgmental, and disarmingly personal narrative to which even its few panning critics (Donald Davidson most conspicuously) conceded certain undeniable virtues.

The book was not perfect. It was more about the Carolina piedmont than about the South writ large; its analyses of women and blacks revealed Cash's lack of close association with both; it could have benefited from a little more documentation—some hard data, some citations, some notes—and at the very least, it needed a bibliography. Sometimes the Cashian flights of rhetorical verbalizing were like Roman candles, a triumph of style over substance.

But forget all that. W. J. Cash evoked the South as few writers before him had done. Drawing from a full bag of literary devices—first- and second- and third-person perspectives, monologue and soliloquy, satire and irony, dialogue and description, detachment and engagement—he could turn a phrase, paint a picture, spin a yarn. He had an organized sense of where he was going with his argument, and he knew how to keep it moving. Above all, he had a point of view; he made independent observations, passed judgment, came to conclusions. Like Myrdal's *Dilemma* and the nonfiction works of Du Bois and other writers, Cash's *Mind* had a moral dimension. Myrdal, with all his credentials and an army of aides, had made his pronouncements from the distant safety of New York and Stockholm; in contrast, Sleepy Cash was just an ordinary guy standing alone in the heart of darkness, saying things about his beloved and benighted Southland that made his own countrymen wince—and then nod in reluctant agreement and even admiration.

It was the white masses that populated lynch mobs, he said, but it was the upper classes that inspired and protected them, and the failure of this "better sort" was the genesis of the South's undoing, its original sin. The Old South planters, the textile barons, the politicians and bankers and cotton brokers who controlled the region and kept it in feudal backwardness were not really aristocrats but erstwhile dirt farmers just a step or two up from the frontier. The New South was really the Old South in spruced-up garb. The white ruling elite created the illusion of a class-free society by uniting all whites in dominion over the blacks—and the lowly whites, out of a misguided sense of gratitude and superiority, were willing to fight and die for a social system in which they had no real stake. Cash saw through the Rebel-rousing Old South myth perpetuated in literature and history; he saw the hand of the state and the church and the academy in it too, and Yankee acquiescence, if not outright chicanery. In Cash's essentially tragic view of Southern history, the common mindset of the white South conformed to a "savage ideal" that bonded most of its citizens to a narrow interpretation of the past, the present, and the future. And there he left it:

> Proud, brave, honorable by its lights, courteous, personally generous, loyal, swift to act, often too swift, but signally effective, sometimes terrible in its action—such was the South at its best. And such at its best it remains today, despite the great falling away in some of its virtues. Violence, intolerance, aversion and suspicion toward new ideas, an incapacity for analysis, an inclination to act from feeling rather than from thought, an exaggerated individualism and a too narrow concept of social responsibility, attachment to fictions and false values, above all too great attachment to racial values and a tendency to justify cruelty and injustice in the name of those values, sentimentality and a lack of realism—these have been its characteristic vices in the past. And, despite changes for the better, they remain its characteristic vices today.

His friends in Charlotte loved Jack Cash, and out of a sense of loyalty if nothing else, they also loved his book. They were delighted when he married a vivacious divorcee, Mary Northrop, in December 1940, just two months before *The Mind of the South* was published. The friends were proud, too, and even their doleful colleague managed to smile, when strongly positive and favorable reviews of the book began to pour in from around the South and from the national press. They could not have foreseen, of course, that it would become the best-known and most influential book of nonfiction ever written about the South, never to be out of print in the first fifty years of its existence. All they knew was that it was important and good and true, and that was enough for them.

His friends could not have known, either, that Cash's time was short, but some of them were aware that he was pursued by his own private demons, driven at times to hand-wringing depression and anxiety. He received a Guggenheim fellowship, and in June, he and Mary went to Mexico, where he hoped to begin work on a novel. Within three weeks he was an emotional wreck—paranoid, delusional, certain that Nazi agents were pursuing him. His pleading wife finally got him to see a psychiatrist, but there was no relief. With everything to live for, with so much to give, W. J. Cash could only hear the demons. In a Mexico City hotel room on July 1, 1941, he hanged himself with his own necktie.

There was a certain Southern poignance, a familial quality, to what happened after that. After Mary phoned Pete McKnight back at the *News* in Charlotte to get the tragic word to Jack's parents and his other family and friends, she was left, alone and afraid, in the custody of the Mexico City police. Hours later, the American embassy sent a driver to police headquarters to pick her up and bring her to shelter, on orders of the U.S. ambassador to Mexico. It was more than an impersonal act of courtesy; it was what you would expect from an old Southern gentleman, a North Carolina patrician: seventy-nine-year-old Ambassador Josephus Daniels of Raleigh.

In good time, Cash's ashes were given a proper Baptist burial in the Sunset Cemetery at Shelby, North Carolina, a short walk from the home of his parents and a stone's throw from the spot where another Carolinian of note, the novelist Thomas Dixon, the propagandist of romantic racism, would soon be laid to rest.

Death, like politics, makes strange bedfellows. . . .

. . . That summer [1955] outbursts of random violence against black Southerners spread ominously across the South, as had happened after the world wars. In Mississippi, four people were killed in separate incidents that amounted to nothing less than assassinations, lynchings. One of the victims, fourteen-year-old Emmett Till of Chicago, had been visiting relatives in Tallahatchie County. A young white woman claimed he got fresh with her. Two men, one of them the woman's husband, tortured and killed the boy, and threw his mutilated body into a river. After they had been acquitted by an all-white jury, the men told the whole story to maverick journalist William Bradford Huie, representing *Look* magazine. The case stirred the nation's conscience momentarily, but the attention span was short, and the South soon slipped again into the shadows, out of sight out of mind.

The Washington journalist I. F. Stone summed up this latest manifestation of the American dilemma:

> There is a sickness in the South. . . . Mississippi went through the motions [of seeking justice], and the motions were enough to muffle the weak conscience of the northern white press. . . . Those whites in the South and in the North who would normally have moved to act have been hounded out of public life and into inactivity. To the outside world it must look as if the conscience of white America has been silenced, and the appearance is not too deceiving. Basically all of us whites, North and South, acquiesce in white supremacy, and benefit from the pool of cheap labor created by it. . . . The American Negro needs a Gandhi to lead him, and we need the American Negro to lead us.

Two months later, in Montgomery, Alabama, a black Gandhi with a voice like Southern thunder answered the call.

It was after the second *Brown* decision and the Till murder trial, but before the start of the Montgomery bus boycott, that the Southern Historical Association invited William Faulkner and Benjamin Mays, among others, to discuss the Supreme Court's school decisions at the group's annual meeting in November 1955. The SHA had overcome its traditional deference to segregation in recent years, and on this occasion—an integrated dinner meeting at the Peabody Hotel in Memphis—the historians interrupted Mays with prolonged applause several times as the Morehouse College president delivered an eloquent and impassioned "historical sermon" on the immorality of segregation.

The historians who were chiefly responsible for this session—Bell L. Wiley of Emory University, Thomas D. Clark of the University of Kentucky, Philip G. Davidson of the University of Louisville, and James W. Silver of the University of Mississippi—would long remember with special pride the appearance of both Mays and Faulkner, the latter by then a world-renowned author by virtue of his Nobel Prize. Later, when the South's cancerous racism had broken to the surface, the quiet Mississippian would speak with confused ambivalence about the South's crucible of race. But on this occasion, his brief remarks (and an appended passage he wrote later) were direct and to the point.

"To live anywhere in the world of A.D. 1955 and be against equality because of race or color," Faulkner declared, "is like living in Alaska and being against snow." The only faith "powerful enough to stalemate the idea of communism" is the belief in "individual human freedom and liberty and equality." The momentous question was "no longer of white against black," Faulkner asserted—it was the age-old question of slavery or freedom. It also had to do with repeating the mistakes of the past: "We accept insult and contumely and the risk of violence because we will not sit quietly by and see our native land, the South, not just Mississippi but all the South, wreck and ruin itself twice in less than a hundred years, over the Negro question." He concluded:

> We speak now against the day when our Southern people who will resist to the last these inevitable changes in social relations, will, when they have been forced to accept what they at one time might have accepted with dignity and goodwill, will say, "Why didn't someone tell us this before? Tell us this in time?"

Faulkner was not the first Southerner to "speak now" against white supremacy, and to prepare his listeners for a coming time when segregation would fail and the old social order would be swept aside for the new. He had found enough universal truths in the provincial lives of his fictional Mississippi characters to know that everything changes—that peace and prosperity, mobility and materialism, technology and population growth, and dozens of other factors beyond the control of any man, democrat or demagogue, will inevitably transform a society, ready or not. The segs weren't going to turn back the clock to the nineteenth century anymore than they were going to take Jackie Robinson and Willie Mays out of the lineup, or bar Ralph Bunche from the Harvard campus, or keep Thurgood Marshall from prosecuting Jim Crow, or take away Edith Mae Irby's University of Arkansas medical degree.

Benjamin Mays, standing on the shoulders of such giants as James Weldon Johnson and W. E. B. Du Bois, had been pointing to Jim Crow's judgment day since he assumed the presidency of Morehouse in 1940. Numerous other Southern progressives, including half a dozen or more who died in the mid-1950s, right around the time of *Brown*—Mary McLeod Bethune, Walter White, Osceola McKaine, Maury Maverick, Howard Odum, Charles S. Johnson—had found their own quite different and varied ways to "speak now" in admonition of and preparation for the inevitable demise of segregation, and they had gone on speaking until their voices faded away and new ones filled the silence. Johnson, in a *New York Times Magazine* article in September 1956, just a month before he died suddenly of a heart attack, took note of the thinning ranks of white liberal advocates of civil rights in the tense post-*Brown* atmosphere. The South, "provincial and isolationist to the core," would never reform voluntarily, he concluded—the courts would have to mandate it.

A month after Mays and Faulkner spoke to the historians, events in Montgomery hastened the day of racial justice that would eventually sweep over the South. There were heralds and antecedents to this drama: Two local organizations of black citizens—the Progressive Democratic Association, headed by E. D. Nixon, and the Women's Political Council, led by Jo Ann Robinson, had long been trying to combat racial discrimination in the city. Nixon, a former president of the Montgomery NAACP chapter, was a Pullman car porter with organizing skills he had learned from his revered labor union boss, A. Philip Randolph. Among Nixon's local friends were Aubrey Williams, the *Southern Farmer* publisher, and Clifford and Virginia Durr, the former New Deal attorney and his activist wife (all three of them having been in the news the previous year during their sensational clash with Senator James Eastland in New Orleans). Through Williams and the Durrs, Nixon had met Jim Dombrowski of the Southern Conference Educational Fund and Myles Horton of the Highlander Folk School. Highlander had started summer workshops on school desegregation in 1954, right after the *Brown* decision. The Montgomery NAACP wanted to send a delegate to Highlander the next year. They chose their youth director, Rosa Parks, a forty-two-year-old seamstress.

The rest of the story is now engraved in civil rights history. Rosa Parks was arrested on December 1, 1955, after she refused to obey a Montgomery bus driver's order to surrender her seat to a white person. (On two previous occasions that year, teenage black girls had been dragged from city buses and jailed for alleged violations of the segregation code.) E. D. Nixon was called, and he took Cliff and Virginia Durr with him when he went to the jail to post bail for Mrs. Parks. A boycott of the bus system was announced, and on Tuesday evening, December 5, a mass meeting was held at one of the city's black churches to organize a nonviolent Christian protest group called the Montgomery Improvement Association—the forerunner of the Southern Christian Leadership Conference. It was at that gathering that twenty-five-year-old Martin Luther King, Jr., the newly installed pastor of the Dexter Avenue Baptist Church, was chosen to lead the group, and it was there that he first galvanized and mobilized a following with eloquent, soaring rhetorical flourishes:

> If we are wrong—the Supreme Court of this nation is wrong. If we are wrong—God Almighty is wrong! If we are wrong—Jesus of Nazareth was merely a utopian dreamer and never came down to earth! If we are wrong—justice is a lie! And we are determined here in Montgomery to work and fight until justice runs down like water, and righteousness like a mighty stream!

On the wings of the biblical prophets, a new voice—young, black, and unmistakably Southern—was speaking against the day when a confused and divided South would face the inevitable demise of segregation uninformed and unprepared. For the next thirteen years, Martin Luther King would be the transcendent figure in a movement to liberate the soul of the South.

• •

JOHN EGERTON, who lives in Nashville, is the author of eight books and innumerable articles and essays. His *The Americanization of Dixie*, *Generations*, and *Speak Now Against the Day* are critically and popularly praised as seminal, yet accessible, works in American studies. *Speak Now Against the Day* won the Robert F. Kennedy Book Award for 1995.

CONNIE JORDAN GREEN

NOVEMBER

In the fall of the year
the house calls us
to wash windows
to rake leaves

while she herself—
old house—
squats into the hillside
seventy years
mellowing her lines
until shrubs, trees, house
fit like unmortared stone.

We like to think
we own these walls
that have sheltered our years
to think the thing
grown wild can be tamed
by clean windows
by leaves raked into rows
awaiting the compost pile.

Bread

We go in not knowing
where we'll come out—

anchored by
the smooth kitchen counter
the cold, precise cups and spoons

the bowl old
like something our grandmothers
peeled apples into.

We know the feel—
wooden spoon stirring flour
easy as children's laughter

then our hands into the dough
the rising, the shaping
the warm loaf, aroma binding us

sure as one more day
of baking bread.

Connie Jordan Green is the author of two novels (*The War at Home* and *Emmy*), stories for young people, and poetry. Green's poetry has appeared in more than twenty-five journals and publications, including *Confrontation*, *Cumberland Poetry Review*, *Iowa Woman*, *Poem*, and the anthologies *Some Say Tomato* and *Voices from the Valley*. In addition, since 1978 she has written a weekly newspaper column for the *Loudon (Tenn.) County News-Herald*.

NIKKI GIOVANNI

GRIOTS

I must have heard my first stories in my mother's womb.

Mother loved a good story and my father told good jokes, but it was her father, Grandpapa, who told the heroic tales of long ago. Grandpapa was a Fisk University graduate (1905) who had majored in Latin. As he sometimes told the story, he had intended to be a diplomat until he met Grandmother, but that is probably another story altogether, he being Black and all in 1905 or thereabouts.

Grandpapa loved the stars. He knew the constellations and the gods who formed them, for whom they were named.

Grandpapa was twenty years the senior of Grandmother, so he was an old man when we were born. Grandmother's passion was flowers; his, constellations. One needn't have a great imagination to envision this courtship: the one with her feet firmly planted on earth, the other with his heart in the sky. It is only natural that I would love history and the gossip of which it is composed.

Fiction cannot take the place of stories. Aha, you caught me! Fiction is stories, you say. But no. Stories, at their best, pass along a history. It may be that there was no Ulysses with a faithful Penelope knitting and unraveling, but something representative of the people is conveyed. Something about courage, fortitude, loss, and recovery.

I, like most young ladies of color, used to get my hair done every Saturday. The beauty parlor is a marvelous thing. Every Saturday you got the saga of who was sleeping with whose husband; who was pregnant; who was abused by whose boyfriend or husband. Sometimes they would remember the children were there, but mostly the desire of the women to talk without the presence of the men overcame their desire to shield us from the real world.

My mother's family is from Albany, Georgia, but Grandmother and Grandpapa had moved to Knoxville, Tennessee. We four grandchildren spent our summers with Grandmother.

At night, when we were put to bed, my sister Gary and I would talk and sing and sometimes read under the covers using our Lone Ranger flashlight rings. Of course, we were caught. Grandmother would threaten us and take our rings. We would sneak out of our room, wiggling on our stomachs, to reach the window under which we sat and listened to Grandpapa and Grandmother talk.

Sitting under that window I learned that Eisenhower was not a good president; I learned that poll taxes are unfair. I heard Grandmother berate Grandpapa for voting Republican when "Lincoln didn't do all that much for colored people." I heard assessments of Black and white people of Knoxville and the world. No one is enhanced by this. I'm not trying to pretend they were; there were no stories of "the African" in my family, although I am glad there were in Alex Haley's.

We were just ordinary people trying to make sense of our lives, and for that I thank my grandparents. I'm lucky that I had the sense to listen and the heart to care; I'm glad they talked into the night, sitting in the glider on the front porch, Grandmother munching on fried fish and Grandpapa eating something sweet. I'm glad I understand that while language is a gift, listening is a responsibility. There must always be griots . . . else how will we know who we are?

• •

NIKKI GIOVANNI, a native of Knoxville and a graduate of Fisk, is the author of nineteen books of fiction, nonfiction, and poetry, all but one of them still in print and many of them bestsellers. The recipient of innumerable awards and honors, Giovanni has also been named Woman of the Year by three different magazines, *Ebony* among them. She is now a professor of creative writing at Virginia Polytechnic State University.

BETTY PALMER NELSON

UNFAMILIAR TERRITORY

Charlie Cooper, who was also eight, was the first person Rob met when his family moved to Pattonsburg. Rob had been standing by the car looking at the house, which had a tall point over the door. It was about the same size as their house in Louisville. Some trees around it had branches to climb in, and the grass needed mowing.

But the town was a lot different from Louisville. It was like there wasn't any town. What Daddy called town had one short street with a few stores and a couple of service stations. The marquee on Daddy's new theater stuck out over the sidewalk like the green awnings on the stores. It was hot in the car, and it would be cooler in the shade under the awnings.

His father said it was an ideal location because the drugstore was next to the theater, and moviegoers could get ice cream at the fountain before or after the shows. Mommy said she doubted if there'd be many moviegoers in a town that small. Daddy said there'd be enough. This was not just the only movie theater in town, but the only one in twenty miles in any direction. He said that again: "Yessir, twenty miles in any direction."

Mommy just sighed and leaned her head onto the seat back. Rob hoped she wasn't going to be sicker and have to go back into the hospital.

Then they drove to the new house, and Daddy said, "Velma, we're here."

Mommy raised up and said, "Well, thank goodness. I don't think I could ride another mile." Daddy helped her out of the car and up the walk and through the door.

Rob stayed outside to look around. That was when he saw Charlie looking through the hedge. Only he didn't know it was Charlie then.

Finally Charlie said, "Who're you?"

"Rob McFergus. Who're you?"

Charlie came out of the hedge. His red-striped polo shirt was rolled up in front and showed his belly button. His red hair was short all over his head. "Charlie Cooper. You going to live here?"

"Yeah. My daddy just moved us. He runs the movie theater." Rob had learned this was a plus. Saturday mornings watching John Wayne or Jerry Lewis were prizes to give a friend. Even when the movies didn't make sense and had a lot of kissing, the kids had been impressed when he took them into the projection booth to see the little beam of light that turned into people and things on the screen.

"Yeah? My dad says television'll take the place of movies. We got a television last year."

"Oh, yeah? Well, I've seen television, and it's not colored like the movies. John Wayne's not on television, either."

"Want to come see our television?"

"Yeah, maybe sometime. I got to go now. My mommy might need me. She's been real sick."

"Yeah? What's the matter? She gonna die?"

"I don't know. I don't think so." Rob scuffed up the gravel in the drive. It was round, brown creek gravel, not crushed limestone like their drive in Louisville. "Is there a creek around here?"

"Yeah, a mile down the road. You got a bike?"

"Yeah, but I can't ride it out of the yard."

"Me neither. Tell you what, maybe my pa'll take us to the creek tomorrow. It's too hot to stay in town, and we're too big to play in a washtub."

"Yeah."

Charlie was pulling leaves off a bush. "You got any brothers or sisters?"

"No, just me."

"I got two sisters," Charlie confessed with disgust. "Brenda's about grown. She's finishing up high school this year. She's okay, I guess. *She's* got a *boy*friend." Charlie rolled his eyes and raised his sandy brows. "And then there's Debbie. She's twelve, and she's *awful*. You're lucky you got no sisters."

That night Mrs. Cooper brought over some food for the McFerguses and asked if the next day Rob could go to the creek with them, and his daddy said yes, so he met Brenda. She wore a bathing suit like Marilyn Monroe, and her tits weren't as big, but she was pretty, with blonde hair in a pony tail. She asked Rob where he moved from and what Louisville was like, and she really wanted to know. She didn't want to get her hair wet, so she didn't swim, but she got her suit wet, so he could see where her belly button was. She waded in the edge looking for pretty rocks and shells. Rob found some, and she seemed real glad to get them. She smiled at him. She wore lipstick. He thought Charlie was lucky to have a big sister. Then if his mother got sick, he'd still have somebody.

Debbie was something else again. She was always picking on him and Charlie, bossing them or tattling when they wouldn't do what she said or when they splashed her. Charlie was half right, anyhow: he was lucky not to have a sister like her.

That summer Mommy did get worse and had to go to the hospital in Nashville, just for a while, Daddy said. He stayed with her when he didn't have to be at the theater, and Rob stayed with the Coopers. Charlie went with him every Saturday morning to the theater. Sometimes Brenda or Debbie would go too.

When school started, Brenda walked home with him and Charlie every day. Charlie teased Brenda about somebody named Ronald, and she called Charlie "Copperhead," which he hated, but she was always nice to Rob.

Rob's mother got worse, and Daddy stayed in Nashville except on weekends. Daddy paid Brenda to stay with him. Rob was glad.

Brenda slept in his mother and father's bed. Staying at his house, she was like his sister more than Charlie's. At night she wore short little gowns she called baby dolls, pretty colors with full underpants. She took long baths, and when she came out of the bathroom, it smelled like flowers like her.

One night he had a bad dream. He was lost in the dark, and he tripped and was falling down a deep hole. He woke up sitting up in bed, and he must have cried out, for Brenda turned the light on and came in. "What's the matter?" she asked. Her hair was all rolled up, and bobby pins stuck out all around.

He told her about the dream, and she said, "Sometimes I have bad dreams too. Do you want me to snuggle with you till you go back to sleep?"

He nodded. She turned out the light and climbed into bed with him. It was cold, so there was a blanket under the bedspread, and she put her arm under him and hugged him. He got warm again and was about to go back to sleep when she shifted her weight and said, "I'm sorry, Rob, but your bed's too little for both of us. Why don't you come to mine?"

"Okay."

So they went across the hall and settled into the double bed and got warm again. She felt soft next to him, and the last thing he remembered before sleeping was the way she smelled.

The next night when he tried to sleep, he kept thinking about the nightmare. Finally he got up and crossed the hall in the dark. "Brenda?"

"Is that you, Rob?"

"Yes." He was ashamed to go on; a big boy wasn't afraid of the dark.

"What's the matter?"

"I can't sleep."

"Are you scared?"

"No. I just . . . I might dream my bad dream again."

"Come sleep with me then."

He didn't answer, but padded across the cold floor and crawled into the space she made under the covers.

She hugged him; he could feel her breasts against his arm. "My little teddy bear; come on and cuddle up. Oh! Your feet are cold. Put them against my leg till you're warm again."

He did; he could feel the prickles where she shaved. Pretty soon the warmth filled him and her sweet smell and the softness. He went to sleep then.

The next night he asked, "Can I sleep with you again?"

"Sure," she said.

The next night he didn't ask, but just crawled into her bed after he had brushed his teeth.

On the way to and from school, he had to share her with Charlie. And sometimes

Ronald, her boyfriend, talked with her after school until he had to catch his bus. He was a big boy with big hands. Charlie said he lived on a farm and raised calves. Charlie had seen Ronald's calves once. He had dogs too.

Rob's father came home every Friday to work at the theater that night and Saturday and to see the woman that took the tickets and the boy that swept out the theater and ran the projector when he wasn't there. Daddy would get clean clothes and leave his dirty ones for Brenda to wash and iron before he came back.

Brenda would ask how Mrs. McFergus was, and Daddy always said, "All right. She's going to turn a corner soon and get well."

Daddy would spend Friday and Saturday night at home and go back to Nashville on Sunday. Brenda would come over and fix lunch on Saturday, then go home and not come back till Sunday afternoon. On Sunday Rob and Daddy would eat Vienna sausages out of a can for lunch.

Daddy came home on Rob's birthday, and Rob hoped he would bring the cap pistols he wanted. But he didn't; he didn't say anything about Rob's birthday. Rob told Charlie on Monday, and Charlie told Brenda.

"You mean it was your birthday, and you didn't even get a cake? Poor thing! I'll bake you one."

She did. She made a devil's food cake with chocolate icing and let him lick the bowl. She fried chicken, and she and Charlie lit candles and sang "Happy Birthday" and gave him a copy of *Tom Sawyer*. He already had a copy, but he didn't tell them.

The second Friday in December, Daddy didn't come home. Brenda said he had called her mother. "Your mother's real sick, and he doesn't want to leave her. I'll stay here tonight. But Ronald's coming, so you'll have to go to bed early."

"Okay." After supper he went to his own bed.

He couldn't sleep. He heard Ronald come and tried to hear what they said. But he didn't hear talking much. After a while, he got up and went to the bathroom and looked into the living room. They were on the couch with their backs to him, and Ronald had his arms around Brenda, kissing her. He kept saying, "Oh, baby," and she moaned as if he were hurting her. But sometimes in the movies they did that. She said things too, but Rob couldn't hear what.

He went back to his cold bed. Finally the front door closed, and Ronald's truck started up and drove off. Pretty soon Brenda went to the bathroom, then to bed. She didn't check to see if he was asleep.

Ronald came again Saturday night. The next day, Rob went to church with the Coopers. He sat between Brenda and Charlie but didn't touch her. When they prayed, he prayed that his mother would get better.

When they got back, the Cooper's telephone was ringing. When Mr. Cooper hung up, he came to Rob and put his hand on Rob's shoulder. "Boy, I'm sorry. Your mother died this morning."

Rob didn't say anything. He turned and went out. On the porch, he started running. He fell down once in his Sunday clothes, but he got up and went on. When he got home, he threw himself across his parents' bed. He didn't cry.

Mrs. Cooper came in and made a big fuss over him and took him back till after supper and the Ed Sullivan Show.

That night Brenda asked if he wanted to sleep with her. He said no, but he didn't go to sleep for a long time.

The next day, his father came home. He told Rob they were going back to Circleville for the funeral. "I reckon we'll bury your momma there," he said.

Rob remembered when his dog Abe got hit by a car and they buried him under a rose-of-Sharon bush. Abe had been all bloody from the car, and his tongue had hung out.

"You always said she was going to get well," Rob said.

"Well, son, I hoped she would. I hoped she would." Daddy looked away. "But I reckon she'd rather be with Jesus in heaven."

Rob didn't say anything.

Just before the funeral, he saw her. She was in a metal box, and she had gone away from him farther than the hospital, though she was right there in the box. The preacher said she was happy with Jesus in heaven. So she must have wanted to leave him.

When they put her in the ground in the cold metal box, he cried and pulled Daddy's hand and said, "Don't let them put my mommy in the ground." But they did.

• •

BETTY PALMER NELSON, a native Tennessean who has lived all over the United States, now lives with her husband in Cottonwood, Tennessee, and teaches at Volunteer State Community College. Since 1990, St. Martin's Press has published five volumes of her *Honest Women* series about changing relations between men and women in Middle Tennessee from 1820 to 1980. *Changing Seasons*, the most recent in this series, will appear in 1996; this selection, originally part of that manuscript, was omitted by the publisher.

TOM C. ARMSTRONG

Here, I Neither Ode Nor Threnode Sing

early on in our lives
death
starts stopping by
for brief visits
from time to time
just to get acquainted

later
having thus prepared us
death moves in
into our body
and mind
and lives with us
for a few weeks or months

and then
in turn
has us
move in with him

when
doesn't much matter
at the end
we find
we can live with death

well-acquainted at that point
the body generally eager
the flesh weary
blood and brain tired
recycling old wounds
suffering new

often
even the mind
doesn't mind

knowing that it's had its future
and that memories
are but outtakes
from a film
which
like most
couldn't be fixed
in Edit Bay

aware also
that this certain
curtain closing
is not
a cue for an encore

April and October —Visitation Vision

there's this ghost
visits me every April
he gets bored, he says
spending springtime
surveying grass roots
from the grave
(it's not greener
on the other side)

he comes again each October
it's the most vital month
he tells me
and his last outing
before winter sets in
(he has Raynaud's disease
then, too
ghosts also
have trouble negotiating
the waters of life
solidified and slippery
as ice)

"April and October - visitation vision," by Tom C. Armstrong, appeared in *Pacific Coast Journal* 2, no. 4 (Fall, 1994). Used with permission of French Bread Publications, P.O. Box 355, Campbell, Calif. 95009.

thus
ghost-juxtaposed
I'm more alive and vibrant
in April and October

and do less well
in summer and winter
left alone
hot and bothered
out in the cold

• •

TOM C. ARMSTRONG, a widely published poet, is a member of the Academy of American Poets, the Authors Guild, and the Writers Guild of America. Book editor for *Nashville Life*, he is also a successful playwright and scripter.

RICHARD MARIUS

FROM AN UNTITLED WORK IN PROGRESS

If Charles Alexander had not broken the sabbath, he would not have been witness to murder. He would not then have had a .38 Smith & Wesson hammered to his forehead while a corpse lay at his feet. He would not have made his doomed promise to the killer. He would not have broken his word; he would not have made his blasphemous bet with God. He would have missed everything.

All his life his story would have reminded people of the tale of someone who missed a plane that crashed or those Japanese called out of Hiroshima unexpectedly to the countryside in the serene and sunny early morning of August 6, 1945. Now, more than forty years after the dog-day night in 1953 when Hope Philip Kirby murdered his wife and her lover on the courthouse lawn, people in Bourbon County would recall Charles as a footnote.

"Oh yes, the second oldest Alexander boy was deep in his books at the newspaper office that night. He was a reporter, you know. A prig, if you ask me. Went to summer school up at the university? Went to class in the morning? Drove back to Bourbonville in the afternoon in that smelly old Ford? Wrote for the paper? You remember.

"Took pictures for the paper, too. Don't you recollect? That big black camera. Belonged to Lloyd Brickman, that camera did. Who was Lloyd Brickman? Lord, Lord. He was the one drownded in the lake with that girl? Editor of the paper? Ah well, they're both dead for many a year. Everybody knowed what they was doing out there in the lake when the rowboat turned over. Fished them up out of the water nekkid as couple of dead jay birds. You know what that means, I reckon.

"Anyway, Lloyd bought the camera. And he left the kid that old '37 Ford station wagon. Lord, that jalopy looked like a rolling junkyard. That car give the name to Ugly! The fenders had rust holes in them you could put your fist through, and them wood sides—hell, they rattled like a skeleton falling downstairs.

"Tell you what I recollect about the '37 Ford. That was the last year ole Henry made them with mechanical brakes. Next year, '38, he put in the hydraulics. Now I tell you something about mechanical brakes; they don't quit on you like them hydraulics do. No sir. You tighten them brake cables ever day, and you got brakes. Course, nowadays you got real brakes, things we never heard about in my day.

"What was I talking about? Oh sure. The Alexander boy and the murders. He studied his books in the newspaper office late at night on account of his idjit brother. Older than he was; the idjit was older, I mean. The idjit used to play the Victrola or the radio real loud at night. Liked music, you see. Idjits are like that; they love music. Calms them down when they get frantic. I mean, that's what I hear. Hell, I don't know. Ain't never been an idjit myself.

"Anyway, boy couldn't study at home nights with all that racket. Taken his books with him to the newspaper office and studied right there after work. Only thing was, he kept the Sabbath. Wouldn't study on Sunday. Shut his books up tight at the stroke of midnight on Saturday and didn't open them again until the next midnight brought in Monday. Pious little shit, don't you know.

"Well, not meaning no harm. I'm all for God and the Bible and Jesus and all that shit, and I think it's damn good for kids to say prayers in school. Keeps the meanness out of the little bastards. And hell, this was 1953, and you know how little towns was in East Tennessee back then. Well, I reckon you don't know. But let me tell you about it.

"Back then everybody was religious or pretended to be. Billy Graham was a whooping and hollering and telling everybody the world was going to end and raking in money in big cardboard buckets. You go to a Billy Graham meeting, and you see the dollar bills falling over the edges of them buckets like foam off beer. But the Alexander boy, he was the real thing—on his way to cemetery to learn theology and all that stuff and how to preach, and he was already preaching some, and he wouldn't do nothing to break the laws of God.

That's why he wasn't there. Midnight come. Courthouse clock struck twelve. He shut up his books and walked out the door and locked it and drove home. An hour later, them two was shot dead. They say her husband done it. But nobody could prove nothing. He said he was out on the lake fishing with his brothers, and wasn't nobody to say different. So he went scot free. He's retired now. You see him at the post office sometimes and in the bank cashing his pension check. But he keeps to hisself.

I sometimes want to ask him, I want to say, "Hope? Did you kill them two? You can tell me now. Hell, it's been forty years. Be honest with somebody who ain't going to tell nobody nothing, somebody like me that can be silent as a tombstone. Did you do it? Did you kill them two? Cross my heart and hope to die with almighty God as my witness, I won't never tell."

What Really Happened

That's the way it might have been if Charles had gone home at midnight, when the sabbath—the Christian one—began. But he did not. And because he stayed at his books one more hour, no one can speak of those murders without telling his story. No one who remembers, that is. The murders would have happened anyway. Everybody agrees to that. Just like a football game will happen whether you're there watching it or not.

Hope Kirby's pretty young wife walked into his trap. He shot her dead, and he killed Kelly Parmalee, too. He planned every detail; his brothers helped him.

They were accessories, legally speaking. But in wise restraint the state brought no charges against them. County prosecutor Wilbur McNeil had a sense of proportion. He was sixty years old, and he had to live in Bourbon County. By the time the trial was over, he was through anyway. Washed up and washed out, although he kept on being county prosecutor another five years until he fell dead one afternoon walking back and forth in front of a dozing jury. When he hit the floor, the jury woke up. He's buried in the City Cemetery. Dead a long time now.

The county took Hope Kirby's side. Yes, he was the killer. Nobody doubted that when you got down to it. He was a war hero, and people made excuses for him. They still do. Bataan Death March survivor; escaped from a Jap prison camp; carried his loony brother John Sevier off almost on his back to the hills of Luzon after the Japs beat John Sevier in the head and made him loony.

Hope waged guerrilla war against the Japs until MacArthur came back. Silver Star. Highest decoration anybody in Bourbon County won during the Second War. He was quiet, modest, minded his own business, and didn't drink or smoke. The way Bourbonville looked at it, killing his wife and her lover was his right. Caught them in the act, didn't he? Well, almost. The people of Bourbon County thought that if justice had been done, Hope Kirby might have spent a year and a day in the penitentiary for involuntary manslaughter, come home, taken his place in town, and got back his job at the car works. Nobody would have spoken to him about the thing everybody thought about when anybody saw him.

Part of the blame lies on Wilbur McNeil. Everybody who remembers agrees on that. Wilbur McNeil had a steely heart, and he was ambitious in a crazy sort of way. Putting a man in the electric chair sated something in him. Sport. He could cover up his sporting instinct for death—even from himself—with a phony gravity that made it seem that he hated to do his job, that he did so only out of the oath he had made to uphold cruel laws, and only out of the understanding that if you did not hold the lash over society, it would disintegrate into chaos. He was a drugstore philosopher. Sipping his Coke, he told you how things were and why the world was bloody. It couldn't be any other way.

He was not surprised at the wave of sympathy for Hope Kirby that rolled through the county. Wilbur McNeil knew the world, had seen through it years ago. Nor did he give a hoot for what happened to Charles Alexander. He didn't like Charles Alexander, if the truth be known. He was not pious himself, and he could not understand piety in others.

Wilbur McNeil understood that public office was theatre and that you had to make some gestures to the audience or else be hissed off the stage. From the first he resolved to put Hope Kirby in the electric chair for sport but to spare the brothers for theatre. So Wilbur McNeil.

The linchpin of McNeil's case was the testimony of Charles Alexander. Charles Alexander got most of the blame, gets it to this day when anybody speaks about him. Everybody knew that the boy should not have been there. Bad luck all around. Hope Kirby told his brothers that he was startled out of his wits to see Charles Alexander that night. "It's the one thing I didn't plan for," he said. "The one thing I didn't think about."

Hope had planned everything else down to the minute. On two consecutive Saturday nights he told Abby that he was going fishing with his brothers Joye and Love on the lake. When the Kirby boys fished on Saturday night, Hope did not come home until Sunday morning. On these two Saturday nights he embarked with the two brothers from the little boat dock above Ft. Bourbon Dam in the gray twilight when a sheen of whitish light glistened on the water. Joye sat in back next to the five-horse Johnson outboard motor. He steered. Love sat in the middle. Hope sat in the prow next to the coal-oil lantern. He held his rod and reel and looked abstractedly off in the gloom lost in thought. A dozen or so casual witnesses saw them go churning slowly out into the smooth anonymity of Fort Bourbon Lake. Not for the first time. The waters darkened under the darkening sky. The wake trailed behind them like an expanding silver fan, and overhead the stars came out.

Just past midnight, the lantern dark, the motor cut, Joye let the boat slip to shore under trees hanging over the water, and Hope made his way on foot to a grove of cedars near the old Martel Pike not far from the Martel Church. With perfect timing, his brother M. L. swept out of the dark in his pick-up, slowing down enough for Hope to leap inside. Hope crouched in the front seat, and M. L. drove him into Bourbonville and dropped him in a dark alley near the depot where a couple of silent warehouses stood on a spur line of the railroad, sliding doors faintly illuminated by naked light bulbs.

Hope glided into the square and to the side of the courthouse facing southwest, towards the railroad tracks. He could move like the ghost of someone dead a thousand years. He had practiced silence two years in the mountains of Luzon. A man did not forget talents picked up in a game of life and death. The Japs tortured captured guerrilla fighters to death. Better to kill yourself than let the Japs practice pain on you.

There he sat, back against the brick wall, hidden by boxwoods growing around the courthouse. The brick wall gave off the heat of the day, and the boxwoods smelled like boxwoods, a thick, unpleasant smell in the humid summer night. He sweated. His cotton shirt glued to his skin where he leaned against the wall. He sat still and waited.

Hope Kirby was like his daddy. He had patience. His patience had made him deadly in the Philippines, and he had not lost it. At almost exactly the same time each Saturday night, he saw what he came to see. He heard the Plymouth lonely on the lonely street. He recognized the engine, the swish of tires, the peculiar combination of many sounds adding up to only one car in the world—Abby's car. In seconds she swept around the courthouse and pulled into a slanting parking place as far from the street light as she could get. No other car was in sight. She turned out the lights and waited under the trees. He heard the engine pop, cooling. He could see her face an unfocused white blur in the open window of the driver's side. From up the track came the mournful rise and fall of a freight train whistle, the train bound out of Knoxville to Chattanooga and Birmingham. He heard its distant, attenuated rumble augment.

In moments Kelly Parmalee strode around the building. He resembled a mannequin from his store window, dressed in a tie and a linen jacket, sleek and thin and nervous, looking this way and that, the gesture of a rodent coming out of a hole, the stagey, useless caution that the poor fool must have absorbed unconsciously from western movies where men in funny hats did all their ducking out in the open where the cameras could see them.

Seeing nothing because he did not know what he should see, Kelly Parmalee sped to the car, opened the door on the passenger side, and flung himself inside, shutting the door softly. Hope Kirby saw the two of them embrace, Abby's dark hair gleaming dimly in the dim light. He saw his wife borne down under the window by Kelly Parmalee's body, her white arms uplifted, clasped around his neck. A half mile up the tracks, the train rounded the bend by the cotton mill. The high, panting breath of its Baldwin 4-8-4 locomotive and the rhythmic clanging of its bell and the jubilant shout of its whistle and the following clangor of the cars rolled in waves of sound over the square. Just as the engine exploded past, the great white clock in the courthouse tower struck one, a crash of time across the rooftops of the sleeping town.

Kelly Parmalee helped Abby Burdine Kirby out of the car, her hair and clothes already disheveled. He led her across to his store on the square, the two of them oddly substantial in the dim light shed by the electric street lamps. He unlocked the door, and they disappeared inside. The train rolled by, spaces between the cars flashing against the background of feeble lights between the tracks and the river, and suddenly the caboose passed, a faint glow in the windows, a coal oil-lamp probably, and on the back of the caboose a red light gleamed and was gone, and the sound dropped off, dwindled, softened, and decreased into a murmur receding, the train blowing for the bridge across the river six miles south, and passing into silence, heading south.

Hope Kirby waited. In an hour they emerged. Kelly Parmalee put his head out, looking this way and that. He said something into the opaque obscurity of the store, gesturing impatiently. Abby came out in languor, looking across the square so that if she had known what to look for she might have seen her husband's face gleaming behind the boxwoods. They passed close to him walking towards the Plymouth.

"I don't want to go home, honey," Hope Kirby heard her say one time. She seized her lover's hand. Kelly Parmalee replied anxiously, in a low voice, urgent but indistinct to Hope Kirby in his hiding place. Abby reached up to kiss him. Kelly Parmalee pushed her away. He shook off her hand and hurried off, disappearing around the courthouse heading up Kingston Street, to the safety of home where his wife slept unknowing in their bed.

Abby stood for a few moments looking after him, her pout visible even in the weak light, an attitude of body more than an expression on her face. Hope Kirby could have spoken to her, and she would have heard. But he remained silent. Kelly Parmalee did not look back. Hope Kirby thought, "She is in love with him." He was not angry; he was surprised. He knew Kelly Parmalee only by sight, but he thought the man was an effeminate fool. More than anything else, he felt emptiness opening inside him, a pit, bottomless and dark, and the emptiness inside the pit had weight that squeezed his chest and his stomach and for a moment made it hard for him to breathe.

After the second Saturday night, Hope Kirby talked it over with his brothers and with his father. They sat on the porch of Pappy's little house with its garden out in the country towards Varner's Cross Roads, and Hope told what he had seen. Nobody said anything for a while. Pappy looked off into the distance with a studious expression and ran his hand over his smooth chin and thought, and his sons waited for him to say something. It was Sunday afternoon, and you could smell the sun baking the fields beyond the deep shade of the verandah where they sat in hard wooden chairs. Everything was still. At last Pappy looked at his eldest son and shook his head, a little jerk of decision. "Only one thing to do, boy. You got to kill her. Kill them both." Pappy spoke quietly in a dead sure tone.

"I figured you'd say that," Hope said.

"Hit's the onliest way they is. You got to be a man; she done you wrong. They hain't nothing to do but kill her. Too bad. I liked her."

"I liked her, too," Hope said.

"Well, hain't no use thinking about it. You got to kill her."

That was it, judgment without appeal. The third Saturday night Hope sat against the courthouse wall holding a .38 revolver on his thigh, and he waited. The blued metal joints of the Smith & Wesson were so closely fitted you could scarcely see them. In the Philippines he had a Colt .45. He got it from an officer who died. The Colt .45 automatic was a canon; the Smith & Wesson was a thing of beauty.

He had scouted the square. The moon was full and standing high in the sky, but under the canopy of oaks tall and densely leaved around the brick courthouse, the darkness was softly thick, and on the side where Hope Kirby sat, only a couple of widely spaced street lamps dimly glowing shed any illumination under the trees.

Nothing moved except an occasional car or truck passing through on Highway 11, and Highway 11 ran by the front of the courthouse, where the courthouse lawn was wide, and he knew Abby would park her car in back, on this side that faced the railroad. Here, between the courthouse and the railroad, nothing broke the stillness.

Tonight a 1937 Ford station wagon was parked at an angle near the place where Abby would come. It looked abandoned, a wreck, a worn old rattletrap country people drove until it wouldn't run any more, and then somebody towed it to a junkyard, and it rusted and rotted, and weeds grew up through holes in the floorboards, and pretty soon it was covered over with green, and a tree burst through the roof, and fat snakes lay sluggish on the rotting fabric seats when the sun came through the blue safety glass of the windows.

Something vaguely familiar about the station wagon; Hope Kirby could not place it. He dismissed it. He sweated. His clothes were soggy, and he could smell himself. An unpleasant smell. The air was as thick as oil. The radio had declared triumphantly that humidity during the day had been 94 percent and that the temperature had been 101—the hottest August 23 on record. Something to be proud of. Tennesseans could endure hell.

Hope Kirby waited. Above him in the oaks, millions of katydids sang, their steady, monotonous throbbing like a soul of the universe struggling to say something it had not yet thought out.

Hope Kirby sat, embracing his knees, alert and patiently watchful. He thought a worm could not burrow in the ground without making a noise that he could hear, and the katydids made his ears ache. He heard the train far, far up the line, farther than anyone else in Bourbonville might have heard it, the faintest suggestion of a rumble like distant thunder, continuous in a storm. His heart beat regularly, slowly, his self-control so perfect that he thought sometimes that he might be able to stop his heart merely by willing it.

He remembered Jap patrols coming through the Philippine forests, how silently they moved, how in the face of their silence he found a deeper silence of his own and carried his men down into it, down and down, until the instant when he sighted down along his BAR and squeezed the trigger. He always felt a sadness swirling with him in that silence; he felt it now.

He heard the mournful, extended hoot of the locomotive entering the block five miles away at Martel, and the distant, indistinct rumble shook the air faintly, augmenting, and he heard Abby's Plymouth. She drove into the parking place next to the old Ford, stopping with it between her and her watching husband. Almost at once Kelly Parmalee came gliding around the courthouse from Kingston Street and went to her car. The train hammered through Bourbonville at five minutes past one, blowing for the crossing by the depot. Hope Kirby thought it would take two bullets—easier than the Japs in the Philippines. Abby and Kelly Parmalee would not expect him; they would not shoot back.

He would kill Abby first, he thought. If he did it fast, she'd not know she was dead. One minute alive, the next gone wherever the dead go. He wanted Kelly Parmalee to know. He hated Kelly Parmalee because Kelly Parmalee was forcing him to kill Abby.

◆ ◆

RICHARD MARIUS is the author of numerous books, including *After the War* and *The Coming of Rain*. A native of Tennessee, he now lives in Massachusetts, where he is director of expository writing at Harvard University.

ISHMAEL REED

OPEN HEART

True love is
When you lose ten pounds
He loses five
On the day they cut you
He couldn't eat

True love is
Your idle fox car
And your fickle garrulous cat
looking as though they haven't
A friend in the world

True love is
Your daughter and your
Husband holding you up
You're taking your post-
Operative steps
The infusion pump
"IMED 980"
Is leading the way
They pretend that
You're the queen and
It's parliaments' first day

True love is
You lying in bed
Tubes sprouting from you
like the Orchid stems on
Your night table
You are as vulnerable
As the flowers that Nancy
Sent
The note attached said
"Water Immediately!"

True love is
Your husband watching
The color return to your face
The radio is tuned to Monterey
The nurses say that they can't
locate your veins, but he manages
To find your fragile hand
He's listening to A. Henricks
scat a Thad Jones solo and catching

Brando in "The Fugitive Kind"
It's playing above your sleep

The weather inside the movie
is like the weather of life
It rains in black and white

Outside the walls of
Kaiser-Permanente
The silence is dry
The drought drags on

◆ ◆

ISHMAEL REED, a Chattanooga native, is professor of English at the University of California, Berkeley. His novel, *Mumbo-Jumbo*, and *Conjure*, a collection of poetry, were both nominated for a National Book Award; the latter also was nominated for a Pulitzer Prize. Reed is a cofounder of the Before Columbus Foundation, a national organization that has been instrumental in furthering the work of new and emerging writers.

MARILOU AWIAKTA

HONOR TO THE FOUNDING ELDERS OF OAK RIDGE

In Celebration of "Tennessee Homecoming '86"

> I spend a lot of time with the elders. They've lived long enough to move beyond the ego to the calm. I need their counsel.
>
> —Chief Wilma Mankiller, Descendant of Outacite (Ostenaco), "Mankiller of Great Tellico" (Tennessee)

Chief Mankiller's words make me think of you—the Founding Elders, my parents and their contemporaries. Because of you there's an Oak Ridge to come home to. Thank you for homemaking—and for what you continue to do, homekeeping.

I remember you in the frontier days when we all came to Oak Ridge—in the 1940s and early 1950s, the time of my childhood and youth. Most of you were in your thirties then. Although atomic energy was the keystone of our community, even the word *atom* was new to the public mind. Looking at Oak Ridge from the outside, many people considered it a dangerous, futuristic place, as remote and alien as a space colony floating in the blue-hazed billows of the mountains. To us it was home. While we children played, you worked. Worked hard, creating the root system for dwelling, school, and church; for laboratory, society, and city government. And all of it "from scratch."

I don't see how you did it, especially now that I'm doing the same kind of work. I didn't have to start from scratch. When I married and moved to Memphis in 1957, the city was flourishing like the green bay tree, its "rooting" six generations in the past. However, in researching my second book, *Rising Fawn and the Fire Mystery*, I went back to 1833, when Memphis was a pioneer town, a gateway to the West—to the future—as Oak Ridge was a gateway to the Atomic Age in the forties and fifties. I discovered that whether it has a population of one thousand or seventy-five thousand, a frontier in any century is a raw place—a hurly-burly, physically primitive, dangerous, invigorating, lonely, freewheeling, "do-for-yourself-or-do-without" place. For a family to survive, the parents and other elders must have courage, stamina, shrewdness, faith—and an earthy sense of humor. When I tell you what I saw in Memphis in 1833, you'll know why I often smiled and thought of you and our early days together:

"Honor to the Founding Elders of Oak Ridge," by Marilou Awiakta, appeared in *These Are Our Voices* (Oak Ridge, Tenn.: Children's Museum of Oak Ridge, 1987); and was reprinted in *Selu: Seeking the Corn-Mother's Wisdom* (Golden, Colo.: Fulcrum Publishing, 1994), 142–52. Used here with permission of the author.

- Dirt streets—mud if it rained—and holes in them big enough to drown an ox (or swamp a car).
- Small, look-alike houses, mostly of logs.
- A few stores, a hotel: rough-hewn, square or shoebox shaped, strictly utilitarian.

Overall, a drab-looking place, except for close-drawn woods and the Mississippi River.

We had woods and the Great Smokies, but structurally Oak Ridge was drab, too, with its ash-gray houses and barrack-style public buildings that were painted such a boring green color that we all made fun of them.

Federal ownership. A big difference from privately-owned Memphis. Humor in both places, but in Oak Ridge, government bureaucracy was a major target. You made jokes like these:

"How many men does it take to pick up the garbage?"

"Ten. Two to take the top off the can. Two to carry the can to the truck. Two to dump it. Two to carry it back. Two to put the top back on!"

"How long did they take to paint the inside of our house?"

"Long enough to raise a litter of pups. First the 'ceiling crew' came. Two weeks later the 'wall crew' came with flat paint. Two weeks after that the 'spotters' came to touch up the walls—with enamel!"

"Wait a minute. That's only four weeks. Takes six for pups."

"Well, it took me two weeks to get used to the shiny spots!"

"The red tape around here is so bad that if you want to make a baby, you have to fill out a form—*in triplicate*!"

"Humor is the saving grace," Mark Twain said. And you had it in abundance. In the midst of hardships, you created fun (as your Memphis counterparts did) with laughter, dancing, plays, picnics, parties, music, clubs, and visiting with relatives and friends. By example, you taught us children not only the value of work, but also of the "saving grace" so necessary for perspective—for survival.

You were good horse traders, too. And Tennesseans have always admired the ability to cut a shrewd, fair deal. The government needed you for the Manhattan Project, and you laid the terms on the line—among them, the best teachers for your children. And we got the best. Never mind that the buildings were rough in the beginning, the education going on inside was second to none. And you supported the work as parents, teachers, counselors, and interested citizens. Also, federal ownership was an advantage for education—money poured in; whereas in Memphis, the pioneers had to begin with a privately funded class (for boys only) in a house and build from there. On that frontier I would have grown up illiterate.

Pioneer churches were freewheeling, building-wise; people had to use available structures, which led to some funny situations. For example, Memphis Methodists, whose favorite axiom was "Whiskey leads to dancing," had to meet for a while in the Blue

Ruin Saloon, so-named because its gin gave regular customers a blue tinge to their skin. In Oak Ridge, after an ecumenical period of taking turns using the Chapel-on-the-Hill, religious groups found other quarters. We Methodists went to Sunday school in the high school above Jackson Square, then hurried down the hill to the Ridge Theatre for church, where it was dim and cool and the seats were soft. This state of affairs shocked some "hard-pew" advocates, one of whom I quoted to my father:

It's a Sin and a Shame

"It's a sin and a shame,"
said Miss Mabel Travain,
"these children are churched in a movie.
With those billboards they'll sink
and grow up to think
that God looks like Clark Gable!"

Daddy laughed when he heard,
"Why, the woman's absurd . . .
You can think better than that.
How much worse it would be
if you grew up to see
that God looks like Miss Mabel!"

As you did elsewhere, you elders "kept your eye on the mark . . . steady as you go." From watching you, we learned to walk in balance, which included the ability to cope with the swarm of different people.

Memphis had "the swarm" on a small scale—less than one thousand residents—but a constant flux of people with different origins: Native American, European, and African-American. They came to trade, unload cargo, settle, or head west. (Some also came to raise Cain.) Since material resources were few, inner resources had to be many.

Oak Ridge had a *big* swarm—people from all over the United States came to settle among Appalachian families, like mine, who had lived in the area for generations. Oak Ridgers had a common purpose—to work on nuclear energy. And fortunately, government security kept many of the worst "Cain-raisers" at bay. But the fission of the atom in the laboratories was mirrored in the community. There was high energy and high confusion. Life had to be sorted into an orderly pattern. It was up to the elders to create the pattern.

One of the best parts of it was that everyone had a similar lifestyle, regardless of occupation. Our neighborhood on South Tampa Lane was typical: families were involved in science, construction, city government, cafeteria management, the ministry, teaching, accounting. A business entrepreneur lived in a D-house next to a grocer who had converted a school bus into a "rolling store." When it wasn't en route, the bus was parked in front of the family's flattop house. Needless to say, the rolling-store kids were the most popular on the block.

Neighbors worked and played together—kept each other company. In hot weather everyone was outside a lot, for we depended on mountain air-conditioning. In cold weather, tending the fire was a constant family chore, just as it had been for Memphis pioneers. While their major heat came from a fireplace, ours came from a coal furnace. Remember how the coal was dumped in a closed bin near the furnace, just inside the house's back door—which faced the street (always confusing to non-Ridgers)? Almost everyone came in through the back door and tracked coal dust through the kitchen into the living room. Fire was a *presence*. It had to be fed regularly in daytime, banked at night, stirred up in the morning. Parents taught children its ways, and every family member old enough to be responsible took a turn firing the furnace, as we took turns with other chores.

Our pioneer life was a hands-on, communal experience that included the joy of just being alive. After years of fear and horror, World War II was over. The dark clouds had rolled back, the breeze was tonic-fresh, the sun full on our faces. For a season we rejoiced and were glad.

Then the wind changed. As it seems to do on every generation's frontier.

In Memphis, the change came in the late 1830s, when the federal government shoved the natives (Chickasaw Indians) out west to make way for Big Power, Big Money—the cotton industry. The city grew past its sapling stage and branched into "good" (wealthy) and "bad" (low-income) neighborhoods, into divisions of class and race, into the "we's," who had power and money, and the "they's," who didn't. Some elders thrust to one side or the other. But as Memphis leaned in the wind, the wisest elders found their counterparts among the newcomers and began shoring up the roots of the community in every sector. Only a few elders, however, recognized and warned against the deadly borer making its way toward the city's heart—slavery. It caused damage that Memphis leaders of today are still working to heal.

The primary segregation in Oak Ridge was of a different kind—what we had was a season of high and bitter crosswinds, when the city swayed with change. It corresponded approximately to my youth, 1950–60. When the fence came down in 1949 and real estate gradually transferred to private hands, the city began to take on color—literally, in paint and construction, and figuratively, in business and political patterns. Slowly, the population stratified, neighborhoods changed. Private wealth was not the catalyst. Science was. Federally, and therefore locally, the push was for scientific research, education, and development. As one high school student put it, "Science is *it* in Oak Ridge." The change in the wind was good in many ways, but there were drawbacks.

Some elders noted the change away from an egalitarian climate by saying, "It was more fun in the old days when we were all in the same boat." Children younger than I complained that they had lost their "roaming grounds." Property lines often extended into the woods, which formerly had been communal areas; some people put up fences. It was becoming difficult to play in the hollows and hills without trespassing.

As a teenager I felt a bitter edge to the crosswinds, a bitterness that through strands of family, education, business, and politics webbed out from Oak Ridge to the surrounding area. One wind came from the direction of "outsiders" (mostly scientists) and the other from "natives" (mostly nonscientists). They sounded like this:

Outsiders: "We've done everything for these people and they're still backward."

"They're so uneducated they don't even know what the word 'science' means."

"They don't articulate properly."

"They don't have any 'culture.' Just listen to that Grand Ole Opry stuff they call music."

"As for the University of Tennessee, who ever heard of it?"

"Bunch of fundamentalists."

Natives: "They're looking down on us, but we're not looking up to them—and it gets their goat."

"You have to have three degrees to get them to sit down, much less listen."

"They're all book learning and no sense. Show them a rock slide coming down the mountain, and they'll show you a map that says there's no rock there."

"They come in telling us who we are and what to do like the world began with them. But I'm here to say different."

"They talk about our university like it was nothing."

"Bunch of atheists."

Extremes from both sides. Not from everyone, certainly, but from enough to create the kind of root-loosening crosswinds that no tree, no community, and no individual can long withstand without severe damage. Someone had to shore up the roots while the wind blew its course.

The wisest of you Founding Elders did just that. You had already begun a network of cooperation between outsiders and natives, between the laboratories and the University of Tennessee, and between neighbors. You strengthened those ties by years of patient work—by homekeeping. You explained to the young that not all people in any group are alike, or, as one native put it, "One braying jackass don't make the herd." You said that in time the season could change for the better. And today in Oak Ridge, who could deny that you were right? At least on the surface, many institutions reflect mutual cooperation and understanding, among them the Museum of Science and Energy, the Children's Museum and its Regional Appalachian Center, Oak Ridge Associated Universities, and various service groups. I have no way of knowing about that vast labyrinth beneath the surface, where politics, history, religion, and human relations intertwine and where traumas from seasons past reverberate for generations.

I only know that for me the damage took twenty years to heal. In the "time of bitter crosswinds," I was a sapling. Unlike the elders, I didn't have the girth and tough bark, the far-flung roots and spreading branches to hold me to balance. All I had was my long, tenacious taproot of highlander heritage that my parents kept packed tight in the earth of my homeland.

My shorter roots were tearing loose. I swayed one way, deeply angry at the disdain poured on my people and our culture. Then I swayed to the other, defensive of friends and elders—so-called "outsiders"—who were not as some natives described them. Adding to the degree of sway was the fact that I was born in Knoxville and living in Oak Ridge, a child of the mountain growing up with the atom. Could such opposites ever meet in peace?

Exacerbating the conflict of loyalties was a conflict of worldview and communication. Appalachians and Cherokees—my relatives—are symbolic peoples. We view the world in cosmic connection, where the tangible is a reflection of the intangible, of the spirit. We speak of this connection in images. Science, on the other hand, is based on facts that can be demonstrated and proven. It tends to create an objective mindset, which speaks literally and views imagistic thought as subjective, primitive, unreal, and romantic. What I was experiencing was the basic conflict between the intuitive and the analytical mind, but at the age of sixteen I had neither the knowledge nor the power to define it as such. I only knew it was painful—a stone blocking my way, for the path I had chosen was poetry.

I asked advice from Papa, my maternal grandfather. A Methodist minister with a live-and-let-live philosophy, he was six feet tall and square-handed. Earlier in his life he had mined coal, then taught Greek and Roman history at Hiwassee College to pay for his education there. He listened sympathetically as I described the bitter crosswinds. "The government and some outsiders make the natives feel shoved out," I said. "And they *literally* shoved out the old pioneer families in Wheat, Scarboro, Robertsville, and Elza to make room for Oak Ridge. Some of the tombstones in the Wheat cemetery go back to the 1790s."

"And back then," Papa said, "the settlers were the 'outsiders.' This was Cherokee country . . . had been for hundreds of years. Chota was their capital, over at Tellico. The settlers called the Indians 'uncivilized' and heathen. The government made them walk the Trail of Tears to Oklahoma. But the Cherokee knew a secret. The settlers had to learn it. And these new folks in Oak Ridge will too, if they want to last. *The mountains have been here a long time*."

I took his meaning. "People come and go . . . seasons come and go. Mother Earth abides and heals. Hold on . . . work patiently . . . wait. . . ."

But I wanted action. I wanted the stone out of my way. "In that case," Papa said, "you'd better be like water. Flow around it. Or vapor yourself and rain down in another place."

Which place? The French teacher at Oak Ridge High School, Margaret Zimmerman, suggested the answer, for she gave me a vision of the land of Pascal, where "the heart has its reasons that the reason knows not of." A land linked to Appalachia through Huguenot immigrants who intermarried with the Scotch-Irish and Cherokee. Historically, the French, Scots, and Native Americans have been drawn to each other by their similarities: devotion to family, a cosmic connection to the world, imagistic language, fierce independence—and a humorous pragmatism based on the "long view" of events. A fusion of these genes runs high in my blood, and when Margaret Zimmerman said, "the heart has its reasons . . . ," every cell in my body demanded, "Go to France!"

From that moment I was outward bound, driven by the need to find an equilibrium between heart and mind, mountain and atom, art and science—and a language to express the balance. Eleven years later, in May 1964, I stopped in Oak Ridge to take my final bearings for France. Dr. Margaret Mead, the distinguished anthropologist, was also in town to give her critique of the community. I heard her describe the need for balance in Oak Ridge in much the same terms as I defined my own.

But what I felt as "bitter crosswinds," she called "a vast gap between intellectual scientist and uneducated native . . . eggheads and fundamentalists . . . those highly educated for the modern world and those culturally deprived." She said, "You [scientists] are 'missionaries to the natives.'" Never once did she suggest that natives might have valuable knowledge to exchange, although with her on the stage was one of our wisest elders, Dr. William G. Pollard—physicist, Episcopal priest, director of the Oak Ridge Institute of Nuclear Studies—a man reared in Knoxville. Beside him, representing the wisdom of non-natives was Alvin M. Weinberg, humanitarian, director of the Oak Ridge National Laboratory. Dr. Pollard's face was calm, unperturbed. Maybe he would tell her, "Margaret, the mountains have been here a long time."

I couldn't. I had to pack. I was traveling with our two daughters, who were under five years old. Paul had gone ahead to his duty station at Laon Air Force Base, which was in the middle of sugar beet fields ninety miles northeast of Paris. The only housing available for us there was a small government trailer with a lean-to built on it. And I would be flying the Atlantic alone with the children, not in a luxury jet, but on a government transport. It all sounded like another frontier to me. But now I was responsible for the homemaking and homekeeping. It was heartening to find my parents and other elders spinning the web of life as you always have—with courage, stamina, shrewdness, faith, and humor. Unchanged also were the mountains, the Ancients who, from generation to generation, teach the art of survival to those who will listen.

I carried my strand of the web to France, where thanks to you elders and the knowledge coded in my genes, I remembered how to spin my part of the pattern. I discovered that stone and water form one of Nature's most beautiful combinations. By its weight and mass, the stone alters the course of the water. And water, with its patient flow, changes the shape of the stone. Together, they sing magnificently. As Science and Art once used to do. I also experienced being the "outsider" and came to bless the "bitter crosswinds" for all they had taught me about human relations. Most important, I finally understood and could say to myself, "I am a Cherokee-Appalachian poet. To find the 'eye of my work'—the center—I have to come home."

You elders were there to meet me, in the summer of 1977, sharing your wise counsel and support as I began to write *Abiding Appalachia*. Because you had been honest with me as a child—telling me exactly what the atom can do to help or to harm and what our responsibility is for its use—I found the point where mountain and atom meet.

Now it is 1986. I've just returned from the Cherokee National Holiday in Tahlequah, Oklahoma, where the mountains are so much like ours in East Tennessee. Seven generations after the Trail of Tears, as elders at that time foretold, the Cherokee are strong again—sixty-five thousand in the West and eight thousand in the East. Twenty-two thousand relatives and friends came to Tahlequah for the Holiday, which had the theme, "Honoring the Cherokee Family."

At the powwow, held on the athletic field of Sequoyah High School, Chief Wilma Mankiller called for a dance to honor a distinguished elder of the nation, saying, "Without his counsel through the years I would never have become chief." Paul and I joined the throng of people circling the slow, steady beat of the drum in rhythm with an ancient song. Children mingled with elders, matching their steps to the pattern. I thought how mysterious the web of life is, how real the strands that connect us all. No matter how wide the web spins, circling round and round are children and elders of the present, of pioneer times, of centuries when none but native people lived on the land. I danced in honor of them all.

But especially, I danced for you.

◆ ◆

MARILOU AWIAKTA, a Knoxville native who grew up in Oak Ridge, Tennessee, and lives now in Memphis, is of Cherokee-Appalachian heritage. Recipient of the Distinguished Tennessee Writer Award and the Award for Outstanding Contribution to Appalachian Literature, Awiakta is profiled in the *Oxford Companion to Women's Writing in the U.S.* (1994).

CHARLES WRIGHT

ARS POETICA

I like it back here

Under the green swatch of the pepper tree and the aloe vera.
I like it because the wind strips down the leaves without a word.
I like it because the wind repeats itself,
                    and the leaves do.

I like it because I'm better here than I am there,

Surrounded by fetishes and figures of speech:
Dog's tooth and whale's tooth, my father's shoe, the dead weight
Of winter, the inarticulation of joy . . .

The spirits are everywhere.

And once I have them called down from the sky, and spinning and
        dancing in the palm of my hand,
What will it satisfy?
            I'll still have

The voices rising out of the ground,
The fallen star my blood feeds,
                this business I waste my heart on.
And nothing stops that.

Two Stories

Tonight, on the deck, the lights
Semaphore up at me through the atmosphere,
Town lights, familiar lights
                                        pulsing and slacking off
The way they used to back on the ridge outside of Kingsport
Thirty-five years ago,
The moonlight sitting inside my head
Like knives,
                    the cold like a drug I knew I'd settle down with.
I used to imagine them shore lights, as these are, then,
As something inside me listened with all its weight
For the sea-surge and the sea-change.

• • •

There's a soft spot in everything
Our fingers touch,
                              the one place where everything breaks
When we press it just right.
The past is like that with its arduous edges and blind sides,
The whorls of our fingerprints
                                          embedded along its walls
Like fossils the sea has left behind.

From *The World of the Ten Thousand Things*, by Charles Wright (New York: Farrar, Straus & Giroux, 1990).

◆ ◆ ◆

This is a story I swear is true.

I used to sleepwalk. But only
On camping trips,
or whenever I slept outside.
One August, when I was eleven, on Mount LeConte in Tennessee,
Campfire over, and ghost story over,
Everyone still asleep, apparently I arose
From my sleeping bag,
opened the tent flap, and started out on the trail
That led to the drop-off, where the mountainside
Went straight down for almost a thousand feet.
Half-moon and cloud cover, so some light
As I went on up the path through the rhododendron,
The small pebbles and split roots
like nothing under my feet.
As I got closer,
moving blindly, unerringly,
Deeper in sleep than the shrubs,
I stepped out, it appears,
Onto the smooth lip of the rock cape of the cliff,
When my left hand, and then my right hand,
Stopped me as they were stopped
By the breathing side of a bear which woke me
And there we were,
the child and the black bear and the cliff-drop,
And this is the way it went—
I stepped back, and I turned around,
And I walked down through the rhododendron

And never looked back,
                                        truly awake in the throbbing world,
And I ducked through the low flap
Of the tent, so quietly, and I went to sleep
And never told anyone
Till years later when I thought I knew what it meant,
                                                        which now I've forgot.

◆ ◆ ◆

And this one is questionable,
Though sworn to me by an old friend
Who'd killed a six-foot diamondback about seven o'clock in the
        morning
(He'd found it coiled in a sunny place),
And threw it into a croker sack with its head chopped off,
                                        and threw the sack in the back of a jeep,
Then left for his day's work
On the farm.
                        That evening he started to show the snake
To someone, and put his hand in the sack to pull it out.
As he reached in, the snake's stump struck him.
His wrist was bruised for a week.

◆ ◆ ◆

It's not age,
                        nor time with its gold eyelid and blink,
Nor dissolution in all its mimicry
That lifts us and sorts us out.
It's discontinuity
                            and all its spangled coming between

That sends us apart and keeps us there in a dread.
It's what's in the rearview mirror,
smaller and out of sight.

◆ ◆ ◆

What do you do when the words don't come to you anymore,
And all the embolisms fade in the dirt?
And the ocean sings in its hammock,
rocking itself back and forth?
And you live at the end of the road where the day starts its dark decline?

The barking goes on and on
from the far hill, constantly
Sticking its noise in my good ear.

Goodbye, Miss Sweeney, goodbye.
I'm starting to think about the psychotransference of all things.
It's small bones in the next life.
It's small bones,
and heel and toe forever and ever.

◆ ◆

CHARLES WRIGHT is a native of Pickwick Dam in Hardin County and grew up in Tennessee and North Carolina. Winner of many honors and awards, including a Guggenheim Fellowship in Poetry, the National Book Award, and, in 1992, the Award of Merit Medal from the American Academy of Arts in Letters, Wright has been professor of English at the University of Virginia since 1983.

BOB SUMMER

Jim My Father

There have been three Jims in my life—Jim my brother, an All-American youth who became an air force officer; Jim, the FFV (First Families of Virginia) golden boy and marine captain with whom I spent an intense summer the year President Kennedy was assassinated; and Jim my father. Each of these remarkable men left his imprints on me in various ways. To a large degree, my life has been a reaction to the example of a maleness society deems orthodox, which my older brother set for me to follow. Jim the sensitive FFV scion ennobled me with a vision of what two men can find together if fate smiles upon them. But although my father and I were not close for much of his life, he is my life's greatest loss.

Oh, don't worry, this is not going to be another of those "I Never Sang for My Father" types of reminiscences. An outwardly unaffectionate man, at least until he was well into middle age, my father would be embarrassed by that. So even if such maudlinness were my style, it would be inappropriate to his memory. Instead I want to sort through our perplexing responses to each other, to see if I can find the answer to why it is that I have missed him so much since he died in early 1977.

Is it guilt? Yes, I am sure there is some of that, but I am just as certain that that is not the entire reason. Indeed, our tentative approach to each other, and for a span of time almost total alienation, was rife with complexities. He had many qualities I admire in a person, mixed, as in most of us, with some of a baser nature. And when I was very young, probably up to the time I was in the third or fourth grade, I kept him on a pedestal. I favored him in looks, people told me, and even then I was aware from family stories that he had triumphed over an early life of hard knocks. In the South, storytelling—our vaunted, but not wholly positive, oral tradition—does more than just entertain; it passes down myths. And the stories told by uncles, aunts, and my grandparents that focused on Daddy left me with a virtual reverence for him. . . .

. . . Daddy, who inherited the late Victorian code of "manly" restraint, did not easily show his tender side; he did not even cry at his mother's funeral. But he had provided much of her livelihood, since his brother with whom she lived on the family homeplace was a poor manager and another brother was left an invalid from the gassing inflicted upon him as a foot soldier in the trenches of France during World War I.

Daddy, in short, was the only son she had to depend on. Indeed, compared to other relatives still living in the Dutch Fork (where he had grown up), he had done quite well for himself. And by the time of her death, he had advanced to become a section foreman in the large plant he worked at in Oak Ridge, the East Tennessee site the federal government chose for the Manhattan Project, which developed the atomic bombs that were dropped on Hiroshima and Nagasaki to force the Japanese to surrender, ending World War II.

A job in Oak Ridge was enviously sought after by workers across the South, and the fact that Daddy had landed one added further to his reputation back home. Now certainly his job as an electrician was a much lesser one than those of the scientists at the Oak Ridge National Laboratory, who oversaw the diffusion of uranium, Oak Ridge's purpose. Nonetheless he was proud of the small part he had in the national effort, and he had an abiding loyalty to both the place and his union. After all, Oak Ridge provided him with the best job security and highest income he ever had or probably dreamed of having.

To be sure, Oak Ridge did not make him a wealthy man. But he was able to buy there the only house he ever owned and settle with his family into a community, albeit one much different from that in which he was raised. The stark new town the army had built almost overnight in the aged Tennessee hills gave him—and us—a hard-earned security.

The piano he bought, ostensibly for me, symbolized the attainment of all this, although Mama was the impetus for it. Her sister, whose husband found an Oak Ridge job about the time Daddy did, had purchased one in nearby Knoxville for her daughter. Mama and Aunt Fannie always played their own private keeping-up-with-the-Joneses game, and when I saw the spinet model in my aunt's house, I knew it wouldn't be long before we had one sitting in our small living room too. Not that I didn't want it. I had my aspirations too, and, happily, when I began my weekly lessons my teacher said I showed promise.

Maybe Daddy got some satisfaction from my developing talent. I hope so, but he never said and didn't attend my recitals. What did spark his excitement, though, was my brother's growing involvement with sports, especially football. Fall Friday nights saw Daddy, with Mama and me in tow, in the bleachers at Blankenship Field, along with other workers from the Oak Ridge plants, lustily cheering on the town's favored sons as they clashed with opposing teams from area high schools. . . .

. . . I guess I realized I was overshadowed, although I tried to pretend it didn't matter that Jimmy's exploits made anything I did pale by comparison. My inclinations were more artistic, I rationalized. Anyway, the pedestal atop which I had set Daddy in my childhood had long been toppled. No longer did I laugh at his stories. And although he may have single-handedly raised his status, I noticed we were still considerably below the economic and social level enjoyed by the scientists and plant managers who lived in the larger, better furnished homes I envied. I was uncomfortable to be alone with him, since I always seemed to unleash his anger. At night, on the other side of the thin wall separating my and Jimmy's bedroom from theirs, I could overhear him questioning Mama about why I did this, why I wasn't better at that. When he tried to teach me to drive it was, predictably, a disaster, and I failed the first test I took for my driver's license. . . .

. . . On the other hand—and that was to me the baffling thing about Daddy; there was always an "on the other hand"—he lent me the down payment for my first house (after Mama's intercession on my behalf). And he was generous with hospitality; no one ever left our house hungry or thirsty. He bought canned food for our church, Grace Lutheran, to give to needy families, in addition to the tithe he annually made for what he called the church's good work. And after he retired, he became active with Grace Lutheran's project for the resettlement in Oak Ridge of Asians whose lives had been made chaotic by the regionwide catastrophe brought on by the Vietnam War. It was the first such project in Oak Ridge, and many people there—including Mama—initially did not approve of bringing non-Caucasians into a mostly white, middle-class town where the political allegiance had shifted from Democratic to Republican. Despite that, Daddy argued the resettlement was commanded by the church's mission.

Thus he enthusiastically helped gather furniture, clothes, and other household items for the Mouas, the family from Laos the church pledged to sponsor. A home was found in a housing project, a menial job for the father (a former Laotian army officer) was located in one of Oak Ridge's scientific facilities, and individuals were assigned to help them become acculturated. So when the family of ten arrived in Oak Ridge the year the United States celebrated its bicentennial, all was ready for them to begin their lives anew, far from the refugee camps they had left behind.

Even if neither Daddy nor I had forgotten the past perceived wrongs our life together had wrought, both of us had mellowed and by then were learning (or perhaps relearning) how to talk with each other. He never questioned why I had not married, since he had not done so himself until age twenty-nine. To him that (as well as sex in general) was a private matter. Instead, he always wanted to know about my jobs and the places where I lived or visited. Geography and demographic facts fascinated him, and each year he bought an almanac to supplement his world atlas.

That year I was back in Oak Ridge for Christmas when Daddy, over Saturday breakfast, broached the matter of a holiday gift for the Mouas. Mama dismissed the idea outright; he had done enough for them already, she declared, and besides she had more than enough to do to finish getting ready for Jimmy and my sister, who would be coming in shortly with their families.

Undaunted, Daddy mused that a basket of pecans, apples, oranges, and tangerines would be a gift all the Mouas could enjoy, and he turned to me and asked if I had time early the next week to drive him over to the farmers' market in Knoxville. I leapt at the invitation, and early on Tuesday we headed out on our little expedition. On the way over, he reminisced about what would have been happening in the Dutch Fork at Christmastime when he was growing up.

The older he got, the more vividly he elaborated on his memory of those early years. "Papaw, tell us about ole times," was his grandchildren's key to getting his stories started. And since he was reared on a farm he was right at home in a farmer's market. I knew that, while filling the bushel basket we brought with us, he would exchange stories with each of the farmers there. Indeed, he enjoyed that swapping so much that it was late afternoon before we were headed back to Oak Ridge. And the temperature was dropping so that it was much colder. The TV weather forecast on the evening local news raised the specter of snow, the season's first, but when we finished supper and were leaving with the brimming basket for the Mouas, I thought the air lacked enough moisture for that.

Someone from the church had called Mr. Moua to tell them we were coming, and their outside porch light was on for us. And when we knocked on the door, I could hear him telling his children, I guessed, how to act. Then when he opened the door, he smilingly welcomed us with gestures and faltering, staccatolike English. Meanwhile, I glimpsed his wife shepherding the children out of the small kitchen into the living room

Daddy, talking loudly and deliberately, explained why we had come and signaled for me to follow him in. I looked for a Christmas tree under which I could set the basket, but there was none. So I set it in a corner of the small room, exchanged smiles with Mrs. Moua, and watched the children align themselves in descending order according to height (and perhaps age) beside their parents.

Daddy continued talking, as if sheer volume was enough to make himself understood, and Mr. Moua responded by bobbing his head up and down with small punctuating laughs. But the smallest of the children, a young boy and his younger sister, didn't know whether to direct their attention to us or the gift basket in the corner. What their mother wanted, though, became clear when the little girl reached to touch an apple and was reprimanded with a pat on the head and a stern look. But once again attentively assembled, each child followed their father's lead by arranging their hands together, palms pointed upward. Daddy looked befuddled, and for a second I thought he was going to follow their example before he dropped his hands down to his side.

Mr. Moua began talking. He and his family, he said to Daddy, were honored by our visit and grateful for the gift. He then bowed to Daddy, and his wife and children followed suit. I looked at Daddy, whose perplexed smile revealed his uncertainty about how to respond. But, his voice calmer, he answered by saying we were happy they had come to America and wanted to wish them a Merry Christmas. Then he extended his hand to the much smaller Laotian. "You thanked me your way," Daddy remarked, "but I'll answer with mine." And he went down the line, bending and grasping in his hand that of each member of the family, wishing everyone a Merry Christmas.

That little ceremony seemed all that was called for. Noting we had interrupted the family's supper, we took our leave so they could return to their kitchen table. Mr. Moua saw us out, while his wife tried to muster the children back to their evening meal. But the basket was a magnet drawing their curiosity, and as I left I saw they were hovering over it, perhaps, I later realized, because in their temperate homeland they were unfamiliar with apples.

We had not stayed long enough to remove our coats, and Daddy, after exchanging goodnights with Mr. Moua, hurried back to the car. I added my own "Merry Christmas" and followed. But on the way out, I noticed that a light from a source other than the one on the porch was widening in front of the house. Looking back toward a large front window, I saw that littlest girl, probably standing on a chair, holding up a curtain with one hand while, in the other, she held an apple.

When I got back to the car and climbed in on the driver's side, Daddy too was watching the scene. What was he thinking? I wondered. When I first saw the little girl in the window, my first Christmas memory—a large decorated cedar in Pa Joe's house, brightly lit with colored lights and shimmering with tinsel—suddenly came rushing back to me. Was Christmas imagery from the Dutch Fork in Daddy's mind also? Was he hearing ol' Mims and Holly blazing Christmas greetings across the Piney Woods with shotgun blasts rather than the customary firecrackers? Was he remembering his mother's once-a-year pineapple upside-down cake?

I didn't ask. Nor did I hear his usual, "Let's get going." He seemed to be silently relishing what was happening. The faraway gleam in his eyes told me that, and I was certain Christmases in other times and places were resonating with us as we sat there on the fourth night before Christmas, 1976. How strange that this exiled family from halfway around the world could be the agent for bridging the gap between Daddy and me.

I switched on the engine to get some heat into the car. Then, when I pulled on the headlights, the beam of light picked up flakes of a beginning snow. And across the way, Daddy and I saw the little girl being joined by an older brother who held an apple in his hand also. Both were wonderingly looking out at the snow and us, and time for a precious moment was seamless. Christmas present and Christmas past were joined, and Jim my father and I were together.

Silent night. Holy night.

• •

BOB SUMMER, southeastern correspondent for *Publishers Weekly* and president of the Southern Book Critics Circle, is a native of Oak Ridge, Tennessee. Associated for many years with university presses at Columbia, the University of North Carolina, and Louisiana State University, he now writes and reviews for a number of the country's major newspapers and journals.

ISABEL JOSHLIN GLASER

BASKET-BLASTING

A fast leap
And she leaves the court,
Slicing through space
Like a rocket moonbound,
Motors firing her feet.
She's leaning, curving, letting go,
Whamming the ball through
So the hoop rattles
Like it's storm-sick.
And her teeth ache
And the hairs on her arms
Rise antennae-straight
And her skin tingles
And the whole world's cheering!
  Then Ms. Downs repeats
    the question . . .
And blang! —she's back,
  sitting, red-faced,
In Sixth Grade Social Studies
Grabbing for the aftertrail
    of words.
And she answers, "Kenya?"

Inheritances

I woke to: no fingers
and stories damping-off
      like messages
in bottles at sea . . .

a time of extensions
my forehead unshuttering
      its pencil
my eyelashed trying all
      typewriter keys
my tongue extending

      its plot
its woman-theme
breath after breath
daughter to daughter

a time of endings
little for him, helf-orphaned
beyond a certain heritage
      of stories broken
at this male point . . .

"Inheritances," by Isabel Joshlin Glaser, appeared in *Tennessee Voices Anthology* (Memphis: Poetry Society of Tennessee, 1981). Used by permission of the author.

my son who must stand
    in the cold
white waves of his room
    inventing parables
to explain his island
the sea erasing its sands.

• •

ISABEL JOSHLIN GLASER, an Alabama native and graduate of George Peabody College at Vanderbilt, has lived most of her life in Tennessee. With publishing credits in fiction, nonfiction, and poetry, she has served as president of the Chickasaw Branch of the National League of American PEN Women and in 1991 was named Poet Laureate by the Poetry Society of Tennessee.

JEANNE McDONALD

THE MARK

Sometimes a man's life can change in a day. Sometimes when the dark unravels and the pieces of the morning begin to blend together in the light, a man will wake to find he is a different person from the one who had lain down in a familiar bed the night before, and nothing he can do will change what happens after that—not action, not reflection, not prayer.

From a distance you would have seen a small boat bumping across the broad sparkling lake, spanking the flat water with a metronomic rhythm. From a distance the sound of the motor would have seemed subdued, almost plaintive in the resonating whine that trailed out behind the wake like a long, coaxing lament. The whole image in fact would have seemed idyllic—the blunt prow of the outboard dividing the smooth bronze surface of the water, the dark pencilled edge of the shore shouldering the bank where the trees rushed by in a tender blur of green—locusts, sweetgums, dogwoods, and maples.

But the man in the boat, enveloped in noise and thus deaf to it, was nursing a private pain, and that morning he was consumed with a loss that seemed to him like a wound no longer fresh but not yet closed. He sighed and breathed in the damp, ripe smell of the water. Then he pointed the prow away from the main channel and into his favorite cove. There he shut down the throttle and let the boat drift. Until he killed the motor he had not been aware of its deafening noise, but now the absence of sound was stunning.

Miller Sharp knew the cove well. He had come there with his father since childhood. Even in the dark he could have found the place where the bass fed—a pale, thick cluster of submerged stumps that had once as tall locusts shaded the driveway of a working farm before the government had flooded it and turned it into a lake.

He closed his eyes and lifted his face toward the sun and let the current carry him until the boat bumped against the bank. When finally he leaned over to drop the an-

"The Mark" is excerpted from a novel-in-progress, *A Random Natural Occurrence*.

chor, he was startled by what he saw. For a second he had mistaken his own reflection in the water for the image of his father, Hollis Sharp—the lean body long and slightly bent, the face open and intelligent, a wide, deep brow.

He interpreted the reflection as a message, and it came back to him then—a memory of himself as a child, out on this very lake with his father for the first time.

He is six or seven years old. Six—because it is the year he gets the leather baseball glove for his birthday and he wants to stay at home to test it. Sulking, he sits in the bow of the old wooden rowboat with the broad lake circling and the sky blue and buoyant, but when his father stands up to cast the first line, the air becomes electric with excitement and anticipation. The water swells, reflects the incandescent light. As the line leaps above the water, as lithe and sure as a dancer, Miller feels the wonder of it. It spins out like truth—the beautiful long loose cast from his father's arm, the sweet and graceful follow-through, the line rippling in supple crescents and loops and then straightening and stretching into a crisp clean connection when the line stings the water.

Across the cove a fish leaps silver in the sun. His father laughs. "Christ, look at the size of that son of a bitch." Miller laughs, too, caught up in the contagion of pleasure. Everything his father says has weight and balance and beauty. Everything he utters owns the ring of truth. "In the old days," he tells Miller, "when they taught you to fly fish, they made you hold a book under your arm, to keep the cast controlled. Now, hell, you can use your arm, your shoulder, whatever. It's a matter of control." He squints into the sky. Miller notices that his father's shadow is foreshortened in the sun. Hollis looks down at Miller. "Remember, son, you don't cast the fly, you cast the line. Concentrate on the line and remember that the line creates wind resistance. Factor that into your cast. See? Control it, that's the trick. There's a feel to it. It's a forward, stop, motion until the line straightens itself out. You'll learn to recognize the second that happens, the very second. Trust me on that. You'll get it eventually. The cadence can't be fixed, though. It's intuitive. When you feel the slack, you sharpen your pull to get line speed. Aim it high, about eight feet above the water. You want your line high in the air so it can straighten out completely by the time it hits the surface."

It had seemed like a miracle that first day, the magic his father worked, and when Miller himself was able at last to fall into the rhythm of the cast, he knew it would forever thereafter be a part of his life. His father, though, was gone—six months now since the heart attack. Sometimes on the lake where they had spent so much time together, Miller believed he could feel the old man's presence. Sometimes the boat would tip as if with a shifted weight and Miller felt *something*, a warmth, an energy, that seemed comforting and familiar.

It was possible, he told himself. It was possible. He would believe anything to get the old man back, if believing was what it took. He shook his head and leaned over to open his lunch box to take out the tube of sunscreen his wife had given him. When he opened the box, the sun struck the glass bottle under the plastic-wrapped sandwiches. It was his occasional comfort now that his father was gone. Not yet, though. He did not need it now.

He had been fishing for an hour when he suddenly noticed voices nearby, first low and then rising, peppered with sharp laughter. He shaded his eyes and saw them fifty or sixty yards up the shoreline—six kids settling in on a dock probably not their own. There was no sign of a boat. They must have parked their car on the road above and walked down through the woods. On second glance he saw that they were older than he had first thought—in their early twenties, perhaps. One girl balanced a baby on her hip, and an older child clung to her leg. Miller noticed her because of her pale skin—it had the sheen of alabaster—and hair so dark it seemed to glint blue in the sun. She was looking his way, but with the light in his eyes he could not tell if she was staring at him or simply facing downstream.

Miller decided to cast a few more lines and then move on. *Let it go,* he thought, *they're up to no harm, just a day in the sun.* He noticed that one of the boys had lassoed the limb of a tree with a thick rope that was knotted at the end to make a foothold. The first swinger grabbed the rope, closed his knees against it, and spun out over the water. His shrieks of excitement bounced across the lake and then he released the rope and plunged into the water. *That does it,* Miller thought. When the rope swung back, a girl grabbed it, climbed higher on the bank, then leaned into space and swept out over the lake, her long laugh tumbling into the air behind her. She let go of the rope at the highest point of the arc and her body hung for a second suspended in sunlight, as if time had stopped momentarily.

Miller blinked, his eyes swimming with sunspots. He had lifted his anchor when a skinny blond boy stood up and grabbed the rope. The dark-haired girl shifted the weight of the baby in her arms and looked down at the other child. "Look, Sister," she said, "your daddy's gonna fly. He's gonna fly right out over that water, just like Peter Pan."

The boy laughed and moved as if to kiss the girl but he was constrained by the length of the rope he held. He seemed to be estimating the empty space of dock between them, but the girl remained fixed where she was. The boy turned his head and spat into the water. Then he pushed one foot against the bank and started running down the length of the dock. When he released the rope, his feet were still churning the air, as if he were running in space.

Lighter now, and slower, the rope swung back, a lazy length of gold drifting in the sun-drenched light. It bumped softly against the tree trunk a few times and finally hung motionless. The girl walked idly to the end of the dock and peered into the water.

"Hell. You see that run?" said one of the boys, laughing. "Jimmy Duane coulda gone straight on to the Olympics. He coulda gone to Barcelona."

The others laughed, too. A broad concentric circle spread on the surface of the water.

The child looked up at her mother and asked something, but Miller could not make out the words. The girl shook her head and looked downstream toward Miller. Then she said, as if for her own validation, "He's play-acting. He's just down there trying to scare us. He'll be up in a minute." Her voice was deep and throaty, like a country singer. She hoisted her baby higher on her shoulder and sat down by the ladder, her long feet dangling in the water. She wore faded blue jeans cut off at the thighs and a sleeveless tee shirt the color of a pale green apple. Her breasts were high and round and her hips were straight as a boy's.

One of the other girls started to chant in a sing-song voice, "Jimmy Duane is drown-ded, Jimmy Duane is drown-ded."

There was hesitant laughter.

"I'll bet he swam underwater to the other side," said one of the boys. He hunkered down and peered into the water. "Shit."

The girl with the baby leaned forward from the waist, addressing the water where the boy had jumped in. "Jimmy Duane," she screamed, "you get the hell out of that lake and get on up here. Get on up here right this minute, you hear?"

They all watched the surface. Silence expanded. Waves generated by the boy's plunge had moved downstream, nudging Miller's boat. He held his breath.

"The way they do it in the movies," said one of the boys, "is they get them reeds and stay underwater and breathe through 'em?" He phrased his observation like a question, lifting his voice at the end of it.

Nobody answered him. Nobody else was talking anymore. Miller noticed that he himself had been holding the anchor rope so tightly his fingertips were white.

Finally the girl said something soft, something that seemed more contemplative than communicative. Miller thought he heard her say *Oh sweet Jesus*. "Go in, somebody," she ordered. Her voice grew louder now but quavered. "Maybe he is drowned. Maybe he hit his head." She leaned out over the water again. "Jimmy Duane, this is not funny. Get back on up here, damn you."

Her voice bounced along the bank of the cove.

In Miller's head a small vein began to throb. Slowly, deliberately, as if he should not make a sound or a false move, he carefully laid his fly rod down in the bottom of the boat.

He waited. They all waited. Upstream, the other two boys eased into the water and swam in slow circles around the area in front of the dock. One went under briefly and then reappeared, shaking water from his long hair. The three girls hunched together, watching. The child peered over the edge of the dock. "Where's my daddy?" she said. "Where's my daddy gone?"

Abruptly, Miller swung his feet over the centerboard of the boat and jerked the starter. The girls on the dock snapped their heads in his direction and began to wave him toward them, as if they could pull him closer with their frantic gestures. Miller's heart pounded as the boat sliced across the water toward the dock. All the time he kept thinking that he did not want to get involved, it was not his affair. He kept scanning the water, hoping the boy would pop up, laughing. *Got you that time, didn't I?* he would say.

Son of a bitch.

A long minute had gone by since the boy had gone under, maybe two. Miller killed the motor and when the stern of the boat swung toward the dock, he heaved the anchor in. The dark-haired girl shifted her baby to the other hip and leaned forward. When she reached out to Miller, he saw a dark bracelet circling the small bones of her wrist.

Then he realized that what he had thought to be a bracelet was not a bracelet at all, but bruises—the skin of her wrist stained green and purple. He stared, momentarily transfixed, and then one of the boys suddenly yelped and scrambled up onto the ladder. "Shit, oh Christ, he grabbed me," he gasped. "He tried to pull me under." His eyes were wide, his mouth gaped. Miller felt shock and contempt for the boy's terror, as if some basic primeval flaw had been exposed in his naked countenance.

He acted then without thinking. He ripped off his sneakers and dived in. The shock of the cold water stunned him for a second and then he lowered his head and began to kick. Below the surface the lake was murky and foreboding and his own heartbeat thundered in his ears. In his chest his breath gathered like a clenched fist and he pulled hard against the water in order to stay down. Overhead there was a pale light but the lake floor was dark with the ominous shadows of rotting stumps. Miller's lungs began to burn. When he came up, one of the boys was screaming. "Over there. His hand came up."

Miller gasped and went under again. His head pounded in the roaring silence. He swam with blind, awkward strokes and suddenly a weight fell against his back so abruptly that in his panic he opened his mouth to protest and he swallowed water. Something grabbed his hair and jerked his head back and Miller realized that the drowning boy had clamped his legs around his body, riding, mounting Miller's frame as if to climb his way to safety.

Down. He was going down. He flailed his arms, straining against the pressure of the water and the weight against his back. He could feel himself sinking and he bit hard at the hand that covered his face and then he didn't know how it happened, he was suddenly free, thrust upward as if propelled, and when he broke through the surface a net of water blurred his vision like a cataract and the air seemed solid with screaming.

Jesus God he was up, he was alive. He sputtered and pulled himself up onto the first step on the ladder and drank in long rough drafts of air.

The dark-haired girl grabbed his arm. "Did you see him?" Her mouth was pulled down at the corners, anchored in terror.

Miller looked away. He shook his head and droplets of water rained from his hair. The metallic taste of the lake was on his tongue.

"Hurry," the girl ordered, "Hurry up."

Miller kept anticipating something he was not even sure he had seen—how could he have seen it from behind?—the boy's face—yellow in the eerie light, mouth open, eyes rolling. His long blonde hair had floated around his head like a ragged aureole. The girl screamed something else and Miller plunged in again. He swam away from the place where the boy had fallen against him and he hung suspended in the dark golden water, moving his arms slowly, letting himself sink and rise, sink and rise.

He was biding time.

Sink and rise. Sink and rise. Below him in the dusky labyrinth of the lake he could make out a pale form rocking in the current. He heard the thick hollow drumbeat of his own pulse in his ears and his brain raced in a wild delirium. He could die there, he could die for a stranger who had tried to climb to life on his very back. From somewhere far off he heard a chambered sound that he recognized as his own internal moaning. He was so tired now. The pale light was hypnotic and he thought how easy it would be to open his own throat to the lake, to drink in the amber water and let himself drift down toward the grassy floor. To dispel the mood, he swam to the surface for a breath of air, then descended toward where he had seen the boy on the floor of the lake. He stroked downward and touched flesh—this time a flat plane—the back, maybe, or the shoulders. His first impulse was to jerk his hand away but suddenly he understood that the boy was face down now, bobbing gently on the floor of the lake. Miller pushed against the weight of the water and moved his hand along the body, searching for a handhold. He found the belt loop of the boy's cut-off jeans and pulled, but the body was incredibly heavy, filled with water—the lungs, the stomach. Waterlogged.

Oh Jesus, help me, Miller thought. *I waited too long.* He pulled again, and the body would not be lifted. Miller's blood thundered and his head throbbed with pain. He pushed away and burst to the surface. The group waited on the dock, watching the water. "I found him," Miller sputtered. "I found him."

They stared at him, stupefied.

"Will you for Christ's sake help me?" Miller cried. He coughed and something bitter pushed up in his throat.

One boy shuddered and slid hesitantly into the water. He followed Miller down, his hand brushing Miller's back for guidance as they descended. Miller reached back to grasp his wrist and in the murky gloom he fitted the boy's hand to a belt loop and he took another loop, and with their burden they struggled up toward the light.

The girls screamed as they reached out to help drag the boy onto the dock. Miller shuddered. "Turn him over," he gasped as he pulled himself up the ladder. "Get the water out of him." His own body now seemed as heavy as the boy's. For a second that he hoped was imperceptible, he looked for the bite mark. It was there—an unmistakable ragged crescent just below the boy's thumb, bright against the pale gray color of his skin. The others were too hysterical to notice. They were pulling at the boy's arms, calling him, cursing, imploring God to save him. His wife held the baby and leaned close to her husband's face, screaming his name. Miller pushed them aside and rolled the boy over onto his back. Then he pinched the boy's nose and put his mouth to the cold blue lips and began to breathe.

It was almost impossible to establish a rhythm with the others pulling and crying. He tried to wave them away with his arms. He thought it must be like this in hell—terrible noise, horror, and confusion.

He kept pushing his breath into the boy's mouth. When he paused between breaths, he could not keep from looking. In those frenzied seconds he saw the mark of his own teeth and the flesh around it dark and discolored, but there was no blood. It was as if the blood had drained out of the boy on the lake floor. Miller wanted that blood back now—to start a pulse, to make the heart start beating. Panic mounted in him. He felt sick and dizzy.

He straddled the boy and began to thump his chest. Occasionally he felt the throat for a pulse. Nothing. The young wife squatted beside him, moaning. "Jesus Lord almighty, Jesus Lord almighty."

Miller nudged her away with his shoulder and turned the boy on his side once more. A thin trickle of water drained from the pale lips. *So much water,* Miller thought. *So much water.* For a second he felt frozen with exhaustion and confusion, and then he forced himself back to the business of pushing his breath into the boy's lungs. *Breathe, rest. Breathe, rest.*

He lost track of time and the motions became automatic. *Breathe for three seconds, wait for two, breathe for three, wait for two.* He must have worked at it for ten, fifteen minutes. Finally he looked up at the others. "Can somebody take over for a while?" he said.

They backed away.

Miller shook his head. It was too late anyway. He looked at the wife. "I think he's gone," he said. "He was under too long."

"No." Her black hair fell across her eyes. "You keep on trying, you hear me? Do you hear me?"

Miller started to speak, but the girl howled and struck out at him. Miller saw her hand coming and hunched his shoulders as he waited for his punishment. He deserved it, he thought. The blow glanced off his ear and shoulder, so that it was not nearly as painful as it should have been. And in the moment he closed his eyes he saw as a negative image the bruises bracketing her wrist.

"Adra, stop it," somebody cried.

Miller got to his feet. His knees were shaking. "I'll report this at the marina," he said. "Stay here on the dock. I'll send help." Somebody held the wife as Miller jumped down into his boat and started the motor. He swung about so sharply that he nearly swamped. All he could think of was to get away, to leave behind the squalling women and the ineffectual men, the terrible din and bedlam, and most of all, to escape the scene of his shame and failure.

He opened the throttle and the boat ripped across the cove and into the open lake, and it was then and only then, with the wide silver sky above him and the summer sun reflecting on the broad green expanse of water before him, that he let himself believe it: from that day on, his life would never be the same.

◆ ◆

JEANNE MCDONALD, whose work has been published in *American Fiction* and *Special Report: Fiction* and anthologized in *Lovers* and *Love's Shadows* (both from Crossing Press), was the 1990 recipient of the Tennessee Arts Commission's Alex Haley Fellowship in fiction.

ROY NEIL GRAVES

PENTECOSTAL WOMAN

Seeing you here and there, in the dress you made
knee-length, collared and three-quarter sleeved,
with pocketbook, sensible shoes,
and uncut hair molded into the high bun
that testifies to the years of your devotion;
seeing your spectacles,
your eyes worked back from reading Scripture
into your unadorned face;
seeing you always in profile in the checkout lane
and at the sidewalk sale,

I see your ancestors
the Hesters and the women beside men with rakes
and I think of your brighter sisters
my mother and the lady across the road
and wonder what you are like
in bcd with your hair down
and how God got so far into the interior here
where the corn is high enough to hide in
and summer and everything in us
preaches indecorous ripeness.

"Pentecostal Woman," from *Somewhere on the Interstate*, by Roy Neil Graves (Memphis, Tenn.: Ion Books, 1987). Used with permission of Ion Books. This work also appeared in *Appalachian Journal* 3, no. 4 (1976): 398.

Fall Sowing

In fall, too, clover and wheat seeds
arc out fast from the cyclone seeder, and
one shines then too, the beautiful machine
marching a sight-line toward a yellow tree,
cutting swaths of feather-edged nothing,
crisscrossing like a loom part,
hand-cranking, spring organ grinder early out.
Seeds swirl out in the old patterns.
Invisible seeds like clover fly with us,
barely ahead of the freeze.

Thus we stroll on into the cool evening
cranking this old contrivance ourself,
misting like faith the air moving with us,
cluttering ground with minuscule goods.

"Fall Sowing," from *Somewhere on the Interstate*, by Roy Neil Graves (Memphis, Tenn.: Ion Books, 1987). Used with permission of Ion Books. This work also appeared in *Mountain Review* 3, no. 1 (1976): 38.

To the Family We Left at the Truckstop

We hope that there are rides to Indiana tonight,
    and jobs, and good cheap places to live.

We hope that the truckstop restaurant
    was the place to find the good ride.

Maybe that one long ride to Indiana
    will come along in the cool of the night.

We hope that the little girl will keep being good
    and sleep on her plastic board
    even in the sun, even during the long wait.

ROY NEIL GRAVES II is a native of Medina, Tennessee, and professor of English at the University of Tennessee at Martin. He frequently presents critical papers, as well as his own poetry, at professional and learned conferences. In 1987 he was the winner of the second Mid-South Chapbook Competition for his volume, *Somewhere on the Interstate*, from which the poems included here are taken.

"To the Family We Left at the Truckstop," from *Somewhere on the Interstate*, by Roy Neil Graves (Memphis, Tenn.: Ion Books, 1987). Used with permission of Ion Books.

VICTOR M. DEPTA

THE SILENCE OF JUNE

How silent the earth is
on a country road
in the somnolence of grass and the weeds
the rustling in the tree line
silence on silence
but for the starlings, field sparrows and the cowbirds
immemorially excited

like children's chatter, bus stop
the audience before the hush as the curtains sweep
silence on silence
the few crickets, the plaintive owl
but for the faint hum somewhere
a tiller, a semi, a train in the distance—
how silent the earth is

so I walk the railroad tracks to the bridge
and climb down to the creek
full, now, swollen with pickerelweed, cutgrass and reeds
a sandbank, mud and gravel
and since I cannot imagine God
to speak to

I imagine a friend with a twelve-pack
a voice like a mandolin
a banjo out of the case
all folderol in the world's sorrow as we drink
as we kick up sand
and holler.

Country Road

Empty as a gully
a realty sign, baled acres, a seedy lawn
a mind-shambles, ultimately, a falling in
melancholy as a tilted shed
rusted wire, a barn swaybacked—
each drifting away
lisping ballads like cirrocumulus

that's my way
about as glamorous as a spore
whereas some anger, some empty heart has a snout
tusks, and stalks about
hog-lion among honeysuckle
UZI, the shuddering
and the sweet holes in the meat
of meaninglessness

while at the center
the house with the brickless chimney
the shingles blown away, the windows gone
split clapboard, flaking paint

"Country Road," by Victor Depta, appeared in *West Branch*, nos. 21–22 (1988): 72–73. Used by permission of *West Branch*, Bucknell University, Lewisburg, Pa. 17837.

rabbit bones on the porch, bits of fur
the wind, *look to yourself*
it whispers
look to yourself

◆ ◆

VICTOR DEPTA has published three collections of poetry and one novel, as well as numerous essays. He holds the Ph.D. from Ohio University and is professor of English at the University of Tennessee at Martin.

SAM PICKERING

Blue Caterpillar

I took the *New Yorker* to the first rehearsal. I had started reading an article describing the murder of a partner in a distinguished New York law firm. The man led two lives, one public and heterosexual with a family, the other private and homosexual. A piece of rough trade killed the man in a sleazy motel in the Bronx, stabbing him thirty-two times. I didn't finish the article. The spire of the church in Lebanon rose clean above the common, resembling a sharp white cattail pushing through a green pool. Dressed in leotards and tutus little girls bustled out of cars and fluttered into the church, mothers and fathers swirling about them. In the good afternoon sun the article seemed dank and soiling, and before going into the church, I dropped the magazine into a garbage barrel at the edge of the green, a blue barrel with a swinging, hinged top, the kind that makes second thoughts and retrieving trash impossible for all except the simian.

June and the "annual concert" of the Lebanon School of Dance had arrived. Nancy Baldwin the director divided the concert into halves, selections from the *Sleeping Beauty* ballet for the older girls and then, for younger girls, ages three through nine, *Alice's Adventures in Wonderland*. On Friday the 18th of June and again on Saturday the 19th, the students performed. Sixty-seven girls and one adult dance in *Alice*. Eliza was the Queen of Hearts, and I was the Blue Caterpillar. I was excited. Never had I been in a ballet. Fifty-two years is a long time to be a chrysalis, and I was eager to split the pupal shell, pump up my wings, and flutter through an auditorium. I am not light of toe or hind leg. Upstroke and downstroke, glissade and passe de chat were beyond my furnace, and the best I did was bask at the corner of the stage like a satyr of hairstreak, wings folded and body sideways to the audience.

In truth my costume was so heavy that I could hardly manage a hop, much less the slow bob of a swallowtail. Instead of ballet shoes, I wore bedroom slippers, the brown kind sold by L. L. Bean, stuffed with wool and costing forty-five dollars. I also wore a green athletic shirt, presented to people who ran a road race in Norwich, Connecticut, in 1985. Since Eastern Savings and Loan, the sponsor of the race, was printed in big white letters across the chest, I wore the shirt inside out. On my head sat a green bathing suit. Stuffed with cotton, the suit rose to a point. Through the leg holes on the sides poked antennae, two curved ten-inch springs, atop each a Ping-Pong ball dipped in silver glitter. For the performances I bought my first pair of tights. I wanted a yellow pair, but the only color that TeeKay's in Willmantic sold that fit me was gray. Still, I enjoyed wearing them, and when I first put them on, I leaped through the house, plucking, I said, apples from silver trees. Domestic reviewers did not rave. When I stopped, rising to a soutenu, my arms cradling a bushel of golden apples, Eliza turned to Vicki. "Ugh," she said, "I hate that lump that men have in the front when they wear tights." "I know," Vicki answered, "but it is not a very big lump. At least that one isn't."

At the performance I wore blue bathing trunks over the tights, and the lump was not visible. Even if the mole hill had been a mountain, the audience would not have noticed it, for, draped over my shoulders and trailing after me, was an ancient brocaded curtain. In a previous dramatic incarnation at the Rectory School in Pomfret, the curtain had stalked the stage as a dragon. Stapled on as trim was a thirty-seven-inch tail thicker than an eiderdown. While a heavy yellow beanbag was attached to the end of the tail, a ruffle of diamond-shaped orange scales ran up a seam to the back of my neck. Despite their reptilian attributes, my costume remained a curtain, lined and so heavy that I sometimes thought it still contained rods, and not plastic rods but heavy walnut or brass rods, removed from a great-aunt's country estate. Stitched across the body of the curtain were gold designs, some resembling thin, leafless Chinese trees, others onions sliced in half. At the bottom of the curtain hung a deep border. Green cord twisted through the border in a series of doodles, all of which turned into eights the longer I looked at them. While a double row of green tassels switched above the floor, a strip of lead half an inch tall insured that the curtain would not wobble lightly out of presence.

At the Bench shop in Willmantic I bought makeup, for two dollars a tube of luminous blue Harlequin Colors cream makeup, a white grease crayon for a dollar, then for $1.95 a black "Eyebrow Eye-Liner Pencil." Before each performance I painted my face, neck, and ears blue. With the eye-liner I blackened wrinkles and crevices. Afterward I colored my eyelids white and highlighted my cheekbones and forehead. Next I drew a white line along the center of my nose over the tip and down to my upper lip. Lastly I clipped two plastic earrings to my ears. The earrings belonged to Eliza. Gold-colored and two inches in diameter, the earrings formed bright circles, making my caterpillar seem swashbuckling, transforming him from the larva of a dull swarthy or dun sedge skipper into that of a fritillary, maybe even that of a spicebush or tiger swallowtail.

I began my *Adventures* by walking down the aisle of the auditorium. I carried several vertebrae of tail in my left hand; in my right I held one of Francis's school notebooks. Vicki covered the outside of the notebook with red and green paper, the kind of paper used for wrapping presents at Christmas. Inside were prompts for my "steps." Once I reached the stage, I opened the notebook and read an excerpt from Lewis Carroll's poem "Which Dreamed It?" Afterward I sat on an orange mushroom-shaped stool at the left front corner of the stage. The stool was so low that my knees were almost as high as my chest. Surrounding me were four cloth mushrooms borrowed from the School of Puppetry at the University of Connecticut and ranging in height from one and a half to two and a half feet tall. After I arranged my curtain, the dancers tripped down through the theater like dreams. The youngest children were bumblebees in yellow leotards and black tutus speckled with gold sequins. Attached to their shoulders were gauze wings. Fluttering behind the bees were butterflies, five dressed in lilac and three in apricot. Close behind them hopped rabbits, pink and white ears flopping over their heads. Next came the dodos spinning in bright colors, green, yellow, purple, red, and blue. Once the dodos slipped through the curtain, a garden of flowers bloomed, daisy chains of creamy petals wrapped around their waists. Next came diamonds wearing sashes decorated with red sequins. When the hearts danced into the theater wearing long white dresses, my own heart leaped up. To love a child as much as I loved the bright Queen of Hearts was almost painful. Alice was the last dancer to slip down the aisle. When she approached me, I wriggled, startling her, and asked, "Who are you?"

My role was small. I introduced nine dances by reading short excerpts from *Alice's Adventures*. I spoke a total of seven hundred and thirty-six words. Although I did not leave the stage during the ballet, I tried not to move. I was merely gena and mandible, the horny functional stuff of a caterpillar. The dreams, to use Lewis Carroll's words, were "golden" on the stage and in their parents' eyes, and I did not want to drain "the wells of fancy dry" by calling attention to myself. Only once did I leave my mushroom, and that was to retrieve three little bees who strayed far from hive and choreography to bumble about dangerously near the front end of the stage. When the curtain closed at the end of the ballet, I gathered my costume and walked to the middle of the stage. I started to go behind the curtain, but then I turned around and facing the auditorium asked the audience, "Who are you?" Three minutes later I led Eliza out for her bow. The caterpillar had vanished. I was now Daddy—proud, adoring Daddy.

. . . The Blue Caterpillar was wrong. Knowing place is more important than knowing self. When a person knows a place, not only does he become part of that place, but others get to know him so well that questions about identity are meaningless, having almost nothing to do with daily life. Sometime during winter, my lawnmower froze to death. By the time I bought a new mower, the yard was a hay field. In order to cut the grass I pushed the handle of the mower down to my knees, thus lifting the front wheels and the front half of the blade a foot off the ground. Then, hunching over, I leaned forward and, inching the mower along on its back wheels, attempted to cut off the top third of the grass. Every ten or so feet, a bale of hay clogged the blade and the mower shut off, exploding in an aneurysm of clanging and acrid white smoke. I was trying to restart the mower for the twentieth time when suddenly a tractor appeared in the yard. On it sat a man who took care of lawns for his living. "Mr. Pickering, you don't know me," he said, "but while I was driving by just now I saw you trying to cut the grass. You are never going to finish the lawn, and so I am going to mow it for you for free. Will it be all right," he added, as he turned his tractor, "if I dump the cuttings in the woods behind your house." "Yes," I said.

Two days later Dave knocked at the screen door. "Sam," he said, "I've got something to show you and the children." I don't know Dave well. Like me he swims, and I see him a couple of mornings a week at the university pool, where we chat about college doings. Dave had never come to my house before. I didn't think he knew where I lived, and I could not imagine what he had in his car. An old leather briefcase sat on the front seat of the car. Piled next to it were its former contents: two books, a stack of loose papers, a notebook, and yellow pencils in a rubber band. As I looked in the car window, the briefcase shrugged. Dave reached over, picked the case up, unzipped it, and took out a box turtle. "I found him on the road," he said, "and I thought you and your family would like to see him before I turn him loose." Years ago I wrote an article for *Yankee Magazine*, describing a person who rescued turtles from roadsides and who placed signs along highways reading, "Turtle Crossing. Please Slow Down." Once or twice a year since the appearance of the article, neighbors telephone and ask me questions about turtles. In truth I am a bit of a turtle person. Since childhood I have rescued turtles from roads. Only last week I stopped traffic and removed a painted turtle from the middle of a state highway. Box turtles have finer feelings or at least they are capable of more aristocratic restraint than painted turtles. Dave's box turtle did not soil his briefcase. Not having a satchel in which to place him, I put the painted turtle on the floor of my car. Before I turned him loose in Tift Pond, he created a lake and several creeks of his own, urinating almost nonstop.

The Memorial Day Parade is, as a friend put it, "the event of events" in Mansfield. The route of the parade is short. Starting at Bassett's Bridge Road, participants march a quarter of a mile along Route 195 past the old graveyard. On Cemetery Road the parade turns right and proceeds a tenth of a mile to the new graveyard. Along the route mothers and fathers sit in folding chairs, and children play atop old stone walls. The parade itself isn't lengthy, this year consisting of a handful of marchers representing the Eastern Star, Lodge No. 14 in Windham, Connecticut, one of whose members wore a top hat and looked like Abraham Lincoln; the mayor riding in a jeep driven by a retired Army sergeant; a smattering of veterans; a five-man color guard; and two bands—one from the middle school, the other from the high school—playing old favorites: "Anchors Away," "Yankee Doodle," and "The Marine Hymn." Following the bands were five antique cars; volunteers with the Eagleville Fire Department, triangular patches sewed on their left sleeves depicting a white eagle spreading its wings, under which was printed "We Protect"; nine trucks manned by fireman-pumpers, a hook-and-ladder, and also a small green truck with "Forestry 117" printed on the side in yellow; then a pickup truck towing an aluminum boat equipped with an outboard motor, used to rescue people in difficulty on ponds. Most marchers were children, Girl and Boy Scouts, Cub Scouts, and Brownies. One Cub Scout pulled his sister in a Radio Flyer decorated with small American flags. A Brownie pushed a baby carriage crammed with a zoo of stuffed animals. Marching behind the Scouts in happy disorder were children who played baseball in the town recreational league. Among them were Eliza and Edward—Eliza wearing a blue shirt and a blue cap, on the front of the cap a white M standing for Mansfield; and Edward wearing a green shirt, yellow letters on the chest spelling **TCBY,** the name of the yogurt store that sponsored his team.

In front of the stone walls along the parade route, daisies bloomed. Red-winged blackbirds nagged at marchers from perches atop cattails in the shallows of Echo Lake. Standing beneath a sugar maple in the graveyard, the mayor introduced the speaker, a colonel in the Army Reserve. The mayor promised that the colonel's speech would be brief. "When he loses the attention of the Brownie Scouts," the mayor said, "he cuts it off." In his talk the colonel implied that the United States had lost a sense of purpose and maybe identity. He asked God to "give us a vision." No, I thought. Visions are too distant and abstract. People need to see and appreciate the immediate. Identity and purpose do not lie beyond the horizon. They inhabit backyards. Instead of being handed meaning, people should seek it themselves. Wonderland does not lie inaccessible in dream or down a rabbit hole. When a child flutters awkwardly across a stage and smiles at her daddy, that's Wonderland. When a man hides behind an oak at the edge of a baseball field and watches his son bat, that's Wonderland, too. Wonderland is a boy, a good science student standing in a graveyard talking to his best friend about computers, in the background a nice man praying for a vision, a red-eyed vireo singing, sunlight yellow on hemlocks, the new growth molting, flickering like candelabra.

• •

SAM PICKERING, whose recent books include *May Days*, *Still Life*, *Let it Ride*, and, in 1994, *Trespassing*, teaches English at the University of Connecticut in Storrs. A native of Nashville and a graduate of the University of the South at Sewanee, he has recently completed *Walkabout Year*, about his time in Australia.

RICHARD TILLINGHAST

FATHER IN OCTOBER

When the smell of freshly sharpened pencils had lost
Its power to intoxicate, when our first
Infatuation with September had slackened—
With its satchels and homework and new teacher;
When the leaves of the late-blooming chrysanthemums
In our frost-finished back garden had blackened,
One morning my mother would retrieve our winter
Hats and scarves, our gloves and heavy raingear.
My father would go up to the attic, bring down the storms
And snug them in, between ourselves and the weather.

One hundred years of our family had lived
Beneath that house's airy ceilings, had sat
By a grate where coal sputtered and glowed in the glass
Cases where my grandfather's books were shelved—
Shakespeare, the Brontes, Dickens, Sir Walter Scott.
And the house told stories, of interest only to us:
The well, sealed after Uncle John drowned a cat.
The deep-cut initials my older brother carved
Above the stairs. The bed my mother was born in.
Every dip in the floorboards spoke, every curious stain

"Father in October," by Richard Tillinghast, appeared in the *New Republic* (March 10, 1995), 40. Reprinted by permission of the author.

Remembered. To marry my mother, my father found
In 1932, was to husband her house
Its *fin de siecle* wiring was a fireman's nightmare;
What was airy in June was drafty in December.
"Manage," "Simplify," his granite New England
Eyes said. Those Willifords must have seemed another
Species altogether—with their Southernness,
Their leaky roof, their Eastlake furniture.
There was hardly a marble-topped table that didn't wobble,
Or a chair that couldn't have used some glue or a nail.

Saturdays he'd be up by six. First
A shave, and with his shaving brush he'd soap
Clean the lenses of his gold-rimmed glasses.
Then he'd collect himself over coffee and make a list,
Numbered and neat, of his day's projects in the shop
He had built out back under the hickory trees.
A nimbus of sawdust surrounding his concentration,
He'd turn a chair-leg on his lathe, cut out
A bracket or brace with his jigsaw, then fashion
A toy pistol for me, or a paddle-wheel boat.

Daddy's real work was engineering. His own
Dreams and epiphanies came to him, I imagine,
In the language of his calling—straightedged and clear
As a blueprint, verifiable by time and motion
Studies. His few inventions that made a profit,
The many he drew in his mind but had to give
Up on, lived a life pristine and platonic—

Not subject to half-measures or the change of season,
Not battered by weather or in need of repair
Like the mortal house I judged him master of.

Six Mile Mountain

The ground held more stones than dirt. No arrowheads,
No shaped flint-chips rose to their pick and shovel.
No one had disturbed these rocks since God and the glacier
Laid them down in anger.

They attacked the shelved-in limestone with their pick,
And flecks rained dryly down on dead oak leaves.
Dogwood misted the woods, forsythia brightened.
The stores in Six Mile were selling flowers for Easter.

Tears fell into the hole they were digging.
They sweated out last night's whiskey and grief.
In the high air's stillness that hard metallic ping
Ricocheted off tree trunks, bare and obdurate.

Finally the earth's coolness breathed up to them.
Little winged things flitted in the air above
The grave. Thumbnail-sized black butterflies appeared.
Black-capped chickadees perched on the black limbs

And answered the sharpened cries of pick and shovel.
The day warmed. Mare's-tails flared across the sky's
Bland cerulean. In the air-drifts
That skimmed the ridge a hawk glided, watching.

• •

RICHARD TILLINGHAST, a Memphis native, is the author of five books of poetry, most recently *The Stonecutter's Hand* (David Godine, 1995). A professor of English at the University of Michigan, Tillinghast is a frequent contributor to such periodicals as the *New York Times Book Review*, *Washington Post Book World*, and *Partisan Review*.

ARTHUR FLOWERS

FROM *ANOTHER GOOD LOVING BLUES*

I am Flowers of the delta clan Flowers and the line of O Killens—I am hoodoo, I am griot, I am a man of power. My story is a true story, my words are true words, my lie is a true lie—a fine old delta tale about a mad blues piano player and a Arkansas conjure woman on a hoodoo mission. Lucas Bodeen and Melvira Dupree. Plan to show you how they found the good thing. True love. That once-in-a-lifetime love. Now few folk find the good thing; most folk struggle through life making do—you can learn to love most anybody thats good people. Truth be told its probably best that way because when you find true love my friend its strictly do or die.

My boy Luke Bodeen wasn't even thinking bout no love that bright springly morning he first saw her walking on the dusty little main and only street of Sweetwater Arkansas. But the moment he saw her he wanted her and needed her—she took his breath, she took his heart.

Spring 1918. The Mississippi delta. Bodeen 37 and in his prime. Known to be silver-tongued delta bluesman, Luke Bodeen had left more good women grieving in more towns than he cared to count. But this one touched him. Somewhere deep. Boy didn't know what he was stepping into when he tilted his Stetson just so and crossed her path.

"How do mam, I'm Luke Bodeen. You interested?"

She kept walking, proud little round head cleaving the air. Thick pretty head of hair he couldn't wait to put his fingers into. He matched her stride-for-stride, and their rhythm was a good one. She turned then to look at him and he stumbled into the massive brown galaxies of eyes that saw a mite more than he was comfortable showing.

"A bluesman," he told her, "and a good one too. Outta Memphis Tennessee mostly, but I been around. I come to town with the traveling medicine show."

He paused, poised for an opening.

"Melvira Dupree," she said, "conjure."

He stumbled again. Conjure? Didn't know if he was ready for all that. But he looked her over again and he liked what he saw.

"Well I declare you ain't like no conjure I ever seen."

"Is that so bluesman, and how many have you seen?"

"Oh I seen plenty conjures gal, I'm a well-traveled man, I been to New Orleans, St. Louis and Chicago Illinois, been to New York City, Paris France, Timbucktu and Rio de Janeiro. I done downhome blues wherever the four winds blow. I come back home regular though cause I'm just another good old boy delta born and bred. Warn you up front that I ain't never tossed my shoes under no woman's bed for long. When the blues call I'm liable to answer."

He smiled at her, a bright warm sunny day in the middle of March, a hint of springs to come. She looked him over again with those funny eyes of hers . . . a good spirit, healthy, vigorous . . . she could see that he would be, shall we say, a troublesome man . . . but still . . . there was something about him that spoke to her in that special way. And seeing as she hadn't been any further out of Sweetwater than her traveling spirit had took her, all this talk about getting around intrigued her.

Now Bodeen knew he was being judged, felt her digging. Deep too. Naturally his first urge was to block her, but he found himself just letting her look and hoping she liked what she saw. She, of course, blinked and looked no further—between men and women a degree of mystery is often appropriate.

"I seen hoodoos and conjures of all persuasions," he told her with a downright bodacious grin, "but I ain't never run across one like you. Don't bother me none you understand, I'm here to claim you and if you really conjure, then you know I'm talking true. I likes you gal, I likes your style, really truly I do."

He offered his arm and a big old country courting smile.

She laughed with a newfound pleasure and took them both. Most of the men in Sweetwater were afraid to talk to the woman in her.

"You ain't half bad yourself bluesman."

Her throaty voice was a tickle, a challenge, a music that bewitched him. He preened under her obvious approval like a old bantam rooster and commenced to sang himself a brand-new blues.

I'll bring you sweet southern loving
in a old tin cup
pour it on your body baby
then I'ma lap it all up
everyday
Show you how much I love being your man.

"Gon git you too," he sang, "gon git you good, cause I don't mind working at it."

She just as tickled as she can be.

"Do tell . . . bluesman."

They stopped in front of the Sweetwater General Store and she rested her hand lightly on his arm.

"I thank you for your company Mr. Bodeen, you are kinda cute."

"O I'm a lot more than cute. As you shall see when I come a courting. Course I ain't gon pester you none just now, though. Just enough to put me on your mind some."

She went inside, laughing pertly over a curved brown shoulder bare to the sun.

"You don't know you want to be on my mind bluesman."

"Oh yes I do," he sang after her. "I ain't scared of no conjure, what you gon do, hoodoo a man the blues already claim? I'll be seeing you around Miz Melvira Dupree."

Now it would be safe to say that the good coloredfolk of Sweetwater Arkansas were scandalized and mystified when their conjure woman took up with that blues-singer, when he stayed on after the medicine show left town and moved into her little place out there on Sweetwater Creek.

The local lads were understandably upset with him. They wouldn't have minded a chance with that fox Dupree, but she was known to have a temper, and any old fool know that courting a conjure woman with a temper is a chancy thing. The two of them bickered and fought about as much as they laughed and loved, always mad at each other about something. Any day now folks expected to see that boy hopping round like a toadfrog or wiggling on his belly like a snake. But whatever he was doing, he was doing it right. Melvira Dupree changed up on them. She walk down the street smiling at folks and greeting them good morning just like a regular neighbor. But it was when she started hanging out down at the local jukejoint where Lucas got a job barrelhousing every Friday and Saturday night that folks really commence to commenting. Girl started flouncing that big impressive boodie of hers and having herself much too good of a time for the puritans from the old school, who couldn't quite recall a conjure woman quite like this one. Of course the older Sweetwater women, elders all who didn't miss very much, would poke each others ribs when they saw her walking around town glowing. They knew a recently satisfied woman when they saw one. After all a good man is still hard to find and even conjures appreciate good loving.

And that boy Bodeen, he just as snug as a hog in fresh summer mud. When he wasn't all knotted up mad at her, he could be seen walking around with his thumbs hooked in those red suspenders and grinning proud as a brand-new fool.

Scandalized as they were at their conjure lady taking up with a bluessinger, of all things, you could tell he loved that woman something truly fierce. A buncha Sweetwater women like the way his lean brown fingers caressed music out of those cold piano keys and wondered what music he coaxed from a woman's warm body, but he went home to Melvira Dupree each and every night. Took his money home each and every week, too, like a natchural man, and wasn't never fool enough to try and raise up his hands against her. They did fuss a lot, but folks come to decide that they just liked to fuss.

So the good coloredfolk of Sweetwater Arkansas gave their grudging approval. To this day Sweetwater folk are known for being bighearted, and there just ain't no counting for a conjure's taste noway.

Course what folks saw from the vantage points of their big wraparound porches wasn't the whole story. Never is. Any good story is always at least 4 or 5 stories deep. And since this a good story, I expect you to pay close attention to the weave of it. Even they couldn't tell the whole story. But what they did come to understand deep down in once starved and lonely souls, is that when you do find yourself some of that real good loving, if you got any sense at all, you hold on to it.

Truth. I swear by all thats holy.

◆ ◆

ARTHUR FLOWERS, a native of Memphis, is cofounder of the New Renaissance Writer's Guild and the Griot Shop. The author of *De Mojo Blues* and *Cleveland Lee's Beale Street Band*, as well as *Another Good Loving Blues*, Flowers now lives in New York City, where he teaches at Medger Evers College.

MALCOLM GLASS

WITNESSING

Some of us are called, by circumstance,
into the folds of an elect, to witness
those moments everyone else in the world,
by the same blind chance, missed:

Leroy Wilton, short-order cook
at Lasseter's Cafe, who just happens,
as he drives I-40 south of the city,
to catch, in the corner of his sight,
two small aircraft swallowed, mid-flight,
in spectacular conflagration. He brakes
onto the shoulder, craning to look hard,
and sees, flung from the fire-ball,
a bundle of fabric, growing, suddenly,
arms, legs, flailing.
                              This one moment
cants Leroy's life askew, and he lumbers,
from that time forward, in a hobble,
his shoulders and neck bent, heavy
with the words he must rehearse over
and over for listeners by the drink
machine at work, in the bar Friday

"Witnessing," from *In the Shadow of the Gourd,* by Malcolm Glass (Minneapolis, Minn.: New Rivers Press, 1990), 44–45. Used by permission of the author.

night, over the Saturday poker table.
Or Deborah Lopez, who finds, on a walk
by the river late in April, a skull,
ragged and gnawed by dogpack, thus ending,
fortuitously, the search for Jennifer
Stinson, abductee, and thus beginning
Deborah's clueless wandering in search
of language to carry her beyond mere
narrative, beyond logic, beyond fear.

And Randy Brown, driving the steep,
swift descent of Vermont Highway 15
into the maw of coincidence, first
on the scene: a runaway truck come
to its twisted conclusion in a ravine,
and the driver, who had leapt free,
for a moment, at least, until the back
wheels splayed him across the asphalt
like a lamb on a chopping block.
Years later, Randy still drives holding
hard to the right of center, still
piecing together some theory, or other,
to explain the intersections of clock
and compass, the dire circuitry between
the heart and the inexplicable

These witnesses have never known
the listener who nods a *yes, I know*,
soundless and echoing clear against
the ribs, have never seen anyone

whose eyes mirror the gaze that once saw
grim fiction come alive in death.

It never occurs to this small and scattered
band to gather for Witnesses Anonymous
meetings, to huddle Tuesday nights
in a Fellowship Room or a Lutheran
basement to spill the words again,
to straighten the account once and
always, to know their listeners feel
the same shiver and twist of the spine,
to know they are sure of nothing else.

MALCOLM GLASS directs the writing program at Austin Peay State University, where he is coeditor of the literary journal *Zone 3*. The author of two poetry collections, he also has had poems and stories in the *Sewanee Review*, *Poetry* (Chicago), *Reader's Choice*, and *Prairie Schooner*, among others.

RICHARD SPEIGHT

THE PANCAKE MAN

I have no idea when the tradition started.

Who knows why some things become "traditions" within families, while other things occur once and are forgotten? It just happens, I suppose. All I know is that by the time my oldest daughter, Barby, was no more than five or six years old, the tradition of the Pancake Man was already firmly entrenched. She's grown and married now, which means that this little bit of family lore has been around for a long, long time.

There was a day, however, when I thought for sure that the Pancake Man had died, and that's what this is about. It isn't about how the tradition started. It's about how it almost ended.

Let me begin my setting the record straight. I am, in fact, the Pancake Man. The one and only. Accept no substitutes.

Before Barbara and I started having children, I had a vision of what I wanted fatherhood to be like. I wanted to be a "pal" to my children and more besides. I aspired to be a dispenser of wisdom, a benevolent guide who would lead his children along the mine-infested pathway to maturity, gently nudging them this way and that, helping them make the journey safely. It was a big job; it would take a big man to do it. I never once envisioned myself in a role as mundane as that of the Pancake Man.

Why did the Pancake Man catch on? Why did he become a legend in his own time?

Maybe it was because I appeared so out of place in the kitchen, even in that role. My being in there for any purpose, even something as innocuous as making pancakes, must have seemed like a big deal to our little ones. Perhaps it was because I attacked the task with such obvious enthusiasm from the very first. I couldn't just go in there and make pancakes. Oh, no! I had to assume a second identity, step out of my unimaginative self and enter upon the task with a flourish. I had to make it fun, exciting, and extraordinary. I couldn't just do it.

"The Pancake Man," from *The Pancake Man & Friends*, by Richard Speight (Nashville, Tenn.: Dimensions for Living, 1992), 11–19. Used by permission of the author.

My enthusiasm was a carryover from my childhood. As far back as I can remember, I have loved pancakes, especially buckwheats. I would stack them up, cover them with butter, watch the butter trickle down the side of the stack as it melted, then soak them in syrup from a metal can, the one that looked like a real log cabin. I would cut the stack into wedge-shaped sections and stick my fork through the whole wedge, so that each delicious bite consisted of layer after layer of still-warm pancake, laced with butter and soaked in syrup.

It was more than a meal. It was an experience. I almost salivate when I think about it. Even now I can't drive past an I-Hop without getting an urge to sit down to a stack of buckwheats. It was altogether natural, then, that I would want the same kind of memorable experience for my children. Thus it is no surprise that the legend of the Pancake Man was born. I made it fun, because for me, it was fun.

Early on, the Pancake Man became a regular Saturday morning visitor at our house. I would take my place in front of the stove at the drop of a suggestion. The cast iron griddle of my youth had turned to Teflon and the little metal log cabin had become a plastic squeeze bottle, but the same great smell still filled the house, and the same sense of satisfaction still accompanied the completion of the meal. I derived great pleasure from knowing that the good feelings from my childhood were being appropriately preserved and passed along to the next generation.

The simple thing, of course, would have been to just make pancakes and skip the silly stuff. Why have an alter ego? Why assume a separate identity? And how did that title, the Pancake Man, come about, anyway?

It sort of evolved, actually.

As in many families, our children were usually up first on Saturday morning. Often as not, they would come racing into our bedroom and pile onto the bed, ready for some fun.

One Saturday morning, one of them brought up the subject of pancakes. Instead of doing so in the usual way, however, he or she, I don't recall which, asked in complete innocence if the Pancake Man could come that morning. I grabbed the ball and ran with it. I told them that I'd heard that the Pancake Man was in town, and that if they would wait in the breakfast room, who knew what might happen? Once they had scrambled off, I slipped into the kitchen, donned an apron and a chef's hat, grabbed a spatula, and burst through the door to the breakfast room. Voila! The Pancake Man was born!

After that, the routine was set in concrete. At some point on Saturday morning, one of the three would ask that all-important question. "Daddy? Do you think the Pancake Man will come this morning?" That would set the other two off. "Yeah, Daddy! Do you think there's a chance? Can you get him to come? Try, Daddy! Please!"

"I hear he's in the neighborhood," I'd reply once more, eager to play my role.

Was there ever a time when he couldn't come? Are you kidding? My heart would melt faster than a dollop of butter on a hot buckwheat whenever they started in with the game. Forget about sleeping late! Forget about a quiet cup of coffee and a relaxed session with the paper! Of course he'd come! Bolstered by their infectious enthusiasm, I'd mentally assume my "other" identity, arm myself with spatula and ladle, and head off in search of the pancake mix. No sooner would the first round of cakes be bubbling on the griddle than our stairstep trio of tykes would come marching in, ready to chow down.

For a while, there was an official outfit. On that first morning, I had conscripted the red-checkered apron and chef's hat Barbara had bought for me to use in my role as Outdoor Grill Man. That ensemble quickly became part of the game, but after a while it no longer mattered what I was wearing. From time to time I would inject variety by making pancakes of different sizes or by making them in the shape of the children's initials, but by and large, it was just regular pancakes and a room full of happy people.

Sometimes I would be asked to play the role of the Waffle Man. This is a somewhat more sophisticated version of the standard Pancake Man tradition and one that carries with it considerably more risk. Remember, I'm a professional. You shouldn't try this at home.

It's pretty hard to mess up a pancake. I've flipped a few clean off of the griddle in my time, but for the most part, pancake errors are few and far between and are seldom noticed by the ones waiting to eat. If you mess up a pancake, you can make another in a hurry and cover your mistake. But when you are standing in front of a lone waffle iron, the pressure is on.

Think about it. Three little faces turned toward me like so many open-beaked birds in a nest, depending on me to fill their needs. Three hands holding onto junior forks. Three sets of eyes watching my every move; three button noses soaking up the delicious aroma steaming from the cooking waffle. Then comes the moment they've been waiting for.

I jiggle the handle cautiously, then confidently pull upward. The waffle splits in the middle, each half permanently stuck to its respective side of the waffle iron. I smile lamely. Disappointment fills the room. Depression becomes my companion.

Believe me, it has happened more than once. It takes a while to recover from a trauma as big as that!

The Waffle Man is high-risk business. The Pancake Man managed to survive, however, and through the years, pancakes evolved into a kind of comfort food for our family. The Pancake Man became an important part of our existence.

Time passed, as it always does. Days became weeks, weeks yielded to months, and months mystically blended to form years. Before we knew it, our three stairsteps had grown up and were beginning to wander off in different directions. Barbara and I clung to the past, wishing with all our hearts that we could stick our fingers in the hourglass and stop the painful, inexorable passage of time.

Then came the fateful day.

It was Saturday after New Year's, not too long ago. That's when it happened. I had been up for a while. Everyone else was still in bed. I was sipping coffee in the quiet of our breakfast room. All of a sudden the idea hit me. Why not surprise the children? It's a tradition! And it's been such a long time. They'll love it! Really they will.

I stepped into my imaginary phone booth, ripped off my everyday image, exposed the bright-red "P" on my chest, and emerged as the Pancake Man!

What a great idea, I thought, as I scurried about, making preparations. Barby, our oldest, would be moving back to her dorm at Vanderbilt the next day. Lindy, the second in the line, would be flying back to Davidson College at the same time. "Bet they don't have anything this good at school," I mused as I plopped the Teflon griddle on the computer-regulated, heat-sensitive burner, and turned the switch to 450 degrees. Richard, the youngest, was still a year away from college, but I knew he'd appreciate this surprise every bit as much as his sisters. I decided to let Barbara sleep late. This would be daddy's special time with the children.

Visions of Ozzie and Harriet filled my head as the familiar sweet smell wafted through the house. I eagerly anticipated the coming experience. The four of us would gather around the table, hum "Getting to Know You" in three-part harmony, then sink our teeth into a delicious stack of pancakes. What a warm, wonderful family moment it would be.

A few minutes later, I began knocking on bedroom doors.

I started at Barby's room. There was no response. I knocked again. Still no response. I eased the door open and stuck my head in. The place was dark as a tomb.

"The Pancake Man is here," I chirped. Her answer was a low, gutteral moan. "Come on to the kitchen when you're ready," I added cheerily, easing back out and closing the door.

Lindy's room was next. Again, no response to my knock. When I cracked the door, a shaft of light fell across her bed. "Lindy," I sang out. "The Pancake Man is here!" I thought I detected the slightest upward movement in one of her eyelids, but it slammed shut so quickly it was hard to tell.

"Lindy, the Pancake Man is here," I said less cheerily. You should have seen it. One hand came out from under her covers, followed by the other. They moved slowly upward toward her pillow. Then in one smoothly executed, world-class maneuver, she simultaneously flopped from her back to her stomach and flipped the pillow over to cover her head.

"Come on when you're ready," I said. My voice had all the confidence of a principal inviting a student to drop by the office for a little discipline.

I wasn't daunted. It was a temporary setback, that's all. After all, weren't our children known to be legendary sleepers? They actually die for a while; their bodies become one with the bed—a single unit dedicated to a single purpose.

I headed for Richard's room. His head was already under his pillow. There must be some kind of underground warning system at work, I thought.

"Rise and shine," I called out. "The Pancake Man's in town. He'll be along any minute."

"What time is it?" Richard groaned.

"Almost ten," I responded, my enthusiasm waning.

"You're kidding!" he cried out, his tousled mop of unruly hair pointing in every conceivable direction. "What're you doing up so early? It's Saturday, for Pete's sake!"

I headed back to the kitchen, turned the temperature under the griddle to simmer, put some plastic wrap over the batter bowl, and returned to my morning newspaper.

Finally, they began to wander in.

Richard came first. His eyelids drooped and his jaw sagged. He didn't even turn on the Saturday morning cartoons. He just sat there, teetering on the brink of unconsciousness.

Lindy came next. She forced out some cheerful words, but I could tell that her heart wasn't in it.

Barby finally appeared. The other two seemed downright peppy compared to her.

She had sent her body as her official representative, but had left her mind and her spirit in the sack.

The three of them sat in stony silence while I stacked up the cakes and placed them in front of their semicomatose bodies. They ate in silence as I scurried about. The only sound was the clinking of forks and the gulping of milk.

One by one they got up from the table.

Richard said nothing. He just walked over to me, patted me gently on the back, then returned to his room.

Lindy carried her plate to the counter. "Thank you, Daddy," she said, one eye still firmly closed.

Barby gave me a hug. "I love you, Daddy," she said. I thought she was going to fall asleep on my shoulder, but she managed to regain consciousness and headed back to bed.

The kitchen was deathly quiet. I started to clean up. That's when I noticed it. Lindy and Richard had only picked at their food. Fully half of their pancakes remained, a soggy reminder of their noble effort. Barby's plate was clean, but moments later I found her pancakes sitting dolefully in the sink, still stacked, untouched. They looked as sad as I felt.

Everything changes, I thought. Nothing remains the same. The Pancake Man has outlived his usefulness. He has died a natural death. It's time to let him rest in peace.

Winter came and went, and I thought no more about it. The children were in and out, sometimes at odd intervals, and not always at the same time. I purposely avoided all recollections of that experience. I didn't want to remind myself of the melancholy feeling that had come with it.

In April, Lindy came home for her spring break, ready to rest and recuperate. She had a good week, resting a lot, visiting friends, and sharing a few laughs with us old folks, too. On her last Saturday morning I cooked pancakes again. I left out all the fanfare, though. Enough is enough. Don't make a big deal out of it, I reminded myself.

We had a nice conversation while she ate. Then I wandered off to do something else. When I came back a while later, Lindy had finished and had cleared the table. There was one plate still on the table, however. It was at the place where I sit.

In the middle of that plate, sitting on a napkin, was a single cold pancake. On that pancake, Lindy had drawn a happy face with a red magic marker. It wasn't an ordinary happy face. It had glasses, a pointed nose, and a forelock that hung down over its forehead. It looked suspiciously like me!

On the napkin, she had written these words:

Thanks, Pancake Man! . . .

◆ ◆

RICHARD SPEIGHT, a Nashville trial lawyer and former assistant district attorney turned writer, is the author of a number of crime novels and story collections. His *Desperate Justice*, published by Warner, was an ABC-TV Sunday Night Movie in late 1993, under the title *A Mother's Revenge*.

MARGARET SKINNER

The Buoyancy Factor

I never said I could fly. A close read of the article proves that I never said any such thing. The newspaper photograph shows me hovering above the power lines all right, but just being *up there* is not the same thing as flying.

The foreshadowing of my rise above ground came one day last spring when I ran to catch the tail of a red kite. It caught my eye from the car window as it skittered across a vacant lot grown up with bright green fescue. I stopped the car, got out and ran for it, drawn like a hummer to hibiscus. The kite shimmied and teased, dragging its long yellow knotted tail through the wavering grass as I stumbled, reaching for it. Just as the wind rustled the kite and swept it forward, I caught hold of a knot and held on tight with both hands. I ran fast to keep it, the wind pushing hard at my back, when suddenly a powerful cross-current shot the kite upward—me along with it—and I tread air just long enough and fast enough to be airborne three feet above ground for several seconds, before a gust of wind snatched the tail out of my hand and blew the kite high in the sky.

Though I hit the ground with a thud, my quick rise-and-fall was nonetheless exhilarating, and I thought about it on the days that followed. Something was building inside of me, a welling so strong that I set upon each day as if embarking on a strange and mystical journey. Mostly, I thought about sex.

I'd read that women at midlife sometimes feel a surge of passion—an old garden variety flower suddenly producing a show-stopping bloom. I hardly knew how to assimilate this phenomenon. In the past my desires for the carnal were minimal. In a one to five ranking of my favorite activities, sex, at best, had come in fourth, behind reading, music, and swimming, followed by walking. In truth, walking had nudged sex into fifth place more often than not. No more. Through my veins the blood now ran so fast I could feel its coursing heat, a passion unbridled. Sex rose to number one and sensually held its place. Nighttime was the right time, and I was in my prime.

Bob, my husband, owns a company that cruises timber, a job that keeps him away in the woods for long periods, but then he comes home and stays put for weeks at a time, enjoying the amenities of civilization. Our two children are grown and gone.

Quite taken with surprise over my suggestions of amorous adventure, he'd say, "Suits me, Sarah," and move toward the bedroom.

The pulsations that began in my lower extremity soon swam wildly throughout my entire body, like a school of bloodfish. Effusions of the night were no longer enough. A desire for sex became my motive for rising each day, and I left gaps in my routine to accommodate any possibility that might arise.

As a freelance copyeditor, I work at home, so taking a sex break during the workaday impinged on my schedule alone. At odd hours of the night I made up for the lost time when I'd wake from an erotic dream, pace the floor in order to settle down, then go at my work for several hours. I persisted even while doubting the quality of the copyediting done on the heels of a sex-driven dream; when a paragraph dealt with something physical, I'm afraid I edited out sterile words such as *pleasure* and suggested substitions that were inappropriately sexy—*lust* or *concupiscence*, even though these words often held no meaning in the text. In the margins of the manuscripts I alluded not only to romance with drawings of birds and flowers, but also to vulgarity and lewdness in the faint penciled doodlings of naked bodies. In the past I'd always considered Freud's idea of penis envy with derision, feeling the misery caused by my shortcomings only in a fishing boat with no way to go. Now I drew the apparatus with abandon.

The sex drive broke through the limits of my own past and now carried me forward to a new place in time where the fullness of my true self might freely bloom. The hard part was deciding how best to harness the wild thing and develop its potential. I tried to cluster my thoughts in order to make sense of them.

To unleash my power, I concluded, would require Bob's cooperation in such illicit activities as *swapping partners* and *group sex*, which would ultimately train me for *team* sex. But I was compelled to ask myself how *do* these people find each other? So besides the problem of identifying potential participants, issuing invitations and overturning Bob's good character, such orgies would also demand that I, too, strip off the demeanor of grace worn over a lifetime. In truth, even soft porn offends me.

Still and all, the portents of love stood first and foremost as the dominant function of my life. At forty-nine I expected to deflate, so explaining this surge of adrenaline might come easier if the passion were directed toward one individual, the great lost love-of-my-life, for instance. But I'd never had one in the first place. Ironically, Bob's snappy libido now seemed placid when compared to my own new shades of Venus. Although Bob tried valiantly to keep up, I just about killed him. "Whoa," he'd say.

For Bob's sake, I started swimming almost everyday at the Y in order to weaken the force of sex. In college I was on the women's swimming team. I never cared about winning any race. I was in it for the water. In water your thoughts are insular. No one can get to you. In fact the coach was constantly peeved at me because I never heard his whistle when he blew it. "Time to get out, Sarah Gorda. You're shriveling up." But I wasn't shriveling. I was preserving. I was doing the breast stroke and could have kept on doing it forever.

Now the daily swimming took the edge off during the daylight hours, but as darkness fell my thoughts of sex became more liquid. At night I dreamed of erotica with a strange new love, replete with veils and violins and roses, only to wake in the morning light to review the brevity of Bob's lovemaking. He was a mere stand-in, until the leading man showed up.

An affair seemed in order, so much so that I took stock of the available men: first the widowers—including Albers the tyrannical editor I often worked for who I envisioned as a whip and chain man, Biggs the yard man whose sexual preference was suspect even before his wife died, Mossy the egg man whose virility seemed to diminish along with the decreasing sales of his eggs, and Mayhood our next-door neighbor who for the most part viewed the world through the eye of his camera, so much so that he was just one step above a peeping Tom; then the bachelors—both the mail carrier Johnson who didn't know my name after five years on the route and Sam the plumber who had eyes only for the American Standard, all prospects mere sub species of Lothario. I was tempted by a handsome homeless man on the street carrying the sign WORK FOR FOOD, but quickly considered the prospect of AIDS, paid him a small sum for the bright color of his blue eyes, and drove on to the Y.

I was stuck with Bob. That my commitment to monogamy was powered by the convenience of a bird-in-hand stood as a giddy understatement. As the expression goes—I did the best I could with what I had to work with.

Still, I lusted for something more. Between the cool sheets I lay in a sweat beside Bob in the dim morning light. He snored softly as I groped for an answer. Then I heard a crow caw, and I left the bed to look out the window.

In the garden below the Stars-of-Bethlehem bloomed among the spent daffodils. Bob had dished the wildflowers from the floor of the forest and presented them to me several years back. I planted the corms and since that time, they appear each year in late spring like clumps of onions among the startled flowers and soon after the buds shoot up all at once, offering a starry surprise.

I walked down the stairs and outside, my bare feet stepping lightly on the pebbles of the garden path. The wonder and excitement of spring warbled and buzzed from the grasses and trees as nature reinvented itself, the energy of renewal an erotomania that aroused me as I breathed its intoxicating perfume. With each deep breath I bobbled, then suddenly felt myself rise off the ground. Still in the upright position, I was suspended over the May apple and columbine that grew along the edge of the fish pond and I saw my own reflection in the water, hovering there like the Lady of Fatima wearing brown shorts and an old white shirt. Exhaling, I quickly descended and landed in the water, scattering the goldfish. I waded for a few moments, taking it all in, and felt the drag of my wet shirttail trailing from behind me, the tail of a polliwog. Quite pleased with myself, I squeezed water from my shirt and tried it again. Breathing deeply, I again lifted off the ground in one effortless movement. Holding my breath, I stayed there in place just over the Stars-of-Bethlehem and dwelled on them, smiling and dripping. By just breathing in and out, I could rise and fall at will.

I felt as one with the world, almost the same as when I swam—removed from my element and yet fused with it. I tried swimming in the air. With my arms stretched out front, I planed off and floated forward. The kick of the breast stroke looks something like a bullfrog's. Up Out Down Back. I started in on the kick, and at the same time pushed the air away from my body, propelling forward as if in water. And I put my head down when I exhaled and looked up when I breathed in, and in this way took in the scene below while still keeping track of where I was going without bumping into trees and bushes. Coordination between arms, legs, and oxygen intake saves energy—hardly ever does a swimmer drown while doing the breast stroke, and I reasoned that in the air the same motion would prevent me from free falling. Obviously the principle held true, for I was floating around the yard now, up and over the fish pond, snowball bush, the forsythia hedge, and the garbage can. An earth and air sensation, that's what I was—alive! Dynamic! The adrenaline inside of me was the factor; like helium it had filled me, and I was lighter than air—I was *Up There*. I was *Buoyant*.

I circled over the garden, higher now, higher than most insects—and looked down on butterflies, dirt daubers, and bees. The crows cawed loudly from the top of the sycamore, and I knew it was because of me. I skirted the drip line of the giant oak and then I stroked upward, taking many deep breaths for the rise.

Reaching the roof of the garage, I rested for a moment on the apex, and spied on Bob as he combed his hair in our bedroom. I was struck by the familiarity of his slender form in the distance. I swam toward the power line for a better view. As I watched him, I thought of his footsteps as soft as an Indian's and remembered the strength of his voice. I breathed his *essence*—as warm as a hot air balloon—and hardly noticed the hazy figure of my neighbor, the ever-ready Sam Mayhood, when he jumped out from behind his japonica hedge and snapped me with his Polaroid.

All this fuss about flying still lingers. After years of submitting photos and accompanying stories to the press, Mr. Mayhood finally succeeded in getting his by-line, at my expense. There I was on the front page in my old tattered shorts, my shirttail billowing like a sail. No one would guess that it was sex that got me up there and sex that brought me down.

That Mayhood owned neither a zoom lens nor a video camera was my salvation. But members of my own family determined that it was me—"no one else would wear those old things," my daughter said on the phone. "It's you all right," said our son. "Your bony knees. Your feet." My son and daughter wanted to sell tickets to a repeat performance. Even Bob failed me. Imagining the joys of early retirement with an oversexed wife, he saw dollar signs and wanted me to float above Memphis wearing a costume of red, white, and blue on the 4th of July for a large fee. But no one—not even my family—could prove it was me.

I held them off, insisting that it was trick photography. I told Bob that if I could fly that's what I'd do. Right out of here. Fame is fleeting and almost always disastrous in the end, especially over something sensational. Today the local newspapers; tomorrow the supermarket tabloids. Then comes degradation and ruin. I have since stayed on ground, flat-footed and stubborn, and attempted as much poise as any person could muster under the pressures of celebrity. "Was it really you?" I smile at such questions and try my best to look incredulous.

But on that day, while airborne, I was all of the things I could see and feel—land, water, air, people, fish and birds. In other words, I, Sarah Gorda, was a *woman evolving* and nothing else mattered but that life was growth and change, particles fusing one with another in continuum. And as I watched Bob combing his hair there in the bedroom, wearing his old khaki pants and Saturday's black T shirt, the sight of him seemed somehow arresting, and I wanted very much to be there with him, to speak of the woods, of water and of air. What's more, I knew I would lose the buoyancy, that I would plane off, sputter, then stop, and that he would love me still, not as an antiquity in the Museum of Air and Space, but in spite of it.

I forgot to hold my breath and suddenly I hit the ground hard like a sharp spade thrust into gravel.

"You okay, Sarah?" From the window, Bob looked down at me, an old verity alive in the frame. I felt myself growing out of feet mired in pebbles as I struggled to stand. Beside me the white Stars-of-Bethlehem reached for the sky from which they had fallen.

◆ ◆

MARGARET SKINNER, a native Memphian, has taught fiction writing at the University of Memphis. Her novels, *Old Jim Canaan* and *Molly Flanagan and the Holy Ghost* were both published by Algonquin Books of Chapel Hill, North Carolina. Currently, she is at work on another novel, *Little Walter*.

JACK HURST

NATHAN BEDFORD FORREST'S FINAL DAYS

In July of 1877, the controversial and debt-plagued Confederate hero, Nathan Bedford Forrest, was trying to regain his health at Hurricane Springs, Tennessee. Hurricane Springs was the latest of a succession of reputedly restorative spas to which Forrest had traveled from a leased island plantation near Memphis that he had been operating with inmates of the Shelby County Jail. Former aide Charles W. Anderson visited him at Hurricane Springs and was struck by a new "mildness, a softness of expression, and a gentleness in his words that appeared to me strange and unnatural," Anderson later recalled. . . . When Anderson inquired about the change, Forrest explained that he had "joined the Church and [was] trying to live a Christian life."

Anderson remained at Hurricane Springs several days, during which Forrest decided "that the water was not benefiting him, but he spoke hopefully of recovering his health." Mary Ann Forrest, however, was fearful. She told Anderson that her husband had "an unnatural appetite and seemed always to crave food unsuited to him." . . .

[Forrest] returned on July 27 to Memphis . . . [but] by August 10 some of the convicts who had been working on his farm were reported to have been moved to another one, and on August 14 he departed again. Two weeks later, the [Memphis] *Appeal* reported that "General Bedford Forrest is quite ill at Bailey Springs, Ala. He has been confined to his bed several days, and his condition is anything but encouraging." A physician, C. K. Caruthers, was called to consult with him there and later remembered the patient was "too feeble to mix with the crowd" or go to the dining area; he whiled away the hours, Caruthers said, playing cards on one of the galleries with [Memphis newspaperman Matthew] Gallaway, Memphis Congressman Casey Young, and "a steamboat captain."

The August 30 [Memphis] *Avalanche* carried a notice so grim that even the *New York Times* saw fit to reprint it. It noted that for months Forrest had "been afflicted with chronic diarrhea, and a malarial impregnation has brought on a combination of diseases which makes his case hopeless. . . . His life has been one wherein he became inured to exposure, and this gave him a confidence in his powers of physical endurance which perhaps was unfortunate." The item went on to report that on the President's Island plantation "he has given his farm his strict attention. Often till 11 o'clock he would be out in the poisonous night air seeing to his stock" and giving "everything his personal supervision. The result is he lies now a shattered man on the verge of the grave. Beef tea is the only nourishment he can take, and he is gradually growing weaker and weaker."

While he was at Bailey Springs, apparently, another prominent wartime associate arrived to pay his respects. General Joseph Wheeler, his graciously forgiving fellow cavalry commander, had not seen him for several years and could not help noticing the same "startling change" Anderson had observed. He looked "greatly emaciated . . . and the pale, thin face seemed to bring out in bolder relief than I had ever observed before the magnificent forehead and head." All the lines and "suggestion[s] of harshness had disappeared, and he seemed to possess . . . the gentleness of expression, the voice and manner of a woman." Once more, he tried to rally. On September 8 the *Appeal* quoted the Florence *Gazette* as reporting that he was "improving," and shortly afterward he wrote a letter to another old friend and ex-staff member, George W. Adair of Atlanta.

Bailey Springs, Sept. 15, 1877

Capt. G. W. Adair:

My Dear Sir: I have just persuaded my wife to write you a few lines. I have been lying here flat on my back for a month, unable to get up without help. I feel now that I am just passing out of a most terrible case of sickness, which lasted me about 12 months. My disease has been inflammation of the stomach and bowels. I am too weak to walk about without help—only weigh about 120 pounds. My symptoms now are all gone, and the doctor thinks I will soon recover . . . ever your true friend.

N. B. Forrest

Forrest may have been putting up a front to Adair. To an even closer friend, Gallaway, he seems to have been more frank, speaking "of his readiness to meet his God and his inward cravings for rest from the battle of life, which to him had been fierce and full of bitterness." He told Gallaway he was "extremely anxious to live for useful purposes and to make another fortune, which he saw in sight, for his wife and only son," but "to his confidential friends he invariably touched in the small hours the same Aeolian chord that murmured of failure, the nothingness of life, and death as a desire." The September 21 *Appeal* reported that he "is recovering and will soon be able to leave Bailey Springs," and a week later the newspaper described him as "rapidly recuperating" and soon to return home. On October 2, Forrest arrived back in Memphis and stayed at the home of his brother Jesse. . . . "General Forrest, though weak, is much improved and will rapidly recuperate," the *Appeal* said.

Such lines were wishful thinking. Coming home from Bailey Springs on a train, he had had to "lean . . . upon the shoulders of friends as he dragged himself from the cars to the carriage," the *Avalanche* soon reported, and although he went from Jesse Forrest's house back to President's Island, it wasn't for long. His weight dropped to "scarcely more than 100 pounds," and the Reverend [George T.] Stainback [pastor of the Memphis Court Street Cumberland Presbyterian Church] hurried to visit him. . . . Stainback found a man who knew his time was gone. Money and such stubborn lifelong vices as cursing and card playing seem to have been on his mind, and he talked about the debts he still owed on earth and elsewhere. "I've worked hard and may have killed myself," he told Stainback, "but in the providence of God I am in a way to discharge soon every obligation I owe to man." He "regretted" many things "said and done . . . in the presence of others" during his brief religious period that didn't look or sound very Christian, he told Stainback. Nevertheless, he said, "'I want you to understand now that I feel that God has forgiven me for all"; and then, lifting up his emaciated hand, and pointing his finger to his breast, with a smile upon his face, said, "Just here I have an indescribable peace. All is peace within. I want you to know that between me and . . . the face of my Heavenly Father, not a cloud intervenes. I have put my trust in my Lord and Saviour."

Within days of Stainback's visit, the recent convert was returned to Jesse Forrest's house in Memphis, this time borne on a litter. Friends came to pay their respects. One was Minor Meriwether, with his son Lee. The ghostly appearance of the man who had loved children seemed to frighten the boy. "Don't be afraid, Lee," Forrest whispered. "Your father is my friend. Come closer. Let me look at you." The boy moved timidly to the bedside and—decades afterward—remembered Forrest's hand running its thin fingers through his hair. "A fine boy, Colonel," the patient pronounced weakly. "I hope he will live to be a true son of the South." As they left Jesse Forrest's house that day, Lee Meriwether would remember later, his father's eyes suddenly brimmed with tears. "Lee," he said, "the man you just saw dying will never die. He will live in the memory of men who love patriotism, and who admire genius and daring."

Jefferson Davis, a Memphian at the time, came by on the afternoon of October 29, but by then Forrest had slipped so far he seemed hardly to recognize the President of the tragically flawed nation whose labored and ultimately aborted birth had made his fame and ruined his life. Davis left, but Minor Meriwether returned to keep the death watch, and it was Meriwether who about 7 P.M. heard the patient speak his last coherent words. Unlike those of Lee, Jackson, and several other fellow Civil War titans, they did not concern a mind's fevered return to the scene of distant onslaught; his fantasy did not appear to have galloped back in time to the frustrations of Fort Donelson and Shiloh, the exhilaration of Brice's Cross Roads, the hounding of Abel Streight, or the maddened vaulting of the walls of Fort Pillow. Fighting had been so commonplace in his life that such military moments merely faded into the rest of the mosaic of struggle. All he sought in his final hour was succor in suffering his last defeat. Characteristically, though, the final words formed a command, a last assertion of his lifelong assumption of the right to tell others what to do.

"Call my wife," he ordered. Then he died.

Jack Hurst, a native of Maryville, Tennessee, covers the Nashville music industry for the *Chicago Tribune*, which he joined in 1975. In addition to his life of Forrest, Hurst is also the author of *Nashville's Grand Ole Opry*. He currently resides in Lancaster, Tennessee.

with thanks for your love of poetry — Jeff Daniel Marion 31 August 1996

JEFF DANIEL MARION

Song For Wood's Barbecue Shack in McKenzie, Tennessee

Here in mid-winter let us begin
to lift our voices in the pine woods:

O sing praise to the pig
who in the season of first frost
gave his tender hams and succulent shoulders
to our appetite:

praise to the hickory embers
for the sweetest smoke
a man is ever to smell,
its incense a savor
of time bone deep:

praise for Colonel Wood and all his workers
in the dark hours who keep watch
in this turning of the flesh
to the delight of our taste:

praise to the sauce—vinegar, pepper, and tomato—
sprinkled for the tang of second fire:

"Song for Wood's Barbeque Shack in McKenzie, Tennessee," from *Lost and Found*, by Jeff Daniel Marion (Abingdon, Va.: Sow's Ear Press, 1994), 26. Reprinted with permission of Sow's Ear Press. This work also appeared in *CrossRoads: A Journal of Southern Culture* 1, no. 1 (Fall, 1992): 34.

Praise we say now for mudwallow, hog grunt and pig squeal,
snorkle snout ringing bubbles of swill in the trough,
each slurp a sloppy vowel of hunger,
jowl and hock, fat back and sow belly, root dirt and pure
piggishness of sow, boar, and barrow.

The Man Who Made Color

For the memory of my father, J. D. Marion, 1915–1990

Consider the lilies, we have been told,
they toil not,
neither do they labor.

But I have sweated in the fall sun
to plant this hillside
in a cascade of hues, held
in a ring of rocks I have carried
from the river.

Long ago on my first day of school,
the teacher asked, "What does your father do?"
"He makes color," I said.
"Oh . . . I see."

But she did not see the man
who stood before vats of color
deep as flame
and dipped his finger in,
touching paper, testing the tack
of ink.

"The Man Who Made Color," from *Lost and Found*, by Jeff Daniel Marion (Abingdon, Va.: Sow's Ear Press, 1994), 17–18. Reprinted with permission of Sow's Ear Press. This work also appeared in *Southern Poetry Review* 34, no. 2 (Winter, 1994): 8–9.

I saw him believe in the truth
of touch, the message only his fingers
would tell, color splashing
across rolling sheets of labels:
Bugler, Del Monte, Van Camp,
School Days, Lucky Strike.

Consider these lilies, father, their color
a swash of words I roll across
my tongue—*Harbor Blue, Open Hearth,*
Spindazzle, Kindly Light. They sway
on their long stems but a day.
They know no grief, no loss,
only a tumble of color,
season to season, across this hillside.
Their blossoms unfold bright as flame,
ready for your touch.

JEFF DANIEL MARION, a Rogersville native who teaches writing at Carson-Newman College in Jefferson City, Tennessee, is the author of four collections of poetry. The recipient of many honors and awards in poetry, he has received a Literary Fellowship from the Tennessee Arts Commission.

ANWAR F. ACCAWI

THE CAMERA

Over the past forty-seven years, I have had my share of burning bush experiences, but my first encounter with the camera will always be one of the most unforgettable.

I was five years old when I saw one for the first time, but I will never forget how I felt as long as I shall live. This is how it happened: Uncle Wadi', my father's youngest brother, came up from Beirut, where he was going to school at the American University, to see his mother, Grandma Mariam, and to spend some of his Easter holiday with us. My father was "between jobs" again, and Grandma had let us stay with her at her house in Magdaluna, a quiet hamlet perched like an eagle's nest in the nettles-infested hills about ten kilometers east of Sidon.

It was great to have Uncle Wadi' home again because he was a lot of fun. Actually, he was a lot more fun than my father because Aammo (Lebanese for uncle) always showed up with fascinating new gadgets, and he would take the time to tell me about them and explain to me how they worked and what they were used for. He was the one who introduced me to the gramophone—the kind that you had to wind up with a crank—and he was the one who gave me my first pocket knife.

Easter Sunday, 1948, was Resurrection morning and as good a time as any to have a religious experience, which I did! After a sumptuous dinner of chicken stuffed with rice, and a yoghurt and cucumber salad, Aammo announced, in a mock-ceremonial voice, that he would be taking pictures of those who wished on the deck above the cistern. As soon as we heard it, my brother, Munir, and I made a dash for the deck, followed by our two sisters, Mary and Mona, whose dresses were new and stiff and made swishing sounds every time they moved. We all limped a little that day, as we always did on holidays, because our new shoes were stiff and they gave us blisters.

Being the first-born male in the family, I got preferential treatment and was to go first. Aammo made a big thing out of posing me, telling me how to smile and how to tilt my chin a little this way or that and how to hold my hands just so to keep from hiding the shiny brass buckle on my new belt. The air crackled with excitement. My hands shook. My breathing became shallow and rapid. My knees felt deliciously weak. This was . . . magic! I felt very much like I did the first time I sneaked into the Catholic church behind the Presbyterian cemetery, against my father's express instructions, and smelled the incense and heard the priest, standing in the warm glow of candlelight, chanting in a strange and melodious language as he expertly swung a smoking brass bowl that dangled, like a yoyo, from the end of a yellow chain. I remember shivering a little when the priest's eyes met mine, and I knew, immediately, that he knew I was Presbyterian. The feeling that came over me was strange and new, like nothing I had ever felt before. It was a mixture of excitement and . . . fear. I loved it!

That Easter morning I had the same feeling again as I stood under the unblinking glassy gaze of the two-eyed black box in my uncle's hands. It wasn't that I had never seen a photograph before because I had, quite a few. The walls of the eastern room in Grandma's house were plastered with pictures of dead and dying folks who looked vaguely familiar, but who could not have possibly been any relatives of mine because they looked clean, blemish-free, and trustworthy. It was just that I had never really thought about how those pictures were made or what they were made with. I may have even seen a camera or two before, but not known what it was that I was looking at. Or it may be that that particular Sunday I was ready to receive my "camera revelation." Of course, I did not quite understand why I felt the way I did at the time, but now, when I look back at that glorious day, I think my experience was nothing short of a "biblical encounter." There I was standing in the presence of a man who was about to freeze time and snatch a moment from an ever-vanishing world and hold it . . . forever. Like Joshua, whose story Grandma had told me time and time again, my uncle stood poised and ready to stop the sun dead in his tracks. I was so awed I forgot to breathe. Though I was only a kid at the time, yet I knew that I was partaking of something strange and wonderful and not totally without . . . sin!

When Aammo finally pressed the little shiny button on the front of his little black box, I heard a faint click. I could have sworn that at that moment one of the glass eyes, the one on the bottom, blinked. It winked at me and I was bewitched. Right there and then, I fell in love with the camera and have been ever since!

◆ ◆

ANWAR F. ACCAWI was born in Lebanon of a family believed to be descended from French Templars who went to Jerusalem during the Crusades. Married to a native Tennessean, he taught English as a second language at the American University in Beirut until the civil war there forced his departure. He and his wife now live in her native LaFollette, Tennessee, while he works as a full-time instructor at the English Language Institute, University of Tennessee at Knoxville.

ELIZABETH COX

THE THIRD OF JULY

The night kept up one of those almost-silent rains until dawn, and now the mist rose and leaves showed their waxy shine. Nadine combed her hair, but decided not to wash it. She pulled on her skirt and the blouse with cornflowers, and put away the pile of sewing she had promised to finish before tomorrow. Nadine was a seamstress. People brought their clothes for her to hem and make alterations.

Today was the third of July. Harold had left early for the field and would work late so he could take off all day on the Fourth. Nadine prepared a lunch for herself and another one for Miss Penny. Two days a week she took lunch to Miss Penny, and she would take it today. The old woman was like a mother to Nadine, ever since the year her own mother died when she was nineteen. The year Bill was born too early. She put chicken salad and sliced tomatoes in a small basket made by Bill when he was six years old. She placed two pears inside and thought of the day he handed it to her.

Nadine Colby had been married for thirty years, but on this morning she wrote a note to Harold after he left. *Dear Harold, I have rented an apartment in Mebane and if you want to see me you can call and ask to come by. Things cannot go on as they have.* She signed it, *Love*.

A shaft of sunlight moved into the bedroom as Nadine packed her bags and put them into the car. She had already paid a month's rent for an apartment ten miles away in Mebane. Her sister lived nearby, but Nadine did not like her husband, so the apartment was a perfect alternative.

She left the note in a conspicuous place on the counter. Harold would see it when he came in. She fixed some dinner that could be heated up—a plate of meatloaf, potatoes, and creamed corn. Nadine wondered now if he would still take the whole next day off.

Her reason for leaving was based on one small happening: Harold came in one night, and though she knew who it was when he got out of his truck and started toward the house, Nadine thought he was someone different. His hair stuck up on one side and he carried his cap which he usually wore into the house and threw down on the hall table. But on this particular evening she thought he was a stranger, someone coming with bad news—telling her Harold was dead, or hurt. She imagined herself falling into the arms of this stranger and letting him hold her. All of these thoughts came in a few moments while Harold opened the door and said, "Whoa! It's hot!" Then she recognized his voice.

That night Nadine couldn't sleep. She lay next to Harold beneath the sheet and wondered what her life would be like without him. If she left, it would have to be quickly and quietly, as though there had been a murder she could do nothing about.

He was foreign to her now, as was Bill. Her son was thirty, and had been the reason they got married. Harold and Nadine planned to have four children, though Bill was the only one.

The last time he came home Nadine said, "You don't look a thing like your daddy anymore, you know that?" She picked him up at the airport on Easter weekend. "Not a thing like him. And you used to favor him so strong."

"Lotta changes," was all Bill said.

"No one but me would know you were even kin."

Bill rode next to his mother with his long legs cramped in front of him. He had offered to drive, but Nadine insisted on doing so herself. She wore a navy blue dress with a large white pin at her bosom, bought especially for Bill's visit. She felt pretty as she drove him home.

Bill was a salesman for MetroLife Insurance Company and he had purchased this car for his parents—a Chrysler New Yorker. He had driven it into the driveway one Saturday and said it was theirs. Everyone in town knew Bill was wealthy, and that he had bought them the car.

Their son came home on the Fourth. He also made regular visits for Christmas and Easter, but this year he would not come in July. Nadine told him he was getting stingy, though she meant self-centered. She had loved telling people how Bill always spent certain days with them, and how she could count on him. But now Bill lived with a woman executive in his insurance company, and they were going off somewhere for the Fourth.

"I don't know what's going to happen if that woman gets pregnant," Nadine told Harold.

"They'll probably get married like we did." Harold didn't think things had changed all that much, but he remembered when Nadine had seemed soft. Her softness had unraveled with the years, and he felt left with just a thin wire of who she was. But he never mentioned it. He loved his wife, even her sharp tongue. And he loved the way she sometimes exploded with laughter at something funny he said.

Yesterday at breakfast, Harold read the paper and Nadine stared at the page which blocked his face. She imagined how he might speak to her, if he knew she was going to leave. *Nadine*, he spoke in her mind, *Don't leave. Please don't.* He would beg. He would kiss her, then kiss her again, hard.

Yesterday when he put down the paper, he asked, "What're we gonna do on the Fourth?"

Nadine didn't know until that moment how much she wanted out. She did not want to spend the Fourth of July with him. She would write the note on the third, and let him go. As she thought of it, she felt like the ghost of someone, more than a real person.

"Anything," she said.

Harold kissed her cheek and left for the field.

Nadine washed the breakfast dishes and poured the rest of her coffee into the azalea bushes. She wanted to pick up the dry cleaning in town before going to Miss Penny's house. She placed the note where Harold would be sure to see it.

She had not gone five miles before coming upon an accident. A Ford Station Wagon had speeded past her only a few minutes before, and Nadine marveled at how this grief might have been her own. When she arrived at the wreck there was still a vibrancy lingering, as after a bell.

The car collided with a truck carrying chickens. It was the kind of crash which occurs in the movies where an audience roars with laughter as some fat farmer gets out stomping the ground and flapping his arms and elbows about—moving as the chickens themselves might move.

She hoped to see that now, even looked for someone to climb out of that screaming chicken truck, but as she drew closer she saw the driver tucked over the wheel. The station wagon's front end looked crumpled and the man driving had been thrown clear. He lay sprawled in the road. Nadine heard him groan for help and felt glad the car had not been her own.

She looked both ways for help, but no one was coming in either direction. She could not hurry toward the accident, her arms and legs felt like rubber bands. The man in the road was barely conscious. She stood over him, then squatted and placed her fingers on the pulse of his neck. She had seen this done on TV.

"My family," the man said. It was a question. He pointed toward the car as though he thought maybe Nadine hadn't noticed it yet. His head lay turned at a peculiar angle.

"Quiet now. You lie quiet." She patted the man's shoulder as if he had a contagious disease, then she moved back. He pointed again to the car. There was no sign of blood and Nadine hoped he was all right. "I'll check them for you," she said. The man seemed grateful to her, and closed his eyes.

The man in the truck was still slumped at the wheel. Four crates of chickens had fallen onto the hood. One of the chickens still flapped around, but less now. There were more crates in the ditch where others squawked and fought to get free.

She heard another sound that came from the back seat of the car. Gurgling. A woman weighing almost three hundred pounds lay across the back seat. She had been sleeping when the accident occurred. Her head was on a pillow and she lay covered with a lightweight blanket which was soaked with blood. Nadine, who always turned away from such sights on TV or in a movie, opened the door of the car.

The woman was drowning, the gurgling noise came from her own throat which lay exposed by a low-neck dress, her skin white, supple. Nadine ducked into the back seat to help, and she thought how this woman must be about her own age. The effort for breath came closer now. But the woman's hands jerked as a child's do in deep sleep, and the top of her head was pushed askew, so that it hung precariously like a lady's small hat about to fall off.

Without even thinking, Nadine reached two fingers into the woman's throat and began to dig out debris. She dug again and again as though she were clearing out the hole of a sink. The woman began to cough and as she did her eyes opened—unseeing.

Nadine could see the place where the forehead split. She reached to place it straight, and the man from the road called out again the question about his family. Nadine said, "They're fine. You be quiet now," and it was the calmest voice she had ever heard. She continued to clean the woman's throat, making her cough a few more times before the breathing came back. "You'll be all right," she told the woman, in case she could hear.

A young boy in the front seat curled slightly forward. About sixteen, Nadine thought. She got out to open the other car door, wiping her hands on her skirt. Some of the chickens wrestled free of their crates and walked around in the road. Another one had flown to a low branch. She glanced again to the man at the wheel of the truck. He hadn't moved. She wished he would.

She searched the highway again, but there was no sign of help. As she opened the front car door, she expected to find the boy as she had found the woman, but only a small amount of blood trickled onto his shirt and pants. The dashboard had struck his chest and he leaned forward onto it like a mannikin. He wore shorts and his strong legs had planted themselves to the floor as he braced for the impact. His arms caught the dashboard, but had fallen to his side as the dashboard caught him. The windhsield shattered and coated him with a shower of glass that spread fine as Christmas glitter. Nadine wondered if he had ever played football.

When she looked up, she could see Emmett Walker coming across the field. She felt happy to see him though she did not usually wish to see Emmett. In fact, she went out of her way to avoid him. Emmett wore coveralls and his red hair was almost completely gray. His arms and face, though, still exposed his freckles from boyhood. Once, for three weeks, Nadine and Emmett had been sweethearts. Nadine could not imagine that now.

"I heard the crash from the field," he said. "Are they all dead?" He stared at the boy's shimmering back.

"Seems so," was what Nadine said, forgetting about the man in the road. She held her mouth as though it were full of food, then pointed to the back seat where the woman lay. Emmett peered through the window without commenting.

He turned to the chicken truck. "What about him?"

"I don't know." They walked toward the truck. Nadine wondered if she would be left here all day with Emmett and what she would do. They had seen each other in town, and at gatherings they spoke pleasantly. Now they were suddenly talking in concerned tones and moving together as parents through a room full of sick children.

Emmett pried open the door of the truck. The man's face was hidden by the horn, but his eyes lay open and his lips moved in an effort to speak.

"Listen," said Emmett, and he put his head closer to the steering wheel. "He's not moving. Something's wrong with his neck."

They went to each of the bodies, Nadine speaking low, explaining. But as she started to open the door of the car where the woman lay, they heard a siren approaching.

Emmett put his hand on Nadine's shoulder and pointed to the ambulance coming over a far hill, arriving more slowly than the siren made it seem.

"I called the hospital," Emmett said.

Nadine went to stand beside the man in the road. He began to scream the name of his wife, "*Mamie, Mamie*."

"Shhh," she told him. The ambulance driver and his attendant secured the stretcher beneath him, then called for Emmett's help. The man asked again about his family, and Nadine said not to worry. "Everything will be taken care of now."

"Somebody's still in the truck," Emmett said and pointed to the tucked figure. "He's not moving." The attendant nodded and motioned toward the car, as if asking a question. Emmett shook his head and the driver reached into the back seat to check the woman's pulse. He stared boldly at the odd hairline.

"She's still alive," he said to Emmett.

Emmett peered through the window, as if expecting the woman to sit up, say something.

"Wouldn't be though." The driver directed his eyes toward Emmett. "Who did this? *You*?" The floor was full of Nadine's work.

Emmett looked at Nadine. She had her back to them as though the whole scene were something she had not yet witnessed—her back rigid, cocked for protection.

"Hey, lady. You do this?"

She retreated the way a child does who has been reprimanded, her tongue in her cheek, worried. She nodded and held their admiration, then walked toward them as fragile and blue as smoke.

"Well, you saved her life, lady." He spoke softly and to the side, so that only Nadine could hear him, then he amended his statement. "Might have saved her life."

It took all three of them to lift the woman from the car, then Nadine stood back as they tore the front seat apart, trying to pull the boy from the dashboard. She wished she knew his name, and hoped she had saved Mamie's life. They placed the son in the back of the ambulance, and Mamie next to him. The man from the chicken truck was strapped near the front. Everyone looked dead.

As the ambulance disappeared, Nadine and Emmett stood beside each other. What followed was a silence as pure as that between lovers. Then Emmett faced Nadine and she turned to Emmett, and they resembled people who see their reflections in a mirror, slouched in a way they never imagined themselves.

Nadine opened her mouth and said, "I hope that woman lives. You think she will?" She wondered if she should take Emmett's hand or touch him, but didn't.

"Yes." He went to the truck where chickens were scattered in the road. They had stopped their squawking. One was still in the tree. "I'll drive these over to Hardison's Poultry." He pulled the crates together. "What's left of them." He picked up the crates from the road and climbed into the truck. He turned the key several times before hearing it catch. As he drove off, he waved goodbye and Nadine waved back. She walked to the car and checked the salad. It was still cool.

Miss Penny was watching TV when Nadine arrived. She didn't hear the knock on the door, so Nadine walked in and called to her. Miss Penny was folding towels and placing each one beside the chair, fixing them like small bales of hay about to be stored in a barn. She was watching a game show.

When she lifted her head to respond to Nadine's voice, the pupils of her eyes were large and gave an expression of spectral intensity—hollow, not sad. A cataract operation had made them sensitive to light, so the blinds and drapes were pulled. The room, after the full sunlight of the road, seemed to Nadine unusually dark.

"I'll put this in the kitchen." Nadine patted Miss Penny's chair as she walked by. She wanted to scrub her hands and wipe her skirt clean.

"There's a man on here who'll win ten thousand dollars if he can answer this last question," Miss Penny said. Nadine took it as a silencing. The TV blared the question and the announcer declared him winner. Bells rang, people clapped and cried and Miss Penny told her, "I could've won me ten thousand dollars." She pushed herself from the chair to go to the kitchen.

"Don't know what you'd do with it," said Nadine. She watched the old woman hobble to the kitchen and fall into a chair.

"I'd buy me something."

"Don't know what you need." Nadine spooned salad onto plates and set two places at the table. Her tongue felt dry and she asked Miss Penny if there was some iced tea. Miss Penny pointed to a pitcher. She always made tea and took out the ice trays before Nadine arrived, but today Nadine was two hours late and the ice was mostly water. They put slivers that remained into the tea and sipped it.

"I had the right answer," Miss Penny persisted. She tasted the salad and Nadine gave her a napkin.

"You can't spend the money you have now, let alone ten thousand dollars." They helped themselves to the tomatoes. "What would you spend it on?"

"I'd pay somebody to look after my dogs."

"You don't have any dogs," said Nadine, " and don't need any."

"I would if I had all that money." Miss Penny's words, though simple, were true. "I'd need a lot of things." She thought for a moment, chewing her food with meticulous care. "I'd get some dogs. Not the regular kind, but show dogs. The ones you can train and take to shows."

"You'd like that?" Nadine asked, surprised to find a new interest in a woman she had known as long as she could remember. She thought there were no more surprises left between them.

"Show dogs." Miss Penny's face flushed at the thought of it. "I always have wanted to do something like that."

Nadine wished to say something about the accident, to tell someone what she had done and how she wasn't afraid to see Emmett anymore. "There was a wreck," she began and leaned across the table so Miss Penny could hear. "Over near Hardison's Poultry. A truck ran into a station wagon. The whole family got hurt." Miss Penny reached for more slices of tomato. Her face had not yet lost its flush. "It was pretty bad," Nadine said. "A man and his wife, a boy about sixteen."

"What?"

"Their *son* about six*teen*." Nadine spoke louder. "He was killed right off, but the man might live, and the woman." She stopped leaning and slumped back. "I don't know about the woman though." Nadine's gaze shifted to something outside the window.

"*Ten thousand dollars*," Miss Penny said. Her voice emphasized each word equally.

From the kitchen window Nadine could see bags of web in the crabapple trees.

"Tomorrow's the Fourth of July," she told Miss Penny. Neither of them turned away from the window.

Nadine washed the few dishes and put away the bales of towels into the hall cabinet. She decided not to go to Mebane, but to go back home. "I'll put these pears in the refrigerator." She held up the pears. Miss Penny's eyes unclouded and hardened clear as stones.

On her way home, she picked up the dry cleaning and stopped at the pet shop to look at dogs not yet full-grown. On Tuesday she would buy one and take it to Miss Penny. He would outlive her by six years.

The note to Harold had not been touched, but she left it propped against the sugar jar. The house looked older now. Each object seemed to have a separate life of its own. When Nadine saw herself in the mirror over the fireplace, she became aware of the frame around her face.

She called the hospital, but the line was busy. She had already unpacked her bag and put the clothes into drawers where they had been—her blouses, her good blue dress, two nightgowns, a sweater, four pairs of shoes. She put her umbrella in the hall closet, and went to sit across from the large picture window.

Twilight made the room silver, drapes shimmering like creek water. The late sun dropped halfway from sight, going down behind trees like some wild head, and Nadine wondered if everyone wished for life to be different.

When the phone rang, it was Emmett. She heard his voice and her mouth worked itself into a smile. He called to tell her about Mamie and Robert Harkins. "The man will live," he said. "And the woman, she'll live too." For one moment Nadine could not even straighten her legs. "But that boy, he didn't make it. He was dead when we saw him."

"What about the man in the truck?"

"His back was broke and some ribs. But he's all right, or will be." Emmett coughed as though he didn't have much to say, but wanted to think of something. "The truck driver was Buck Hardison's nephew."

"Why, I think I know him," Nadine said. "I think I met him once when he was a little boy." She wanted the conversation to go on, and she thanked Emmett, so he said she was welcome. "You were fine help," she told him through the silence in the cord. "I mean, really," and she spoke as if trying to convince him of something important.

"Well," said Emmett.

Nadine watched the sun go all the way down and wondered if Emmett had turned to see out his own window. "It's getting dark," she said.

When they hung up, Nadine sat until she could see nothing but her own dark reflection in the window, and the reflection of the lamp beside her. Harold would be in soon. She decided to wash her hair. She was bending her head over the sink and rinsing for the second time, when she heard Harold come in.

"Nadine?"

She wrapped her hair in a towel and went to the kitchen. Harold held the note that Nadine had not thrown out. He held it, but didn't say anything.

"You want something to eat?" she asked him.

Harold said he did.

Nadine did not get the covered plate of meatloaf and creamed corn. Instead, she took out some flounder and began to prepare it for baking with lemon and butter. She cut up new potatoes to go with it, and told Harold about the wreck.

She told him about the man, the boy, the woman she saved, the truck driver who was Buck Hardison's nephew. She told him she had seen Emmett, and how they had worked together. Her telling went from the time she took out the fish, cooked it, and then sat down with Harold to eat.

The note lay on the counter as they talked. Harold had carefully placed it next to the sugar, face down. He listened attentively and ate everything Nadine put before him. When she was through washing the dishes, he walked up behind her to turn her around. He slowly unwrapped the towel from her head. Her hair was damp and frizzy; and he rubbed it dry with his hands.

◆ ◆

ELIZABETH COX, a professor of writing at Duke University since 1985, is the recipient of many awards, including one MacDowell and two Yaddo Colony fellowships. This story appeared in the O. Henry Award Collection in 1995. Her most recent novel, *The Ragged Way People Fall Out Of Love*, is available from North Point Press and, in paperback, from HarperCollins.

ERROL HESS

WATERMELONS

Rubenesque watermelons brought by JC Bells in his red logging truck. "Sell 'em," he said, "for whatever you can get, and we'll reckon up later."

How to keep twenty watermelons at a slow-paced country store, with too little refrigeration?

The spring house was half fallen down. It hadn't been used in as long as any of us could remember. Old man Miller who built the place and first kept the store had used it, his son, Kenneth, said. But since then it sat idle till the roof rusted thru in places and its back side settled as the creek's many floods washed out under its foundation.

But the concrete floor was there under a ton of silt, and once we mucked it out for a couple of hours with a bucket we could climb down to the concrete without too much trouble.

The water was cold enough in August it almost hurt my feet, so it became my daughter's job to go lift out a melon whenever anyone bought one. They weighed about sixty pounds apiece, and it was all a twelve-year-old girl could do to push them up the wall and onto the doorsill. They floated, so she didn't have to reach clear down to pick them up. The water was about knee deep.

We were left with seven the follwing Saturday night when Bells got back from his week's logging. A crowd was gathered at the store, sitting on the bench that ran along its front, and on the concrete base where there were once gas pumps.

Bells laughed when I asked what he wanted for his share. We'd sold them for $4 apiece, because they were early, and because nowhere else would you get melons so big as from Chuckey. We split the sales in half.

Then I asked what we should do with the rest of the melons. "I don't know how much longer they'll keep," I said.

Bells laughed again. He was a stout man, about my height, who won bets he could hold back a Percheron horse with his bare hands holding its traces. He could do it, alright, anybody could, the way he did. He stood behind a tree or telephone pole and drew the traces tight on a motionless horse. A little like getting a car up over a high curb it's tight against.

He was about half looped, I judged, from the amount of red in his face.

"Tell you what," he said, "let's have a watermelon eating contest. Anyone wants to enter can put in a ten spot. It don't count to eat part of a melon. You gotta finish it."

I didn't have anything to lose because I'd made more than that on the melons, so I took him on, after a few minutes of his teasing with no one willing to bet ten bucks, just to entertain the crowd.

We pulled the seven remaining melons out of the spring house. Bell's teenaged boy helped my daughter, or, rather, didn't let her get her feet wet.

We lined them up on the old gas pump base, got a butcher knife out of the store, and each split a melon to suit our way of eating.

Just then, Bell's oldest son, Bobby, said, "Let me in on this one, daddy."

Bells laughed. "Sure, son. There ain't no second prize, you know. . . . I almost forgot, no pissing. The first one to go to the toilet loses."

I quit halfway thru the smaller half of my melon. I couldn't get pumped up, somehow, about a melon eating contest, maybe because I'd already eaten a whole one that week by myself.

But Bells and his boy went at it, steady-like; like they were going in the woods to cut logs all day.

The crowd watched and joked with the contestants, sucking on sodas or nibbling a piece of the melon I'd left unfinished. They smoked or chewed, and leaned forward, intent to watch father and son compete.

"I'll give odds that neither of them finishes a second," I joked, when they were an hour along, and each still had a good-sized piece of melon left. Bells pulled out a fifty-dollar bill.

"Hey, I ain't got that kind of money to bet."

He held it around the audience. "Anyone else want to wager?"

He knew they wouldn't, of course. Tobacco sales were a long way off, and these were all farmers. Most of them owed me six months worth of groceries.

Bells let out a big belch and went back to eating.

The boy was nineteen or twenty, just married, not rich enough to quit living at his daddy's. He was saving up to buy a used trailer, he said. He would have liked to quit working for his daddy, but couldn't find other work anywhere. The economy was in a slump, and the only skill he had besides timber was a body mechanics course at the high school.

He stood to gain twenty or lose ten. Not enough to buy that trailer. The crowd, the women anyway, were mostly rooting for him. Some of the men, who themselves still hadn't been bested by their sons, were identifying pretty strongly with Bells.

I was tickled I'd come out of the deal sixteen bucks ahead, hard for anyone to believe who'd ever had any business with Bells. And, after word of this got around, I'd have a good crowd at the store next Saturday night, for sure. So I was feeling pretty benevolent, and rooting for the boy to win.

Bells was eating with his pocket knife, slicing the melon off with a great show, leaving only white rind behind, spearing big bites and licking the juice off the knife as he took each bite.

Now, almost done with his first melon, he was still eating big bites, but his preparation for each bite was much slower, and the seeds now shot out of his mouth one at a time—still aimed at the Coca Cola sign or a stray pop bottle or the shoe of some little kid.

The boy was keeping up, with quiet determination. His bites were quite small, but he never quit chewing.

Bells finished first, and immediately picked his second melon.

"Hey, wait a minute," I said. "Why don't you two call it a tie and split the money? It sure ain't worth getting sick for fifteen dollars."

"The boy ain't finished his yet; don't get in no hurry about calling it a tie. Guess I will wait for him afore I start another."

His son was about stalled, with a two-inch-thick slice and the bowl at the end of the melon left. The struggle each bite caused was evident. He was using every bit of control he had to keep his hand from shaking.

I looked over at Bells. He sat rigid as a statue on the concrete pump base.

I had to excuse myself and go across the creek to the outhouse. Returning, relieved, I could imagine how much fuller they must be than I was, and wondered how they could stand it.

As I passed, Kyle Parsons whispered, "Gotta hand it to that s.o.b., he'd keel over before he'd quit."

When I got closer to Bells, I could see big, isolated globes of sweat on his forehead. His son was still eating, very, very slowly. The boy's face was twisted like someone had just kneed him in the groin.

I could see some of the crowd was squirming to hit the bridge themselves, but none would leave and risk missing the ending.

"Anyone want another Pepsi?" I asked. "I'll fetch it if you do." Something about the crowd's lust over these two's suffering made me want to remind the crowd of their own full bladders.

There were a few polite no's, but mostly looks that told me that my charity wasn't appreciated.

The boy had finished the smaller piece first, the cap at the end. He started on the final slice.

"That piece is at least two inches thick, and eighteen across," I reckoned out loud. "Is that a gallon of water? Must be at least half a gallon."

The boy started the piece faster, like he could get it over with in a minute, but after three bites he stopped, remained for a long minute completely still except for the increased twisting of his face, and then began to shake.

The trembling began in his hands, and from there reached out across his whole body. Hell, it made me feel so bad just watching, I would have given him twenty dollars to get him to quit. But of course I couldn't. We all looked away from the boy and to his father, to see if he would relent.

Bells sat there like a stone frog. Now his eyes were squeezed shut.

I cussed them both. "The stubborn bastards. Why should I feel sorry for either of them?" Still, I was long past enjoying the spectacle.

Not so the crowd. It was like the still frame image of one minute at a cockfight. There was no action for them to react to with body english, so they were sympathetically frozen, mirroring their choice of contestants.

Watching the crowd, I could tell who was for the boy. He once again moved slowly, eating again, and his supporters' bodies moved in slow random motion with him. The old man's followers were arrested still.

Now, over half the last piece was eaten, and a flurry of whispers moved along the audience.

I couldn't stand to look at either contestant now, so, except for an occasional glance at the remaining watermelon, I just watched the crowd.

Its anticipation increased, just as towards the end of a cockfight, when the witnesses know it can't possibly last much longer. The crowd became more restless, more disturbed, till it reached the point where it became a greater threat to me than the suffering it craved. Like I might do as well to fuel its flame. Just then, as I rose to go back into the store, the whole bunch rose with me, giving me, that second, quite a fright.

Then I saw what moved it. A liquid darkness spread out from where the old man Bells sat on the concrete, just as his son was eating the last bite of melon.

• •

ERROL HESS, a resident of Bristol, Tennessee, is founding editor of *Sow's Ear Poetry Review*, organizer of a local writer's workshop, and a founding director of the Appalachian Center for Poets and Writers. His many publications include an award-winning animated children's film based on his story, "Joey Learns to Fly,' and the anthology, *A Gathering at the Forks*.

STANLEY BOOTH

FROM "REDNECK," AN ESSAY

Some years ago, a national magazine asked me to tell them about rednecks, because rednecks, they said, were doomed. Not sure whether to feel honored or insulted, I declined, since we are all doomed, and the true redneck, whose spirit is tougher than mulehide, may be a little less doomed than most. Still, each year there are fewer of them, as there are fewer mules, while ever all around us falsity, plastic, and the short con increase.

Last summer, as I drove across the Southeast from the Georgia sea islands to the Arkansas Ozarks, I saw "For Sale" signs on so many farms it began to seem that the entire South was on the auction block. In the last ten years, one third of the country's family farms have been sold. Even my friend and Ozark neighbor, Newton Jardin, a scarcely movable object, is wearing a bill cap that says, If Dolly Parton Was a Farmer She'd Be Flat Busted Too. If the redneck is doomed, well and good, many people might say, but the redneck is a link to sanity in a world that needs all such links it can get.

Though the redneck is no longer an essentially Southern phenomenon (the Playboy Lodge at Lake Geneva, Wisconsin, was more rednecked than the Holiday Inn at Eufaula, Alabama, which makes it one of the more rednecked spots on earth, almost but not quite in a class with the Crosstie Supper Club, between Waycross and Fort Mudge, Georgia, where my cousin the bootlegger Ransom Booth was shot with five .22 long rifle bullets and killed the man who shot him and lived, still lives, to tell the tale). His origins are in the tidewater states of the South—probably, to my mind, in the state of Georgia, part in the sixteenth century of the great wilderness known to the *conquistadores* as La Florida. Ponce de León had come in 1513 and Panfilo de Narváez in 1528, but the Indians drove them away, and it was not until Hernando de Soto came in 1538 that the Spanish discovered the single captive survivor (four others had escaped La Florida with their lives) of the de Narváez expedition, a gentleman from Seville named Juan Ortiz, the original redneck.

The inhabitants of North America can be divided very roughly into red, white, and black people. ("The Chinee," as Uncle Remus said, "got to be counted long er de mulatter.") In time the whites nearly wiped out the red inhabitants, but some of the whites and some of the blacks learned to emulate, in certain things, the Indians. Actually all of civilization learned to emulate the Indians in one way or another—by smoking tobacco, eating corn, or taking quinine—but Juan Ortiz was the first white man forced to adopt the Indian's relationship with the land, to live like a North American savage, smoking the calumet, eating sweet potatoes and opossums ("the little dogs that do not bark"), not living as the whites did in America—that is, by stealing from other people or attempting to convert or enslave them. De Soto and his men came with all these ambitions, preaching to the Indians, chaining them, feeding them to dogs, followed as they came in the *conquistador* fashion by a trail of buzzards in the sky; but by the time they reached the Mississippi River, the chief Tuscaloosa and his people had stripped them of nearly everything they had except a hundred baby pigs, and they were almost as naked as the pigs.

Their dreams of conquest shattered, they settled down beside the Mississippi and raised corn. But de Soto would not give up his maniacal search for gold, and so they crossed into the rough, swampy Arkansas bottomland, where de Soto broke his heart and health. He died in Arkansas, as did Ortiz, who had served as de Soto's interpreter, and those few of his men who remained alive left La Florida, badly beaten.

Hurt and angry at the treatment they had received from their red brothers, the white men did not invite the Choctaws or Chickasaws to attend Mass again for a hundred and thirty years. Finally the whites returned, some to kill and steal and enslave, but those who were to live best upon the land did not forget the lessons of the Indians. Once in South Georgia a pregnant woman was talking to an older woman friend—I will not tell their names—saying that she did not know how, in their poverty, she and her husband could feed another child. The friend rebuked her for her lack of faith and said, "Don't you know that every time the Lord makes a possum, He makes a tater?" But I am getting ahead of my story.

The Spanish returned, the English and French came, the English slowly squeezing out the other colonists. The vast wilderness which men like Daniel Boone had only begun to explore instilled even white men with the desire to be as autonomous, as free, as the Indians. While tamer spirits settled the northern shores and richer men secured tobacco and rice plantations in the Southern tidewater, "long hunters" like Boone, men without wealth or the temperament to work as hired hands, traded in furs and speculated in the land of Tennessee and Kentucky, living on the land like Indians, manipulating its ownership like whites, pursuing the dichotomy that apparently will last as long as there are rednecks.

Being rednecked means, or has meant, being close to the land; this suited Daniel Boone, but destiny has visited redneckery on an entire people, whether they wanted it or not. The invention of the cotton gin about twenty years after the American Revolution made possible the establishment in the fertile Southern backwoods of the great cotton plantations, some of them really rich and a few even elegant. Almost all of them, though, were destroyed in the Civil War by the Yankees, those white men who had remained the whitest.

Yankee civilization—mechanical, evangelical, dangerous—could not coexist with the Southern agrarian system, based on human slavery. Each system had, to say the least, its drawbacks. Many Southerners, like Robert E. Lee, believed slavery wrong; and there were northerners, like General William Tecumseh Sherman, inventor of the *blitzkrieg*, who were not opposed to it. The War was not fought to end slavery (seventy per cent of white Southerners had no slaves), though nominal slavery ended during its course. The Civil War was fought, as the Revolution had been, for independence. To Lee's father, "Light Horse Harry" Lee, one of Washington's favorite generals, the Revolution had seemed—as it had to Washington himself—a matter of Virginians, with some help from New Englanders and a few Philadelphians, overthrowing a colonial yoke. Robert Lee, who had been superintendent of West Point, fought the Union as his father had fought the Crown, standing together with his neighbors on the issue of self-determination. When his health was gone, lost in the War, and he took over the presidency of Washington College, an impoverished school, left a ruin by the Yankees, with forty students and a faculty of four, Lee in defeat was as unassumingly noble in aspect as he had been astride Traveller at Manassas. The spirit of the South was not broken by the War, but the South's economy was shattered, its great houses burned, the plantation lands broken up, many of the planters gone, the social structure literally leveled so that nearly all white Southerners became, as if by a chemical process of reduction, rednecked. There were in America a number of other people, shaped on other frontiers as the country moved west, who could be called rednecks; but in the postwar South, forced to start over again from the ground up, almost every white man—and woman—showed at least a little pink around the gills.

The century was almost ended before the South could begin to recover from the damage inflicted by the War and the punitive and confiscatory taxation of Reconstruction. The Radical Republicans' corrupt military carpetbag governments stole from the little substance that remained to the Southerners and humiliated them in every available fashion, increasing many times the Southerners' one final possession—that is, pride. For thirty postwar years, the Southerners resisted force of all kinds, including the bayonet, used in a manner intended to re-form them into Yankees. When the carpetbaggers left, they left behind a people who were desolate, dirt-poor as they used to say, but who were at once more united and more independent than ever.

And yet, in spite of their independence, their desire to be as unlike as possible their Yankee brethren in the Union who had brought them again to the status of frontiersmen, they were, or felt, forced by the times—the Yankee century—to become increasingly like the Yankees in order to survive. In the early 1900s, Southerners began building cotton, iron, and tobacco mills, hydroelectric plants, and hundreds of other industries. The towns grew. World War I brought increased production and profits. Southern rednecks began to acquire such trappings of modern civilization as automobiles, plumbing, and phonographs to play Jimmie Rodgers and Carter Family records. Then the Depression cut production, and wages dropped. Once more the Yankee system had put the rednecks back on a sowbelly and hoecake diet.

Roosevelt's New Deal programs slowly raised the rednecks' living standard, but at the cost of further encroachment of industrial civilization into what had been, under optimum conditions, a way of life in which harmony existed between man and nature. Some religious fundamentalists in the South believed the National Recovery Administration eagle symbol to be the mark of the beast prophesied in the book of Revelations. Fanatics they may have been, but still there was a germ of true perception in their belief. Roosevelt's reclamation of the South exposed the rednecks to ever-increasing danger of annihilation by assimilation. World War II accelerated this process, and in the immediate postwar years, redneck culture, the strongest, the most basic, white ethnic culture in America, became more pervasive until 1953, the year when Hank Williams, whom many consider the finest flower of redneck music, died. In the next year in Memphis, Boss Crump, the South's archetypal High Redneck politician, would die, and Elvis Presley would appear, a "hillbilly cat" who sang like a black man, who bought his clothes at Lansky's on Beale Street, where the black pimps traded, who had been regarded as "different" at all-white Humes High School, who broke through America's color lines so that its popular culture would never be the same again. It was in the same year, naturally, that the Supreme Court outlawed school segregation. The world had changed, and distinctions of race, of urban and rural cultures, were vanishing.

I began by saying that redneckery is no longer essentially Southern, only to talk about it as if it were. This I will continue to do, because, though a type of behavior vulgarly thought of as rednecked—the behavior, for example, of sailors on leave—exists throughout the world, Southern rednecks, being triple distilled, are the redneckedest of all. I have also, with all proportions kept, like Capablanca writing a book on basic chess without telling the reader how to move the pieces, omitted to mention the most basic and literal meaning of the descriptive term we are considering.

Rednecked: because of the sun on the back of the farmer's neck, making the skin brick-red and cracked as the dry clay soil of middle Georgia and Alabama in the dog days, when the leaves of roadside trees are coated with layer upon layer of the finest, most pervasive, mouth-drying, nose-stinging, eye-scratching, gold-pink dust.

Rednecked: because not even the farmer's hands, likely scarred and deeply calloused, nor his face, dark under the pale band of skin between his hairline and the line on his forehead just over his eyebrows to which his straw hat reaches, become as red as his neck, that part of him (since the rest of him is protected by, say, Wolverine brogans, Tuf-Nut overalls, and a Duck Head blue chambray work shirt buttoned all the way up) most exposed to the merciless sun and equally merciless mosquitoes, horseflies, deerflies, yellowflies, biting gnats, wasps, hornets, bees, and the other tiny savage creatures that swoop and stab in the scant breezes of the Southern summer. Of redbugs, ticks, and chiggers I will say nothing, since they do not especially favor the neck, except that they are eternal and cannot be protected against. . . .

. . . The word *redneck* to outsiders represents the raw, crude, unsophisticated, and savage, and this is not completely inaccurate. But how, if the word has any real relation to its roots, can we call unsophisticated a twelve-year-old man like Jesse Root of near Burnt Fort, Georgia, who when we were growing up would go into the woods with a rifle and two bullets and come home two days later without ever firing a shot, having eaten in the woods (as he also did at home) better than celebrities eat at 21? . . .

. . . A redneck, even one on the right side of the law, bears watching, because he will surprise you. Jesse Root, who attended school rarely and under duress, not at all after he was fourteen, can hardly write his name, but the Lord called him to preach, and for a while he led tent revivals in Jacksonville. Luckily the Lord released him from his obligation, and the last time I saw him he was living near Waycross, driving a lumber truck. I say luckily because among rednecks preaching is not considered one of man's most desirable occupations. "I have preached," a great-uncle of mine once said, "and I'm not too good to do it again."

The redneck's opposition to preaching, an activity that involves one man's prescribing behavior for others, arises from the independent depths of his heart. A redneck could hardly be an adherent of any highly organized religion because he would insist, if he could read, on interpreting God's word for himself. The redneck has traditionally preferred the King James version of the Bible, believing if that version was good enough for Jesus, it's good enough for him. The prohibitions of redneck Protestantism result from the strenuousness of life in a primitive environment, where eternal vigilance was a necessity, where the choice was between dissipation and survival. Only prohibitions that matched the real condition of his life would have been tolerated by the redneck. Many times I have heard it said of someone in the South who took it upon himself to offer too-personal advice that he had "quit preaching and gone to meddling." The first characteristics of Yankees I was told to watch out for were that they are Rudely Outspoken and season their food too high.

Once I asked Dan Penn, who grew up in a junkyard in Vernon, Alabama, wrote the rockabilly hit "Is a Bluebird Blue" when he was fifteen, and whose career has been uphill ever since, what exactly was the special gift of Southerners like himself. Penn, unshaven, looking hungover and seedy, wearing a green baseball cap with the bill over his left ear, twirled the ukulele he had been clasping to his bosom and said, "They won't let nobody tell them what to do."

Even a pale modern redneck has memories, from his own observation or bred into him, of a past when man did not live in boxes and obey the whims of machines; when God turned on the light in the morning and everything a man saw, smelled, heard, touched, or tasted had a life that was in both a real and apparent manner related to his own. It was not indifference or recalcitrance but a profound sense of the complexity of life, of the vast mystery of even the few acres he occupied under the extremity of the sky, that caused the farmer in the story to reject the advice of the government agent who attempted to tell him how to manage the place better: "I ain't farmin' good as I know how now."

In the old redneck way of living, a man took his orders from his own perception of the order of the natural world, a world filled with innumerable amazing forms and conditions of life that make vivid the true redneck's life and language. A real redneck is never simply happy; he is happy as a dead pig in the sunshine, grinning like a possum eating yellowjackets, smiling like a mule eating briars over a bobwar fence. When he is unhappy he is down in the mouth, has the mullygrubs, and feels as blue as bluing. When he is in trouble he is between a rock and a hard place; his ox is in the ditch; he has plowed up a nest of snakes. When he is well, he is fine as frog-hair and mending; you couldn't kill him with a stick. Should his health decline, he is not just sick but *low* sick, sick as a dog, feels like he has the misery. . . .

. . . Of a redneck with money, other rednecks will say, truly or not, that he is broke out with it, 's got boocoos (beaucoups) of it, he don't care if syrup goes to a dollar a sop. For most old-fashioned rednecks, money is scarce as hen's teeth, and when one's money runs out, he is broke as a haint. Then push comes to shove, and it is root hog or die pore.

Though the South is fertile and bountiful, too many rednecks, faced with this choice, have died poor. Over the years, through successive generations and catastrophes, the land has been removed from the rednecks and the rednecks from the land. There are more jobs in the towns and more money, but there is not the old closeness to life, to living things. It is this closeness that the urban or suburban redneck descendant tries to recapture with his speedboats, hunting and fishing trips, barbecues, rodeos, and pilgrimages to Graceland and the Grand Ole Opry. To understand the heartbreak of the modern redneck, you would have to work the graveyard shift at Kellogg's and seeing the clock at 3 A.M. think of what it would be like now on the hillside among the rushing creeks and branches with the whiskey burning in your veins and the hounds baying and the big moon shining bright through the big trees, while beside you on a vast conveyor belt, little puddles of corn dough harden as they cook into little meaningless crunches, as nutritious as the boxes they will occupy, as unlike real corn as the box is unlike a tree.

It is in fact impossible for any culture to be sound and healthy without a proper respect and proper regard for the soil, no matter how many urban dwellers think that their victuals come from groceries and delicatessens and their milk from tin cans. Andrew Lytle wrote those words in 1926, and they are truer now that the diseases of the cities have increased in number and intensity. . . .

. . . And yet the city's siren song has lured away the country folk until now there are only a few of the real old rednecks left, living at the ends of the WPA farm-to-market roads, where the struggle continues.

As a young man, pursued by the urban horrors (in my case, publishers, women, and the police), I went as far into the country as I could go. I lived in the Boston Mountains of the Ozark Plateau, in the one Arkansas county the railroad never reached. My nearest neighbor, a quarter-mile away through the woods on Low Gap Mountain (half a mile away by the mud-and-gravel, spring-overflowing, loblolly-pitted Arkansas superhighway between our places) was Newton Jardine. The Jardine family had lived on the same few mountains for so many generations that Newton had hardly any notion where they came from; it was as if his people had always been a part of the mountains. But Newton's mother and father were dead, his brothers and sisters had left the hills, and of them all only Newton was still there, at the end of a road a car could not climb, right up at the ridge, where the weather comes from. Newton lived in a three-room house made from untreated grey porous boards that were taken off another old house, he told me, it's just no tellin how old them old boards are.

For most of Newton's life (he was then in his early forties), he worked on his pa's place and then on his own place, never having a regular outside job. After he married, Newton spent most of his days climbing trees with a chain saw for the local electric co-operative, working all day and still managing to keep cows, pigs, chickens, dogs, cats;

to raise hay and a garden; to fish; to hunt; to find mushrooms, ginseng, and rattlesnakes. Newton weighed 132 pounds and was as hard as an Arkansas rock.

But even Newton came down the hill. You needed at least a pickup truck with a strong low gear to get to Newton's old place in the dry months, and in the winter snow and ice too often made it impossible for even a truck with four-wheel drive to get feed to the barn. The last winter they lived there, Newton's wife Opal, walking up the rocky road with a sack of groceries, fell on the ice and banged her head pretty bad. So Newton built another house, down the hillside. It was much more accessible (and conventional, a tight white frame house), and that was one of the reasons, I think, why Newton, who had spent most of his life acting on the principle that the thing to be was inaccessible, called it "Opal's house."

"I'll come back off up here to the old place when she gets put out with me," Newton said before they moved, knowing he wouldn't, and wondering how he would sleep in a tight house, and would he feel the same bathing indoors in a bathtub. The new place was not far away, but sleeping in the wood shanty up at the ridge, hearing the rain on the tin roof, Newton felt closer, just a bit closer, to the way man lived on the land when he lived as the land dictated, not according to his own will even, much less the will of advertisers, manufacturers, and police, but according to a much more complex will, of which he was, with the rain and trees, a part.

We would sit sometimes on Newton's porch (the boards of the porch bleached white from a million washings, shrunken away from each other, soft rough-textured old boards) as the sun dropped over the ridge behind us and the green hills stretching out before us darkened into distant blue. You did not notice the light changing until the first firefly flashed, and then their cool yellow flashes were everywhere as the light all faded and the stars came out and we sat on Newton's time-shrunken porch boards in the darkness, as if suspended in eternity, the stars and the fireflies equally near, drifting and flashing in time.

"When will you get into your new place?" I asked him.

"By fall, if the Lord's willin' and the creek don't run dry. Just before this place falls down."

"This place will be here when we're gone," I said.

"Yeah," Newton said. I could barely see his face in the darkness, his eyes dark as an Indian's looking at the old house, invisible around us. "I hate to leave it," he said.

◆ ◆

STANLEY BOOTH, a graduate of the University of Memphis, is a professional writer and photographer. Much of his work deals with the lives of musicians and has appeared in such periodicals as *Esquire*, *Rolling Stone*, the *London Times Literary Supplement*, and *Playboy*, as well as in his recent books *Till I Roll Over Dead*, *Rhythm Oil*, and *The True Adventure of the Rolling Stones*.

BILL SWANN

School

The boy threw up on the way to school,
Regularly,
A matter of course,
Compass-setting.
The stink of decomposing plankton
Would rise into his blowholes,
And make his bright eyes water,
Make the sidewalk swim.
His almost hairless body, half-formed,
Wet cetacean eyes casting about,
Sought protection, not ritual,
Not emesis on neighborhood lawns.

His mother protected him when she could,
Let him swim in her shadow,
Helped him feed, hid him
When she herself was not in danger,
The denounced whore, the common slut,
The bright-eyed nurse.

He scraped his way along sidewalks
Thinking six times nine, four times three,
Thinking bile-tinged thoughts.
He thought of the school cafeteria, steaming,

Windows fogged,
A place that sometimes had no food for whales.
He thought of home and crashing waves,
The leaping thrashing father,
Heaving himself up, up into bright air,
Leaping high and falling back into the sea,
Killing what lay below him,
Denouncing the whore.

He wondered how it could be
That at home only she loved him,
While at school many, many loved him.
Even the ladies in the cafeteria,
Even on the days
When there was no food for whales.

He thought of children, tiered and glowing,
Standing on stairsteps that reached
All the way to heaven,
Reached so high the air was thin and shimmering
Where the oldest stood, singing,
Singing in the school's foyer,
Singing oh little town,
Singing with no fear of megaliths
Falling, white-crusted, waves driven asunder
Gulls sent screaming, panicked,
Their wingtips slapping foam.

He thought of his teacher who loved him,
Who loved his grey skin,

His smooth grey skin,
Who gave him stamps and stars.
At night, rising to breathe,
He saw her stars among the stars,
Her stamped cat shapes upon the constellations.

At night, rising to breathe,
He knew he wanted to live in school,
Breathing the dust of tempera paints
And construction paper forever,
Far from falling fear,
Far from barnacled screams.
He knew he wanted to live, and live, and live,
Without bile, without flagellae,
Beyond the horizon, among the stars.

◆ ◆

BILL SWANN is a circuit court judge for the State of Tennessee, a position he assumed in 1982. Judge Swann has published extensively in journals and law reviews on legal subjects. He has also written weekly columns for the *Knoxville Journal* and the *Knoxville News-Sentinel*.

LAMAR ALEXANDER

FIND THE GOOD AND PRAISE IT

"It helps to talk a story," Alex Haley said. We were far out in the Pacific, three weeks before Christmas 1987, two of only eight passengers on a German freighter, and my friend was teaching me yet another lesson.

We had completed dinner and climbed to the second deck to admire the stars. Then Alex settled against the railing and began "talking" the story of his grandmother, a slave named Queen, and Queen's father, an Alabama plantation owner of Irish descent. He would practice a phrase, then polish it, all the while judging my reaction to each serving.

We would be thirteen more days to New Zealand, and the captain had said we would not see land—not even an island—for twelve days. These long voyages were the way Alex had found time to write *Roots* and *The Autobiography of Malcolm X*, two books that changed the way we think of ourselves and made Alex seem a member of almost every family.

The stars seemed to dance as the freighter rolled and Alex talked. "It took twelve years to write *Roots*," he recalled, "searching to find Kunta Kinte, to understand what those stories meant that I had heard as a boy on my grandma's front porch. For days I rode in the belly of the ship, trying to imagine what it was like when one of every four captured Africans died in those hulls trying to hear their shrieks in the wind. I dug and dug and kept trying to find a way to use all of the research. I was broke, down to eighteen cents and two cans of sardines. Once, standing on the stern of a ship just like this, I thought of jumping. The water seemed so inviting, so peaceful. It would be the end of my misery. I could see no way out of the mass of material that eventually became *Roots*."

"What made you finish?" I asked.

"There came a time—maybe I was halfway done—when the book took over," he said, "just swept me ahead with it, something like a stream rushing. The book became itself, and I became merely the instrument that made it happen."

I believe Alex Haley was put on earth to teach the lessons of *Roots* and then left here for a while longer to remind us of some other important lessons.

Our family first met Alex Haley in 1980. I can still see this friendly bear of a man cuddling our newborn son, Will. Alex was—at that moment—the world's most celebrated writer, and I was governor of his native state, Tennessee. *Roots* had won the Pulitzer Prize and was being translated into thirty-seven languages. The TV version had become the most watched miniseries in history.

Everyone seemed to know him. Once, walking in a Philadelphia hotel lobby, we heard, "Hell-o, Alex!" and running to greet him came "Dr. J," the basketball star Julius Erving. One night in Los Angeles, two young men accosted Alex and one looked up and said, "Hey, it's Mr. Roots!" So, instead of money, they demanded his autograph, And here, in the midst of our Pacific voyage, the ship's radio crackled with an urgent message. News had somehow reached New Zealand that Alex might be on board. "Would Mr. Haley consent to an interview?"

No one who spent the night at our governor's mansion in Tennessee—not even the president of the United States—created the stir among the employees that Alex Haley did. He had time for each one; Dr. J., the young men in L.A., the New Zealanders, the cooks at the mansion. One of the first lessons I learned from this famous man was that he wanted to know each one of them just as much as they wanted to know him.

Late one night on our voyage, I asked him, "What is it about *Roots* that has affected so many millions of people?"

"Kunta Kinte's struggle for freedom, I think," he said. "It seems to help others struggling."

The Rev. Jesse Jackson explained it this way: "He made our grandparents superstars." I know when I heard Alex tell his grandma's stories, I began to pester my oldest relatives to learn what my ancestors had been doing seven generations earlier. When I heard how his Aunt Liz, rocking on the porch telling stories, "could knock a firefly out of the sky from fourteen feet with an accurate stream of tobacco juice," my Great-Grandmother Sadie's snuffbox became a prize.

Alex also taught us that these superstars came from super places we often take for granted—our hometowns. Each night during our voyage, after "talking" his stories, Alex would disappear into his cabin to work on a book about his hometown: Henning, Tenn., pop. 973.

The more Alex's fame spread, the hungrier he seemed for his own roots. Quietly, he purchased his Grandpa Palmer's house—the one with the front porch where he first heard the stories of Kunta Kinte. He paid for the upkeep of the graveyard where "Chicken George" is buried; it still has the fence down the middle—whites buried on one side, blacks on the other. In 1983, he bought a farm outside Knoxville, at the edge of the Great Smoky Mountains.

Living at the edge of the Smokies—so different from the cotton fields of Henning—he began "talking" new stories about pioneer men, strong-willed women. Those of us whose families had always lived in those mountains were enormously complimented when such a great man discovered superstars in our midst.

What we finally came to understand was that, to Alex, everyone was a superstar. Walking in Knoxville, he met Joseph Rivera, discovered that he was an adult learning to read and encouraged him. Within a few months, Joseph Rivera was another superstar, the subject of a story by Alex in the Sept. 2, 1990, issue of PARADE. Cabdrivers, university students, out-of-work neighbors—all might find themselves guests at the Haley farm, seated at dinner next to, say, Oprah Winfrey or Quincy Jones.

Alex's favorite lesson was that the most important superstars of all were family. No one in our house ever felt quite so important as when Alex would visit. "Now, let me see that essay," he would say to Leslee or Kathryn, our daughters. "My, with just a little work, that could surely win a prize!" To our youngest, who had been experimenting with a video camera: "Will, you have a real talent. You, know, that's how Steven Spielberg started. I think I will tell him about you." Or, after a trip with our teenage son, he would confide: "You would have been proud of how polite Drew was, how many people were impressed with him."

In 1988, I became president of the University of Tennessee. I was happy that this meant I could spend more time in Knoxville, closer to Alex. I was at his farm in December 1990, when President Bush telephoned to ask me to become the Secretary of Education.

I saw much less of Alex once our family moved to Washington. But, whenever I was on the spot—which was more often now—I found myself thinking, "What would Alex say?"

As Secretary of Education, I found opportunities almost every day to pass along Alex's lessons. Sometimes I would produce for students a typed page of Alex's *Roots* manuscript, almost obscured by green ink corrections, and tell them what he told me: "Some of those chapters I rewrote 15 times, 20 times, 25 times. I wanted it to be right." The teacher's face always brightened, as if to say to the students, "I told you so."

When I would salute an outstanding school or teacher, I usually began in this way: "My dear friend Alex Haley has a saying, which I am putting into practice today—'Find the good and praise it.'"

In the classrooms of Los Angeles, following last spring's troubles, teachers struggled to find ways to help children of different backgrounds and races learn to respect one another—and how to react if someone does not respect them. I told them how Alex handled such matters. How, because of his race, his jobs in the Coast Guard during World War II were limited to the kitchen. One job was serving coffee to the captain, who usually was so busy reading magazines that he ignored the server.

But one day the captain observed, as he lifted his cup: "There's a good article here by an Alex Haley. Same name as you."

The server replied, "I am the Alex Haley who wrote the article." After that, there were fewer calls for coffee, many more for conversation with the author.

It is worth telling about this man who co-authored *The Autobiography of Malcolm X*—whose grandmother was a slave, whose blacksmith grandfather was not permitted to own land, whose brother attended the University of Arkansas Law School in a basement classroom set apart for blacks—that I never heard him say one angry word about this country or about any other person because of that person's background or race.

In September 1991, Alex and I and my son Will sweltered in 100-degree heat at the opening game of the University of Tennessee football season. Alex was breathing heavily, I noticed, perspiring more than even a slightly overweight, 70-year-old diabetic with an impossible schedule should.

A few months later, my wife, Honey, and I were in Memphis, listening as Attallah Shabazz, the oldest daughter of Malcolm X, spoke about the unwelcome call that had come last Feb 10, telling of Alex's passing: "My first thought of my godfather was how he had always said, "Find the good and praise it," she said. "And then I thought: One less call, one less trip, and we who demanded so much of him might have had him for a few more precious years."

I once told Alex that I hoped he would speak at my funeral, because it would sound so good. I did not want to speak at his. But it came my turn, so I said, "He was God's storyteller. We loved him so much, we just used him up."

Later that afternoon, family and friends crowded inside Henning's New Hope C.M.E. Church. I was certain that most everyone there thought at least once of another of Alex's lessons: "When an old person dies, it is like a library burning."

After the service, we proceeded to Grandpa Palmer's house and stood waiting by the porch. Early daffodils decorated the yard. Every now and then, we would hear the awkward winching noises of the contraption that lowered the mahogany casket—that eventually brought the gravestone etching into view: "Find the Good and Praise It."

The crowd huddled as a drizzle began. A bugler played taps. The explosions of twenty-one guns hurt our ears. A flute playing "Amazing Grace" soothed them. Then came the rumbling and the whistle of the train. Honey whispered, "Isn't it nice that he could be here to hear the train?"

And, as we drove home, Honey said what I had been thinking: "Standing there, I felt like everyone else had disappeared and that there were his great-aunts and grandma on the front porch rocking, and Alex was there—Alex was there, just telling me another story."

A month after Alex died, I was to address the Gridiron Dinner in Washington, D.C., an annual assemblage of the nation's Establishment. The other speakers that night were to be the stiffest competition: Texas Gov. Ann Richards and President Bush. So I decided to play the piano and sing satirical verses about politicians and to rely on a little help from my friend. I closed in this way:

"My friend Alex Haley used to say, 'Find the good and praise it.' He especially liked to say that to people who were busy finding everything wrong with America. It was a powerful message coming from the grandson of slaves, from the man who wrote *Roots* and *The Autobiography of Malcolm X*.

"I used to think about it every time Alex told the story about John Newton, the slave trader, and how he saw the light and wrote one of the world's greatest hymns, 'Amazing Grace.'

"I thought about it again last month as an African flute played the melody of that great hymn and we buried Alex Haley next to the front porch where his grandma and great-aunts first told him the stories that became *Roots*."

Then, on the piano, I played "Amazing Grace."

The crowd of a thousand insiders did something they rarely do—they rose and applauded. I was thinking: "Thank you, my friend. It's more for you than for me."

I was not surprised earlier this year when Will, now in seventh grade, told me that he had chosen to read *Roots* for a class assignment. Some evenings he and I have been reading it together.

When we came to the page where slave traders surprise Kunta Kinte in the canebrake, Will sat straight up, just as I did when I first read it. When Kunta is struggling in the filth and death of the slave trader's hull, we struggled too, trying to imagine it. For both of us, of course, the best thing has been that on each page our friend Alex comes alive again.

After we read and before I turn out the lights, I usually pause at Will's desk, where he keeps the mounted plastic fish that arrived in the mail soon after he caught what Alex assured him was "the biggest catfish ever seen" in the Haley Farm pond. On the wooden base of this trophy, there is a strip of white paper carefully cut out and taped, with a neatly penned inscription: "To Will, my favorite fisherman—Alex Haley." To Alex, everyone was a superstar.

◆ ◆

LAMAR ALEXANDER literally walked a thousand miles across Tennessee in 1978 to become its governor. After two terms as governor, he became president of the University of Tennessee in 1988; three years later, in 1991, the U.S. Senate unanimously confirmed him as President Bush's Secretary of Education. He lives in Nashville, where he is counsel to the law firm of Baker, Donelson, Bearman, and Caldwell.

ROGER R. EASSON

SANTA WAS A WOMAN: A CHRISTMAS STORY

The warm earth gave way easily as James pushed his spade in deeply, all the way up to the metal roll which marked the upper limits of the steel. The soil was variegated: black loam, light gray clay, clumps of mulch, streaks of the sharp red river sand he'd added last spring, old roots left from the pumpkin hills last summer, worms, grubs, every now and again a small burrow where the mole had run.

He had worked hard to build the fertility of this garden patch, tilling in leaves and mulching grass clippings every year for the last six, and now, he was once more turning under the top four inches and bringing up the bottom three.

It was too early for the Martins, he recollected, but then he had not cleaned out the Martin houses, which still sat on their tall perches by the back fence. Perhaps tomorrow, *he thought as he continued the repetitive spade work. . . .*

His dream of spring and spade work was broken by a loud noise on the porch. Roused from his slumber before the fire, James did not want to rise up, did not want to go out and check.

Probably that branch damaged in the ice storm last February has finally given way, he surmised.

Nothing to worry about.

All during the day a light rain had fallen in Shelby Forest beyond the front door of his cabin. Even though it was unseasonably warm for December, he'd built a fire in the fireplace.

It was, after all, Christmas Eve, and what would Christmas Eve be without a fire, he'd thought as he gathered the kindling. On the hearth, fire dogs held the glowing embers of logs burning slowly but completely.

Above on the rough-hewn mantle from three hooks hung the stockings his late wife had made for their sons. There was no reason to hang them anymore, except it made James feel more at home with this season. David and Andy had not come back from Vietnam, and Mikey . . . well, Mikey was a disappointment in anybody's book. He was a Republican hack working for a conservative gun lobby. James felt his liberal Democratic values had been betrayed utterly, and the two of them could never be together without getting into a political fracas. Even at this time of the year, they avoided each other's company.

James dreaded Christmas. Even so, he'd gotten out the green depression dishes Margaret had collected over the years. It made him feel good to set the table for the five of them; though there was never any way those chairs would hold his family again.

James thought he was like the votive candles which guttered low in their puddles of ivory wax as they cast long red shadows across the mantle: about burned out.

As he heard the old clock chime midnight, he settled back into the soft folds of corduroy when the second heavy thump on the porch roused him to action.

Damned pigs, was his first thought. *They're back for what's left of my garden.* There were wild pigs in Shelby Forest. They were feral pigs, lost from farmer's herds generations ago, returning to their porcine roots. They were tuskers and sows who turned the soil of his garden with their febrile snouts, so sensitive to buried tubers and fungus. The thought of pigs tearing through his garden was recoiling as he emerged from the still waters of his deep sleep.

He roused himself uneasily. It had not been long since his prostate surgery and he was still sore. But two thumps could not possibly be a tree limb falling. More curious than afraid, he went to the back window, expecting to see broad black pig backs, wet with the winter rains, nosing around in the dark soil. But there were no pigs. He felt he'd heard them sure enough. So he went to the front window, pushed back the drapery, only to see a large woman draped in a heavy red blanket, or at least what seemed like a red blanket at the time, sitting on his porch swing.

He went to the door and opened it slowly, unsure what to say at this time of the night. She was a big woman. The rusty chains which suspended the swing from the iron hooks in the ceiling protested the weight they were forced to bear. A low grinding noise echoed through the porch roof as if they had been sounding boards of an old drum as she gentled the swing.

She raised up to look at him, and then he saw them. She was nursing twins at her ample breasts.

Collecting his facilities after this shock, he began again with the standard greeting required on opening doors to strangers: "May I help you?"

"No need," she said in a voice gravelly with longing. "It's hard to manage the truck and feed them at the same time. Your porch looked inviting—so I thought I'd just rest a spell here. Hope you don't mind."

He looked out into the drive where an old black pickup truck sat; on the side door "Vicksburg Stables" in ornate scroll work hung above the large letters of "Racing Pigs."

"Mind? Not in the least. Come in, please won't you? I've a warm fire and no one to share it with. You look chilled and I'm sure your shoes must be wet from tramping across the wet grass."

"Well thanks. Suppose I will set by your fire, but as you can see I've no shoes to dry." She held up a large brown foot, it was bare, and dry. In the porch light, golden hair gleamed from the knuckle of the great toe.

She rose up with difficulty, gathering her bundled charges and swept into the house, settling into Margaret's love seat opposite his archair. She gave a great heave trying to arrange the twins and the blanket all at the same time. One of the infants uncoupled itself and stared at James with amazing blue eyes.

James closed the door, turned on a few lamps, busied himself with small matters. When he finished, he asked the question obligatory when meeting the newly born: "How old are they?"

"About two months," she answered as she settled back.

"Would you like me to hold that one for a moment? It's been so long since I've held a little one."

The mother looked at him for a long moment. It was a knowing look, as if a door had been opened and then shut again. Balancing the other in the crook of her arm, she gestured with an elbow for him to take the tow-headed infant with the blue eyes.

James settled back into his chair, cradling the infant to his chest and stroking its golden hair with his free hand. Its little hand waved through the air, and little gurgling noises, such as babies make after they have been fed, gave accompaniment.

"Do you think I should burp him?"

"Sure, if you want," the mother said.

James carefully moved the infant to his shoulder and began the practiced movements he had known when he had given this service to his own three.

"Guess you never lose the knack," he said with a smile, a look of contentment glowing on his face.

She seemed to have no modesty at all with this feeding of babies. There was an easy casualness about it, although she had tucked the free bosom back into her dark dress. James began to watch this woman more closely as the warmth of the infant he held pressed into him. She was big. She was dark-skinned, but he could not say her features were either African or European. She was not merely beautiful. Her hair flooded down her shoulders as she let slip the blanket she'd clutched so close to her earlier. It was an oily black, so black it seemed to have the glint of gun metal blue. And it was braided in an odd way, quite unlike anything he'd ever seen.

She began to croon and to sway, rocking the child at her breast. Her great thighs swung back and forth as the melody swam up through her flesh seeking human company. James thought to himself, he'd never known heavy women could be so beautiful. She caught his eye and motioned for James to return his charge to her arm. The little one was beatifically asleep, but as he passed it over to her, a little foot fell out of the blanket.

James reacted as if he'd been shot: it was a little pig's foot.

The mother caught it and before she tucked it back into the cloth, she kissed it. With an easy grace she unburdened the breast the child had begun to squeal for. James began to doubt what he'd seen. The dim light from the fire was playing tricks on his old brain. Then again. . . . It was not long before he convinced himself he had been an old fool. It was late after all.

"So where do you come from?" he ventured.

"Been up to Covington," she said. "I'm heading home to Vicksburg. I don't usually travel alone, but no one wanted to come with me."

"I see," said James, but he really didn't, and he decided not to press the issue. The silence settled down between them again, and the twins wiggled closer as they sucked.

"What's a racing pig?" he asked. "Your truck says 'Racing Pigs.'"

"Oh, it's something I do in the summertime. I take pigs to county fairs and race them just like greyhounds. Folks don't know how fast pigs are. Sometimes, I train pigs to take the harness and run in pairs hitched to a small cart. The real challenge is when I hitch them up in a team of twelve to pull a wagon or a sleigh. I have the twelve hitch with me. I'll show them to you when I leave."

"Never heard of racing pigs. That's a new one on me," James said, wanting to know more and yet aware of her fumbling with the twins and how she probably had better things to do than talk to an old fool.

Still, he tried to make conversation again. "Is there anything I can get for you?"

"Do you have any spring water or well water? I can't stand tap," she said.

James knew what she meant. The chlorine had always bothered Margaret, too.

"There's a spring way back of the property," James offered. "It runs fresh this time of year. Swallowhead, people call it. Comes out of the bottom of an old Indian mound. Feeds into a small lake around the back side of the mound. I like to take the boat out and murder bait now and again. It's probably what's left of an old horseshoe bend after the river moved further west . . . there's a wooden bucket somewhere. I'll go fill it for you."

"I think I've heard about that spring," the mother offered. "But that's asking too much, and it's so late. Don't you have some bottled water? That would do just as well."

"Sorry, no Perrier. I won't be a second. Walk will do me good."

That was not true: he did need exercise, but not just now with the soreness in the groin. Nevertheless, he got up, put on his jacket, grabbed up his big field light, caught up the wooden sap bucket Margaret had kept silk chrysanthemums in and made for the door.

"Make yourself at home, now," he said as he looked back at his guests. Over his shoulder he'd noticed the mother was crooning again.

Never did get her name. No matter, she's not going to do any mischief with that load in her arms. Glad for the company.

The night air was brisk but not chilling. The grass he crossed as he entered the forest whispered under his boots. Sharp pains came less frequently as he strode out across the land. In the darknesss he thought about the portion of earth he owned and wondered who would own it after him.

Swallowhead spring had been the site of many wonderful summer afternoons. The boys had built great forts on the mound's summit. James marveled as he recalled the great times they had in the cool water on hot summer days.

He'd always thought himself fortunate to have acquired property with this mound on it, one of the last old Mississippian Culture mounds that had once dotted the Mississippi shore. Most of the local examples had been leveled as Memphis edged north and south along the river's banks.

After he and Margaret had taken over the summer house when he retired, they would sometimes take a bottle of wine to the top and watch the sunset. During one of those afternoons, Margaret had told him about the cancer, and how she was ready to go "home," as she'd called it. As she grew weaker, they'd sit for hours in the sun on the mound and watch the river. When she left him finally, he'd planted a pink dogwood on the summit near the bench they'd used on those long afternoons. For some reason, he no longer went up to the summit, he realized as he walked.

As he came upon the spring, he could hear the grunting of pigs in the night air. He smiled at the confirmation of his initial feeling about the sound which woke him. He delighted in the sound of the rushing water as he savored the coolness of the night. Catching up the clear freshness, James stood up to begin the half-mile walk back to the house.

Then he saw it. The light seemed to burst up over the roof of his house. He picked up his pace, disregarding the pain in his side, emerged from the forest, and crossed the long lawn from the mound to his house more quickly than seemed reasonable.

As he rounded the side of the house, he saw she had the truck lights on, and was arranging the little ones into the front seat. He'd not noticed the odd way the truck had lots of little lanterns hanging from thin poles fencing in a huge sack which sat uneasily in the bed. The red blanket she wore now revealed how it was held by clasps into a coat: her hair was stuffed into a red hood, trimmed in dark fur. Twelve gray and black pigs ringed the truck, quiet and watchful. They weren't hogs; not old enough: shoats, more likely. They were most unpiglike, James thought.

"You've come at last," she said. James handed her the bucket and her big hands gripped it. Holding it full to her mouth, she drank deeply. "Would you give my lads a drink, too?"

James thought it quaint that she'd call the pigs "lads."

"There's a wooden trough in the truck. Would you get it out and pour the water in it for them." Sure enough there was a hand-hewn wooden trough about two pigs wide. He was sure there would not be enough for all twelve to have a drink. But as he poured water from the bucket, the trough filled to the brim. When they drank, there was an awful noise and water spilled everywhere. Yet, as they drew back, the trough was only half empty. They stood uneasily, watching James, as if waiting for some sign to break and run.

"Could you help me get them back into the truck? There's a plank in the truck bed that makes a ramp. They'll go up pretty well. But they can't jump," she laughed.

James obliged, and sure enough the pigs climbed into the bed of the truck and began to squeeze in close together. Several of them pressed against the heavy sack, and others hung their front hooves over the side of the truck to get a better look at James. But they didn't make a sound. All he could hear was the sound their hooves made on the metal truck bed and the rough soughing of their lean pig-bristled flanks rubbing together as they jockeyed for position before the journey resumed.

James placed the plank and the trough back in the bed of the truck, sliding them along the side. When he forced himself to turn away to look again at the woman, he saw she was rummaging around in the great bag in the truck bed searching for something. Finally with a great laugh she retrieved a leather bag and held it aloft.

"Got it!" she shouted. Turning around, she handed it to James and said, "This is for you. If any one asks, just say it's from Santa Claus."

She did look a little like Santa, he thought. From the cushion of the bag he drew out a great red cup, very plain. Painted around its lip were twelve black pigs harnessed up to an ancient wagon driven by a huge woman who was suckling twins at her breasts. For some reason, James held it as carefully as if it were made of gold.

"Remember me," she said as she clambered into the cab of the truck. "If you come to Vicksburg, come to my place beneath the hill. I'll have work for you to do, if you want it. We have racing pigs in the summer, but the best time of all is in the winter. A man's never too old to learn to race pigs."

What an odd thing to say, James thought as he waved happily when she drove out of the yard through the wet earth. The little lamps danced like fireflies behind the truck as it disappeared into the forest. James was alone again, holding the cup to his chest like a sacred relique.

"Racing pigs," he said to himself. "Imagine that. Pig races. What in the world would an old man like me do with racing pigs?" But then he noticed he didn't feel old any more. There was bounce in his step as he went back inside to call Mikey.

"Bet he's never heard of racing pigs," James said out loud to no one in particular. "Imagine the look on his face when I tell him Santa is a woman."

◆ ◆

ROGER R. EASSON, a widely published Blake scholar and a former editor and publisher, is now associate professor of English at Christian Brothers University in Memphis, where he directs the Writing Center.

SUSAN WILTSHIRE

THE AUCTION

Liza Myatt leaned forward in her aluminum lawn chair, looking intently at Len Barker over by the sugar maple. When she saw his index finger flick imperceptibly the fourth time, she knew that the auctioneer, Colonel Burns, only had to add the usual flourishes to his routine before the pie safe would be sold.

It was the nicest thing she had. It was made of oak and was more elaborate than pie safes usually are. She had bought it with her egg and butter money nineteen years ago when the Moultons sold out. Colonel Burns had been the auctioneer then, too, and she had decided then that he would handle things for her if she ever needed it. His auctions were a cross between an ice cream social and a political rally. He had already introduced five local candidates today, two of them getting special notice because he used to play ball with them or their daddies. And he could sweet-talk one more bid like a preacher at altar call: "Still cheap at the price."

She was glad the Barkers got the pie safe. They had helped her since Orman went into the nursing home in Richardson nine months ago and had sent over their two boys this morning to help her move the rest of her things out onto the yard for the sale. She was so grateful for their help that she pretended not to notice when twelve-year old Jake tossed two sterling silver teaspoons into a paper bag of knickknacks he was carrying out to the auction table.

She was pretending not to notice a lot of things today. The July heat, though she was mostly used to the heat. The size of the crowd, a little smaller than she and Colonel Burns had hoped for. Mostly she was pretending not to notice the looks on people's faces when they glanced at her, the concern from the people who knew her and the pity from those who didn't. They were the ones who bothered her the most, the pitying city folks who didn't know her from Adam.

You could tell which ones they were right away. It was the nervous way they stood,

"The Auction," by Susan Wiltshire, appeared in *Alive Now!* 23, no. 5. (Sept.-Oct. 1993): 40–45. Reprinted by permission of the author.

always looking around at the crowd but pretending not to. A couple of men wore Co-op hats and blue short-sleeved jumpsuits, the kind you get for $17.95 at K-Mart in Richardson, but you just knew it was the idea of farming they liked more than the work of it. It was the women, though, that she resented the most, the kind who are nearly happy because they have almost everything they want.

Liza had gone to enough auctions to know how it worked. The women would get a little jumpy at first and buy something too high that everybody knew was as cheap as it looked. Then they would gather themselves up and lean right into it, narrowing their eyes like a man at a poker table. They would pass the afternoon piling up the small victories they could win here, since they couldn't even play any games that mattered at home.

Billy Mitchum, Colonel Burns' assistant, was holding up a yellow Rubbermaid dishwashing pan filled with odds and ends. Liza saw that it included her lighted make-up mirror, the only trifling thing she had allowed herself during those years and maybe the only vanity she owned. Billy had trouble getting the bidding started. He finally sold the whole batch for $2.00, but not before Liza remembered the day she bought the mirror on sale at Walgreens in Memphis.

That was the time she had gotten on the bus and gone to the city by herself. Orman hadn't wanted her to go off, but of course he never did. She knew that was because he was more worried about himself than her. She had wanted to get Luke's baby shoes bronzed, though, and there wasn't any place in Richardson that could do it. It felt so good to be out on her own that day that she nearly laughed out loud when she sat down at the counter at Walgreens to order a cherry Coke and a hamburger.

That was the day she realized she was no more or less alone than she had been before Luke was killed nine years earlier in the car wreck coming home from his construction job in Jackson. She had thought her life was over then, and for a time it was. The silence between her and Orman had widened, and after a while he started talking about leaving her even though he never did. But when she got off the bus from Memphis at the one-stop store late that evening, her heart was lighter than it had been in years. It had taken her that long to pack up her sorrow and let it be.

Now Billy was holding up the guitar Orman gave Luke for his fifteenth birthday. It was just about the only thing that ever passed peaceably between them. Orman could never play it at all. He had bought it at a pawnshop in Nashville around the corner from the Opry in one of the few fanciful gestures of his life. When the tobacco dried up the next year, that's all they had to give Luke for his birthday.

Luke never really took to the guitar either, but Liza leaned back and smiled to herself as she remembered the warm spring evenings when Frank Mays would come over and sit with them on the front porch. Frank had learned a few chords from his Army buddy on the ship headed to Tunisia in late '43, and he could put them together in a moving way with tunes he had heard his father sing.

Frank was different from the rest of the men in the valley. He paid attention to things, and he listened to what she said. When she occasionally browsed in the county library in the basement of the courthouse, she noticed that his name was signed on most of the check-out cards in the back of the books.

The sun was slanting behind the house now, and the crowd had moved over to the furniture under the other sugar maple. Colonel Burns started picking up the quilts piled on the bare mattress of their old iron bed. Liza leaned forward intently, watching carefully now.

The first quilt, a double wedding ring, sold for far too little, she knew. City people were collecting quilts these days without knowing much about them, but the woman who bought this one got a lucky bargain. The second two, twin size with a green backing that Aunt Sophie had made, were in bad condition and brought about what they were worth. Then Liza drew in her breath as Colonel Burns spread out the pieced quilt top, trying awkwardly to gather under his long arms the yellow backing and polyester batting, still wrapped in cellophane, that went with it.

This was the only moment of the afternoon Liza had been anxious about. She knew it made people nervous to have her there, and her friend and neighbor Sallie Luton had offered to take her to a movie in Millerstown for the afternoon. No one except maybe Frank could have understood that the sale was oddly a relief for her. Except for the few things she had taken to the little apartment next to the nursing home in Richardson, everything she had accumulated in forty-five years of married life was disappearing this afternoon. Of what was left, only the quilt top mattered.

It was not a pattern anyone recognized because she had made it up herself. Each square had diagonal stripes in all sorts of widths and angles, and every square was different. Except for the back room curtains and a graduation dress she had made for her niece, all the pieces were remnants from shirts she had made for Luke over the nineteen years of his life.

She had started the quilt a year after he died, crazy sometimes with grief and sometimes just numb. She had read somewhere that any grief was bearable if you could tell a story about it or make a story out of it. She couldn't make a story, but she could make a quilt.

When she finally finished piecing together the top, she knew she would never put the backing on it. She had done what she needed to do. Sometimes she would spread it out on the bed, sit in her rocker, and stare at it for a long part of the afternoon. A piece here or there would help her remember a detail about Luke's life she had forgotton, and sometimes the scraps in the pattern would form new connections in her memory of him. In ways she did not fully understand, the quilt top began to solve a problem for her.

When Joey Barker asked her this morning if she wanted to sell it at the auction, she paused only a moment to confirm her decision. Yes. It was time.

Instinctively Liza wasn't sure about the woman standing behind the cot, the tall one with the expensive haircut and the pretty daughter. There was something determinedly sincere about her that didn't settle quite right. She saw the woman eye the quilts, begin to bid on the first one, but pull back after the first round or two; shake her head no on the twins; then pick up interest again when Colonel Burns reached for the quilt top. The woman entered the bidding after the first offer, nodded yes again after the confusion about whether the backing and batting went with it, and finally got it all for seven dollars.

Half an hour later, Liza remembered something. It touched her somehow that she had forgotten this one last thing. She rose from her chair and reached her right hand deep into her pocket as she looked around the crowd.

Seeing the tall woman talking with Wilma Barker, Liza walked up to her slowly. Cocking her head just right, she looked her straight in the eye. "Are you the lady who bought the quilt top?" she asked. The woman replied yes, surprised and a little confused.

Liza drew her hand out of her pocket, extended her arm directly toward the woman, and dropped two spools of yellow thread into her hand.

"Here's what it was supposed to be put together with," she said.

Liza Myatt turned and walked away. Nobody saw the quick nod she gave herself or the fine smile playing across her face.

◆ ◆

SUSAN WILTSHIRE is chair of the Department of Classical Studies and professor of classics at Vanderbilt University in Nashville, Tennessee. The author of many articles and essays in her field, she also has written three books, the most recent being *Seasons of Grief and Grace: A Sister's Story of AIDS*.

RICHARD SCHWEID

CATFISH COUNTRY

It was early in the morning when I left Clarksdale, Mississippi, headed south on Highway 49 toward the heart of the Delta. I had an eye out for my first sighting of catfish ponds, as well as for a place to get a cup of coffee. But the farther I drove, the clearer it became that it was going to be a while before I found either one. The road was nothing more than a two-lane asphalt ribbon, with drainage ditches on either side, running through vast, flat fields of cultivated soil.

Northern Mississippi is divided into two parts by the Bluff, a ridge of land that begins just across the state line in Memphis, Tennessee, and runs like a spine with a western curvature down to Vicksburg. In Mississippi, when people speak of the Delta, they do not mean the true Mississippi River delta, where the mighty river meets the sea south of New Orleans, but rather the low-lying flood plain of the Yazoo and Mississippi rivers, which lies west of the Bluff. It is a level, nearly treeless expanse of land some eighty miles wide and two hundred miles long between Memphis and Vicksburg. When the first white people settled there in the mid-1800s, it was a vast hardwood swamp that flooded each spring. The swamp was cleared, acre by acre, and the flooding was gradually controlled by levees along the rivers.

It was spring when I went to the Delta, and the fields were dry and planted. There were seemingly endless rows of dark brown dirt mounded up, carpeted with the delicate, bright green of new cotton plants barely poking through the earth's crust. There were occasional winter wheat fields coming ready to harvest: huge expanses of waist-high emerald-green plants stretching to a distant horizon, waves of wind rolling across them. Mostly, though, the land was planted in cotton. I drove past mile after mile of ploughed ground, the rows of cotton flashing by the side window of my Volkswagen van with military precision. There were no other cars on the road.

This is deep country, a rural vastness so far back from the rest of America that it feels like a foreign country. The Delta is not on the road to or from anywhere. It is one of those places that has gone its own way, with its own character, its own culture. The only animal life I saw was red-winged blackbirds. They banked up out of the drainage ditches and away from the road as my van passed. Flushed suddenly up out of the ditches, they'd come flying, vivid flashes of scarlet on the shoulders of their wings. The few signs of human life that I saw were unsettling: an occasional tar paper-and-wood shack at the edge of a field, with the ploughed ground coming right up to its walls. I would have thought these places were tool sheds had it not been for the unmistakable signs of human habitation—laundry strung up on a line between two aluminum poles at the edge of a field, or a dog on a sagging front porch scratching at its fleas. These scenes reflected a poverty more severe than that of the inner cities; the tin-roofed shacks called up a bare-bones, rural living and a doing without things that most of us consider indispensable: health, privacy, education.

I passed a gravel turn-out on the right side of the highway where there was a ramshackle little wooden cabin with the word GROCERY painted on the gable. I pulled over, got out of the van, mounted three worn wooden steps to a tilted porch, and went through a screen door into the cool darkness inside. Along one wall was an old soda pop cooler with chipped white paint and "Barq's" written in red script on its side, advertising a locally popular root beer. Next to the other wall was a low woodburning stove, and in the shadowy depths of the tiny room there was a counter. I felt eyes on me from behind it before I made out the small woman sitting there in the sprung easy chair with its ancient floral print upholstery. She was frail, with polished dark brown skin stretched tight over her birdlike bones, her fine grey hair in a plait on top of her head.

She answered my request in a deep Delta accent, slow, thick, and broad, shared by black and white, those intimate and flowing rhythms of unhurried speech as enveloping as the sweet smell of honeysuckle, speech with a resonance that wraps itself around you like smoke. "Used to have coffee in here many years ago, when I sold sandwiches and such, but there's nary a sandwich or coffee now. There's pop," she added, nodding toward the cooler, but I thanked her and left, holding out for coffee.

Farther down the road, I passed a sign telling me I had entered Tutwiler, and I took the first road to the right off the highway. It led me to a dead end in the middle of a town square surrounded by low brick buildings—all there was to downtown Tutwiler. There was a clothing store, a post office, and a hardware store, each still closed at seven in the morning. As I sat in the van and looked at the locked-up, empty town, the front door of a building across the street opened. A sign above the building's window read WONG'S SUPERMARKET. Out of the door came a tall, young black man in a white shirt and black pants. He held the door for a wizened, tiny Chinese woman, who was following behind him. I approached them on the sidewalk and addressed myself to the woman, bending down slightly to do so, "Excuse me, is there anywhere around to get a cup of coffee?"

"We're not open and don't sell coffee here, not here." "I know, but is there anywhere in town where I can buy a cup of coffee?" I asked, an edge of caffeine-deprived annoyance in my voice.

"No coffee here, we're not open yet," she said, insistently, as if I were hard of hearing or spoke some other language.

The man took pity on me. He had a vicious stutter. "Th-th-there's a Jit-jit-jit-ney Jungle down the highway. Th-th-they've got coffee."

A big, dark green Buick Electra 225 was parked at the curb, and he held the back door open for the woman. She was so small that she hardly had to duck her head to climb in the back seat. He got in front and drove away.

Sure enough, there was a Jitney Jungle convenience store less than a mile down Highway 49. I bought my coffee and watched a group of about a dozen black men of all ages, who were standing around outside waiting for someone to come by and hire labor for the day. A pickup truck pulled in, driven by a middle-aged white man wearing a green John Deere cap. He sat behind the wheel, the truck idling in neutral, while some of the men went up to his open window, presenting themselves for work. A handful of them climbed into the back of the truck, perching on the walls of its bed. The truck pulled off, leaving behind some of the men, who continued to stand, smoke, and wait to see if a day's wages would come their way.

I finished my coffee and got back on Highway 49. The road runs south, straight as a string. It wasn't long before my other morning's wish was fulfilled. Catfish ponds began to appear in fields beside the road: rectangular ponds, three times the size of football fields, sparkling in the sun. Each was surrounded by a graded levee wide enough to drive on in a pickup truck. A sign told me I was crossing the line into Sunflower County. Right on time, I thought to myself, looking at the catfish ponds. This was what I had come to see. They gleamed in the sunshine, big watery fields within fields. I was on my way to Indianola, the seat of Sunflower County, to learn about catfish farming.

Since childhood, I have been fascinated with farm ponds; the sight of them touches me in a way perhaps possible only for a city dweller, someone who loves to sit on the bank beside water and fish but who lives in too urban an environment to have a readily accessible place to do it. That there were people who actually had their own ponds was powerfully impressive to me, even as a child. Swimming pools did nothing for me, but the idea of having your own wild piece of water was remarkable. For the pond-owners, I realized, it was no big deal—a place to let cows drink and to go fishing for a little bit when there was nothing else to do; but to have such a pond on the land where one lived seemed to me like riches.

The first farm pond I ever swam in belonged to an aunt and uncle in the North Carolina country. It was full of leeches. The first time I saw it, on a childhood visit, my cousins urged me in for a swim, then stood around giggling behind their hands as I stood for a long time barefoot on the bank, toes squishing in the mud, water dripping slowly off my bathing suit as my aunt picked the black, shiny leeches off my chest, back, legs, arms, and thighs and dropped them in a pail to be left in the sunshine, and scolded her children. Each leech she picked off left a blossom of blood behind as it was pulled loose from my skin. Even with such an unpleasant initiation, I spent many an hour of subsequent visits to my relatives fishing in that pond or just sitting beside it, watching its life: the birds, snakes, frogs, turtles, and dragonflies.

I was in Sunflower County to see what a whole land of farm ponds was like, to see what kind of world could encompass hundreds of farmers harvesting the water, making their living from the water. The notion of a part of the country where substantial numbers of people spent their days farming fish fascinated me. It evoked a respectable labor that combined two of humanity's oldest occupations: fisher and farmer.

This was not my first trip to look at an aquacultural industry. I had been to southern Louisiana to see how people farmed crayfish ("crawfish" to the Cajuns) in flooded rice fields, and Martha's Vineyard, Massachusetts, to meet scientists who were growing lobsters in pens. Compared to catfish, crayfish and lobsters are small potatoes as aquaculture products. They are minor league efforts that have yet to make enough profits to guarantee long-term viability. . . .

◆ ◆

RICHARD SCHWEID is a native of Nashville who grew up in the family's retail bookstore business. A former writer for the *Nashville Tennessean*, he now makes his living as a freelance journalist. His books include *Hot Peppers* and *Barcelona: Jews, Transvestites and an Olympic Season*.

RICHARD JACKSON

HEARTLESS POEM

It is true that my heart does not exist.
It is absolutely true that the birds are not mine,
the river will not stop for me, the leaves will not
stop aiming for the very ground where I stand,
that I cannot hold the smallest amount of air
in my hands. The closed fist of the moon
punches its way through the lake.
Someone else might talk about the moon as a heart,
but that's all I'm going to say about it.
On this night when the stars begin their lies
about the light beyond them, when the young men
from Tuzla are hanging from lamp posts
in place of lights, I am here to tell you
my heart has never existed.
The only feelings I have ever heard of
take to the highway with the carts
and trucks of the other refugees.
Why do you think you need to join them?
If it were a violin my heart would not rest
between anyone's chin and shoulder. It would
sit in a pawnshop window for someone's supper.
On this night when my heart does not exist

"Heartless Poem," by Richard Jackson, appeared in *Bloomsbury Review* (Winter, 1994-95). Reprinted with permission of *Bloomsbury Review*.

I eat out of the hands of yesterday.
If it did exist, the fist of my heart would
grab the hanged man by the collar of his soul
and turn him away from his own death.
But who can say anything about the soul?
The soul, too, is just another migrant.
I have heard that the soul and the heart are
the two best scavengers of whatever past
you have discarded by the side of the road.
You can find them sneaking around in some orchard
behind the smoke a farmer uses against the frost
or plucking the hanged man's weight like a pear.
See, it is not so hard to say something about nothing.
The stars are already leaking their light into dawn.
But I can tell you that my own heart has never existed.
That's all I'm going to say about it.

Do Not Duplicate This Key

It is not commonly understood why my love is so deadly.
At the very least it uproots the trees of your heart.
It interferes with the navigation of airplanes like certain
electronic devices. It leaves a bruise in the shape of a rose.
It kisses the dreamless foreheads of stones.
Sometimes the light is wounded by my dark cliffs.
Around me even the moon must be kept on a leash.
Whenever I turn you will turn like a flower following
the day's light. Sometimes I feel like Ovid's love,
hiding behind the clouds and hill, waiting for you
to happen along some pastoral dell thinking
what I might turn you into next. Then I remember
the way he turned himself into a drooling bull to scour
the pastures of Arcadia for Europa. Forget myth, then.
Forget Ovid. According to Parcelus, God left the world
unfinished from a lack of professional interest
and only my love can complete or destroy it.
Sometimes I come home, open a bottle of Chalone
Pinot Blanc and listen to the Spin Doctors'
"How Could You Want Him (When You Could Have Me)?"
My love is so deadly because it holds a gun to every despair.
But this is not the case everywhere. In some places
the heart's shrapnel shreds our only dreams. Even
the trees refuse to believe in one another. Sometimes

it seems we've put a sheet over Love and tagged its toe.
Someone thinks it lives in the mother of the Azeri soldier,
Elkhan Husseinar, because she puts, in a jar on his grave,
the pickled heart of an enemy Armenian soldier.
This is love, she says, *this is devotion*.
Someone else assigns Love a curfew. There's the 25 year
old sniper who targets women in Sarajevo to see
what he calls "their fantastic faces of love"
as they glance towards their scrambling children.
This is when the seeds desert their furrows for rock.
This is when Despair pulls a Saturday Night Special
from its pocket and points it at the cashier in the 7-11 store.
This is when it seems each star is just a chink in our dungeon.
It is at this hour that I think entirely about you.
My love is so deadly because it wants to handcuff
the Death that has put all our lives on parole.
I myself escaped long ago from Love's orphanage.
I invented a world where the moon tips its hat at me.
I have this way of inventing our love by letting
my words rest like a hand on your thigh.
I have this way of gently biting your nipples
just to feel your body curl like the petal of a rose.
Even when I sleep you can detect my love
with the same instruments scientists use to see
the microwave afterglow of the Big Bang that created
the universe. My love is so deadly
the whole world is reinvented just as Parcelus said.
I love even the 90% of the universe that is dark matter
no light will ever embrace. Rilke died from the thorn
of a rose because he thought his love was so deadly.

My love is so deadly it picks the blossoming fruit tree
of the entire night sky. I can feel, in the deepest part
of you, the soft petals stir and fold with the dusk.
So deadly is my love
the call of the owl is thankful
to find a home in my ear. The smoke
from my cigarette thanks me for releasing it.
The tree changes into a flock of birds.
So deadly is my love other loves fall asleep in its throat.
It is a window not attached to any wall.
It is a boat whose sails are made of days and hours.
It rises like Botticelli's Venus from the sea.
This is not some idle myth.
In fact, it has been discovered that all life
probably began on the surface of deep sea bubbles
which came together in Nature's little cocktail party
carrying most of the weird little elements we are made of,
the kind of molecular sex that excites chemists.
My love is so deadly it starts spontaneous combustions.
The whole universe grows frightened for what comes next.
The sky undresses into dawn then shyly covers its starts.
Sometimes I think your love is a compass pointing away.
Sometimes I discover my love like the little chunks of moon
they dig from under the antarctic ice. My love is
so deadly it will outlast Thomas Edison's last breath
which has been kept alive in a test tube
in Henry Ford's village, Dearborn, Michigan. Even the skeptic,
David Hume, 1711-1776, begins to believe in my love.
My own steps have long since abandoned their traces.
My own love is not a key that can be duplicated.

It knocks at the door of the speakeasy in Sarajevo
and whispers the right word to a girl named Tatayana.
This, of course, was from before the war,
before everybody's hearts had been amputated from their lives.
Now my love abandons all my theories for it.
This is why my love seems so deadly.
It is scraping its feet on your doormat, about to enter.
Sometimes you have to cut your life down
out of the tree it has been hanging in. My love is
so deadly because it knows the snake that curls inside
each star like one of Van Gogh's brush strokes.
My love is so deadly because it knows the desire of the rain
for the earth, how the astronomer feels watching
the sleeping galaxies drift away from us each night.
I am listening to your own rainy voice.
I am watching the heart's barometer rise and fall.
I am watching like the spider from your easel
My love is so deadly, birds abandon the sluggish air.
Their hearts fall from trees like last year's nests.
The smoke awakens in the fire. The rose abandons the trellis.
My love is so deadly it picks the locks of your words.
And even tonight, while someone else's love tries
to scavenge a few feelings from a dumpster, while someone
lies across the exhaust grating like a spent love,
my own love steps out from my favorite bar under
a sky full of thorns, weaving
a little down the sidewalk, daring the cabs
and after-hours kamikazes like someone stumbling
back into a world redeemed by
the heart's pawn tickets, holding a pair of shoes
in one hand, a hope that breathes in the other.

◆ ◆

RICHARD JACKSON, UC Foundation Professor of English at UT-Chattanooga, is the author of three books of poetry, the most recent being *Alive All Day*. He is also the author of two critical books and an anthology of Slovene poetry and is on the international PEN Sarajevo Committee.

GAIL DAMEROW

The Invitation

Wirt examined the invitation to his son's wedding as if he had never seen it before, when in fact he'd been studying it regularly since it came in the mail day before yesterday.

If there was one thing Wirt resented, it was being put on the spot, and this invitation had him on the spot. He had no more chance than a 'possum in a cage to go to California for a wedding, or for anything else.

No matter how many different ways he added it up, flying out for the wedding would cost him two steady months cutting firewood. Three, if you counted any kind of gift. Wirt eyed the gnarled hands framing the invitation. They didn't have that much wood cutting left in them.

He knew better than to tell his son the real reason he couldn't go. The boy would send a ticket, never thinking his father didn't have cab fare from the airport, much less money for a motel. He didn't even own a suit that wasn't frayed at the cuffs or a pair of shoes that weren't sloping at the heels.

He'd be a disgrace. And an embarrassment. Why couldn't the boy see that?

He threw the invitation onto the table, watched it slide across the slick plastic tablecloth. On the front was a black and white etching of a woman in a long gown seated beside a top-hatted dandy driving a horse-drawn carriage.

Wirt snorted. Wasn't that just like a young'un to run off and live in a . . . what did the boy call that thing . . . a condo? . . . and waste all his wages boarding horses in some other fellow's barn.

Wirt heaved himself away from the table, hitched up his sagging overalls and trudged out to the barn to check on his mare. He'd tell the boy he couldn't leave because the nag was due to foal. His son wouldn't argue with that. Besides, it was the truth. Partly.

One problem solved, Wirt wrestled with the other—what to do about a gift. Anything he sent was bound to look pitiful next to the fine things sure to come from *her* side.

If he had all the money in the world, Wirt wouldn't know what kind of gift to get.

The boy had left home out of high school. Grew up in the army. When his hitch was up, instead of coming home he'd headed west to California to make his fortune.

Not that Wirt could blame him. Working the farm had never been easy, and the income wasn't worth spit. No, he couldn't blame anyone for backing away from rocks and clay and uncooperative weather. Wirt himself couldn't say what it was that bound him to the land.

He entered the barn and the spotted mare nuzzled his shoulder in greeting. He rubbed her neck and whispered into her ear, "What kind of world is it when your only son lives clear across the country?" The mare tossed her head and nickered in sympathy.

"Leastwise he calls every week, don't he, girl?"

Wirt led his horse up the grassy knoll, lush with spring fescue. While she grazed, his eyes wandered down the honeysuckled fence row dividing the pasture from the poplar forest beyond. They'd spent many an hour flushing rabbits here, he and his son. He could still picture the kid's happy grin when he bagged a cottontail for supper.

The mare flicked her tail and moved away. Wirt directed his steely gaze over the hollow to the greening poplars covering the distant hills beyond. In all the world, this was his favorite spot.

"Should have built here, back when me and Eta was starting out," he told the mare. But she was munching grass now, too busy to listen.

No use thinking on it, Wirt reasoned. He'd lived out his life. Eta was gone. So was the boy, in his own way. The house, the barn, the fences—all were running down. He was only one man. One tired, slow old man. Someday the place would grow up to weeds, like so many of the neighbors' had.

"What's the use of keeping a place up," he asked the mare, "if your boy's off in California, fixin' to marry some strange woman?"

The mare raised her head and watched idly as Wirt made his way back toward the house. He got as far as the old Chevy truck and paused in sudden thought. He turned and studied the knoll through clear grey eyes. The mare had gone back to nibbling grass and flicking her tail agianst flies.

Reaching a decision, Wirt climbed into the rusting pickup and searched the seat for keys. The old girl started on the first try. He patted the dash affectionately and steered down the dusty road toward town. There he'd have papers drawn, deeding his son half the farm—the half that included the knoll.

He was certain the boy would resent the gift, take it as rebuke for not having stayed home where he belonged. But Wirt could see no choice. He had nothing else to offer. It was the land or nothing, and he couldn't live with nothing.

After the attorney had done his work, Wirt stopped at the drugstore and picked out a fancy card to enclose the deed in. Mailing it off gave him a great sense of satisfaction, even though he felt sure there'd be trouble yet to come.

He was sitting at the table, nursing a cup of coffee and wondering how to make things right, when the inevitable call came from California.

"Dad?"

"Hello, son."

"Dad, it always amazes me how you know the right thing to do."

"Well."

"We never dared dream of owning land. Dad, we're coming home."

◆ ◆

GAIL DAMEROW, a native of Colorado, came to Tennessee in 1981 and now lives on a small farm in Jackson County. She is the editor of *Rural Heritage*, an international bimonthly magazine for devotees of draft-animal power.

ARTHUR SMITH

After Dinner with a Beautiful Woman, I Wade into the Rolling Tennessee

OK, I'll be a fool for you, for now, head over
and into—sung, usually,

Those things too stupid to be said, and here I am,
living out a love letter with

Anthems in my heart—
the clamor of you, of blade and blossom

Slick on a rumpled hillside and the river running
high with the summer rains—

The physical world no longer
what I bicker with

To keep back some imagined
horror of the truth, but rather,

Every moment now with you, the moments freed and tumbling,
and no one wistful on the bank waving or counting.

"After Dinner with a Beautiful Woman, I Wade into the Rolling Tennessee," by Arthur Smith, appeared in *Crazyhorse* 42 (Spring, 1992). Reprinted by permission of the author.

Kudzu in Winter

Nothing as dead as, dead-beat
Beaten back—vines like pylons
Braided limb to limb, rigging

On a ghost ship, the dead and living
Webbed as far as the eye can see—
Fog on the hills, and cabled pines,

And a few stumps like dock pilings
After the dock's rotted and the engines
Everywhere have blown, and the heat's

Seeped out and is gone, the silence
Louder than the engines ever were.
—And whatever being right had to do

With anything, and whatever beauty,
What on earth made me think it wouldn't be
Just like this at the heart of winter—

Everything not bitten back burned
With cold, and everything not burned
With the cold feeding from it?

◆ ◆

ARTHUR SMITH, a native of California, is associate professor of English at the University of Tennessee at Knoxville. He has won a National Endowment for the Humanities Creative Writing Fellowship, two Pushcart Prizes (XI and XIII), and the Theodore Morrison Fellowship in Poetry for the 1987 Bread Loaf Writers' Conference. His poetry has appeared in such magazines and journals as *The Nation*, the *New Yorker*, *Georgia Review*, *Poetry*, and *Kenyon Review*.

LISA ALTHER

FROM *FIVE MINUTES IN HEAVEN*

While Jude watched from the kitchen doorway, Mr. Starnes, in faded overalls and clay-caked work boots, got out of a rusted red pickup truck and lifted a burlap-wrapped ham from the back. Jude grimaced. Clementine would take slices off it and soak them in water to get the salt out, and Jude and her father would have to eat it with grits and biscuits for the rest of their lives. Mrs. Starnes, wearing a floral housedress and leather oxfords with thin, white socks, carried a foil wrapped cake. Since Clementine had already gone home to Riverbend for the night, Jude went out on the back porch to greet them.

"My dad's on the phone right now. He'll be out presently."

"My gracious, Jude, haven't you grown up, now!" said Mrs. Starnes. Her hairdo looked as though she'd removed her rollers and forgotten to comb out the hair.

"Yessum."

"I declare, if you don't look just like your daddy," said Mr. Starnes, propping one boot against the bottom porch step.

Jude frowned, preferring to look like her mother, since her father was nearly bald. Mr. Starnes's boot smelled of manure.

"Where's your shirt at tonight, honey?" asked Mrs. Starnes.

Jude shrugged, crossing her arms over her scrawny chest. "It's too hot."

"I'll bet you a dime you won't run around without no shirt in a few years here," chuckled Mr. Starnes. His eyes were as washed-out as his overalls, like clear cat's-eye marbles.

It had rained at the end of the afternoon, forked tongues of lightning striking the distant mountaintops as though the sky were a lake swarming with angry cottonmouths. Then, as the sun shone through a gap in the banks of black clouds, a rainbow had appeared, arcing across the river right down into Mr. Starnes's tobacco shed. At Sunday school, the preacher said a rainbow was God's proof that, even after trying to drown everybody for being so wicked, He forgave them. Sometimes God acted like a big baby.

But now the sky had cleared and the sun had set, turning the faraway mountains the color of grape jelly. Bullfrogs had started to croak in the reeds along the riverbank and fireflies were flickering like birthday candles among the leafy branches of the sweet gums in the valley below.

"That daddy of yours," said Mrs. Starnes, "we think he's pretty special."

"Yessum," said Jude. Now she'd have to hear about each stitch her father and grandfather had sewn in these people's mutilated bodies, each ancestor whose life they'd saved by operating by lantern light with a carving knife on a kitchen table in a remote mountain cabin during a thunderstorm, after a journey across a swollen creek on horseback in the middle of a midwinter night.

"Yessir," said Mr. Starnes, "I recollect the day my paw lost his arm in the combine. . . ."

Jude's father appeared in the doorway in his usual white dress shirt, open at the throat, sleeves rolled to the elbows. Sighing with relief, Jude picked up the foil cake from the porch floor. "Thank you, Mrs. Starnes. My daddy and me loves your cakes." Sniffing the foil, she detected caramel frosting, her favorite.

Her father looked at her with a raised eyebrow to indicate that she'd made a grammatical mistake. As she carried the cake into the kitchen and cut herself a large slice, she tried to figure out what it was. Shrugging, she went into the back hall, where she'd been playing Ocean Liner, which Molly had taught her that afternoon. They'd pasted numbers on all the doors for cabins. Striding down the hallway munching her cake, she lurched from side to side on her peg leg. A storm was brewing in the nor'west and it was time to batten down the hatches, whatever they might be. She steadied herself with her free hand against the cases that held her father's arrowhead collection. On his days off, they drove the Jeep down into the valley and dug up the moist black silt by the river. As they sifted the soil, he told her about the people who had lived in the valley long ago—the Mound Builders, the Hopewells, the Copena, the Cherokees, each tribe replacing the previous one, all the way back to the dawn of time, when the valley had formed the floor of an inland ocean full of bizarre sea creatures. When the ocean dried up, the Great Buzzard swooped down from heaven to scoop out the mountain coves with its wing tips.

The arrowheads and grinding stones had been made by the Nunnehi, the Cherokee Immortals, Jude's ancestors who lived underneath the mountains and at the bottom of the river and who came to help their descendants when they were in trouble. In autumn, when the whining winds from the north whirled the leaves off the trees, you could sometimes hear them murmuring to one another in the Wildwoods. And in the summer when you cast your line into the river for fish, if it got snagged, you knew the Nunnehi had grabbed it just to remind you that they were always there. And sometimes when the water was really calm and the breeze stirred tiny corduroy ripples across its surface, you could catch a glimpse of the roofs of their houses on the river floor.

As the Starnes's truck pulled away, Jude's father took her sticky hand to lead her into the den, unaware that the swells were running high and their ship was about to capsize. "My daddy and *I love* your cakes," he said. After turning on the radio, he sank into his brown leather armchair. John Cameron Swayze was talking about soldiers being brainwashed by the Communists in Korea. "Oh, Lord." her father said with a sigh. "Poor, suffering humanity."

"Why do they always bring us those awful hams?" asked Jude.

"That's how they're paying me for Mr. Starnes's appendectomy."

"Money would be nicer." She stroked the back of his chair. The leather was crazed with age cracks like the inside of an ice cube.

"No doubt. But they don't have any. Besides, some people consider country ham a delicacy."

"Not me."

"Yes, I know." He smiled.

"Daddy, why are some people so mean?" Jude straddled the arm of his chair, facing the back. It was her new horse, named Wild Child. The other arm was Molly's, which she'd named Blaze. That afternoon, they had been lassoing Molly's boxer, Sidney, in midgallop with pieces of Clementine's clothesline. Time after time, they played "Git Along, Little Doggie" on the record player—until Clementine marched in and turned it off, announcing, "Miss Judith, if I hear 'yippy tie yay, tie yo' one more time, I gonna bust all your daddy's furniture into firewood and chase y'all round the backyard with a carving knife." Impressed, the girls had switched to Ocean Liner.

"Well, I guess they're mean because they're unhappy."

"But you're unhappy, and you're not mean."

He looked at her. "What makes you think I'm unhappy, baby?"

"Because you miss Momma."

He frowned and lowered his head. "That's true. But I used to be happy when she was here. Maybe that's the difference. People who've never been happy are mean. The rest of us are just sad."

She could smell his aftershave lotion, like cinnamon toast. Leaning over, she licked his cheek. The stiff hairs prickled her tongue and the cinnamon lotion tasted disappointingly bitter, canceling out the sweetness of the caramel frosting.

"Don't, Jude," he said, frowning and wiping his cheek with his hand. "That tickles."

Wrinkling her nose, Jude tried to scrub the terrible taste off her tongue with the back of her hand. Then Wild Child reared, hurling her off his back and into her father's lap. Leaning her head against his chest, she shoved a thumb into her mouth and felt his heart thudding against her cheek like a frog's throat.

"Baby, don't suck your thumb, please. It'll push your front teeth out. You'll look like Bugs Bunny."

Jude giggled.

"Don't you think you should wear a shirt?" he asked. "You're getting to be a big girl now." He patted her pale smooth belly.

"I don't want to be a girl."

"How come?"

"Girls are too boring."

"So you want to be a boy?"

"No. Boys are too scary."

"Well, what do you want to be, then?"

"I want to be in heaven with my momma."

LISA ALTHER, who now lives and writes in Vermont, is a native of Kingsport. The first of her novels, the 1976 bestseller *Kinflicks*, was loosely based on her experiences in her hometown. Her most recent novel is *Five Minutes in Heaven*.

F. LYNNE BACHLEDA

REPORT FROM INSIDE THE LORRAINE: WHAT'S CIVIL ABOUT THE NATIONAL CIVIL RIGHTS MUSEUM?

Like Dealey Plaza in Dallas, the Lorraine Motel in Memphis will forever bear a spiritual bloodstain. No amount of whitewash, abrasive, or polish will ever redeem the horror of the cold-blooded murder that occurred there on April 4, 1968, when James Earl Ray fired on thirty-nine-year-old Dr. Martin Luther King, Jr., as he stood on the motel's second-floor balcony.

At the site of the Lorraine, however, the $9.25 million National Civil Rights Museum (NCRM) nobly attempts to transform a spot of senseless death into coherent inspiration. The museum project has soaked in skepticism, jealousy, and controversy for years. Poor people were turned out of their homes; a lot of money was spent on a minority-favored shrine.

As it turns out, it was arguably both a good sacrifice of housing and a proper investment of Tennessee tax dollars. Other low-income housing exists in the city; some of the exhibits utilize the latest in dynamic museum techniques; and the tourist appeal can only boost a Memphis that seems to need any form of economic aid. Most importantly, here is a story that needed telling in permanent exhibit form—an interpretation of civil rights history in the United States of America over the last century and a half.

Unswervingly, King's life consecration adds a prevailing silent power that further exalts the stories in the displays. Those stories, and there are a multitude of them, are not simply of Martin Luther King, Jr. Rather they are of the innumerable efforts, including other sacrificed lives and livelihoods, that produced the triumphs of the civil rights movement.

The museum begins, not at the assassination site on the balcony of the Lorraine, but at street level. The massive, black, sky-lit sculpture in the entrance by Michael

"Report from Inside the Lorraine: What's Civil About the National Civil Rights Museum?" by F. Lynne Bachleda, appeared in *Number: An Independent Quarterly of the Visual Arts* (Memphis, Tenn.), *Fifteen*, vol. 4, no. 3 (Fall, 1991): 31–32. Reprinted by permission of the author.

Pavlovsky, its struggling figures spiraling upward in relief, is an obvious indication that, in the main, this is a story told about African Americans and their relentless contentions to be free. At first glance, the polished black granite floor surrounding the sculpture seems to echo the same refrain. But in that blackness, there is also whiteness, which shines by turns, as metaphor. Both parts of the whole, both races, are present.

The exhibit path is absorbingly labyrinthine and spiraling. The interpretation of the early years of the movement, especially, here beginning in the mid-1800s, relies heavily on text and photographic reproductions rather than on three-dimensional artifacts to tell the story.

This is a museum of many paper artifacts, obvious for their ordinary character. That is appropriate. The battle for civil rights has no militaristic legacy of uniforms, cannon, maps, and proud portraits of conquering generals. Preserved here are legal briefs and petitions; calls to meetings in churches; song sheets from organizing workshops at the Highlander Center in Tennessee (where black and white lived and worked together in an extraordinary fashion); FBI sheets for the three missing voter registration workers; and scruffy typewritten newsletters that carried the high impact, real-life drama of the Montgomerys, Selmas, and Little Rocks. The paper artifacts, so often so plain, are curiously stubborn beyond their fragile composition.

Greater dynamic value, however, lies in the large installations that include a full-scale lunchcounter, two buses (a vintage Montgomery city bus and a Greyhound literally burned out to recall the fire-bombed Freedom Rides), and a late 1960s Memphis garbage truck, now very rare—only six exist.

The themes of the lunchcounter, the Montgomery bus, and the garbage workers' strike (the reason why King was in Memphis) share a fast-spreading museum exhibit technique—the use of monochromatic (here a compromise grey), full-scale human models. Like a jump into hyperspace, these figures leave mannequins and dummies in the dust of the past. Far beyond specific faces, the detailing includes wrinkles, differentiated fingernails, body hair, and clothing specifics that convey texture and weight to an amazing degree. These are complemented by similarly finely reproduced jewelry items like wrist watches, eyeglasses, and necklaces, the individual links of which are easy to discern. The net effect is that these "individuals" are startlingly and eerily "real."

At the lunch counter interpreting the sit-in demonstrations, visitors will be able to sit at the counter across from the dignified, racially mixed protestors. Working in the museum to catalog the artifacts before it opened to the public, I took advantage of the opportunity to stand behind the sit-in figures alongside their historical counterparts, two silently jeering hecklers. With a chill, I realized how vulnerable were the necks and backs of the sit-in demonstrators, how much courage it must have taken to sit facing forward, not knowing what sort of unseen abuse might be coming next.

There are various accounts of why Rosa Parks decided she had had enough of riding in the back of the bus. Some say she was just tired; some say she attended a workshop at Highlander and that the event was a staged, planned act of defiance. The point is, she did take a seat in the forbidden white zone, thereby initiating the first great success of the movement—the Montgomery bus boycott. As I boarded a real bus, passing the grey driver figure, I could see her sitting alone and still, somehow both meek and resolute. To exit the bus exhibit, I walked within inches of her plaster representation.

(It does closely resemble her.) Strangely, dignity radiated from the inanimate figure.

The garbage workers' strike exhibit can be viewed from two levels in the museum—head on and looking down—symbolic, perhaps, of the perspectives of the workers and the people of Memphis. A column of the haunting grey figures of African-American men with bold red and white reproduction signs hanging around their necks proclaim the obvious and the overlooked: "I AM A MAN." Fascinating from the point of view of a museum environment, the striking protestors are surrounded by "clean" garbage.

With subtlety, the exhibits climb, and at the physical and sacrificial apex of the museum are two rooms recreated from the Lorraine Motel. One is a pristine bedroom. The other—full of coffee cups, ashtrays, glasses, newspapers—is the site of an informal meeting among King, Jesse Jackson, and Ralph Abernathy. Originally side by side, the rooms have been separated and a glass wall in each allows examination.

The furniture pieces in both rooms are originals from the Lorraine, although the bedspreads, curtains, and rugs are reproductions. The headboard in King's room is purported to be the one that he rested against. From a ghostly and vivid photograph, the Reverend Doctor looked straight at me from against what seems to be that very same headboard.

Even with the room air-conditioner on, King's room feels too quiet. An unearthly commonness lingers. Looking out from the window, I could see the wreath that commemorates his fateful place of death, the "D'ARMY IS A SELL-OUT" banner (referring to D'Army Bailey, a key backer of the museum effort and chairman of the board of its foundation, which will operate the completed facility), the sporadic spurt of white joggers who seem to sail past, and the perennial stream of tourists of all races who slow or even stop to take snapshots, waiting for the chance to go inside.

For the room of a man of such courage, leadership, and oratory, King's is painfully plain, even near tacky, with its now-dated minimal faux French Provincial furniture. But, in a way, the unadorned ordinariness underscores the point that King was just a man, just a single human being, in most ways like the thousands of others whose stories also are told here, the people who made the civil rights movement move forward.

From King's room I watched as a worker installed a foot-square section of concrete from the original balcony into the re-poured sidewalk behind the death-venerating wreath. I could discern the faint bloodstain still there more than twenty years later. I felt intensely and uniquely American—fascinated, horrified, sad, and hopeful. In short, I felt so much, I hardly knew what I felt.

Leaving Dr. King's bedroom quieter than when I had entered it, I encountered a handsome dark African-American man who was touching up the grey paint around the outside wall of King's room. White even for a white woman, I passed in stunned contemplation, murmuring to him, "This is a very powerful place." With a calm reflecting his assurance and pride, he replied softly and even tenderly: "Yes, it is."

"Take it easy," I choked out, overcome with old-fashioned gratitude and inspiration, as I turned to drive back to Nashville.

"You, too."

From the outside, it might be tempting to write off the NCRM as a tasteless testament to the site of a single martyr. From the inside, it's clear that people are going to change for the better for having been here. We humans need to know more about this kind of courage, manifested in thousands of American citizens who said, "This is wrong, and it's got to change. Starting with me."

That's what's civil about the National Civil Rights Museum.

◆ ◆

F. LYNNE BACHLEDA is a freelance researcher and writer in Nashville. A religion reviewer for *Publisher's Weekly*, she also writes for various regional and national visual and media arts publications. She wrote the historical interpretation for the Tennessee Bicentennial Mall.

WYATT PRUNTY

THE WILD HORSES

The horses imagined by a boy
Who cannot get himself to sleep
Are grazing so deep within a story
He cannot say what it means to keep
Such things inside and at a distance;
They are a silent governance
He feels but cannot name.
The horses change, and are the same.
They run miles farther than the meadows
In which he sees them run. They have no shadows,
Are unceasing, and they never die.
What he feels when watching them is like a cry
Heard somewhere else, and neither pain
Nor happiness in it, but sustained
Like a long note played in an empty room.
And that is how he waits for sleep, which soon
Takes him deeper than the fastest animal
As he tunnels clockwise in a fall,
The meadows rising through him, then gone
Somewhere above, until alone
He sees the horses turn in one long curve

That rounds them back where nothing moves,
And he knows that they were always blind,
Running from what they heard each time
The wind would shift, running away
Because they could not see their way.

To him, the horses are beautiful and sad;
They are a celebration made
Out of the way they end, begin again,
A morning's bright imperative sustained
Long after dark. They are a walling out
By looking in, what opens when he shuts
His eyes, the body's quiet allegory
By which it knows itself, a story
Told against the body that it cannot see.
The horses run because they're free
And incomplete, while poised somewhere between
The half-light in the hall and what he's seen
Inside, the boy wakes or sleeps, or turns against
His sleep, naming a larger self that rests
Invisibly, yet in sight of what it sees,
Rests without feeling, in the calculated ease
Of someone small, afraid, and fragile,
Alone and looking out, flexed but agile.

Learning the Bicycle

For Heather

The older children pedal past
Stable as little gyros, spinning hard
To supper, bath, and bed, until at last
We also quit, silent and tired
Beside the darkening yard where trees
Now shadow up instead of down.
Their predictable lengths can only tease
Her as, head lowered, she walks her bike alone
Somewhere between her wanting to ride
And her certainty she will always fall.

Tomorrow, though I will run behind,
Arms out to catch her, she'll tilt then balance wide
Of my reach, till distance makes her small,
Smaller, beyond the place I stop and know
That to teach her I had to follow
And when she learned I had to let her go.

A Note of Thanks

Wallet stolen, so we must end our stay.
Then, while checking out, the wallet reappears
With an unsigned note saying, "Please forgive me;
This is an illness I have fought for years,
And for which you've suffered innocently.
P.S. I hope you haven't phoned about the cards."
I wave the wallet so my wife will see.
Smiling, she hangs up, and smiling she regards
The broad array of others passing by,
Each now special and uniquely understood.
We go back to our unmade room and laugh,
Happily agreeing that the names for "good"
Are not quite adequate and that each combines
Superlatives we but rarely think.
For the next three nights we drink a better wine.
And everyday we go back through to check
The shops, buying what before had cost too much,
As if now Christmas and birthdays were planned
Years in advance. We watch others and are touched
To see how their faces are a dead-panned
Generality, holding close
The wishes and desires by which we all are gripped.

"A Note of Thanks," from *The Run of the House*, by Wyatt Prunty (Baltimore, Md.: Johns Hopkins University Press, 1993), 26.

All charities seem practical to us,
All waiters deserving of a bigger tip.
And, though we counter such an urge,
We start to think we'd like to meet the thief,
To shake the hand of self-reforming courage
That somehow censored a former disbelief.

Then we are home and leafing through the bills
Sent us from an unknown world of pleasure;
One of us likes cheap perfume; the other thrills
Over shoes, fedoras, expensive dinners;
There are massage parlors and videos,
Magazines, sunglasses, pharmaceuticals,
Long distance calls, a host of curios,
Gallons of booze. . . . Only now we make our call.
But then, on hold, we go on sifting through
The mail till turning up a postcard view
Of our hotel. Flipping it and drawing blanks,
We read, "So much enjoyed my stay with you
I thought I ought to jot a note of thanks."

• •

WYATT PRUNTY's poems and essays have appeared in such periodicals as the *New Yorker*, the *New Republic*, *American Scholar*, *Parnassus*, the *New Criterion*, *Boulevard*, and the *Yale*, *Southern*, *Georgia*, and *Sewanee* reviews. He is the author of five volumes of poetry. Notably, *Fallen from the Symboled World* was published by Oxford University Press in 1990. He currently serves as Carlton Professor of English at Sewanee, where he teaches poetry writing and directs the Sewanee Writers' Conference.

JOHN BAIRD

DEATH AND CANDLEWAX

There was once a summer when it rained every day. No one else minded; they welcomed wet weather, even prayed for it occasionally. Only small children resented rain and the confinement that went with it. I moped through the bedroom window and watched puddles grow in the chicken yard behind the house.

Aunt Mabel had it all figured out and offered instruction on the subject: "God sends the rain and you should learn to be grateful for it."

I had studied all of my funny books to the point of memorization and was incredibly bored. Mammaw and Aunt Mabel were canning tomatoes and had been at it all day, eclipsing any chance they would play Chinese Checkers or Old Maid, and I was left to amuse myself. When I wandered aimlessly through the kitchen, Aunt Mabel grabbed me by the shirt sleeve and undertook to improve my attitude.

"This will make the watermelons," she observed. "You love watermelon."

Truly I did, but it was within the imagination to want watermelon and clear skies as well.

It was bad enough that the day had been lost to thunderstorms. That tragedy was complicated by the revelation that the entire household would overdress and spend intolerable hours at O'Malley's Mortuary. I suppose I should have been glad to lose only one day and not two. The wake could just as easily been held on a pretty afternoon and ruined it as well. I was not consoled, though.

My meanderings through the kitchen were noticed about the dozenth time. Normally I knew better than to complain of nothing to do; something totally unpleasant would be arranged—like breaking green beans. I knew there were no beans in the house, but Mammaw was resourceful and could always come up with something.

"Why don't you go ahead and give him a bath," she told Aunt Mabel. "Maybe he'll sit still for twenty minutes while we get ready."

"I don't need a bath," I protested. "I haven't done nothin' to get dirty."

"Anything," they said in chorus, and soon I was seated resignedly in the bottom of

Mammaw's big iron bathtub with Aunt Mabel singing hymns and getting shampoo in my eyes.

"Be still," she demanded. "You can't go to the funeral home looking like a street waif."

As far as I was concerned, there was precious little point in going to the funeral home in the first place. The neighbor woman was dead, wasn't she? From what little I knew of the matter, she could hardly benefit from visitors. But it was not up to me: almost nothing was.

So I sat in the middle of the back seat of Pappaw's Studebaker between the old women and watched the sun try to come out through episodic showers. Mammaw had an expansive behind, and Aunt Mabel's spread out luxuriantly over the mohair until there was scarcely room for me in the car.

"Looks like it's going to storm again before we get to town," Uncle Ambrose suggested, and I sank dejectedly into the cushion.

He was right, and when Pappaw stopped at the curb to let us out, the drops were large and resonant against the roof of the Studebaker. Once outside, I was seized by both hands and went skipping up the steps between the women, pulled like a marionette on strings and fearing my shoulders would dislocate before we got inside.

Aunt Mabel always stank of lilacs, and Mammaw fancied jasmine. There had barely been time to habituate to their cologne in the confines of the sedan, and I knew that the mortician's anteroom would be as intense as a greenhouse with cut flowers and cosmetics. Why did people want to smell like flowers? Personally, I preferred dry straw and cow manure, but no one had thought to bottle it.

We entered the mortuary looking like a pair of crows quarrelling over the carcass of a dead rabbit. Someone opened the door from the inside, and we were absorbed by the crowd.

There was an immediate reception by the embalmer's wife, a matronly fat woman about the same age as Mammaw. She had an antiseptic air and was always in an attitude of dismay because the funeral home was full of dead people. Actually, I suppose she would have been even more discomfited had it not been.

"And how old is he now?" Mrs. O'Malley sniffed. I could have told her myself, but no one seemed to value my opinion on the subject.

"Almost six," Mammaw advised her.

"And will he go to school this year?"

That seemed likely enough; I was certainly being threatened with it.

"His mother wants him to start, but we all think he should wait."

I wondered if a child anywhere had ever had his own judgment considered in such matters: no, of course not.

"My granddaughter starts this year."

"I haven't seen her in ages," Aunt Mabel interjected. "She can't be old enough to start school."

"You just wait here," Mrs. O'Malley enjoined and disappeared from the foyer.

It was only the first instance of what I knew was going to be an insufferable several hours. Mammaw and Aunt Mabel were already gravitating toward the appropriate parlor, impatient to join the throng of kindred souls who had convened there. The room would be tightly packed with lacquer-haired, middle-aged women, and every one of them would accost me that evening repeating the same inane nonsense that had already begun: "How old is he?" and "Does he go to school yet?" I should have worn a sign around my neck: "Six; not yet, lady." Those who had plagued me long enough would consider themselves familiar and demand attention. I could envision it already: pancaked and rouged cheeks, heavy red lipstick that got all over you, noses laden with camphor-soaked fever blisters. And you had to oblige them, it was simple good manners. The dead woman had been typical of the lot.

"Give me a hug and a kiss and I'll give you a wintergreen Lifesaver."

I hated wintergreen and would not have kissed her voluntarily for all the candy in East Tennessee.

"Go on, now, give her a kiss; isn't that nice," Mammaw would insist, and I would aim for the high point of the jawbone, seeking to outmaneuver the minty, scarlet orifice. But there really was no escape.

Pappaw and Uncle Ambrose came in behind us, having secured the Studebaker. They had tarried in the parking lot long enough to have a nip, and the bourbon was discernible on their breath even above the plethora of odors in the foyer. Aunt Mabel must have perceived it also, as she gave the men a hard look. We had lingered in the vestibule as long as was appropriate, and Mammaw seemed anxious to get into the parlor and talk about the dead woman. She was fussing over the register on the dais when Mrs. O'Malley returned.

"This is my granddaughter, Sally," she beamed, drawing the reluctant child into the foyer.

Salvation! Someone my own age and even better. Sally energized from behind her grandmother and our eyes met. I was smitten instantly, like never before or since.

She was radiant, with soft, umber hair pulled away from her face and secured above her ears and green eyes that reflected electrically emerald highlights. Sally was dressed for the occasion in a brown and yellow cotton dress and patent shoes accented by white knee socks. The nearest I had seen to that pretty was a day-old Hereford, and the calf did not even come close. I was in love. It was wonderful.

And all of my affections were immediately reciprocated. Sally was made up for the receiving line, but I saw through the deception at once. Her arms and legs were tanned about the same shade as my own. One knee was freshly skinned and Mercurochromed. There were a dozen very distinct freckles across the bridge of her nose. This was a creature who spent no more time languishing around a funeral parlor than was absolutely required of her. It struck me that she was not entirely comfortable in her finery and would have much preferred jeans or pedal-pushers. Then the eyes flashed green and the corners of her mouth turned up. We were being introduced, but I did not hear the particulars and neither, I think, did she. It was an immediate fusion of spirits; the moment was rapturous. She loved me, too!

If beauty were not enough, Sally was resourceful as well. We had barely seen one another's hearts when she came directly to my rescue. Mammaw and Aunt Mabel seemed startled when the little girl grabbed my hand and took me away with her. There was a moment of contention, but Sally meant to have her way and no objections could preclude it.

"Wait," Mammaw insisted, then gave up: "Oh, all right, but play quietly. Go upstairs and don't get dirty. We'll only be here a few minutes."

I knew perfectly well they would be a minimum of two hours. It no longer mattered; they could celebrate death all evening for all I cared now.

Then we were away, hurrying down the central hallway of the mortuary. The stairwell to the upstairs living quarters was at the end of the hall just in front of the back porch screen. We were about to go up when the complexity of the building caught my attention. Besides the ground floor, with its multiple parlors, there was an annex built onto the rear of the house. The garage that housed the mortician's hearse and flower truck was joined to the dwelling by a windowless isthmus and had two levels. It was unique architecture and must have been designed for some particular purpose.

"What's that?" I wondered aloud, tugging at Sally's grip before she could lead me upstairs.

"That's where they 'balm people," she revealed. "You have to be 'balmed before you're ready to be dead. Do you wanna see?"

Getting bombed seemed an odious prospect. But if Sally had no fear, neither did I. Her mouth tightened into a secretive line and her eyes got bigger. She fairly glowed, assuming the seductive demeanor that I would eventually learn to cherish in naughty little girls of all ages.

"C'mon," she urged and ushered me willingly through the screened door.

The laboratory was attainable via an exterior staircase built onto the back porch. We entered a warehouse of caskets and vaults representing all price ranges. A few were open, exposing white linen and diminutive pillows. It was the first time I had seen a coffin empty. Sally hurried through the storeroom to an imposing steel door that I figured was the mysterious room above the garage. The door was heavy and the hinges moaned.

Inside was a narrow stainless table with a high-intensity light just above it. The floor was tiled and the walls lined with cabinets. Everything was cold and sterile with a faint taste of formalin in the air.

"This is the place," Sally said.

"How do they bomb people in here?"

"They put you on the table and 'balm you."

She climbed upon the gurney and pointed out an apparatus suspended from the ceiling. Apparently bombs did not require to fall very far. I wondered if they closed the door first and how much noise the procedure made.

"What good does it do to bomb dead people?" I questioned.

"They have to be 'balmed," she insisted.

We examined the contents of the laboratory at some length. There was a refrigerated closet-like appliance at one end of the room. Sally opened the door and chilled air rushed out.

"No one here," she noted. "Mrs. Schultz was here yesterday, but they 'balmed her and took her downstairs."

Now I was skeptical. You awaited bombing in the icebox? Anomalies multiplied in my mind.

"C'mon," Sally said, "we'll go see Mrs. Schultz."

So we did, creeping downstairs to discover the funeral crowd now packed into the chapel on the west side of the mortuary. Mrs. Schultz was laid out in the east parlor and would not be eulogized until the following day.

She was an elderly woman, emaciated in death. The hands were folded talon-like at her waist and were the color of kindergarten paste. Sally fetched a folding chair, and we stood on it together with an arm around each other for support.

Mrs. Schultz did not look as though bombs had fallen on her, but she certainly did look dead.

"Touch her," Sally encouraged and guided my hand to the face of the corpse.

The skin was cool and the consistency of the flesh unnatural.

"She's not really there; she's gone to Jesus."

The body lacked luster and was totally, completely inanimate. No, Mrs. Schultz was not there, wherever else she might have gone. I pressed a finger against her mouth, but the lips would not separate even with pressure. All I managed to accomplish was to smear her lipstick.

"The eyes won't open either," Sally advised, and we tried them too, feeling the round orbs under the lids and ruining the careful makeup.

"She looks like she's made outta wax." I observed, and then revelation overwhelmed me: *of course, wax*!

Here was a substance I was familiar with. Every Christmas, Aunt Mabel got out her molds and cast little evergreens and angels with cotton wicks. Mrs. Schultz looked fabricated. Bombing simply converted flesh to wax.

Granted, Mammaw said that you turned to dust when you died, but she was mistaken. Mrs. Schultz was clearly wax, not dust: just like the Christmas candles Aunt Mabel made. Then I thought of the museum and my theorizing was confirmed.

It was in Gatlinburg—a biblical wax museum. Every summer I was dragged through it several times. Regardless of who came to visit, that was where Mammaw wanted to take them. If the Anti-Christ himself had come to Sunday dinner, she would doubtlessly have insisted on driving him to Gatlinburg to see a wax Jesus afterward.

Actually, you would see about a dozen wax Jesuses. He was the central figure in every scene, surrounded by molded disciples or pharisees. I had never paid much attention to the attraction, wanting only to have the tour over with so I could change into comfortable clothes and get back to the barnyard or the creek bank as soon as possible. Standing there with Sally, I wished I had attended more closely to the secondary characters in the biblical garden's exhibition. Were they dead?

You died and were changed into wax and went to be with Jesus. A semblance of rational sense was emerging from chaos. I disliked the museum, but it was certain that I would visit it again soon. Then I would pay heed to the anonymous background figures, fully expecting to see Mrs. Schultz cast as a bit player among the multitude that Jesus fed. I took another close look at the body so I would not forget her features. Hopefully, no craftsman would think to fix that accipitrine nose before she went to Gatlinburg. I knew I would recognize it even in a crowd.

Sally's mischievous air had returned. It was intoxicating.

"C'mon," she said.

We hastened back to the storeroom and began to practice being dead. Sally found talcum powder and we patted each other ashen. The effect was not exactly correct.

"We won't look right 'til we're 'balmed," she lamented.

"Get in and le'mme see how you look," I invited, and Sally thought it a splendid idea. She climbed a packing crate and eased herself into a large black sarcophagus with snowy linen. I felt a pang of remorse as she lay back in that attitude of finality the dead always adopted.

Sally was obviously not dead. Though heavily powdered her face was animate, and I could detect her breathing. Even so, it was worrisome, and soon I begged her to open her eyes and be vibrant again. My concern earned me that addictive smile.

"Now le'mme look at you," she said, and we changed places. The spectacle had much the same effect on her, and before long she shook me back to life.

"Don't play dead no more," she crooned, "I don't like it."

The scene was blissful there among the mortician's wares. I could have stayed in the house of death forever, but as I lay beneath the hypnotic green eyes, the door of the storeroom flew open and a trio of avenging matriarchs burst in. I have been caught in compromising positions with females since, but none so horrifying or unwelcome as that first one.

"Here they are," Mrs. O'Malley shrieked, and seeing what we were about compounded her outrage: "Oh, my stars! What are you doing? Get out of there!"

I hurried out of the box where the pristine furnishings were now wrinkled and soiled with talc and dirt from our shoes. Mammaw had me by the upper arm immediately. She was a strong woman who could wring a chicken's neck in one coordinated wrenching, and my shoulder was sore for two days.

Sally was in tears. I only caught a glimpse of her as I was swept away. Mrs. O'Malley was berating her granddaughter vehemently, and I feared for her safety.

Then we were outside in the rain. I suppose the drizzle saved me an immediate whipping. Aunt Mabel waddled to the Studebaker to relate the incident to the men, but Mammaw paused long enough to give me some advice.

"Pappaw will have to pay for relining that coffin," she said menacingly. "I've got a withe at home with your name on it."

I knew she did: green Scotch broom, very supple and unbreakable. She would lock my wrist in a vise-like grip and I would dance around her like a maypole. Mammaw's switches could cut the blood from your legs.

It did not matter. I had endured whippings before for the sake of doing what I pleased. It would be for Sally. No green branch, no cat-o'-nine-tails could hurt me as long as Sally loved me.

We were in the car. Uncle Ambrose was hooting in spite of himself. "The little son-of-a-bitch did what?" he roared. He had to stifle it all the way home.

Well, I took the whipping as bravely as love could. It was thorough, too. For several years Pappaw reminded me regularly of the hundred and thirty-eight dollars and fifty cents he was obliged to pay the mortician for relining the ruined coffin.

I did not see Sally again for many years. Circumstances moved her family in one direction and mine in another. Then I happened to meet her on the street. Her hair was the way she wore it as a child, and the eyes were expressive and bright. She had married a machinist, and they had two children. We laughed about the way we had once played with things macabre.

"Keep in touch," she said, but we did not.

It was almost as long before I saw her the next time, also on the street. She was in the company of her grown daughter, and when they neared, I felt an old foreboding like the time I viewed her as an unlikely little corpse in the huge black coffin. Sally was very thin and carried her right arm across her chest. Her color was sallow and faintly yellow, like . . . something.

The last time was just a short while ago. I went early, well before calling hours. She was in the east parlor where Mrs. Schultz had lain. The O'Malleys had done the work themselves and did it about as well as such a thing could be done, I suppose. They got the hair wrong. I adjusted it a little myself, since no one else was there, pulling it back until you could see the tops of her ears. Her skin was cool and the texture foreign.

This time I knew better than to expect deliverance. Still I was beguiled. Over half a lifetime, memory shapes its own reliquary: Sally, death, and candlewax.

◆ ◆

JOHN BAIRD, who lives in Cosby, Tennessee, has had his fiction published in journals and magazines as diverse as *The Sun*, *Gray's Sporting Journal*, the *Flyfisher*, *Flyfishing News*, *Phoenix*, and the *New College Review*.

MARILYN KALLET

HEATHER AND THE WOLF

for Linda,
with all
good
wishes—
good luck
in
the
school
year!
x
Marilyn
Kallet

All summer I've been too sick
to play with her, fighting with Lou.
He yells I should pull myself
together, stiff upper lip.

Too sick to play, fighting with Lou.
Heather won't sleep in her crib.
The wolf's outside, stiff upper lip.
In the dark it will get her.

Heather won't sleep in her crib.
All night the wolf's howling.
In the dark it will get her.
Heather howls, falls down stairs.

He yells I should pull myself
together, all summer I've been too sick.

In the Face of Solitude

I keep my body here, with me,
reaching out to the still air,
trying to smash the stillness out,
tearing the air's silk
to find out what's beating there.

Stripped to the voice,
who will I be
in the face of solitude?
I am frightened by my skin
that cannot escape.

What is denied to love:
"a fin in a waste of waters,"
the pen in its wake.
The sky goes so slowly,
& the body goes fast.

"In the Face of Solitude," from *In the Great Night*, by Marilyn Kallet (Ithaca, N.Y.: Ithaca House, 1981), 65. This work also appeared in *Ironwood* 9, no. 1 (Spring, 1981): 62. Used by permission of the author.

SAYING GOODBYE

We embraced, there in the parking lot
of the ordinary.
How could I know your arms were arguing last things?
Your cheek in my hair.
For a moment I pressed against you. Goodbyes can be vast.
In a breath, we traded lives. I didn't know you
were a cliff I had reached the edge of.
Your touch echoed.
I simply followed it like song.

MARILYN KALLET is director of the Creative Writing Program and professor of English at the University of Tennessee at Knoxville. She is a former recipient of the Tennessee Arts Commission's Literary Fellowship in Poetry, and her most recent book is *A House of Gathering: Poets on May Sarton's Poetry* (University of Tennessee Press).

THOMAS MCNAMEE

1812

One day, later that spring, Tchula Homa was just coming out of his house into the sunshine when he heard East Wind whinnying madly in the paddock. The stallion was racing up and down, rolling his eyes. Then Tchula Homa looked across the square and saw, or thought he saw, a ghost, dressed in the black suit and white shirt of a white man, walking straight towards him.

"Kills Enemy?" said Tchula Homa.

"Yes," said his uncle. "It is me."

"Shall I invite you into your own house?" said Tchula Homa, reaching for the eagle-feathered staff and holding it out to Kills Enemy.

Kills Enemy waved it away, and came in and warmed himself at Tchula Homa's fire. "This is a new house," he said.

"Yours was knocked down by the earthquake in February."

"Ah."

"Your pipe," said Tchula Homa, lighting it and passing it to his uncle.

"This is good. I'm glad to be home." He returned the pipe to Tchula Homa. "How is everything here?"

"My mother died in the earthquake. Do you have any idea what became of my father?"

"No. I will tell you all I know of what happened. He is probably dead."

"I have grieved for him."

"Tatholah ennobles the ancestors with whom he now sleeps," said Kills Enemy in the traditional formula of condolence. "And how is our dear village?"

"There's less illness now, but many have died. Game is scarce. You were presumed dead, and I was made chief. Of course now you'll take over again."

"Let that pass for now," said Kills Enemy. "I will tell you my story."

"Good," said Tchula Homa.

"It was night when the earthquake began, so I couldn't see anything. I reached for your father's hand, but he was already out of bed. I tried to climb up the bluff, but it was coming to pieces and falling on me. I found some other Chickasaws, and we prayed in the dark for a long time. When the sun rose, the river had turned black, and there were huge whirlpools and waterspouts. Whole trees shot out of the water.

"Then there was a great roaring from the north, and there were flashes of red light—not lightning; fire from the lower world, perhaps—and the river began to flow *backwards*, and a big wave came, and I was swept in. I clung to a cottonwood tree and rode it as far as the Forked Deer River, I think. When the backward current met more water coming from upstream, the river went all the way to the top of the sky, with no air in between, and I began to drown.

"The next thing I knew, I was looking into the face of a white man, on the biggest boat I have ever seen. He wrapped me in a blanket and took me inside a house that was built on top of the boat, where it was very warm, and I slept for a long time.

"When I awoke, there were white people all around. I couldn't talk to them, of course, but I did learn some of their names. The man in charge was called Nicholas Roosevelt. His wife was there, too, called Lydia, and their newborn baby, and their big black dog.

"Now, this boat, Tchula Homa, was the most amazing thing I have ever seen. It moves along at an incredible speed, *without human work*. It was as long as five houses, and wider than two. It made a noise like fifty thunderstorms. Inside the wooden house there was a small iron house, and in this there was a fire bigger than ten Green Corn bonfires, with two men feeding it logs all day and night. On top of the iron house was a great pipe like a hollow tree, with black smoke and sparks and burning coals pouring out of it. Every day they would cut up as many trees to feed that fire as our whole village uses in a winter!

"At the back of the boat, there was a huge sort of drum covered with paddles, which drove into the water endlessly, without ever tiring. And then one day, Nicholas Roosevelt spun the big wooden wheel that steered the boat, and we began to go *upstream!* Tchula Homa, I tell you, these white men know things beyond our conceiving.

"Whole islands had been scalped of their trees. At places the river was filled from bank to bank with dead animals and uprooted forests and the wreckage of flatboats and Indian canoes. Sometimes also there were dead men in the water, and then also Lydia cried.

"After a while we came to a white man city, named for our ancient kinsmen who have now disappeared—the Natchez.

"How can I describe it? Countless white men's houses, some of them as big as small villages, full of room after room! In these houses, everything is shining and very complicated, and you cannot find your way around. There are pictures on the walls so real you'd think you could walk into them. You sit on soft, high chairs, and drink a thing like black drink from tiny cups that gleam like mussel shells, with tiny handles. They showed me how to eat in their way, which is very difficult, with many metal tools. Their food is very strange. But it's good—look at me!" Kills Enemy laughed, and patted his belly.

"And these white people have dozens of Negro slaves, who do all the work. The white people just sit and drink their black drink. The women talk and sew, and the men talk and drink whiskey. They get drunk, but not like the ones at Fort Pickering: these white men laugh and tell stories, and I never once saw any of them get angry when they were drunk.

"Every night I would sleep between snow-white cloths in a bed high off the floor, softer than a dream. Frankly, sometimes I would feel sick and have to lie on the floor to sleep. And even on the floor there were soft rugs.

"There was another earthquake when I was in Natchez, but all that happened was that their lamps flickered, and the white women pulled their shawls more tightly around their shoulders, and the white men poured themselves another drink of whiskey. I'm sure that's because they've tamed earthquakes there as they've tamed everything else.

"They introduced me to many white people. Nicholas Roosevelt had this suit of white man clothes made for me. You see how perfectly it fits?" Kills Enemy rose and walked up and down, and bowed low, and grinned. "*How do you do?*" he said in English, his eyes glittering.

"Then one day when I was riding with the Roosevelts in their carriage pulled by two black horses, I saw some Choctaws, and I got down to say hello, and it was such a relief to be able to talk again that I didn't mind even when they mocked me in my white man suit. Later, I thought about how those Choctaws had laughed, and I began to realize that I was only a curiosity for these white people. And I realized how much I missed my village, and you, and all this world.

"So I went into the bottomlands and made a blowgun as Tinebe had taught me when I was a boy, and I lived on small game. I have been walking now for a long time. There was a third earthquake—very violent, too, no doubt because I was now outside the white man world—and it ripped the earth apart terribly. In many places the road was swallowed up, and there were big downfalls of timber. I am very tired, Tchula Homa," said Kills Enemy, and suddenly he was weeping.

"Uncle, sleep here," said Tchula Homa, indicating his own bed.

Tchula Homa went to find Moon Behind Cloud at the women's gathering-house. She came out, kissed him, and before he said a word asked, "Is it true that Kills Enemy has come back?"

"He's asleep in our bed."

"Will he be chief again?"

Tchula Homa frowned.

"Where has he been?"

"It's a long story," said Tchula Homa.

"Is he all right?" she asked.

"We must let him rest, and then we'll see. He's been among white people, and it may have affected his reason. I think they may have put him under some sort of spell."

"Have you talked to Tsatsemataha?"

"I will. I haven't talked to anybody."

Moon Behind Cloud took Tchula Homa's hand. "You love him very much," she said.

"Yes."

"What's the matter?"

"It's hard to express," said Tchula Homa. "We'll talk tonight."

"You don't include me in your thinking," said Moon Behind Cloud. "You always put me off until you've made up your mind."

He said nothing.

"I love you, Tchula Homa," she said.

"I want to be sure I'm right before I speak," he replied.

"It's easier for you to be alone in your thoughts."

"Yes, alas," said Tchula Homa. "Perhaps you don't want Kills Enemy to be back. I ask myself why it should be important to you if I'm chief or not. You've said that you want what will make me happy. Will the chiefship do that? Or does it just put me in a position to fail the more shamefully?—a higher spot, to fall farther from? The world moves one way while I lean against it, trying to push it back—back to where it was before I was born. Is that not a fool's idea? If I were to seek your counsel, wouldn't you advise me that I'm setting myself up for a fall? You see, my solitude protects my folly."

"What, in your view, is a wife for?" demanded Moon Behind Cloud, her tone more gentle than her words.

He did not speak for a long moment, then took her tiny frame in his long arms. "Ah, dear girl—"

She stiffened.

"Just now," he said, still holding her, "I did try to share my thinking with you, however clumsily."

"I'm still strange to you," said Moon Behind Cloud.

"Yes," said Tchula Homa.

"Shall we stay at Tathonoyo's house tonight," she suggested, "so that Kills Enemy can rest undisturbed?"

Kills Enemy slept through the day and all night and into the next morning. When he awoke, Tchula Homa and Tsatsemataha were at his side. The high priest began to chant a song of exorcism.

"This was just a precaution," said Tchula Homa. "You have been in the white man world."

"Yes, I have, and I have a few things to say about it. Will you kindly convene your council?"

Kills Enemy did not tire now, nor weep. There was lightning in the old man's eyes, thunder in his voice. As he finished the narrative of his journey, Kills Enemy's voice dropped to a grave and confidential softness that forced his listeners to lean forward to hear him.

"Last night," he said, "I awoke from a vision, which stayed with me into my waking, as only the truest dreams do.

"Listen, old men! Listen, warriors! In Natchez, I have seen a future for us. It will enable us to stand against the white man, Tchula Homa, so you should like it. In a word, it is this: the Negro.

"With slaves, we too can plant cotton, and be rich. This cotton is the source of the miracle of white wealth and strength. Let us do as our king has so many times advised us—let us take from the white man only what can make us strong as Chickasaws.

"In my vision I saw our fields enlarged into the forest, which we have always had more of than we need, and hundreds of slaves raising cotton for us and our posterity. With cotton, we will have money, and it is clear that only money, in the end—not war, nor even our sacred purity—can protect us from the white man. He comes to us year after year, offering pittances for this, for that, for whatever he has lately set his mind on getting from the poor Indians, and many of our people have not the strength to resist. Even now, who among us has real power, and can stand up to the white man, and strike bargains with him? Only the Colberts and the other mixed bloods.

"And what is the source of their special ability? It is not English: we can always find interpreters. It is money. And how is it that they have so much money? Is it not their ownership of slaves, and the surplus of crops that those slaves produce in the fields of the capital?

"Brothers, listen. Let us start with a few, mainly women, and breed them. Have we not already bred the finest horse in the world? As the Colberts have shown, Negroes are even easier to keep than horses. They grow their own food!

"And here we are, much closer to the Fourth Bluff trading post than the Colberts, with a good road all the way. There is already booming trade on the Father of Waters. We too could sell cotton to the thousands of white men far away across the oceans.

"How many of you have seen cannons? We had one on the deck of Nicholas Roosevelt's boat, and, let me tell you, it is a weapon of unbelievable power. One cannon ball can blast a crater in a river bank as big as a house. Could we not have cannons, too? Could we not then, some day, regain our ancient supremacy?

"Brothers: I ask you only to think."

The words of Kills Enemy sank into Tchula Homa's heart in slow throbbings of sorrow. This was not madness which had entered his uncle; it was corruption.

◆ ◆

THOMAS MCNAMEE, a native of Memphis, is the author of several books, including *Nature First: Keeping Our Wild Places and Wild Creatures Wild*. He now lives on a ranch near Livingston, Montana, and is at work on a new book about the return of the gray wolf to Yellowstone.

TOM HOUSE

THE BUS HOME FROM NASHVILLE

my guitar went flat
 on the bus home from nashville
after sixteen hours
wedged in its compartment
between a duffel bag and a dryer
 as i slept with my wine-skin
 surrounded by soldiers
going home with permission
and woke up sweating
 with a highway headache
and watched the re-run of the road
repeated through the night.

morning added light to heat
    the mountains blocked
the breeze behind us
    heading east
 into lunch and afternoon
a student in her teens
going home for week-end
from a community business college

"the bus home from nashville," by Tom House, appeared in the National Poetry Anthology edition of the *DeKalb Literary Arts Journal* (DeKalb Community College, Clarkston, Ga.), vol. 1, nos. 2–4 (1974): 104–5. Reprinted by permission of the author.

hopping from one small town
 to another
and i sat behind the window
 as the bus gulped down the miles

and my soul went flat
 on that bus home from nashville
the strings that held it
 attached to me
stretched dull/grew limp
   i couldn't hold a tune
i strained and sighed and soured
as i counted the road signs
 floating past tobacco fields
 and grandchildren
   tapping my toe
as if finally i had
   heard my song
and understood
   its rhythms

The Hank Williams Memorial Myth

i walked off-stage
with ol' hank
and I never did look back
the lights are bright
applause is loud
but proud ain't right
necessarily
and sometimes the guts
of the moment get
all twisted
and you've got to give more
expecting less
and if it ain't on
record or tape
or film does that
mean it never happened
if someone important
you know
don't stamp it his seal say
yeah
this cat was pretty hot

naw I walked off-
stage with ol' hank
that night

so drunk i could have
stumbled   but didn't
and wouldn't   and
surprising them all every turn more'n
they ever could or did me kept
step keeping it
hard beat lowdown
right there
kicking up howling how
making it made sense more'n
anything this moment
really might have meant
and no i ain't saying
demons are gospel but
none of us are sour- ass
sonuvabitches
can kiss mine   he laughed
then took dead aim   shot out
the spotlight

The Exhibitionist Primps

The moon spins on a bar stool.
Dogs curse their collars.

The exhibitionist serves his time
as preamble to hysteria.
Zippers keep him honest.

He's the rough draft of a tough guy;
the prize at the bottom of Pandora's box,
the original Beefcake Kid,

flexing his muscles
(raising his sights)

and there's no one bold
enough to remind him

that sometimes an audience
is the only friend
a naked man deserves.

Tom House's work has included poetry, theater, and opera. A former editor and bookstore man, House has headlined Nashville's annual "Windows on the Cumberland" festival for several years.

MELISSA CANNON

MYSTERIES AT GRANNY'S

On Christmas Eve, a little before bedtime,
I work and work until one final twist
unhinges it. But more amazing than
a first tooth that becomes a shiny dime
is my cousin fainting at the blood-splotched fist
I hold out towards him like a talisman.

◆ ◆ ◆

Sun-speckled, flecked with mud dough, I just toss
my old pocked spoon to pluck mimosa, sweet
pink frosting. Then the spoon's vanished. Heat beads
me as I crawl the yard, run to the house—
I'm sent back, empty-handed. At my feet,
a curve of sheen blinks up from withered weeds.

◆ ◆ ◆

Outside, the rust leaves shiver. I'm a bird
caged here on this still chair, an uncontrolled
twitter along my throat. What's "burying"?
Closed in the ground. "Who? Who?" my only word.
When mama says "Your father," I go cold
and blank as bare sky or a shattered wing.

◆ ◆ ◆

"Mysteries at Granny's," by Melissa Cannon, appeared in *Sing Heavenly Muse!* no. 16 (1989). Reprinted with permission of *Sing Heavenly Muse!* and the author.

I watch for mama. There—her red-checked dress,
her cheek against the glass. But the car whines
past, fading down the highway. And this other
who comes at sunset in spring green? I guess
the fairies lent her. I'm feverish with signs,
with losses: tooth and spoon; father, mother.

THE WHITE HORSE

flicking at the barbed edge of field will stand
one impatient moment more, then strain
to nip persimmons from her half-cupped hand;
he's gone before an evening rain
erases them as it covers the cracked land.

(Her oil shows brown spiked weeds, intensifies
orange fruit spilled over the low bank's
red clay; and, mirroring his flanks,
pale ribs of nacre layered on fiery skies.)
Again, light strokes the bleached sheet where she lies
and lies. What landscape held such shades?
Sienna, pearl . . . memory's a white horse that fades
and turns to dusk across those clouded eyes.

MELISSA CANNON lives and works in Nashville. Her poems have recently appeared in *Bogg*, *Kenyon Review*, and *The Lyric* and have been anthologized in *A Formal Feeling Comes* (Story Line, 1994) and *Sleeping with Dionysus* (Crossing Press, 1994).

DONNA TAUSCHER

◆ ◆

MAWAT

(Vacant land from which a human cannot be heard at the nearest inhabited place is called Mawat.)

Harry Adams has a secret and it touches him, a bit of hermit's grace.

His secretary pauses an instant longer than usual before she rings his extension. His associates hesitate to include him in lunch plans. Even Harry's boss ponders the necessity of intrusion before knocking on his door. Business at the law firm goes on as before, and no one mentions the change in Harry. No one is quite sure there is one.

Change is as subtle as a new part in Sam Goldman's hair, the surprising seams in Lillian Putman's silk stockings. Little differences flash across the office and draw sudden smiles, wisecracks in the hallways. But the change in Harry has everyone's sly and silent attention.

Harry, for his part, eases through the days with the same steady motion of competence. Until he enters his front door at home. Sara Adams has noticed the change and she doesn't hesitate to challenge his entrance with an inquisitive eye. His son is too young for incriminating glances, but Harry feels the welcome home hug laced with the hesitancy of expected betrayal.

What can Harry do? Every afternoon at four Harry takes the elevator to the twelfth floor. He pulls the small janitor's room key from his pocket and enters the musty storage place. In the far corner is a shower stall and toilet. Harry stands on the toilet and opens the 3' by 3' window that frames his head. As far as Harry can tell, it is the only window in the entire building that opens. And so he comes here each afternoon to test the weather, to reach his hand out over the narrow alleyway and to think about Sara and his son. He has yet to grasp when the exact moment occurred that he no longer understood the reasons for going home each night. Yet each day he tries to pull from the rain or the filtered sunlight a point at which that which was so central to his being suddenly became peripheral. These moments with his hand out the window and his

"Mawat," by Donna Tauscher, appeared in *raccoon* 24/25 (10th anniversary issue; May, 1987): 456.

head tilted with concentration have become more real than his entrance each night into family.

What does Harry do? Harry returns to his desk and his briefs with a longing so deep inside that it hastens him home with a punctuality startling in its consistency.

Harry has a secret, and it unfolds itself each evening.

The secret whispers to him gently all day.

Others call out in robust voices, "Harry, how's the Moreiga case coming?" "Harry, what's the court date on Piedmont Industry?" And Harry responds with lucid facts and dates, all the while hearing the faint murmur of Mawat.

Mawat, that distant oasis where Harry seeks refuge each night. "Anne, cancel the lunch date with James tomorrow, will you?" he mouths, and Mawat calls with whistling pines.

Typewriters click out the hectic rhythm of the day and Harry's limbs respond in time. His walk quickens to catch the elevator to the 11:00 A.M. hearing, his arms gather up papers with brisk efficiency. But lilting music from a yellow bird on the edge of the forest soothes the beat of his heart.

He tries to rid himself of the distant land each afternoon, gazing out the window, trying to touch something of his life with a purpose before returning home. Mawat pulls him stronger than the warm kitchen and rich smells, stronger than his wife's desire for conversation, stronger than his son's requests for bedtime stories.

Horns honk in the evening traffic as Harry is pulled along in a dribble of movement. The windows stay closed to avoid the exhaust, and a heater in the winter and an air conditioner in the summer provide a monotonous clime. But the changing winds of Mawat cloak Harry with the seasons.

He enters each evening with an urgency to retreat to his study, briefcase full of the plausibility of his escape.

Sara tells him that Jessie is ready for day care and she is ready to return to work. She tells him this repeatedly, trying to shed the guilt, and he seems unable to respond. He nods, he affirms the decision, he inquires after her job search. She desperately tries to hold his attention for a brief moment before desire gives way to resentment.

Jessie won't finish dinner. "Daddy doesn't like it either!"

"You don't have to be like your father, Jessie," she says looking at Harry.

The crickets are starting their steady song to lure Harry back to Mawat.

Each night the dinner attack gives way to the sounds of evening in the high country.

Harry never excuses himself. He leaves Sara with coffee and Jessie's soiled shirt and enters his study. As the door closes, Harry abandons his control over the day and prepares to give himself over to the rhythms of Mawat.

He switches on the black and white T.V. next to his desk but doesn't raise the volume. He allows the plush easy chair to comfort him, to ease the tension from his shoulders, and turns his eyes to the darkened window. Not one obstacle intrudes on Harry's view of the blackened sky.

The blue T.V. light flickers across Harry's features as he starts this climb to Mawat.

Every night the trail holds surprises, new flowers in bloom, an abandoned limestone quarry. There are many approaches to Mawat and he has explored them all. Tonight he doesn't want to linger on the journey. He climbs straight up, pushing himself through the rugged terrain. As he nears his land, a huge red marmot appears and whistles him welcome.

Harry is enveloped with the joy of homecoming. Mawat never changes, except where Harry lays his hand.

After the climb, the land levels into a small plateau, about an acre as Harry estimates it. The silence is never broken by telephones or police sirens, by pointless questions or a car's noisy exhaust. Only wind in the trees and the tall grass, only a bird's cry or the howl of a coyote on a moonlit night tug at the edges of Harry's attention. He can sing or yell as loud as he wants and the far mountain wall only returns a faint echo, never a neighbor's offended cry.

Harry sings sometimes while he digs in the soil, sun glistening on his sweaty shoulders. He has toiled, carrying rocks and branches from a piece of his land for almost a year. He has tilled the earth and shaped it into a fine garden. He has cut a small crevasse around boulders and small trees for a running stream. He has spread the seed of wild herbs and flowers. He has placed everything in perfect order to bloom into a luxurious garden in the wild. And now he needs only the rain.

He has waited a year. The seasons change; the cold, the warm spring, the heat, the faint chill of autumn, but still no rain. A faint cloud of doubt hangs over the wide spirit of Mawat.

Harry arrives tonight at sunset and sits on a small log bench under his favorite redwood. The smells at sunset are pungent and feed Harry's desire to see his hard work begin to grow. He looks around and finds the patches of high grass turning golden, blazing with beauty in the low light. The grass seems to angle a little closer to the ground, to rustle with a parched rhythm.

A sigh wells up in Harry that he is afraid to release. He doesn't want a breath of disappointment to taint Mawat.

Maybe a small log lean-to near this redwood tree, he thinks. A few quilted blankets over the pine needles, a soft pillow. He could sleep in this deep and silent night and wake rested. He has never spent the night in Mawat, never given himself over that completely. A little fear lingers with the thought, and a yearning.

Harry stands and brushes a light dust from his pants. The sky is clear and the stars are falling into place. He bends his head and makes the descent homeward.

Water is cascading into the bathtub and Bessie Smith is comforting Sara as Harry leaves the study. He'll be asleep before she finishes her nightly ritual.

Days pile up on one another and Harry feels the burden of too many cases and the approach of spring. The pitch of the office is in such high-level frenzy that Harry can barely contain a modicum of courtly reserve. Every day something new is pushed out of kilter. An unexpected witness. Muzak in the elevator. Stern Jerry Franklin in love and grinning through the firm's monthly meetings. Nothing can be counted on. Why did June Resnick dye her hair red? Someone plastered over the window in the janitor's room.

Harry has been deprived of his afternoon reflections and it still hasn't rained in Mawat.

Sara found part-time work at a drug rehabilitation center for teenagers and his son tells excited stories about the day care center at dinner. His wife's pride feels like contempt to Harry, and each evening on the freeway home he half dreads and hopes to find her gone when he arrives.

If it wasn't for the refuge of Mawat, Harry can't imagine what would become of him. And every day something seems to push Harry to his study a little earlier and keep him there a little longer.

Today it was Alan Thomas and his implied accusation that Harry was less than thorough on the Wilson Washington case. That Harry didn't have his mind on business perhaps. Alan Thomas was the first to break the office hesitancy about acknowledging the difference in Harry Adams.

Harry nodded his acknowledgment and felt the sun beating on the rough pine bench in Mawat.

"I see your point, Alan. I've been a little tired lately."

"It's more than tired, Harry."

A woodpecker's steady beat is mingling with the rhythm of Miss Langly's typewriter.

"Don't worry, Alan, I'll give it some thought," Harry says to the empty corridor two hours later.

He takes the stairs down the nine flights and drives around the city waiting for a reasonable hour to return home.

Cars jam every street. A pedestrian crosses against the light and barely misses Harry's fender. Brakes screech and a BMW is assaulted from the rear by a Volkswagon. The damage is minimal, the resulting congestion immense. Harry spends a half hour and clears two blocks.

No question, he was lax in the Washington case. An appeal is in order. Maybe that hungry young lawyer Dullus will take on part of his load.

The freeway entrance is partially blocked by a work crew, and a tight-faced woman in the car next to his honks in frustration every few minutes.

Harry feels a dampness between his palms and the steering wheel. He takes a deep breath to curb the panic of entrapment.

One hour and ten minutes to his garage from the time he enters the freeway. He can't stand the commute one more day. What will he do?

Harry enters the kitchen to the smell of baked chicken and the sound of Jessie marching to his mother's rendition of "Over There." They both turn when he enters and offer him expectant smiles. Jessie runs to him with the obligatory hug and Sara inquires about his day. The scene seems woven with a feigned normalcy.

"About ready for dinner?"

"I'm not feeling too well, Sara. My stomach's upset and it was the proverbial 'bad day at the office.' I just want to rest."

Harry wants to rest, to escape, close the study door, lock the kitchen far behind him. Sara catches the nuance of flight in his eye and nods. Jessie marches behind him as far as the study and abruptly turns and marches back to the kitchen. Harry is seized with relief. The door is closed. He's on his way to Mawat.

He decides on a long trail tonight, one that will take him past the lake on the far side of the mountain. He can splash the cool water on his face before he finishes the ascent. Maybe the trout will be jumping. Maybe the spring fireflies will be out. Maybe he'll see a bear cub.

Harry sees it all and drinks in each detail, mining the mother lode of his desire.

When he finally reaches the summit, darkness has taken Mawat. Coolness is breaking through the warmth and Harry sits on a large boulder to absorb some of the day's heat. He's glad to sit in the darkness and feel the earth's presence, not gaze on its dry, cracked surface. He wonders where the. . . .

The study door opens and closes. Fear knots the back of Harry's neck and he struggles to look up. Sara stands across the room and says in a quiet voice, hollow with suppressed anger, "If you don't tell me what is happening with you, why you come in here every night, why you can't touch me; if you don't tell me, Harry Adams, I'm leaving. I may leave anyway. I just want to hear you first."

Harry looks at Sara, disoriented, confronted. He will tell her. Not as an argument to stay, but because at this particular moment he doesn't have the strength to make any other choice.

He looks at the T.V. screen and softly directs his story to the blue light.

"I'll tell you what I know, Sara, but I don't know why. Things happened and I can tell you how they happened. But why, God knows I've thought about it, but I haven't an idea as to why. I know I've felt dissatisfied for a long while and I feel guilty for feeling dissatisfied. I know I haven't given you and Jessie the support you need. But I don't have it in me, Sara, I lack what it is that could reach you or Jessie. I work, I used to be good at it, but now I have my doubts about that. And I have my doubts about why it doesn't even matter to me if I continue to be good at it.

"I'll try not to be ambiguous, but it's all so impossible. And it seems even more impossible not to say it right now. What it is—how do I begin? A couple of years ago I was researching a case dealing with squatters' rights. Now, don't be impatient, I'm not off on a tangent. I was reading about ancient law and how land could be considered available to habitation. One of the laws went something like this—vacant land from which a human voice cannot be heard at the nearest inhabited place is dead land and can be settled. The Hebrew word for such dead land is Mawat. From the time I read that, the whole concept began to absorb me. I felt that piece of land, far from another human voice, deep inside me. It existed. It was mine. I felt a peace just thinking about it that I hadn't felt in years, an aliveness.

"I began to imagine it, Sara, how it looked, how it felt. At first I wanted to be there and slowly I was there. Not only there, but it seemed to be with me all the time and I wanted to escape there whenever I could, to sit in the quiet, to work the land, to be someplace that was only mine, no one could see me, could hear me. And that is what it is like. I feel as if I exist there, I can feel myself breathe, I can feel my feet touch the ground. I sit in here, Sara, but I'm not here, I'm there.

"I climb different trails there each night. It's just a small piece of land, but I've cleared a portion and made it like those wild gardens we saw in Canada. Do you remember? Boulders, logs, streams, and flowers. I've planted the seed and carved the land. And as soon as it rains it will be more beautiful than you can imagine. Except that it doesn't rain. I can't understand it. How can a place full of life, with a wind that makes such music with the grass and trees. . . .

"I've made it so perfect, yet the rain never comes. I will it to come, I pray for it to come. And it's still dry. And now disappointment touches Mawat too, Sara. I feel this small anguish in me when I'm there as if because of my presence the land has been deprived of the rain. Yet I created the land. Why? There is no understanding, Sara. Just as I could never ask you to understand why I come to the study every night and live somewhere that only I know, that I dream. I'm a crazy man, Sara, I see that now, yet it's the only thing in my life that makes sense. Or did make sense until the land began to dry. Now the seeds lie dormant and the birds' songs seem sad."

Harry pauses a long while with his eyes pressed firmly shut.

"And I don't ask you to understand something that I can't explain, Sara."

And Harry Adams finally opens his eyes and looks to Sara, braced for her contempt. He's astonished. He sees eyes clear with compassion and understanding; an understanding that runs deep, beyond his story into her story. He wonders what inside of him is tearing loose as he glimpses the edge of Sara's story blending into his, falling into a common well of human longing.

Sara walks to Harry, kneels at his chair and puts her head in his lap. She clasps her arms around his knees and begins to sob gently. He is jarred by Sara's soft heaves and he too begins to cry. The blue T.V. light bathes them both.

Harry feels her salty tears wet his hands and soften them. He watches his tears splash into her dark brown hair. And as he lowers his head to kiss this woman he had almost forgotten how to love, he catches the rich, full smell of damp earth.

It was raining in Mawat.

• •

DONNA TAUSCHER, an author of published short fiction, works for the Tennessee Humanities Council in Nashville. She is a past winner of the Tennessee Arts Commission's Literary Arts Fellowship and the Ms. *Magazine* Fiction Award.

PAUL CLEMENTS

THE MATLOCK HOUSE

Even when it was covered by a forest and was part of a vast wilderness, the place where the house was to be built was the focus of a far away but ominous mentality. That mentality moved closer, and a village was built several miles away from the eventual site of the house. The house was built, and as a girl who lived in the house became a young woman, the mentality was growing stronger and the distant village was slowly becoming a city. The woman was eventually drawn into the city and became a harlot, and a century after she had become the city's victim, the house in which she had grown up was to become a victim of the city as well. The city and the mentality of unrestrained acquisitiveness feverishly entwine, and as the headlong growth continues, the harlot becomes more than one of the victims of the city, more and more she becomes its symbol.

The Colony of North Carolina included a vast territory west of the Appalachian Mountains, and although English policy had forbidden the establishment of settlements beyond the mountains, for many years the western wilderness drew the attention of land speculators who desired to invest in the area and eventually to expand their personal fortunes. With the Revolutionary War, the region was opened for settlement, and leading speculators seized the opportunity for which they had been waiting. The power to distribute the western lands lay with the North Carolina legislature, and the speculators, after a long and difficult struggle, not only managed to pass laws which were written to their advantage, but also they were able to control the offices which would administer those laws.

A large portion of the western region was surveyed and set aside ostensibly to be used by the impoverished government of North Carolina as payment to soldiers who had served in the Revolution, but few veterans of the war would receive the land. As had been anticipated, most of the soldiers either were unwilling to move into the wil-

"The Matlock House," from A *Past Remembered*, by Paul Clements (Nashville: Robin Press, 1987). Reprinted by permission of the author.

derness or were too poor to make the journey, and the warrants which entitled them to land grants were bought by the speculators at a fraction of their value. Much of the western land ultimately was claimed by speculators, and some, including members of the noted Blount and Donelson families, resorted to fraud in trying to achieve their financial objectives. Although a few speculators grew wealthy as a result of their activities, a number of others were ruined, and for many of the settlers who managed to come west, the most important effect of land speculation was that it drove up the price of land.

Peter Johnston had been a private in the Continental Army of North Carolina, and his seven years of service entitled him to 640 acres of land in the western territory. Johnston died soon after the war, and his land warrant was sold by his heirs to Philip Philips, a speculator who, along with his partner Michael Campbell, was accumulating a sizeable quantity of warrants. Unlike some speculators who claimed grants in Davidson County and never saw the land they owned, Philips, who owned over fifty area grants in partnership with Campbell, settled across the river from Nashville in McLean's Bend and shared the hardships of pioneer life on the Cumberland. Philips was on his way to becoming one of the region's wealthiest individuals, but he died in 1797, only a few months after selling a 640-acre tract which had been claimed with the warrant of Peter Johnston and was located about eight miles southeast of Nashville on Mill Creek.

The same land was bought in 1798 by George Hartman, who had come to Tennessee from Virginia. Hartman already may have been married when he came to Davidson County, and within a few months of the time he bought the Philips tract, his wife gave birth to a daughter. A number of other children were born over the following years, and around 1820, a large two-story brick house was built to accommodate the family. George Hartman had died by the late 1830s, but his widow, Elizabeth, continued to live in the house, and the land was divided among their nine children, most of whom, by that time, had families of their own. The Hartman house, along with about fifty acres, was sold in 1844, and some of the Hartman children who had made their homes nearby moved away over the years which followed.

George Hartman's daughter Martha had been born about the time the house was being built and was not quite ten when her older sister, Hetty, gave birth to a child out of wedlock. Martha evidently avoided any such scandal and went on to receive a limited amount of schooling before her marriage, at the age of seventeen, to Leonard Burnett. Leonard and Martha were married for about twenty years, but they divorced in 1854 after Leonard was accused of adultery by his wife; and after Leonard left his family in the 1850s, Martha apparently was forced to move into Nashville to support her five children.

When Martha Burnett brought her family to Nashville, it was a thriving place with a population of nearly fourteen thousand. It occupied an advantageous location on the Cumberland River, and its growth was driven by the financial abilities, the shared objectives, and the concerted efforts of a number of its wealthier citizens. The speculators of the late eighteenth century had invested in land and occasionally had taken extreme measures to see that their investments increased in value, and the subsequent generation of investors, including some descendants of the speculators, had followed the pattern of their predecessors. Investments in wilderness land had given way to investments in town lots, bank stock, and local businesses, all of which had a value dependent on the growth of Nashville. As had been the case with the speculators, attention was focused by monied interests on crucial institutions of the government, and the state legislature, as well as local government, voted to allocate public funds which were used to stimulate Nashville's expansion. The turnpikes and later the railroads both were financed in part by public money, and their development led to an increase in the population of Nashville and brought greater wealth to those having investments there. The town had become a small city, but as it had grown it had attracted an increasing proportion of individuals who lived in poverty, including forty-five-year-old Martha Burnett and her five children.

To provide for her family, Martha had become one of the more than two hundred prostitutes who were living in Nashville on the eve of the Civil War. Prostitution flourished and was even legalized locally for a time during the war years. By 1870, Martha was keeping a brothel, which provided employment to her three daughters and was located on Crawford Street, a little to the north of Capitol Hill, near the railroad. The Crawford Street brothel remained in operation through the 1870s, and Martha's three daughters, as well as her sixteen-year-old granddaughter, worked there into the early 1880s. Syphilis was prevalent among prostitutes. Surfacing in an initial set of symptoms, the disease continued to spread internally until the victims died years later from apparently unrelated illnesses. Martha Burnett had taken a dangerous road in meeting the economic situations with which she had been faced, and during the 1880s that road probably had brought death to some members of her family. One of Martha's daughters died early in the decade of a disease that may have had a connection to syphilis, and within two years after Martha's death from uterine cancer in 1887, two more of her children were dead.

During the years in which Martha Burnett was living in Nashville, the house which her father had built on Mill Creek was owned by James Matlock, who had grown up on an adjoining tract of land. James had been born in 1811 and was the son of William Matlock, who, in 1783, had been one of the guards protecting the surveying team that had established the boundaries of the lands set aside by North Carolina for its Revolutionary War veterans. James Matlock, who apparently was quite active in the Tennessee militia and eventually would attain the title of general, had bought the Hartman place in 1848 but had not moved there immediately following his purchase. During his first years of ownership, Matlock was living in Nashville and operating a grocery business, and the house was probably rented, but by 1860 he was living there with his wife of sixteen years, Antoinette Matlock. The Civil War, which caused such a boom in Nashville's prostitution business, brought heavy losses to the Matlock farming operation, and the property was sold, after which James Matlock moved to Montgomery County, where he died in 1873.

From the time it was sold by Matlock until the end of the century, the house, which eventually received the name "Twin Willows," was owned by members of the Harwood family, and from 1914 until 1943 it was the property of A. K. Hill. For twenty-five years following World War II, during a period in which another generation of Nashvillians was engineering Nashville's continued expansion, the old house was owned by Albert

Williams. During that period the routes of the interstate highway system were being determined, and Nashville became one of the few cities in America to have three separate federal highways planned to pass through. In addition to a number of other economically motivated actions, Metropolitan Government, the system which eliminated duplication of city and county services, was instituted, and the Metropolitan Airport Authority was established. The growth of Nashville boomed after 1980, and in 1986, in order to make way for the expansion of the airport, plans were announced for the destruction of the house in which Martha Burnett had once lived.

Heavy clouds begin to drift in above the crowded landscape surrounding the river, and the sky gradually darkens. Thunder rolls in faint tones over the yards and residences of subdivisions, and over the monotonous housing complexes which intrude on the community in growing clusters. The wind surges across the vast network of traffic-filled highways and through the garish clutter of commercial centers, and the bristling signs and billboards shudder as it sweeps on toward the encircled city. As the oncoming storm crests on the horizon, the light coming through the windows of the old house is diminished, and the shadows cast on the floors and walls and ceilings become less and less distinct. The sounds of thunder and of the rising, rushing wind drift from room to room, moving through the house like the spirits of those who once lived and died there, and as the approaching lightning bathes the darkest corners in sudden flashes of illumination, rain begins to fall and a shroud seems to descend over the aged dwelling. The rain is soon falling onto the roof in torrents, and it blows against the weathered walls and pours into the yard from overflowing gutters, inundating the ancient soil. Pools form on the lawn, and, as the lightning crashes, the rain washing from the house flows beneath the wind-lashed trees in growing rivulets, out toward the storm-obscured neighborhood and beyond. The tempest continues until the closing of the day, and as the light fades from the cloud-laden sky, the wind slowly dies away and the thunder grows hushed in the distance. The shroud of rain gives way imperceptibly to a shroud of darkness, and as the clouds gradually drift from the evening sky and the night deepens, the old house seems to stand alone.

◆ ◆

PAUL CLEMENTS is a native of Nashville who now lives in Williamson County, where he remains deeply involved in regional and architectural history. He is at work on a novel.

DAVID SPICER

THE FLIGHT OF THE CEDAR WAX WINGS

For Nancy

Four feet from our kitchen window
the berries of the holly tree slowly ripen
in clusters of green beads no one eats.
Until *they* come, scores, in the March breeze
that listens to the wings as they approach.
Each year my wife and I wait,
worried we'll miss the invasion
of this small army with pointed helmets.
They rest upon the branches
and begin pecking.
Heads move side to side,
chatters exchanging,
eyes already in another place as they gorge
and diminish the tree of its bounty.
I wonder which city was their previous conquest,
how they know a weigh station is here,
and why they remember.
They're more beautiful than the jay or cardinal
because ownership of green is their honor.
They remain a mystery
and ignore my wife and me.
I regret that, but not the tree
empty of red food as they fly away
in one flutter of fifty pairs of wings

toward the next tree in the next town,
marveled at, I hope, by another lover
of birds he cannot comprehend.

WEDDING

An enemy of ceremony, I promised
never to attend funerals, or rituals
that demand vows like so many thoughtless
pronouncements: somehow, they seemed
twins in a society smitten with sentiment
and formality—I couldn't stomach
the tuxedos, gowns, gilt-wrapped gifts,
crying sisters. But this one differed.
Held at the home of the bride's brother
and his wife, it happened because
the future mother-in-law grabbed desire
by its shoulders and shook it
like a bashful child. Besides,
I was the groom, and disbelief my co-conspirator
in the natural act of union with the woman
possessing the true reflection in the mirror
I always studied. I no longer needed to,
not knowing the man who searched for answers
like the rarest birds, stones or stamps.
I didn't know him anymore, perhaps afraid,
proceeding to whatever happened next.
She did, and I accepted that reality,
for choice is the only art framed by concrete.
We decided upon the wedding, the reception,

the guests, but not the flowers, nor the swans,
the food, and the ambience: her suave father
cracked jokes about mice, her brother coordinated
arrangements, his wife a partner in the exchange
that accompanied the rings and most important words
not taken lightly. The guests ate, drank,
small-talked, and we stayed after opening
gifts, the four of us, too tired to say goodbye,
glad of exhaustion. And when we did,
we left, the stars receding above our steps,
the wind waving us down the road
into unknown nights we welcomed with bodies
that waited to open and embrace possibility.

The Woman With the Wild Hair

I'm a married man now,
my wife will see this
because I show her everything,
but I confess I watch
the woman with the wild hair on the avenue
when I drive to work each noon of the week.
She's an apparition and fascinates me,
I don't even know her,
have never discussed ecosystems
over a cup of coffee at Brother Juniper's Cafe.
I can't continue in this fashion,
her fabulous hair teases me in the wind,
dark brown curls spread past
a sweat-suited waist and back.
To know her would ruin
the meaning of the life I repress.
I must do something,
invent a name for her,
yell out the window and leer,
anything except the nothing I grope
when I see her jog briskly,
pumping wrist weights out and up
in the November fog.
Where does she live,
is she married to a rich dermatologist,

should I toss her apples
or forget her like a spoiled plate of spaghetti?
Yes, I've met and loved this woman a thousand times,
a fresh version of the same model
oblivious and aware of men like me
infatuated with the mystery of her,
the woman with the wild hair
who runs the avenues
and dares all of them
to catch her if they can.

◆ ◆

DAVID SPICER works as a proofreader and computer operator at a Memphis printing and graphics company. He is the author of four chapbooks and one book of poetry. He is copublisher of Black Cedar Press/Ion Books and publisher-editor of Ion Books.

LEVI FRAZIER, JR.

THE WITCH DOCTOR

I called him witchdoctor, not because of his strange powers (although I had heard stories of ". . . the lame to walk and the blind to see . . ."), but because people in great numbers believed in him, even after his death. Sometimes I was even tempted to believe.

"All I know is that no sooner than he had died, they put his body in the ground," my mother said. She had made up her mind many years ago that if anybody could pull off the Lazarus trick, Dr. Katz was the person to do it.

"Yes suh! That's the way they did Jesus. They didn't hold his body out of the ground for relatives to come all the way from places like Chicago and Detroit to eat you out of house and home, get drunk, and act the fool. If Mary and Joseph had kept Jesus out of the earth as long as some of these Negroes keep their people out of the ground, the Lord wouldn't have had no cause to raise hisself from the dead; he could've just stayed here and did his work and went on to heaven."

My mother had gone to Dr. Katz as long as she lived in North Memphis, probably as long as Dr. Katz had been a doctor. Now his death seemed so hasty, and his burial seemed as rushed as his death, but Ma Minnie, as my sister and I called my mother, believed that all these sudden circumstances were due to the fact that Dr. Seymore Katz was a great man, a healer of men.

I remember the first time I went to Dr. Katz; I had a lump in my throat, not a sentimental one, but a real lump in my throat that bothered me whenever I attempted to swallow. Driving down Chelsea to the witchdoctor's office, I sensed how helpless St. Blaise's patient must have felt before the good saint miraculously removed the fishbone from her throat. At least she had faith. I had no faith in the witchdoctor and his miraculous healings, but my mother did and that's why we were there.

"Say ahh," Dr. Katz breathed, squinting down my throat, his tongue depressor creeping steadily toward my tonsils.

"The Witch Doctor," by Levi Frazier, Jr., appeared in *Homespun Images* (Memphis, Tenn.: LeMoyne-Owen College, 1989), 217–26. Reprinted by permission of LeMoyne-Owen College.

"It's that football," said my mother, staring over Dr. Katz's shoulder down my throat. "Probably got his wind pipe knocked aloose on that field, but I couldn't tell him nothing. And his daddy's a fool for letting him do it. Act'n proud 'cause his son's playing football."

According to my mother, every illness I've had since joining the football team in the ninth grade has been a result of football. God Almighty couldn't persuade her otherwise.

Dr. Katz acted as if my mother was his assistant, as he passed her his tongue depressor to throw in the wastebasket. My mother took the depressor, ordered me to open my mouth, then took one last look without the Wizard's assistance. After about three seconds, she removed the depressor, shook her head and threw the soggy stick into the wastebasket. She then returned to her seat beside me and became a full-time mother again. I could tell from Dr. Katz's sanguine expression that he had probably been through this ritual many other times with my mother and my older sister Karen.

"How long have you been bothered with this ailment," the doctor said, squatting on a too-small stool in front of me, his green eyes staring into mine.

"About a day and a half," my mother said, staring at Dr. Katz.

"Does it hurt anytime other than when you swallow?" the witchdoctor continued, still staring directly at me.

"No, only when he swallows," my mother said with twice as much feeling as I would have said it, had I been able to get a word in.

I could talk perfectly; it was swallowing that I had the problem with. What made matters worse was that I was fourteen years old, a member (non-playing) of the football team, and a freshman in high school. So I made up my mind that I would answer the next question myself.

"Do you have regular bowel movements?" the doctor asked in a low voice.

"Yes!!" I shouted at the top of my lungs, in a rush to beat my mother to the draw. Both the doctor and my mother jumped as if they had been shocked by a bolt of electricity. Even the receptionist peeked in on us to see if everything was all right.

"It seems like you have an allergy," the witchdoctor stated. "Stay away from all sprays, detergents, colognes, and perfumes," he said, frantically writing a prescription.

"Was this fool crazy?" I thought to myself, as I watched him hand the prescription over to my mother, smiling with relief. This was the first time this quack had ever seen me and in the course of five minutes, he was telling me not to use Right Guard, Jade East, and English Leather, three distinguishable signs and scents of manhood for me and my crowd.

As quickly as he expired some sixteen years later, the witchdoctor shook my hand, then scurried out to his next patient. I was too mad to talk or swallow. This crackpot made my mother feel that I had some type of orphan illness that showed up to claim me after fourteen years of hiding underneath my skin.

"No wonder Black folks stayed in slavery so long," I thought, "believing everything the White man's been telling for years." Both manhood and newly found racial pride were being pushed to the limit.

"I knew it was football all along. You probably allergic to all them weeds and dog mess you been falling in. If you hadn't been playing, you never would have been sick.

Look at you; you can't even swallow." This kind of abuse from my mother, along with my illness, went on for at least a week.

As some kind of masochistic revenge, I refused to take the medicine that the witchdoctor had prescribed. Also, my faith in him as a healer of Black people had reached an all-time low, considering he knew nothing about the biological relationship between Black men, Jade East, and Black women.

So I decided I would suffer a few more days and then go to another doctor, a Black doctor, recommended by a good friend. This doctor could cure anything from a toothache to the clap. I was ready to go.

Two days before my intended visit, my father found the full bottle of medicine prescribed by Dr. Katz.

"No wonder you ain't getting no better; don't look like a pill been touched in this bottle. Here," he said, lifting the top off the bottle, pouring one of the round orange pills into my hand. "It says, 'Take every four hours.' You ain't following instructions. How do you expect to get back out there and play football if you don't hurry up and get well?" He ran some tap water in a jelly jar and gave it to me. I downed the pill and a ton of pride. I felt like an old Catholic being forced to eat meat on Fridays for health purposes.

I had wanted no part of the witchdoctor's medicine, but since I had taken it, I would be even more adamant in slandering him and his cures when it was discovered that they didn't work. I was happy when I laid down on my bed.

When I awoke, it was nighttime. I walked into the kitchen, turned on the light and ran me a glass of tap water in the same jelly jar that I had used earlier in the evening. I had drank the entire jar of water and was on my way to turn off the light when it dawned on me: There was no pain. I swallowed. No lump. I had been miraculously cured. The witchdoctor had struck again.

Sixteen years have passed since my healing, and in those sixteen years, many have touched the hem of his jacket, and according to the multitudes and the multitudes' spokesman—my mother—many were healed, and these many, for the most part, were as Black as the woman who birthed them and as poor as Job's turkey. And they all were appreciative of the wonders he had performed. But as always, there was gossip.

"They talked about Jesus, so you know what folks will say about anybody else." The chief spokesman had taken it upon herself to defend the witchdoctor and his memory.

"And you know that the same people that's talking 'bout him now, is the same ones who was standing in his parking lot at seven o'clock many a Monday morning." As usual, the chief spokesman was right, but it mattered little to those who talked about his young wife, his alleged drug problems, and his wayward son. Black people have always been accustomed to the fallibility of their gods or witchdoctors. If a celebrity or anyone else didn't make a mistake, something was wrong with that person. As a matter of fact, it probably meant that the person had a hidden fault, which in turn meant that this fault was much worse than anyone could imagine; therefore, it had to be uncovered, and eventually it would be. I believe some preachers and politicians actually go so far as to develop incidents or affairs to draw attention away from the real dirt that is being swept under the rug. Considering this, then, Black people expect human nature of their leaders, even demand it at times.

I guess I had reconciled myself to the fact that the witchdoctor had quite a faithful following of my people, but there was one thing that began to bother me about him and his association with Black folk, considering he was receiving all of their praise. It dawned on me that as a child, I remembered seeing my mother and grandmother sit on the colored side of Dr. Katz's office, while all of the White people sat on the White side. At that time, the office seemed to have had as many Whites who needed healing as Blacks. In the last sixteen years, however, the ratio had changed. Now the office was 98 percent Black and 2 percent poor White. Everybody sat on the same side. This fact held little comfort for me. Although Dr. Katz may have accidentally cured me, he was still guilty of treating Black people as second-class citizens or animals to be kept apart from White people. The length of time his office was segregated made no difference to me; the fact that it was at some point segregated made all the difference in the world. After culturally, if not personally, suffering an Auschwitz, how could a person relegate a different group of people to another side of the room, the bus, the restaurant, the toilet, or the waiting room? It seemed as inconsistent as taking a shower with gas instead of water, or covering a lamp with human flesh instead of cloth. Inconsistent. And I had to know why so many cousins, uncles, aunts, and my own mother could put their faith in someone who put them in a corner.

When I stepped onto my parents' porch, my mother greeted me at the door; she was on her way to the grocer's for her weekly shopping, which she had done routinely for the past twenty-five years on Thursdays.

"I'm glad you came by," she said, as if she knew I would be standing on the porch at that particular moment. "I got this condolences card for Dr. Katz' new wife that I want you to see." Although Dr. Katz had been married to his "new wife" for the past ten years, none of his patients, including my mother, referred to her as anything other than "Dr. Katz's new wife." The status of *Mrs. Katz* was reserved for one woman and one woman only, and she died ten years ago in Rosewood Nursing Home.

My mother turned back into the house, searching for the sympathy card on the low-lying oak coffee table in the middle of the room. It wasn't there, so she moved on into the bedroom to resume her search. The odor of home hit me as I stepped into the house. A mixture of pork, Sir Walter Raleigh Tobacco, and Pride Furniture Wax hung thick in the air, coating the gold carpet, the pea-green draperies, and the French Provincial furniture. Had the witchdoctor ever smelled this aroma, except for the slight bitter-sweet scent that clung to the Black bodies that he thumped, pinched, and stuck with needles? Did he ever desire to know these bodies beyond the standard data of weight, age, and medical history? Weren't Black folk taking this hero worship too far?

I was just about to turn on the radio when my mother stepped into the living room.

"I got it," she said, relieved. "It was right where I thought I had put it. Let's go to the store before Montesi's gets too crowded."

Suddenly we were out of the house, in the car, and driving west on Poplar Avenue. I was just about to ask, for the third time, my question about Dr. Katz's segregated offices. It seemed a simple enough thing to do, but I kept balking at the thought of catching my mother and a somewhat sacred memory off guard. Finally I asked.

When my mother did answer, she did so with a slight frown on her face. "No," she said. "I don't recall his office ever being segregated." I knew she was still considering another reply.

Hesitantly, she explained to me that the witchdoctor's office was segregated at one time—"but not for a very long time."

As she told the story, Dr. Katz inherited the office and seating pattern from another physician.

"Why didn't he just change the visiting room and let everybody sit together?" I asked, determined to finish what I had started.

She answered that the doctor just probably let things go on since no one complained about them and everybody just expected colored folks and White folks to be separated; that is, everybody except Tapen.

Tapen was a living legend in North Memphis, as infamous as Billy the Kid or Wyatt Earp. Always noted for a "well-dranked" pint of Henry McKenna in the back pocket of his white coveralls, Tapen had painted his way from one side of Memphis to the other and was on his way back to the other side when he fell twenty feet to the ground and busted his leg. Never realizing he had broken his leg, Tapen drank the last bit of Mr. McKenna, wrapped a torn piece of tarp around his wound, and walked the two miles to the doctor's office, where he was immediately ushered to the colored side of the waiting room to await a miracle.

According to my mother, who got the story from her sister Rene, who was there at the time, Tapen was more in need of a chair than a miracle as he stood among the dark multitudes of the aged, the pregnant, and the helpless.

Two elderly women, who could barely stand, tried to get Tapen to take their seat, but the 6'2" painter only shook his head and motioned with his black and white speckled hand that they keep their seat. He then peered past the office dividing the two waiting rooms and saw an empty chair in need of a patient. Tapen didn't necessarily feel that the chair was looking for a Black or White patient, so he opened the half-door that led into the receptionist's area and walked straight through to the "other side," dragging his loosely bandaged leg across the oriental throw rug. The secretaries were busy typing or looking into file cabinets, so they didn't notice Tapen's migration.

Tapen's entrance wasn't a complete surprise to everyone, as evidenced by two White ladies and one middle-aged White man (with one leg) who stood at attention in amazement when they saw Tapen coming toward them.

"Y'all keep your seat, keep your seat; ain't no need to stand on my account. The name is Tapen; how y'all feeling today?"

Tapen then took a seat and waited to be called in to see the witchdoctor, as a chorus of "Sirs," coming from the receptionist area, begged for his attention.

"I'm sorry, Mr. . . . uh . . . uh . . . I. . . ." The little red-haired receptionist sputtered, trying to make sense of the situation and take control at the same time.

"Just call me Tapen. Is the doctor about ready to see me, ma'm? This leg's about to give me a fit." Tapen noticed that some of the White people were still standing, so he nodded to them to take a seat, which they did, except for the man with the one leg, who left the office running.

"But Mr. Tapen," the receptionist continued.

"Just Tapen, ma'm."

Four years at Southwestern University at Memphis might have taught her many contemporary concepts and ideas, but Tapen was not one of them, and she was determined to take hold of the situation.

"Sir . . . we . . . Aren't there any seats on the other side?"

"Not a one."

"I'm sorry, Mr. Tapper."

"Tapen . . . Like a cane tap'n."

"Yes sir . . . I. . . ."

The receptionist was stumped; she couldn't go on. She felt the White people begging with their eyes for help, and she could sense the Black people laughing at the entire situation. She was right. According to my Aunt Rene, the Black folks were laughing and saying to each other, "How in the hell is she gon' get that crazy nigger Tapen out of the White folks side of the visiting room?"

The receptionist stood in the middle of her island with her arms dangling loosely at her side. As the tears welled up in her eyes, she looked toward the ceiling and said, "Lord, what next?"

According to my mother, who swore she got the entire story from my Aunt Rene, the door flew open and a white stick, with a red tip, tapped around inside the waiting room. The person, led by the stick, stepped heartily but aimlessly into the office whistling Dixie and yelling, "Good morning," to the top of his voice. Colonel Jasper had been a veteran of World War I, which he felt was a northern diversionary tactic to keep the South from declaring her independence again. The Colonel was blinded while participating in the French campaign (of this diversionary tactic). The last thing he saw was a French woman throwing hot water in his face for trying to watch her and her Black lover make love. As soon as he returned to the States, Colonel Jasper joined the KKK. As a matter of fact, pictures had been circulated around town of Colonel Jasper dressed in white robe and hood, wearing dark glasses, holding a white cane with fire red tip while standing in front of a lighted cross. Colonel Jasper was as infamous as Tapen.

Having hailed everyone on the White side, the Colonel yelled past the already stunned receptionist to the colored side of the waiting room. "And how is all you girls and boys doing over yonder way?" he asked, not waiting for a reply. However, had the Colonel taken the notion to listen to the Black half of the waiting room, he would have heard a low chorus of "lowdown bastard," "non-seeing dog," and "mealey-mouth mother——." That may have been the reason he never actually waited for a reply.

The Colonel then wandered over toward his usual chair, tapping toes, ankles, and knees with his cane along the way. Having witnessed the Colonel's dilemma, Tapen took the old man's arm into his hand and guided the Colonel to his seat, which was right beside Tapen.

"Thank you, kind sir," the Colonel said, with more than a hint of sorghum in his voice. "You are a most gracious gentleman. I can tell by your grip that you're also very strong. If my daughter were not married, I would surely give her away to someone as strong and gentlemanly as yourself."

"Why, thank you, Colonel," Tapen said, spraying Henry McKenna fumes in the direction of the old veteran, "but the one I got now is more than I can handle."

"According to your Aunt Rene," my mother said, "the Colonel stuck his nose in the air like a rat when there's a human about." Then a White gentleman on the other side of the Colonel whispered something in his ear that made him turn a shade of red the color of his cane tip, beginning with the ear in which he got the news and moving across his entire crinkly face, except for his lips, which turned a deep lavender.

"Godammit, Tapen, what the hell you doing on the White folk side of the office?" shouted the old doughboy, shaking like a 1955 model washing machine.

"Why, the same thing you doing over here, Colonel, having a seat, waiting for the doctor to see me."

"I don't give a damn who you waiting on, Tapen. . . I been coming to this office nigh on twenty years and the only niggers who come on this side, come to empty the trash."

"Well, I guess that's your problem, Colonel; you, and a great many like you, are used to dealing with niggers and not colored folks. I ain't no nigger, Colonel, and I ain't no garbage man either, so I'm here to be waited on—not to take out the trash."

The Colonel's lips were so purple that his teeth looked blue as he yelled for Dr. Katz to come and put a swift end to this nigger's madness. "Maybe the doctor will let this fool bleed to death or hemorrhage," the old man whispered, pacing the floor like a five-year-old kid needing to pee. "Would serve him right! The nerve of that nigger! After they came back from Paris, you couldn't keep 'em away from White folks, 'specially our women!" the Colonel mumbled. "Dr. Katz! . . . Dr. Katz, come out here. There's an emergency."

When the doctor finally rushed out, he figured the old man was having a heart attack right there in the office. Now both stood there, red in the face, breathing hard, facing each other.

"See for yourself," the Colonel said, pointing in the direction of Tapen. "Don't you see him?"

The doctor looked at Tapen and then looked at the Black half of the waiting room.

"At times like these, I think it's a blessing I don't have my sight . . . Well, what we gon' do, doc?" said the Colonel, finally coming under control.

Again the doctor looked at the Black half of the waiting room and at Tapen, who looked like he was going to keep his seat, no matter what the decision would be. The doctor surveyed the office like a general surveys a battlefield after a major battle has been fought.

"Is this the price we have to pay?" the doctor said, motioning to everyone in the office.

"Godammit! That's exactly how I feel, doc," said the Colonel, a faint smile breaking across his lips. "Now what are we going to do?"

"Nothing," said the doctor. "Nothing at all."

"You . . . you mean to tell me that you're going to let this nigger stay over here with the White folks?" the Colonel quietly said. "Is that what I'm hearing?"

"Your hearing's pretty good, Colonel," said Dr. Katz.

"Well, I'll be damned," the old vet said, walking toward the door like a man with twenty-twenty. "Ain't bad enough the niggers getting uppity, but the kikes joining up with 'em. Goddammit, I figure if you look white, you sure in hell ought to act white." He then opened the door and stepped down onto Chelsea Street, cussing everything kosher, from dill pickles to Moshe Dayan.

According to my mother, Aunt Rene claimed that somebody on the Black side of the waiting room started laughing. (Both my mother and I believe it was Aunt Rene.) "When we were kids, Rene would be the first to laugh at anything," my mother said. "So it was probably Rene that cackled first." But whoever laughed first infected the entire waiting room. Everybody laughed, including the White folks (those who wouldn't come back, as well as those who would).

In the midst of all the laughter, Dr. Katz instructed the young receptionist to open the doors between the visiting rooms. "Since everyone is taking the same medicine, everybody will sit in the same chairs," he said, walking over to Tapen and extending his hand to the ailing painter. They shook like old friends greeting each other after many years of separation. The doctor then helped Tapen to his feet and assisted him in walking into the back to be treated. That was 1954.

Having heard my mother's story, I finally resigned myself to accepting the witchdoctor for what he was—dead or alive—even if he was forced to integrate his office, much like Kennedy was forced to help integrate the South. Dr. Katz was a healer. A healer through faith.

"Some of these Negroes taking this faith thing a little too far," my mother said, on the way back from Montesi's Grocery. "Some of 'em going over there taking pieces of paint from the windows and branches from the bushes in his yard, like that junk is going to help cure them when they get the misery."

There was one thing Mother and I both agreed on. Relics had no power. My first year in med school confirmed that. We both swore that we would never remove a token from that place, no matter how small—not even a blade of grass. We haven't and we never will. But when his office became available after my internship, I grabbed it right away. I reasoned that if a blade of grass could inspire faith, then miracles could be performed in this building.

◆ ◆

Levi Frazier, Jr., is a native Memphian who received his B.A. degree from Rhodes College and his M.A. from the University of Memphis. He is co-founder and artistic director of Blues City Cultural Center in Memphis. His musical, *Beale Street Back Again*, is being produced at the Tennessee Performing Arts Center as part of the State Bicentennial in 1996.

LYNDA HAMBLEN

RETROSPECTIVES

An old woman now,
bone pale from dark rooms and pain,
wrinkled and toothless,
body sagging from the weight of man and years,
hair straggling, clothes rumpled and stained,
she once could catch a horse
and ride him barebacked
across the field.

Old Pilot he was called,
piebald and blind from birth.
How strange to him and marvelous
must have seemed his world:
only smells and sounds
and taste and touch,
and touch most of all—
the cold tin of an oat bucket,
the cool, damp prickliness
of early morning grass,
the firm, pulling hold
of an occasional bridle and bit,
and a woman's knees
clamped stout and strong
in love and control.

THE LAKE LOON

The lake loon warned all the night
Of rain to come.
But we braved the morning
And laughed at noon
When thunder filled the sky.
In the evening we returned
Soaked with that day's sum
Of water and surprise.
In the night the loon laughed too,
While we restlessly dreamed,
Hearing from afar, outside of sleep,
The echo of laughing cries,
Hollow against the moon.

LYNDA HAMBLEN is a resident of Union City, Tennessee, and is the president of Writer's Ink. She has had poems, essays, and reviews published in *Alura*, *Beanswitch*, the *Confluent Education Journal*, *Writer's Ink*, *Cats!*, and the *Union City Daily Messenger*.

ALAN LIGHTMAN

FROM *GOOD BENITO*

After the rocket launch at the Galloway Golf Course, Bennett began to realize that he was better suited for theory than for experiment. Bennett pondered things. He was a ponderer. He wondered why the sky turned red at the end of the day. He wondered why soap bubbles formed in nearly perfect spheres, why all snowflakes had six sides. He wondered why a spoon halfway in water appeared to bend in two, why chalk squeaked. He wondered why a spinning top didn't fall over but instead slowly gyrated. He wondered why the sun didn't burn up, whether outer space went on forever. He wondered why clouds formed high in the air and not on the ground. He wondered how sap could rise in trees, against gravity, what made rainbows, what made the dark lines on the surface when water was poured in a bowl. He wondered why upstairs was usually warmer than downstairs.

He lies on his bed in late afternoon. Why must a focusing mirror be parabolic in shape? Why won't a spherical or flat mirror work? Why? There is a logical reason. He must know what it is. Closing his eyes, he imagines various shapes, pictures the trajectories of light rays. Silvered glass curving. Angles. Rows of imaginary lines, perpendicular to the surface as it undulates through space. Bennett, what are you doing up there? Yellow and gold light rays careening at angles to the perpendiculars, reflecting at equal angles, heading back into space, polished glass flexing and curling. Bennett, you've been spending too much time in your room. Come down. Out of all possible shapes, one shape. A parabola, an arc such that each point is equally distant from a directrix and focus. The hypothetical light rays fly in and emerge, converge to a point, converge to a focus. Glass gently sweeping through space. He has to know why.

The world buckled at its knees when Bennett took his first algebra course. He was thirteen. The class began with word problems, verbal applications of the rules of arithmetic.

Mary has three pennies. If she gives two pennies to her younger brother Henry, how many pennies will she have left? Sometime in October, the problems progressed to more thoughtful examples, like: Mary is six years older than Henry, and Henry's age is two-thirds of Mary's. How old is Henry? These conundrums had to be solved by trial and error. Finally, Bennett was taught how to symbolize the unknowns of a problem with Xs and Ys and to display everything in equations. Using the rules of algebra, the unknowns could be solved for in one logical step. What started with a messy statement involving Mary and her kid brother Henry ended with a single, sleek equation.

Bennett wouldn't have been happy with no mention of Mary and Henry. That kind of problem was for the pure mathematician: Consider object A, which is six units greater than object B, whereas object B has a measure two-thirds that of A. No, Bennett was a scientist, and he wanted to begin in the dirt and debris of the real physical world. But he took pleasure in sifting through that world, distilling it, cleansing and purifying it, until he was left with single mathematical equation of inescapable solution.

In his American history class, even after reading the book, the class would argue for days about why the Civil War started. The teacher would argue as well, first giving one reason, then another, walking up and down between the desks, until finally Bennett concluded that no one on earth knew why the Civil War started. It was the same with English and social studies. But algebra was different. There was always an answer, clean as a new Franklin half-dollar. The rules of logic guaranteed an answer. And when you found the answer, there was no arguing about it. You were right, and everyone agreed you were right.

He remembered everything about that algebra class. Mrs. Dixon had gray and white hair, which she kept pinned in a vertical bun. She wore dresses with large colored flowers on them. The floor was linoleum and looked like a checkerboard, with black and white squares. Just inside the door, to the left, was a coatroom with brass hooks on the wall. When someone misbehaved in class, he was sentenced to the coatroom, where everyone soon would hear him trying on other people's coats. Above the middle of the blackboard sat a big red clock, like an eye, reminding the class of how many minutes remained. The desks had swivel tops with grooves to hold pencils. Mrs. Dixon demanded that each student keep a highly sharpened pencil in the groove at all times. The pupils were not permitted to get up from their desks for any reason, including the toilet, except to sharpen their pencils at the back of the room.

Bennett couldn't wait to discuss each new technique in higher mathematics with John after school. John would get impatient and say, Yeah, yeah, I know about that stuff, and then he would bring out some dissected squid's eye or an electrical circuit he was working on.

It is early morning, before breakfast. Bennett stands in his room in his pajamas, looking idly out the window at the Taglias' house next door. A cedar fence separates the two houses. Magnolias grow along the fence. But from his bedroom window, Bennett can see over the magnolias, over the fence, and watch the withered old man slowly walk down the driveway to pick up the morning paper. The old man, the grandfather, speaks no English. Sometimes he mutters to himself in Italian. He leans to the left as he walks, slowly lifts each foot as if it were stuck in the asphalt. He is a tiny, thin stick, and he limps slowly down the driveway each morning, beneath the maple trees, to fetch the paper. It is good weather today, but the old man goes in all weather. Bennett has watched him for years. This morning, he estimates the length of the driveway and clocks the old man's walk with his watch and calculates how long it would take him to walk to the moon.

Bennett's classmates hated word problems. Indeed, they hated math altogether, but they'd rather have a tooth filled than be forced to sit down and contemplate word problems. Bennett, on the other hand, placed word problems on a level with Florida's pecan pie. Word problems were delicious. He devoured them. He convinced the flabbergasted Mrs. Dixon to give him additional problems, beyond the assignments, and when she ran out of problems he created them himself. After school, when the other boys played basketball or loitered behind the Rexall drugstore to smoke and discuss girls, Bennett went home and up to his room to do word problems.

His mother would come out of her bedroom where she'd been resting, wearing her pale amber robe, and stand at the foot of the stairs. Bennett, what are you doing up there, she would call up to him, in a polite voice. Nothing, he'd answer. Then he'd hear some whispering and Marty or Philip would ascend halfway up to the stairs and recite as he'd been told: Bennett, what are you doing in your room? Masturbating, Bennett would answer, don't come up. After a moment, his mother would call up again: Sammy Abrams is such a nice boy, and he's invited you over to play. I don't like Sammy Abrams, Bennett would answer through his closed door. What about Michael Solmson? replied his mother, he's a lovely boy. I don't like Michael Solmson, Bennett would answer. Then, his mother again: You're selfish and you're going to grow up miserable, with no friends. Just like Uncle Maury.

Bennett didn't understand why his mother called him selfish for staying in his room. In those years, and for many years after, he was terribly confused by what people said. One fall, after his weekly allowance was reduced by twenty-five cents, his mother explained that since the family business was doing well, it was a good time to save money rather than spend it. On another occasion, Bennett's cousin Laura, in her early twenties, announced that she was breaking up with her boyfriend because she loved him too much. Could that be what she meant? Bennett learned to hide his confusion and just nod his head. Then he'd go to his room to do word problems. He thought everybody should learn how to do word problems.

One o'clock in the morning. Old man Taglia walks at this hour, unobserved, his house dark and asleep. He limps slowly in the moonlight. There is another light. He looks up to his left, toward the second-floor window. *Che diavolo, ci risiamo*, he mutters, and continues down the driveway.

Bennett sits at his oak desk. They are so beautiful, the equations. Even visually beautiful, but especially beautiful in the mind. Their precision and power are beautiful, and as he begins to understand an equation, he gets the same feeling as seeing a moonrise over trees. In his mind, it is dark and still and then the tops of the trees on the far side of the bay begin to glow slightly, white and soft, and the white gets brighter, silhouetting the trees, and then a small piece of moon appears and the mathematics opens up and contains and shines in perfection. It is one in the morning, but he is not tired. He gains strength from himself. He does not need to go to the library, he does not need to ask other students or grown-ups for information or help. He can be here alone, in his room, with the beautiful mathematics and the moon and figure things out on his own. He can sit here naked at his oak desk with the clean, white paper and work in the absolute certainty and the solitude and perfection. Gliding through the world in his mind, he doesn't worry about his small height or his pimples or his problems with talking or his confusion at what people say. It is a world without bodies. It is a world of clear logic and grace. It is the best part of loneliness, without the sadness.

◆ ◆

ALAN LIGHTMAN teaches physics and writing at MIT. His work has appeared in *Granta*, the *New Yorker*, *Harper's*, and the *New York Review of Books*. His first novel, *Einstein's Dream*, was on national bestseller lists during 1993 and 1994.

DEWEY LAMBDIN

From *HMS Cockerel*

Alan Lewrie turned the packet over and sucked in a cold breath of chill country air, as he beheld the blue sealing wafer, stamped with the fouled anchor and crown. *Admiralty!*

"War wi' th' French, I wager, sir," Will Cony declared as Lewrie broke the seal. His "man" was all but hopping from one foot to the other in rising excitement. "Ever'one knowed h'it wuz a'comin.'"

"Hmmph. Thought the old fart'd retired by now," Lewrie snorted as he noted the inscription below the message. A harried junior clerk had penned the bulk of it, but for the prim signature of the First Secretary, Philip Stephens, who had been First Secretary to the Admiralty since the year Alan Lewrie'd been born!

January 20, 1793
Admiralty, Whitehall

To: Lieutenant Alan Lewrie, R.N.

Sir,
My Lords Commissioners for executing the high Office of Lord High Admiral require your most immediate Attendance, or Response. You are charged and directed. . . .

"Well, damme," Lewrie breathed again. The dawn chill settled lower, to his stomach, not just his lungs. "Bodkins? Do put Anson back in his stall, I'll not ride today. It's—" He dragged out his damascened watch to peer at it. "—Nigh on seven. Harness up the closed coach. I wish to depart for London by ten."

"Be it war, sir?" Cony inquired anxiously.

"No mention of it, Cony. Yet. Something that smells nigh to war, though. I'll see the messenger, now. Do you look to my chest, see what's wanting. You know my needs

Excerpt from *HMS Cockerel*, by Dewey Lambdin (New York: Donald I. Fine, Inc., 1995). Reprinted by permission of the author.

well as any, by now. And lay out one of my uniforms. I'll be up, directly."

"Aye, sir," Cony answered, touching his forehead in a curled-hand salute, of old habit. "Uhm . . . ya wish me t'go wi' ya, sir? Up t'London, that is, sir?"

"Yes, Cony. At least to London," Lewrie smiled, though a bit grimly. "Once I've a ship, though . . . that's up to you. I allow you may be more useful to Mrs. Lewrie about the farm. Farming's what you know best, what you enjoy most?"

"Uh, yessir," Cony shrugged, sounding oddly disappointed.

"No need to take you off to sea," Lewrie rambled on as they went towards the warm kitchens. "Estate agent, overseer . . . and there's Maude down at the Ploughman, is there not?"

"Uhm, yessir," Cony nodded.

Mr. Beakman at the Olde Ploughman was getting on in years, with no sons to inherit the pub. He was a widower, and his Maudie was now of a marriageable age, and both were fond of Cony; almost everyone in Anglesgreen was. Whichever way he jumped, he'd land on his feet.

And do it on dry land, if he's any sense, Lewrie thought.

"I'm Lewrie, sir," he announced to the elegant stranger who was warming his backside by the kitchen hearth, being half-ogled by maids and scullery wenches, who still walked shy of the stranger's threat. "I imagine you'll wish a reply to carry back?"

"That would be welcome, sir," the functionary nodded. "Though I have several more officers to call upon towards Chiddingfold and Petersfield before returning, sir. Naval paperwork, d'ye see, sir. . . ."

"Quite," Lewrie rejoined, grimacing at its necessity, and making the messenger grin, too, over the seeming volumes of correspondence HM Government generated over trifles. "Come to my study. Bring your tea. A dollop of brandy'd thaw your bones, whilst I pen something suitable?"

"Oh, aye, sir!" The messenger agreed heartily.

As they left the kitchen for the central hall, Lewrie espied Caroline and the boys. She stood all but trembling, with a wild cast to her expression, and the petulant, whiny children tucked into her skirts. They couldn't know what was transpiring, surely, he thought, but it was plain enough to them that *something* threatening was playing out.

"Alan . . . dear," Caroline called after him, clearing her throat, almost in a whisper. He thought to pause, to speak a few assuring words to her. But it was her furrow, and her frown, that stopped him. Almost accusatory, she looked, the vexed frown she might bestow on one of the boys when they were unruly, in warning that further such behaviour would call for punishment.

"I'll be with you shortly, dear," he said, instead.

"Is it war?" Alan asked the young functionary after he'd closed the double doors to his study against the rest of his household.

"Not yet, sir," the messenger shrugged, busy at the wine-cabinet. "But they've been calling officers and warrants back for weeks, now. I heard tell the 'Press has been warned, just in case. A 'Hot' press."

"Doesn't say much for me, then," Lewrie forced a chuckle. "I was one of the first recalled in '91, for Nootka Sound."

"Our Lords Commissioners never dismissed some of those called, sir. The Fleet has remained at one-third strength since the Terror in Paris began. And, d'ye see, sir . . . you *are* in the lower half of the Lieutenant's List, so if at a third, sir. . . ."

"Umphh," Lewrie commented, sitting at his desk. He laid out a fresh sheet of vellum and a pot of ink (black required) and took a small penknife to the nib of his freshest quill. He got through the date, his local address, destination, and salutation. Then sat, quite nonplussed, wondering just exactly what the Devil he'd say to Our Lords Commissioners.

Milords—bugger off? he thought sarcastically.

The Navy had not been his career of choice; he could thank his father, far off in Bengal now, with the East India Company Army, for "press-ganging" him into service, for the money he *should* have inherited from Granny Lewrie, long before. He'd never been what one might call a *glad* sailor. Thirteen years of his life he'd given the Fleet, not with much choice in the matter, truth to tell. Nine on active service, midshipman to lieutenant . . . and the last four "beached" on half-pay.

He thought the French had an apt word for these last four years; they usually did, damn their troublesome, rebellious eyes!

Ennui. Boredom and isolation. Shunned and out of his depth as a farmer. And as anchored as Ulysses in his dotage.

Without a war, and one certainly was now coming, in spite of his assurances to Caroline, what would life hold for him? More of Anglesgreen, a leper to his neighbors, until such time, in a misty future, that he outlived Sir Romney, Uncle Phineas, and Harry, and the grudge faded? Harry'd inherit, become baronet, marry some unfortunate mort, and let go his rancour at last? Lewrie *might* become a proper squire, then, with owned, not rented acres, have a right to hunt and fish his own lands, 'stead of waiting to be allowed on others' sufferance; some stooped and greying rustic he'd become, with a fund of tedious yarns, hair growing from out his ears, with a nose that bowed in low *conge'* to his departing teeth! A well-respected, cackling bore, no matter that he bored his audience at the Red Swan at last, 'stead of the Olde Ploughman.

And whilst there'd been war with the French, whilst tall frigates prowled like leopards in the night, bright-eyed and hungry to claw each other, as line-of-battle ships formed to bellow—to make, or to break history—he would have been nothing but a spectator. One far back in the cheap seats, too! He would *farm*! Read the news down from London, the *Gazette*, the *Naval Chronicle*, brandish his walking-stick and *Huzzah* each victory . . . or write scathing letters to the *Times*.

Caroline needed him, though, would prefer this time. . . .

He shuddered with revulsion of his bleak, dreary but respectable civilian future . . . Caroline or no.

No, as his father, Sir Hugo St. George Willoughby, Captain of the 4th The King's Own, Lt. Colonel of the 19th Native Infantry, had said to him once, when they'd met in the Far East. . . .

"Might not have been a *glad* soldier boy . . . but I was a damn' good'un!" He'd told him. Or something like that.

Growl he may, but *go* . . . aye, he believed he would. There would not be a second asking, if he turned the Admiralty down once. And his place on the List would be scratched out, his commission thrown over. Alan Lewrie knew in his heart that there would be no peace for his restless soul if he did not take the King's Shilling, and serve, just one more time.

"Your pardons," Lewrie said, as if coming out of a trance, "but t'is been so long since I penned an official letter, formalities quite escaped me. You found the brandy, I trust, sir?"

"Your rum, sir," the young messenger replied quite happily, baking before the morning fire, a large mug of laced tea in his hand. He had not taken the slightest notice Lewrie might have been delaying, or dithering and hesitant. In fact, what delay he might have at last noticed, he would have enjoyed, so he could warm himself against another cold ride, and make free with Lewrie's fine, sweet, dark Jamaican rum.

"Rum for me, too, it seems." Lewrie grunted in pleasure as he put the finishing touches to his letter of acceptance. "'Clear Decks and Up-Spirits,' seven bells o' the Forenoon." He shook sand over it so the ink wouldn't smudge, folded it carefully, and applied hot wax to seal the outer fold. "There you are, sir. I'll be in London by nightfall, and in the Waiting Rooms by tomorrow morning."

Lewrie went to his wine-cabinet after the messenger departed, and poured himself a glass of dark Jamaican, inventorying his study for items to take along. Would he get a ship of his own to command again, something small like *Alacrity*? Wine-cabinet; fold-leg desk; caddy for tea, coffee, chocolate, and sugar; the extra chest yonder. Fusil musketoon, the Ferguson rifle, the pewter lanthorns down from the garret, and. . . .

No, he thought, taking a bracing sip: I'll go a lieutenant in a wardroom, more'n like. Dog's-manger of a cabin, no room for much beyond my sea-chest and a few books.

He held the glass of rum to the firelight. It was almost opaque, and the alcohol fumes wafted a sweet, lush, adventurous scent of far-off West Indies molasses about his head, rife with promise of potency, of over-the-horizon, beyond-the-sunset, larger-than-life excitements. Honour and glory be damned, he thought: it'll be an adventure!

He took another sip, savouring the rawness of the rum's bouquet. Soon it might be pusser's issue rum, cheap pop-skull, the weary seaman's anodyne. And, with the rum, he could almost begin to sniff a whiff of ocean. Hemp and tar, the steam of the steep-tubs, and the fat off them used as slush on running rigging, the iodine tang of open, rolling seas, the fresh-fish aroma of storm-wrack, and the tide-water mildewed mustiness of harbour-side; of hot sand and kelp, baking beneath a cruel sun on distant strands. The smell of a ship. The dank-cave breaths, wafting up from limber-holes and carpenters' walks, seasoned oak, and sweating iron, ammonial, phosphorous reeks of gun-powder.

Caroline, he thought at last.

What to say to her? Sorry, love, but I'd crawl to Whitehall in a dog-collar, to escape the boresome shit my life's become? Dear as you are, the boys . . . sweet as life is with you . . . 'tis me?

He tossed off the rum impatiently, steeling himself for the hurt words to come. He set the glass on the mantel, reached out and took down his sword. Not a proper officer's slim and elegant small-sword, but a hanger, a slightly curved, single-bladed hunting sword, much like a light cutlass. It had stayed up there, out of reach of inquisitive little hands—young Hugh's mostly; Sewallis knew better.

There was dust on the royal-blue leather scabbard, and it had not received the same strenuous attention their tableware did from the maids. He ran a hand over the slightly tarnished silver lion's-head pommel, the dark-blue hilt wrapped with silver wire, the front and side hand-guards and the belt-hook, formed like argent seashells.

He half-drew it, to test its edge against his thumb-nail. But it was a Gill's, a fine blade, and had lost none of its keenness.

No matter how long it had hung, neglected and idle.

◆ ◆

DEWEY LAMBDIN, a Nashvillian, is a prolific novelist and a former television producer and director. He has been writing full-time since 1988. His novels, all published by Donald I. Fine, Inc., reflect his great passion for the life of the sea.

JUDY ODOM

On Being Shown a Pregnant Sophomore's Ultrasound

You have come
innocent
of spells
and science
to this hour.
We might be
on our knees,
and I
the riddler woman
reading shadows
for you
by a gypsy fire.
My finger
traces
one frail
curve
of darkness,
black
moon
adrift
upon gray
light.

Your diviner,
I conjure
blessing
for you
by that circle
in its fullness
growing,
by the vision
of an ancient
passage
newly charted
on a dark
and newly swelling
tide.

KEVIN

For you
I should have tried
a rap song.
That would surely please you.
But I wasn't raised for rapping
like Run DMC.
I can't quite catch the beat,
I don't like rhyming.
And besides,
I've lived too long
here in these mountains
to feel easy
making poems
out of broken glass
and ghetto jive
and wild erratic horns.
But you,
my son,
you walk the ridges
dreaming asphalt.
The clean smell
of the pine trees
sets you longing
for hot gasoline

and melting tar
and diesel fumes.
You contemplate the mist
that settles in the hollows
and imagine buildings
moored in L.A. smog.
And so,
I give you what I can—
this poem
blending dulcimers
and drums
and keyboard synthesizers.
I sing you
red-winged maple seeds
and dark smoke
drifting
on the same free wind.

◆ ◆

JUDY ODOM lives and teaches in Johnson City, Tennessee. A collection of her poetry, *Blossom, Stalk and Vine*, was published by Iris Press in 1990. Her work has also appeared in *Discovering Place: Readings from Appalachian Writers*, published by McGraw-Hill, and in various journals and other anthologies.

TERRANCE EARL

APPALACHIAN MEMORIES

If anything remained unchanged, fixed, it was the great wood farmhouse, the "Old Homeplace." My parents, my eleven aunts and uncles, myself, and all the other grandchildren would gather there for Sunday dinner. On rainy days, the porch which enclosed the house on three sides became the focus, with everyone fighting over the swing. Suspended from the ceiling by chains, it swung out over the high edge and took your breath away. Sunny afternoons would find a casual gathering in the front yard in the shade of the oaks. Makeshift tables on sawhorses were loaded with covered dishes and there was not much else to do but eat—or maybe play a game of horseshoes. Eventually, great bursts of hysteria would fade into lazy yawns as the afternoon sun moved the shade further and further back. The old folks finally would give up moving their chairs into the retreating shade and would go to the porch. Whoever was left by nightfall would join in a few rounds of hide-and-seek, including the grownups who were rarely found and never would disclose their secret hiding places. But no matter how many people or how bad the weather, the inside of the house was avoided: it was haunted, at least that was what everyone else firmly believed. Sometimes it was necessary to dash to the kitchen or bathroom, but only the daring would go alone—and never at night.

So when my grandmother got cancer and became bedridden, it fell upon the grandchildren to take turns spending the night, since all the children were "too busy with jobs and family." When it was my turn, I insisted that I sleep in Great Grandma Woodward's bedroom beside the front parlor, which had not been slept in since the day she died years before I was born. Originally a study converted to a sickroom, it was viewed through a glass door; everything had been left just as it was at the hour of her death, except that the bed was kept in fresh linens and was immaculately made. A metal pitcher and water glass still sat on the night stand. Except for regular cleaning by Grandma, the room was entered only for short visits by the bold and curious, who seemed to always find the air chilled. The shelves lining the walls brimmed with paperback detective novels with lurid pictures on the covers; I noticed they were replenished over the years and the fleshy women in low-cut, tight-fitting dresses seemed to grow more menacing as I approached adulthood. But mostly, the door was kept locked and several people have claimed a glimpse of a ghost through the swirly glass panes.

Before going to bed that night, I locked the door from the inside with the key which always stayed in the lock. I lay in the bed half-afraid something would happen, and half-disappointed that nothing seemed to be happening. After several hours of trying to read the available literature, I turned the light out, hoping to get some sleep before school the next morning. But darkness feeds the imagination; little creaks and stirrings became screeches and crashes. Remembering reports of the "rapping spirit" and chains in the attic, I got up and pushed a large stuffed chair in front of the closet door. The closet had no ceiling and opened into the attic.

I still couldn't sleep. When the skies began graying before the dawn, I knew I had made it. I relaxed and must have fallen asleep for a few minutes because the sun was just above the top of the hill when Aunt Sarah was knocking on the door. She had come to fix breakfast. I went and unlocked the door and told her "Everything's alright. Be out in a few minutes." She looked at me with a new respect; it was the first time I remember feeling manly. I was smiling as I put on my clothes: it all had turned out as I expected, the world was the way I knew it to be. I had picked up my shoes to carry them over to the chair where I would sit to put them on. And then my heart froze.

The chair had been pushed out and the closet door was standing wide open. With shoes in hand, I backed out of the room, not taking my eyes from the dark interior. I turned and ran to the kitchen on the other side of the house.

I never told anyone about the door, and I basked in the fame and admiration of my accomplishment. But I was shaken. Something had happened which did not fit.

◆ ◆

TERRANCE EARL, a resident of Dandridge, has always been fascinated with word play, in one form or another. His intense awareness of words and their sounds was fostered, he believes, by the Old Testament eloquence of mountain people. This selection is from a novel-in-progress.

JEFFREY J. FOLKS

MID-SOUTH LANDSCAPE

Blackbirds cluster softly overhead,
Their shadows smoking
Like a yearly hankering
A human bitterness
To burn the fields black
To turn the rows of earth with blackbirds trailing,
The unloved insistent ones
With whom one lives.

From *Sow's Ear Review* 2, no. 1 (Winter 1990). Reprinted by permission of the author.

Jeffrey J. Folks

Moment in Rain

Another unquiet spring afternoon
When the sky seems brighter at the sides
Than at the top and the air darkens
And thunder is distant and yet close.
The wind carries steady through
Forests heavy with new leaves.
Then a familiar door opens,
A patient, regular flickering
Of gray shadows of rain.
You work, sitting with the storm
As with an inquiring friend, bending
To her study. The distant population
Steps along the flooded road.

From *Plainsong* 2, no. 2 (Fall 1980). Reprinted by permission of the author.

Landscape

He notices the way the blue hill swells,
offering a white frame house
to the sunrise. The snow hides
among the folds of hills, or behind
the backs of houses.
Melting ice
glances his window, trailing
freezing streams along the glass.
The afternoon's momentary
thaw, when in the same light freezing
begins. The maple buds are still
hard small nipples. Making tea
in the china pot used a thousand
times, he performs the ritual
hopelessly, imagining no other
way but repetition. This time

no dispensation of snug warmth
and tweedy cheer. He cleans the
china, the brown stain
obdurate by habit.

Fall in the House

the delicious pleasure of Fridays in the house
the earliest snowfall ever, but now the sun
emerges, a weak winter sun below low stormy clouds
windy, the leaves still green on the fall trees
though suggesting their willingness to fall
in the sudden cold the house contracts
I hear a ticking, a clicking in the dining room
as the hardwood floors pull apart, contraction
small yellow leaves are swept from the hackberry
the wind rakes them in rows against the house-front

First Mowing

All the details of a father's knowledge
Come suddenly to mind: how not to strike
Hidden objects, how to mow a regular path.
What to think of God. He descends still
Some uneasy web netting my forehead
Trailing from the luminous summer sky
As light as the helicopter seeds of maple.
In its delight of early warmth his hand
On my forehead shares his hoard of
Radiance and sweat. Some towering cloud
Silent in generous rain comes
Tall and boasting above the spring shoot,
Climbers restlessly trellising
From the smoking cycle of my engine
And the grasping arms of level earth.

JEFFREY J. FOLKS has taught at Tennessee Wesleyan College and Indiana University. He has twice served as senior Fulbright lecturer to Eastern Europe. A resident of Knoxville, Mr. Folks's books include *Southern Writers and the Machine: Faulkner to Percy* and *The First of September: Poems*.

From *Old Hickory Review*, 1985. Reprinted by permission of the author.

HENRY SAMPLES

Brotherly Love

He has felt it now for some time, a firm tug, like a hard sleep that holds you in a bad dream. This farm boy now longs for other things. But who will cut him free, and how will he go? And who will watch the land?

He had felt a sharp pull at the funeral home, standing in his best blue suit, styptic pencil covering the shaving nicks on his sharp features. His father laid out before him, sleeping the grin of death in the satin casket, a refugee from obscurity. He now knew he should have said something, but at the time it had seemed so natural that he hadn't mentioned it. Not even at the cemetery, when the wind raked the grave, overturning the carnations and roses, when it kept hammering at his mind: they're burying him with his watch.

Coy Willis sits in a stupor, caught between family and his own demons, thinking of the seventeen-jewel Elgin pocket watch and how the small sweep hand would tick away the seconds. He had seen the serpentine gold chain coiling from his father's vest pocket, ready to anchor the timepiece should the corpse suddenly breathe life and unhinge itself up out of its new home. They shouldn't have done that, Coy thinks. That was too good a watch to bury with a dead man.

Coy's reflections are interrupted by the sharp sting of a bleak February night as his brother Dexter sweeps into the room from the railless front porch. Dexter is dressed in his Air Force uniform and a mackinaw. Coy sits by the steaming Warm Morning stove in his union suit. The room fairly reeks of sweat and cheap whiskey.

By Coy's left foot, away from the heat of the stove, lies a brochure from a midstate auctioneer school. His brother used to make fun of him about his educational plans, and his mother, too, before she took sick. Now he wants to put her in a nursing home and learn a trade.

Dexter crosses the room to a small table and sets down a brown paper sack, twisted slightly at the top.

"What'd you get?" Coy asks.

"George Dickel," Dexter says.

"God-Almighty," Coy says. "That's mighty good stuff."

"It was all he had left," Dexter says. "We's lucky to get, it, this time of night."

Dexter has been to the bootlegger in Valley Forge at two o'clock in the morning. It is the same bootlegger who sold Dexter lukewarm beer when he was in high school. The man was ahead of his time, Dexter thinks.

Dexter tosses his coat and gloves atop a growing pile of garments strewn on the weary sofa. Coy totters to the kitchen and brings back two water tumblers. These he hands to Dexter. "It's cold as witch's tit outside," Dexter says, pouring generously.

"And hot as preacher's dick in here," Coy says.

The two brothers laugh and take a long drink, fire spreading down their throats. Dexter, home on an emergency military pass, will leave in ten hours for his base in Colorado Springs, Colorado. Coy will drive him to the airport in the family truck. A neighbor from the church will stay with their mother while he is away.

Dexter warms by the stove while Coy resumes residence in the wooden rocker. The coal settles in the stove, sending sparks shuttling through the flue toward Canis Major.

"Where's Mattie?" Dexter asks.

"She's asleep," Coy says. "I carried her to bed in the back room."

"They's a time when she wouldn't a stood for one of us helping her like that," Dexter says.

"I know it," Coy says. "It's awful how she's gone downhill."

"You notice it more when you've been away," Dexter says.

Coy says how that is right and the two brothers tilt their glasses again, keeping a solemn vigil on the day of their father's funeral. Their mother is too old and too sick and too asleep to participate.

"Elizabethton sure has changed, ain't it?" Dexter asks.

Coy thinks of the sleeping town of 15,000 nestled near the folds and shadows of the Cherokee National Forest. He remembers when the Camara Inn came, which for a time did a brisk business selling sit-down beer. He knows the date when the Bonanza Sirloin Pit closed. But Coy doesn't say if the town has changed or hasn't. He takes another drink and looks at the picture of Jesus and John the Baptist on the wall. Then he says: "I'm going to sell the farm and put Mattie in a nursing home."

Dexter looks at his brother with disbelief. "You'll play hell," he says. "I'm not standing for that."

"You can raise cain iffen you want to," Coy says. "But I've had all I can stand."

"Our mother is not going to be put in a nursing home," Dexter says, pouring more liquor. "And I'll not have somebody else walking on this land."

"Then you can come back and look after it," Coy says. "I got other things to be doing."

"Like what?" Dexter asks.

"I'm going to auctioneer school so I can open up my own place," Coy says.

"You couldn't sell sex on a troop train," Dexter says. "Your place is here on the farm with mother, especially now that Dolph is gone."

"That's easy for you to say," Coy says, "but I'm tired of trying to look after this place by myself. I'm tired of having to put up with a bunch of cows that have to be milked at

4:30 in the morning, and them just looking for a chance to smack the shit out of you with their tails. And as for mother, I don't see that it's my job to stay here and wipe her ass."

"You watch your mouth, buster," Dexter says.

"Well, it's the truth," Coy says. "The poor woman couldn't look after herself before Dolph died, and I know she won't be able to now."

"Still yet," Dexter says. "You ain't putting her away like that."

"You got any better ideas?" Coy asks.

"No," Dexter says. "But it wouldn't take much effort to think of some just as bad as becoming an auctioneer."

"Why don't you admit the truth? It's easy for you to jump on my ass, but you ain't about to come back here and help do anything about this. You got a family, and they're used to city ways," Coy says. "They won't cotton to a life on a farm, especially one that has a crazy woman on it."

"You say one more word about her like that and so help me I'll bust you in the mouth," Dexter says.

"I ain't afraid of you," Coy says. He stands up, reeling slightly.

Dexter waves his hand and looks away. "Aw, sit down," he says. "I didn't mean nothing."

Coy sits down and takes another drink. Visions of himself and Dexter as boys playing on the cutbank at twilight flash through his mind. He feels the liquor knotting his stomach.

"They's something I got to tell you," Coy says.

"What's that?" Dexter asks, belching loudly.

"They buried Dolph with his watch on," Coy says.

"His Clinchfield Railroad watch?" Dexter asks. "Are you sure?"

"I'm sure," Coy says. "I saw it on him before they closed the casket at the funeral home to go to the church."

"Well, why the hell didn't you stop 'em?" Dexter asks.

"I don't know," Coy says. "I figured they knew what they were doing."

"Well, by-God, I know what I'm going to do," Dexter says.

"What?" Coy asks.

"I'm going out to the graveyard and get that watch," Dexter says.

"You mean dig it up?" Coy asks.

"That's right," Dexter says.

"You can't do that," Coy says. "That's against the law."

"Not to me, it ain't," Dexter says. "I'm just getting back what belongs to us."

"You're drunk," Coy says.

"I am not," Dexter says. "I'm as sober as a judge. You know I could always hold my whiskey."

"That could be," Coy says, "but I ain't going out there in the middle of the night to dig up Pap's grave. We'll tell the funeral home people tomorrow and they can do it, if it has to be done."

"There ain't time for that," Dexter says, "I got a plane to catch, remember?"

"What's the hurry?" Coy asks. "That watch ain't going nowhere."

Dexter throws down his glass with a clatter. It rolls under the sofa, trailing a thick trace of amber whiskey. Dexter crosses to where Coy sits and seizes him by the collar. "Don't you get smart with me," Dexter says. "Now you get your clothes on or I'll beat you to death right where you sit."

A lump forms in Coy's throat and he can see the two of them thrashing on the floor. He knows who will lose if the two come to blows. "Keep your voice down," Coy says. "You'll wake up Mattie."

"All right, then," Dexter says. "You get your clothes on and meet me at the truck. And bring the whiskey. I'll get us a pick and shovel."

"You sure you know what you're doing?" Coy asks.

"You got any better idea?" Dexter asks.

"If I did you wouldn't pay it any mind," Coy says. He falls to the task of finding clothes while Dexter pulls on his mackinaw and heads to the tool shed.

Coy checks his mother before he leaves the house. The pale form moves slightly under the checkered quilt. The room is quiet as death.

Outside, Dexter is waiting under an umbrella of stars by the truck, stamping the ground. He has placed the tools in the truck bed. Coy takes a pull of George Dickel and offers the bottle to Dexter.

"I'd feel better about this if we weren't leaving Mattie by herself," Coy says.

Dexter drinks. "She'll be all right," he says. He takes another drink and screws the cap back onto the bottle.

Coy starts the truck engine, which catches life after a few turns. "Get in," he calls. Dexter slides in on the worn seat, placing the bottle beside them. The two of them ride in silence.

The thin beams of the headlights pierce a black East Tennessee night. "Goddamn," Dexter says. "It's cold as a banker's heart."

The truck rattles past points of local history and family lore. Neither speaks about it, but each remembers how their father use to double-clutch on his way to church, how the truck always bucked until finally their father would shift to second.

The truck rolls onto the church yard. It is bare, although two empty beer cans glitter in the lights, evidence from a back seat seduction under the church elms.

"Let's leave the truck here and walk to the cemetery," Dexter says. "Nobody'll think anything about the truck here, but it might draw attention at the graveyard."

"I already thought of that," Coy says.

They gather the pick and the shovel and the whiskey and walk briskly and wordlessly to the cemetery. Through the black clouds, stars wink a coded message at these watch resurrectors. The whiskey gurgles in the bottle, begging consumption.

The brothers wheel up at the grave, a stark sentinel in the dark. "I'll dig and you shovel," Dexter says. Coy sits down to wait.

Dexter swings the pick over his shoulder like a lumberjack and it falls like a guillotine. It rattles Dexter's teeth when its point strikes the ground.

"They hell fire," Dexter says. "This ground's frozen solid. I never would have thought it."

"This mountain air's hell," Coy says.

"Give me a drink of that whiskey," Dexter says. "This is going to require some elbow grease."

Dexter drinks and tosses the bottle to Coy, who hunkers and watches his brother work, his form outlined on the wall of the mountain. Slowly Dexter works the point of the pick into the earth, tearing toward his father's casket. The pick sounds boom like gunfire in the still of the morning.

Coy sits and takes a long drink of whiskey, his mind now struggling to fight off the cold. He thinks of his father now dead and frozen and squints at his brother laboring over the grave. He sees a village of colored ships nestled on pillars in high mountains. From somewhere afar a light beckons. Coy wonders if the watch is still running and then realizes how disruptive Dexter's plan will be . . . another battle between the two of them, an argument that an invalid mother can no longer referee.

Quietly, Coy stands and swings the shovel in an arc. It hits Dexter slightly behind the right ear and bongs loudly. Dexter grunts softly and falls to the ground, like a side of beef cut down from its rack.

Coy tosses the shovel aside. He looks at his brother sprawled over the grave. A gout of blood pours from his ear. Coy drops to the ground and cradles Dexter's head. He holds the warm body in his hands, clutching Dexter to his chest. The wind howls through the trees, making ghostlike sounds. Coy hears his father's watch ticking like a jackhammer. Dexter's breath comes in forced gasps. "Dammit," Coy says. "Goddam it."

◆ ◆

HENRY SAMPLES is a native of Greeneville, Tennessee. He spent his youth there and in Point Pleasant, Cocke County. Samples obtained his degree at East Tennessee State University and is managing editor of the *Johnson City Press*.

BILL BROWN

Pact

My brother would read my quiet sorrow,
follow me to our room and stand
at the door staring while I sulked
on the bed, head toward the wall.
When I turned to confront him, I'd catch
dirty shorts in my face. "Lighten up,"
He'd say, "you ain't dead yet."

I'd perform my leaping tackle
and he'd tickle me until I gave up,
half silly and drunk with anger.
We'd laugh at my teenage grief,
how goddamn serious I was
about football and Becky Lewis.
She dumped me once a week.

At night he'd fart under the covers,
claim it was an earthquake, and the bed
shook like a life boat in a storm.
Camping at Price's Pond, he found
a black flint arrowhead which he would

"Pact," from *What the Night Told Me*, by Bill Brown (Lewiston, N.Y.: Mellen Poetry Press, 1992). Used by permission of Mellen Poetry Press. This work also appeared in *Passages North Ten-Year Anthology* (Milkweed Editions, 1990).

rub at night before calling a host
of owls around our fire
loud enough to wake the dead.

These frames passed through my head
like coming attractions at the picture show
this morning as I woke to the pastel light
of hospital green. My brother's vital signs
blipped across the screen and his lips
quivered for the words an aneurism
had stolen from his tongue.

I found myself saying, lighten up,
you ain't dead yet, you ain't
dead yet, saying it over and over
until the phrase became our secret pact,
as powerful as black arrowheads,
magic owl calls and his tight grip
on my hand.

AFTERNOON AT CADES COVE

Along the edge of woods
deer crept past us
like the afternoon
toward the ridge barn
where we later hid,
our heads pressed together
behind a board crack
to spy the silent herd
moving between
the shadows of trees
like light flickering
with leaves
and suddenly an old doe
sensed us hidden close,
raised her head toward the woods,
coughed three shrill barks,
and the afternoon almost stopped
that such a startled sound
could burst from grace.

We escaped
the darkness of the barn
and rock-hopped down
a sparkling brook

racing toward the road,
and in an eddy beneath
dogwood buds, we found
a clutch of bones
crowned with a buck skull.
Its hollow eyes
scorched our flesh
as they gazed through us,
past the barn
where we had hidden,
past the wooded ridge
where deer had streamed,
past the slight touch
of spring nestled
in the dark limbs
with the sun.

• •

BILL BROWN, director of creative writing at Hume-Fogg Academic High School in Nashville, has been a Scholar in Poetry at Bread Loaf, a Fellow at the Virginia Center for the Creative Arts, and Writer-in-Residence at Radford University. In 1995 he was awarded a Literary Fellowship (Honorable Mention) from the Tennessee Arts Commission.

DANIEL FOLTZ-GRAY

ACHE

Even before she opened her eyes Evelyn knew he was there with his blanket and little clown, waiting for her to say Jump up, get in the middle. She'd been dreaming about him; she must have heard him at the door. And from his tears and the metallic smell of his breath she knew he was sick, he'd have to stay home. He leaned his head on her chest. Through the nightgown she felt his heat.

"What?" she whispered.

"My throat. It hurts."

She lifted him and laid him between them. She turned on the lamp and looked in.

"What?" Peter said, "What—" He turned and saw the boy.

"A sore throat," she said. She got him some aspirin and stroked his head. When his breathing quieted, she lay on her back and tried to sleep. At twelve she heard the whistle and the first of the cars coming down from the Works, their headlights on the wall, and the rest of the cars. Harry whimpered and she pressed her face against his, to bring him out of the dream. The fever had gone down some. He whimpered again, and Peter turned over and touched the small forehead.

"I've got that interview in the afternoon," he said. "If he has to stay home—"

"Don't worry about it. I'll get somebody."

"Who?"

"I'll find someone."

She got up and went downstairs and made a cup of hot milk. The kitchen was freezing but the milk warmed her. She couldn't think of anyone who could watch him but May Koskin who had done it before but wouldn't take money. Staying home herself was out of the question. If she lost the work they'd be in trouble. They were already in trouble. She washed the cup and put it away and went back upstairs. Peter was still awake.

"Not May," he said. "I won't—"

"I know."

He brushed his hand across Harry's forehead.

"He's cooled off a little. He might be okay."

"He might."

"You must be so tired."

At six the buzzer went off, but she was already awake. She had heard the sound it made before going off, like clearing its throat. Harry leaned up suddenly.

"It's okay. You're in bed with Momma. It's okay. Remember?"

He nodded.

"How's your throat?"

"It hurts."

She climbed down to fix breakfast and felt the first wave of nausea. The bushes were white with frost. She wiped ice from the window with a washcloth. It was March five years before when she'd stood at the sink and seen a family of pheasants in the new snow in the backyard. She had watched for a long time. No one had predicted snow, but there it was. All the roofs were puffed up like comforters. She had switched on the radio and heard the school closings and hurried upstairs to tell Peter he was free for the day and felt the slow movement inside her, the baby turning, stretching.

She called up to them when breakfast was ready. Sam, Peter's father, came down, then Peter and the children. It was already 6:40.

"Harry seems better now," Peter said. He was studying the boy. The boy knew it and lowered his mouth to his bowl and barked.

"Is something wrong?" Sam said.

"He's got a sore throat," she said, "I think strep."

Peter looked at her. "You think it's strep again?"

"I think so."

"How can you tell?"

She looked up from the sink into the grey sky. She was too tired to answer. But if she didn't answer he'd only ask again. "Little white blisters, on his tonsils. Dr. Perrin showed me once. It might not be, though." She turned to the boy. "You have a tummy ache?"

"No, Momma."

"We were supposed to take him back," Peter said. "After last time, he was supposed to have a re-check."

"He gets sick a lot," Sam said. He brushed a rough hand over his grandson's short hair that sprang back from his touch.

"I'll call Rose," she said. "I'm pretty sure she can come over."

"I'll call her," Peter said. "You don't need to bother."

"Well it's just for a couple of hours. I don't guess your interview will last more than a couple of hours."

"Who knows?" he said. "They may take one look at me and ask me to leave."

"If she can't do it, you could try Lois Falco. She might come down." She waited. "I guess you better let Perrin—"

"I know."

She went upstairs. In the mirror, in her work dress and apron, she looked old. She had no heart for putting on makeup. But Crowe insisted they look nice. She drew the tube across her lips and brushed her dark hair. Because of course their customers looked nice.

She heard the door shut and saw Sam going up, huddled for warmth, up to the Works.

She helped Karen pick out clothes and got Harry dressed. She kissed them good-bye. The car started with a little urging. She drifted down past frozen yards already discolored by smoke and soot. At the stop sign the first shoots of grass lay on their backs, black with frost. She turned on the radio. They were interviewing the British newspaperman the Russians had accused of spying and kept in jail for a year.

What did you miss most?

My family.

What was the worst part?

Knowing I would never have the time back with my children, that they'd never be two and five again.

You weren't afraid you were going to die?

No—I never thought they'd kill me.

The car shuddered as she turned onto Greb and shuddered as she climbed the long hill of houses identical to her own. A woman in curlers opened a front door as she crawled past and she glimpsed the worn arm of a sofa, a table. A lamp lit up the damp places on the wall.

All along Butler Street the river lay in a veil of mist.

"Kathy's going to be late," Crowe said when she got there. Already the well-fed faces were wandering in. Mrs. Reed was bent over the cheeses, looking for something French. "Her kid's sick. Can you stay?"

"I can till 12:30. I have to be at the hospital at one and it takes me about twenty—"

"Okay. I know."

Kathy got there at 12:35. By then Evelyn was feeling pretty bad. She wondered if anyone had ever vomited on the cash register.

She hurried out and started eating as she drove. But the food only made her feel worse. She pulled over by the yards and leaned her forehead on the wheel until the sickness passed. It had been weeks since she and Peter had had any time alone. And even that night was nearly ruined by his drinking. He had been so affectionate; but in the morning his head was bursting and all he could talk about was Modick. She raised her eyes and gazed into the scarred bed of a gondola car still lying where it jumped its track a year before. I left the track and can't get back, she thought. I left the track and can't get back.

When she got to her floor, she followed her cart down the wide hall, into the rooms for trash and the laundry thrown in closets. She cleaned sinks and toilets and tubs.

Pushing her cart by the pay phone she heard a man say, "She's dying." She stared, unable to look away. She wanted to say something. But it wasn't the janitor he wanted comforting from. She cleaned what she could and left.

At five she went home. Peter was reading the paper.

"How was the interview?" she said. "How'd it go?"

He shook his head. "They called to re-schedule. Just after you left."

"Oh." She laughed. "All that worrying." She thought—sometimes things work out.

"So when are you going?"

"They didn't say. They said they'd call."

She forced herself to smile. "Well, it's good they let you know. Why did they have to cancel—did they say?"

"Yes. They said." He lit a cigarette and opened to Fashion. There was a big ad for spring hats. "Something about they scheduled too many, they made a mistake." He looked up at her. When he turned the page, a cloud blew from the heaped ashtray.

"You were right," he said at length. "It's strep. Little white pimples on his tonsils."

"Is he okay?"

"He's fine, doing fine. Even likes his medicine."

"His throat's not hurting him?"

"He says it's not."

"When can he go back to the church?"

"Couple of days." They looked at each other. It meant he'd be babysitting. "I can still make phone calls. It's okay."

She went upstairs. Karen was getting him changed. He'd spilled orange juice all down his front. She took over but he wanted Karen. She went into her room to change and looked across the twenty feet of yard to Trillies' window. In the warped glass, against the dark curtain, she saw the shadow at her head like a lump with hair and the light that faded behind her as Peter came in and shut the door.

He lay on the bed and opened the paper.

"Anything in there?"

"Nothing so far."

"Anybody call?"

"They called from West Mifflin."

"Well, that's encouraging."

He dropped the paper and watched it flutter down. "Well, they don't know about me yet."

"How do you know?"

"I could tell. He asked why I left."

"What did you say?"

He shrugged. "What I always say." After a moment he raised his eyes. "He said Modick? You don't mean John Modick? I said yes, the superintendent of schools. He said, well when you had this argument were you acting in—"

"That's what you called it? An argument?"

"Yes." He watched her. "You think I should have been more specific?"

"No. If they want more specific they can ask."

"Right," he said. "Right. So he wanted to know what the circumstances were. So I said to him, well, it was at a meeting, we were discussing Stenglein. The instructor who was dismissed, he says. Yes, that's right, I told him, the second biggest asshole in Pennsylvania. Then he wants to know what the problem was, what my problem with it was. So I told him I was concerned they let Stenglein go without a chance to defend himself. And that led to the . . . argument, he says. Yes, I said, that's when I knocked him down. That's—"

"But what did you say then? Really?"

He pressed his lips together. "I said yes, it led to the argument. He said did I resign at that point. I said yes. So he said he'd have to talk to Modick, of course. I told him I hoped he'd find out about my *work*, too, that I'd taught there five years and done good work and so on and so on."

"You did do good work," she said.

He looked at her.

"No one can question that." She smiled. "Not even you."

He nodded, too quickly, to show that he was okay. "You know the thing is I don't even want that job, I wouldn't have taken it even right out of school."

"It might be better than it sounds."

He shook his head. "I keep thinking about Dad and all his buddies and how they won't take any shit, Oh I'd just had it with his do this, do that, so I took and punched his lights out, he won't fuck with *me* anymore."

"It's different for them."

"Different how?"

"You were a *teacher*." She stared at him. "Are a teacher." She was furious at his father and his father's friends and his own friends who wished him well but would not let him go beyond them. "You're different from them."

"Apparently not," he said.

Karen brought Harry in. She had dressed him. "Good work," Evelyn told her. Harry was holding his shred of blanket to his nose and sucking two fingers. Karen took him out.

"How was he with Perrin?"

"Terrible," he said. "Screamed every time the nurse came in the room. Perrin said changes in season are hard for kids. Not unusual for them to get sick a lot in spring. I told him I hadn't noticed anything about spring. I don't think the man ever goes outside." He raised his slender face, his narrow mouth that only made her more hopeless.

She hung up her sweater. "It's just a sore throat." She felt as if she were lifting the words from her chest, as if each were a heavy stone. She wanted to push those stones at him.

"He never got sick before all this happened."

"Everybody gets sick," she said.

"But it's something we could have done something about. It didn't have to happen."

"It's just a sore throat."

"It's been one thing after another with him."

"It doesn't mean anything."

She went into the bathroom and closed the door. He meant *she* could have done something. She heard him cough and turned on the water. She washed her face and hands and went out and got on the scale.

The scale said 129, a pound more than yesterday. Three more in as many weeks. She leaned down to pick up the necklace she had dropped. The needle jumped. When she stood she felt the weakness in her legs and the wave of nausea and the beating of the hammers.

"Oh, God," she said. She sat on the floor and put her head in her hands until her eyes bloomed with light. After a moment the nausea passed and she breathed through her mouth and swallowed and waited for it to come back. She reached for a kleenex and saw him staring.

"I think I'm pregnant."

It was the last thing they needed now, a child she couldn't take care of.

She looked up and saw his stunned face that had been so happy those other times that seemed so long ago, and saw the hatred in his eyes and knew that he did not remember.

"I can't believe you would do this to us now," he whispered. She could hardly make out the words. "Who was it—some guy who's doing real good?"

She turned and ran. At the top of the stairs she passed Harry, and behind him Karen, just coming out. And then she was outside and in the car, driving too fast past Mrs. Hodil, past Bobby Eckert, past Mrs. Leland whose wave she hardly saw. The little brick houses sped by like rows of yellow teeth. She got on the turnpike and leaned back, and stared ahead. When the steering wheel began to vibrate she slowed down.

She wouldn't have a child she couldn't take care of. Not another child she couldn't take care of.

At the first Donegal sign she realized where she was going. She got off and drove into the darkening country, past Ligonier and out into the fields. On a wooded rise above a pond the dirt path ended. She shut off the engine and waited. A black mare moved its nervous hooves in the sucking mud still frilled with ice.

Once she had known every animal that lived on these fields.

She walked out to the top of the knoll and saw the house lying in its cup of meadow. All the downstairs lamps were on. The drive was full of cars. And in the smoke that rose from the front chimney, she saw the girl who had stood in this spot a hundred times dreaming: Who will my husband be? Who will my children be?

The first breath of frozen wind sent her back. She sat in the car shivering. Night hid the pond and the rough fields. Something moved among the trees and she turned on the lights and saw the mare just before her, saw the heat rising from its back and full nostrils and the mud that spattered the teats swollen down beyond their hoop of ribs.

When the sky above the house finally darkened she started the car and drove out along the stream that fed the pond. On a sheltered bank the headlights found the first purple jonquil just rising from the earth.

The white moon met her as she came through the last of the trees and turned onto the blacktop and she thought of their small faces white with shock and sadness as she ran from the room and down the stairs past them. All the way home their faces hung like the round moon open-mouthed before her.

• •

Daniel Foltz-Gray, a native of Pittsburgh and a graduate of the University of Pennsylvania, teaches writing at Roane State Community College, where he is department head for Academic Development Communications. His fiction has been published in such journals as *Minnesota Review* and *Kansas Quarterly*.

KRISTIN CAMITTA ZIMET

SURVIVOR'S CHRISTMAS

I have been learning to skate over grief.
New ice, of patchy thickness, scabs the pond—
cloudy, an undersky, even in diamond weather.
It sighs, rides low beneath my weight.
Over the gliding hours of holiday
my feet drag and scrape. I keep
trying to balance on your arm, and skid
down to a drowning cold.
My hotcheeked children, voices jingling,
hover and dart away; friends tug me up.
I have been learning to forgive them for
not being you; myself for caroling;
you for your wrapping of mortality.
I wind around me the years thick with love,
a woolen scarf skyblue, invisible,
and slide ahead.
The single-bladed present cuts, sustains.

THE STORYTELLER TO HER HUSBAND

Now shut that book—I know, your favorite,
and one of mine. Bound tight in tender calf,
the edges rubbed in gilt; even the lock
cunning, shaped like a heart; and sewn up,
folded like a wing-clipped dove
one signature of years. How hungrily
you still recount the tale,
breaking it open like a homely loaf
of new-baked bread. Three story-slices:
you see me, win me, keep me
fast in three white rooms,
here in a gray house shelved
beside its fellows on a narrow hill.
And here, dear prince, pudgy and practical,
you still indulge
your quetzal-bird, your goosegirl,
me, your squawking harp
snatched from a giant's kitchen.
Handfed on kindness, here I learn to sing
like the small fire that ducks beneath the grate
this icy night. But shut the everlasting book
and rest. Our pillowed heads
are twin engravings, page and facing page—
yours black-and-white, mine rose,

lit by a brush with things beyond,
a firefly light shaking a jar.
Around my face are spread, glowing in spokes,
my jeweled braids. Listen, the hide-and-seek
of voices weaving tales about my head.
But no—you would prefer a single plait
flat down my back, an anchor line,
a sturdy rope to let you haul on up
Rapunzel's tower, and down onto the flat
of ever-after. Padding about,
you bolt the shutters fast
from blizzard fingers twisting at the latch,
from winter's spite. I'm safe. You'll see to it
no foundling's out there howling at the door,
no riddling crone hawks apples.
Truly, I must have been that lucky fool
who gives away her only crust of bread
to the right beggar, and her fortune's made.
But love, forgive a fool. Tonight again
soon as the lamp's put out, the shutters knock
loud as a dragon's heart.
A hail of voices crackles on the pane.
I start to rise like smoke
straight up the chimney flue
and right on up Bays Mountain. Souls untold
are streaming up from the ravines below.
Mine and not-mine, we melt
cloud into cloud. I rain their heaviness;
release them to the light.
Look, my shadows play

like windy pages flapping round a spine,
near scattering—except a thread of silk
stretches and shines between us—
only look—marking your place
inside me. *Don't* look, then
Just hold on tight. I have to live
not once upon a time, but twice, thrice. . . .

KRISTIN CAMITTA ZIMET, a founding member of the Appalachian Community of Poets, is associate editor of *Sow's Ear Poetry Review*. She has performed and published her poetry in Tennessee, Virginia, New York, Texas, Colorado, and Connecticut. She also writes songs and children's stories and works as a book editor and environmental activist.

LINDA LIGHTSEY RICE

THISTLE MAN

And there came the season of flying, a time my mother Kara would remember all her life, when first she realized that birds, and sometimes people, can fall from the sky and never rise again. Which began with her father and one of the walk-about trips he took when they all lived together, Alice, Reiker, Kara, in a long boxcar suburban house at the edge of the national forest. Reiker worked at night and slept daytimes when the house quivered cellodeep with life. And on days he couldn't sleep he often dashed out the door rabbitscared, leaving behind wife and daughter, to stomp through the woods looking for wild pigs and other dangers.

Sauntering along he was that day, dappled by sun and forestscent, armed with a snakebite kit and that horn to scare black bears away. It was spring and he was traipsing along a path lined with mountain laurel and though it was warm Reiker wore a long-sleeved shirt and a hunting vest (he'd never been hunting, of course) and a fur hat with flaps. It had rained the night before and the rutted path up the mountain was muddy, but sunlight sprinkled lightstars through the trees and they twinkled on the ground as he paused in a clearing, staring across at a distant peak. The gracefully sculpted cone rose like a magic genie out of the clouds. Reiker stared at it for a long time, shook his head and muttered, "Worse batch of poison ivy over there I ever saw."

He continued up the path but soon stopped—froze—when he heard the bleating. Ahead, beneath a bush and caught in a raccoon trap, lay an injured bird. The grayish goose with white cheek patch and long black neck leaned toward him with solemn eyes. Reiker backed away quickly (almost every animal in the woods carried rabies), but the silent eyes begged for help. He inched forward and picked up a stick and prodded the bird, whose eyelids fluttered so hopefully that Reiker forgot himself and pried open the trap and picked up the limp animal with its damaged foot and carried it home.

Kara was seven then—and she was overjoyed, she who was never allowed a pet, and

"Thistle Man," from *Thistle Man*, a novel-in-progress.

she skittered back and forth between the bird on the front stoop and her mother in the kitchen, twirling circles around Alice, describing what the bird was doing—"it's flapping all over"—while Reiker bandaged the mangled foot, holding the bird away from his body.

Every so often the small girl, shaggy bangs flying, eyed her father mysteriously, as though he'd just arrived from a far country, as he crossed into the back yard and began building a cage from chicken-wire and odd lengths of board. This man who said there could be no dog, it might damage a neighbor's garden, and there could be no kitten, it might spray a neighbor's house. This same man was building a home for a bird from Canada. But when Kara hovered about the cage, her father shooed her away and said, we will only keep the goose until the leg is healed, then it must fly away again.

But always, what he didn't count on was love. Nor the male goose who soon swooped into the yard and flew down into the female's cage. Even when Reiker shooed it away, it kept returning.

Kara watched the pair from the porch. "They're in love, Daddy. I asked my teacher. Snow geese stay together for life."

But the father with sunfair hair never spoke of love. He awaited departures. When he was in England fighting a war, his brother in Normandy departed. Before he returned home to the States, his mother and father departed. So each day after the geese arrived, he warily eyed his neighbors, whom he barely knew, anticipating their disapproval, waiting to be reported for harboring wild animals inside his yard. He worried, fumed, paced. And one dark night he went out to make the female leave: the leg was healed, she had to go now. He smashed the cage and the goose squawked off skyward. And Kara cried all the next day, large droopy tears that seeped into the dirt where the cage had stood.

Then the amazing thing happened: the two geese returned to the Mannet yard from time to time, swooping in to say hello, and Kara would run outside and dash along beneath them, giggling. And soon the lovers made, beneath Alice's rosebushes, a nest for eight tiny eggs.

Reiker could see the entire neighborhood covered with geese and knew he would be arrested. But he couldn't get near the nest without the parents diving for his shoulder, his hands. He called an exterminator, who told him to call the wildlife expert at the university, who said to leave the geese alone, that once the goslings could fly the entire family would leave.

The Thistle Man worried and waited, and Kara danced around the nest every afternoon when she came home from school. The eggs hatched and the flightless molt began, and now parents and children both lived beneath the rosebushes, where Alice had buds the size of baseballs that year. Then Reiker's worst fear was realized. Regrowth of the adults' flight feathers began, and one morning when Reiker shooed the mother and father, he frightened them so badly they flew away for good. Leaving eight goslings, untrained and unflown, behind.

Another cage went up in the yard, after Alice pleaded to Reiker well into a long Maying night. Soon Kara was feeding the goslings with a medicine dropper, chatting to them each morning. In time the babies were up and walking and Kara would come home from school and let them out of the cage, and they would trail along behind her as she played.

"We have to teach them to fly so they can migrate north," Reiker said, although what he was thinking now—desperately—was that he had to get these geese gone before he was found out. He was suspicious that the goslings might be harmful to his health, to the emphysema he had diagnosed himself after he quit smoking.

Thus began the flying lessons. Every afternoon Reiker and Kara would tie strings around the goslings' necks and march them into the woods. Father and daughter in the lead, eight small geese on little leashes running behind them. Reiker had found a large flat rock to use as a runway. With the goslings positioned on the rock, Reiker climbed atop it and flapped his arms and jumped off in mock-flight. Kara tickled the goslings from behind to make them imitate Reiker's maneuver and one-by-one they'd run to the edge and flail into the air and crash onto the ground. As a result the runt of the litter had to be bandaged twice.

But, miraculously, one gosling—the one Kara called Henrietta—did learn to fly. After tumbling down off the rock one day, Henrietta crawled into a bush and got stuck. Kara poked a long stick into the bush and Henrietta hopped on and Kara put the stick up to a nearby tree and the gosling grabbed onto a limb—grimacing but determined. Henrietta practiced falling from upper limb to lower limb, while the gang on the ground watched. Kara again placed her on an upper branch and Henrietta actually flew, wobbly and uncertain, to the lower limbs. Next she flew upward, a farther distance than before. Finally, perching high on Olympus, she squawked at her brothers and sisters to start trying it. Her way. But they wouldn't, they went on hugging the ground.

It was almost June now, the geese were growing quite large, and seven showed no signs of wanting, or being able, to leave. "They have to go north," Reiker said every night at the square wooden dinner table where the three Mannets sat, motionless and unspeaking, eating fried chicken and mashed potatoes with gravy in the center which Kara kept imagining was a pond.

She looked up, startled. "Oh Daddy, can't we just keep them?"

"No, Kara. They're wild animals. They belong in Canada in the summer. If they stay here, they'll dirty up the neighborhood. Cause property damage. The neighbors won't stand for it."

No neighbors had complained yet, but still Reiker fumed. Wild things had to be controlled. That evening he walked outside as usual, to check on the geese before he retired, and he found Kara twirling, whirling, swirling, about the fluffy children. She danced as though teaching them to fly. Reiker said nothing to his daughter, only watched and hurried inside again.

A few days later Alice found him in his cluttered workshop late one evening. "What are you building?"

"A glider. I'll show those silly birds what to do." And Reiker bent back over his saw and his plywood.

His wife was surprised. She knew that Reiker had flown a plane in the war, before they were married. But he never spoke about that and would not even board a commercial airline to visit relatives.

Slowly the glider grew. Boards, nails, a box, large canvas wings. It was a small contraption, mostly put together with baling wire. When it was complete, Kara and Reiker again set out for the forest. Henrietta flew beside them, hovering over Kara's right shoulder, but the other goslings had to follow—abjectly—on their tiny little leashes. Deep in the woods Reiker climbed up on a hill, strapped himself into his craft. Kara and the geese waited some distance away, as Reiker ran to the edge of the hill and—stopped. He trembled all over. He turned around and lumped back to his starting position, the glider awkward on his stiff back. Again he ran toward the cliff, gaining speed. Kara held her breath and the goslings squawked. Reiker hit the edge and went over. He fell straight down. All three feet.

"I'm going to have to do something drastic," he told Alice that night. "I can't teach those birds to fly. And they can't stay."

"Shuusshhh, Kara'll hear you." Alice smiled, overjoyed that the geese meant Reiker was spending time with his daughter.

Reiker thought about giving the goslings away, he thought he might be able to interest a farmer back in the hills. But if something went wrong after the farmer took them, he—Reiker—would be responsible. A goose might hurt one of the farmer's children. Reiker tossed and turned at night, watching daylight tiptoe onto the window ledges of his room. Whatever happened would come back on him, who had raised these wild birds. Then he thought—he could give the geese to the university for research. He got out of bed immediately. But when he got in the car to take the geese to town, he couldn't start the engine. The thought of that sprawling campus was too overwhelming.

The next evening Reiker went out to feed the goslings. Their necks were longer now and their feathers fluffier, as they neared adulthood. Snow geese simply could not live in a suburb. There were rules. He watched the birds flit all over the back yard and grinned despite himself, remembering the goslings being pushed off the rock for their first flying lesson.

But the problem came back again—he could not control the geese. Wild things were—too wild.

And he was a man who looked up at the sky and saw only two tones, white moon, black night. That evening he went dark himself and, worrying more, he slipped out into the yard again after midnight. He walked over to the goslings, reached down. His hand touched soft feathers but did not feel them, and so the first went easily. A sharp twist, like his grandmother at the chickens back home, and it was done. Maybe that first inert form frightened the rest. He had to chase the second and the fourth. He began flapping his arms like in the flying lessons and the others came straight to him, children drawn to a family game. Twist, snap; twist, snap; twist, snap. Their necks lay limp. Except for Henrietta, who saw him coming and turned and flew madly out of the yard.

Reiker walked into the mountains and buried the seven goslings under the flying lesson rock, his shadowy form luminized by the silver moon cresting the green mountains as he bent over, curved back into himself, while digging their communal grave. He told Kara the health department made him release the geese atop of Mt. LeConte, but he could see she did not believe him. He told himself he'd had no choice and when her small eyes filled he looked away, wondering if the sooty clouds above them meant a bad storm was coming.

Unnoticed, Kara walked away from her father and sat, still and unmoving, in the back yard, alone. He hovered in the doorway wishing to explain to her—about the danger of wild things—but finally he turned inside without a word.

What Kara would always remember about this, about the morning she danced outside to find the geese were gone, was that the soft flowing treasures that were supposed to be part of her life—inexplicably—weren't.

• •

LINDA LIGHTSEY RICE is author of the novels *Southern Exposure* (Doubleday, 1992) and *The Fireplace Dream* (forthcoming). She has taught fiction writing at the University of Tennessee, Lenoir-Rhyne College in North Carolina, and the Chautauqua Institution in upstate New York. Currently she teaches at the College of St. Catherine in Minneapolis but maintains a permanent home in Knoxville.

JUDITH HAWKES

SWITCHEROO

It all begins the night the three of them decide to switch heads.

They're walking along, it's raining a little, and one of them (afterwards they can never remember who it was) notices that each of their heads actually matches one of the other bodies better than its own. Dee's dark-blue baseball cap seems more appropriate to Marty's body in its green nylon anorak; Ellen's yellow sou'wester obviously belongs with Dee's yellow slicker, and Marty's red ski cap is clearly the mate to Ellen's army fatigue jacket. But it's more than just a question of hats and coats. Ellen's long frizzy hair, Marty's mustache, and Dee's tinted glasses are a part of it, too; and in the light of streetlamps reflected in wet black asphalt, it seems to make perfect sense. They'll just switch heads. Naturally it's the most radical for Dee and Marty, but Ellen ends up having the worst of it.

One of the first things that comes up when they notice, later that night or in the small hours of the morning, that it's actually happened, is just how they're going to define who each of them is now. Is it going to be bodies or heads? Heads or tails? Surprisingly it's Dee (now wearing Marty's body) and Marty (now wearing Ellen's) who vote for heads—surprisingly because in doing so they're abandoning their respective sexual identities and so forth, less surprisingly perhaps because Marty is a computer programmer and Dee has an office job, and they are both oriented, so to speak, in the head. They also point out that it's going to be a lot easier to pass their new bodies off as the old than it would be their new heads (here Ellen's hand fingers Marty's mustache), and that's a strong point. In fact there seems to be no question whatsoever that it's the heads who are running the show. Except that Ellen, divided as she is between Dee's body and Marty's head, has her doubts.

Ellen is a freelance artist, and from the very first moment—or at least the first mo-

"Switcheroo," by Judith Hawkes, appeared in *Elvis in Oz: New Stories and Poems from the Hollins College Creative Writing Program* (Charlottesville: University Press of Virginia, 1992), 336–41. Used with permission of the University Press of Virginia.

ment she becomes aware of the switch, for somehow it happens without their noticing—she has a feeling, or her head does, that this business of switching isn't going to work out, at least not for her. For one thing, Dee, whose body she has inherited, is just a glorified secretary with about as much artistic sense as a doughnut. Ellen never thought much about it before, but now it seems very clear that artistic sense is located not in your head but somewhere in your body, somewhere around the stomach or possibly a little higher. For another thing, Dee is quite a lot heavier than Ellen, and—although one of the other things they decide right off is not to make complaints or recriminations—it's like having to drive a big luxury car when she's used to a small sporty model. Dee, on the other hand, is busy inventing the crash diet that's supposed to have trimmed her down to Marty's shape over a single weekend (it's Saturday night, or early Sunday morning, when it happens)—"Watercress," she keeps saying, "No, bean sprouts. Bean sprouts."

But what's bothering Ellen most of all is what's going to happen to her and Marty. The three of them have been friends for a long time, but recently she and Marty have become lovers. And now here she is with Dee's body, which is bad enough—but there he is with hers, which is worse. She doesn't think she's narcissistic enough to want to make love to her own body just because Marty's head is on it, but she isn't at all sure she loves Marty's body enough to take it in conjunction with Dee's head. The more she thinks about it the more it seems that, in this game of musical bodies or heads, the music has stopped and she's been left out. Because there they are: her body and Marty's probably not caring a bit whose heads they're wearing—that's just the way bodies are. As the feeling grows, she begins to have a sense that she doesn't even like Dee, although before she might have said they were best friends. "Sunflower seeds?" Dee is saying. "Sunflower seeds."

It turns out even worse than Ellen expects. There's no teaching Dee's body to draw; it can't make a straight line even with a ruler; it keeps tidying up the drafting table, and worst of all, it has cravings. Ellen has been a vegetarian since she was thirteen; she's still a vegetarian, however separated from herself she may have become; and to have Dee's stomach craving baloney which will have to pass through her mouth is about the worst she can imagine. Dee also has flat feet. In any case their resolution not to complain to each other's heads about their bodies falls apart almost at once. It seems that Ellen's hands doodle incessantly in the margins of Marty's computer printouts, and Marty's feet are too big for all of Dee's shoes.

"I had to go out at lunch and buy a new pair," Dee says. "Size eleven. Your feet were killing me."

Marty looks under the table at his feet (they're sitting in Ellen's kitchen the following night). "God," he says. "You shaved my legs."

"I had to."

"God," says Marty. He snickers. Dee giggles. Ellen stirs her coffee. She hates coffee, but Dee's body is addicted to it. She doesn't know how they can laugh. Her hostility culminates in curiosity about how they are handling the sex change (it seems that here, at least, she's come out ahead in not having to make that particular adjustment), but she's shy about starting a discussion in which her own body is intimately concerned.

After all, Marty might say something embarrassing. "Your feet can't be the biggest change, Dee," she says significantly.

"Huh?" says Dee, and then purses her mouth. "Oh. Them. Well, I have to watch how I sit."

"You'd better," Marty says, and they're off laughing again.

Later on, when Dee leaves, Ellen asks Marty how he likes being a girl.

"It's great," he says with such a broad grin that she gets the feeling he's enjoying himself—that is, her—in some kind of perverted way that will give her an unpleasant shock when she finally gets herself back. For somehow they're all assuming, with a sort of blind trust, that they will get themselves back.

"Sure we will," he says when she asks him what he thinks. They're sitting on the couch; they're alone, and Ellen is wondering a little nervously what's going to happen next. "Why shouldn't we?"

"Why should we?" says Ellen, depressed by her craving for baloney (she has not yet given in).

Marty looks at her. "What's the matter with you?" he says. "You've done nothing but mope since we switched."

"I hate it," she says. "I hate Dee's body. I want my own back. I miss it."

"What do you mean?" says Marty. He chuckles. "It's right here."

The tears start in Ellen's eyes. "Stop it," she says. "Stop acting like it's some kind of big joke."

Marty stops being horrible when he sees she's really upset. He pats her knee and leans over to kiss her cheek. His mustache tickles in the old way. Ellen turns her head; they kiss; she goes limp. Marty strokes her hair and she leans against him and they kiss again. Marty mumbles against her mouth. "Mmmmm," says Ellen in response. He mumbles again; it sounds urgent this time. She pulls her head back.

"What?"

"I said you're crushing me."

Ellen realizes she's quite a lot bigger than he is. The thought is chilling. She sits up.

"It's okay," Marty says. "We'll just have to be careful, that's all."

Ellen doesn't answer.

Marty strokes her back. "Okay?" he says.

"Don't." Ellen shrugs his hand off.

"What's the matter?" he says.

"I don't want to," she says. "It's disgusting."

Marty looks surprised. "Come on," he says. "It'll be fun."

"Fun?" Ellen says. "Yuk."

Marty assumes a serious expression. "You know," he says, "I think there's something wrong, seriously wrong, if you find me, I mean you, so unappealing."

"It's not me," Ellen tries to explain. "It's Dee. The idea of my body and hers together—"

"Why don't you let me worry about your body?" Marty says. "After all, it's mine now."

"Like hell it is," Ellen says. She scowls at him. "Don't go thinking you can do whatever you want with it."

Marty glares back. "What the hell kind of attitude is that?" he says. "Don't you trust me?"

"No," Ellen says. In such moments the facts are often crystal clear. When Marty leaves, he slams the door so hard that the drafting table tilts and all the pencils roll off onto the floor. Dee's fingers itch to pick them up, but Ellen lets them lie there.

The next night she goes over to her mother's for supper. Her sister Millie is there too; Millie and her mother are having a fight about Millie's boyfriend, who has invited Millie to lunch tomorrow after ignoring her for four months. "He's a bum," their mother keeps saying. "The guy's a bum." Millie, who has been crying, tries to defend herself. "I just want my shirts back," she says. "Mom, he has six of my shirts." Ellen tries to remember if Marty has any of her clothes. Right now it would make sense: they'd fit him a lot better than they would her. Dee that is. She realizes she's eating a lot. Why don't Millie and her mother say anything about how big she is? Don't they even see her? During a lull in the fight about the shirts, her mother gives her a searching glance. "You don't look so good, honey," she says. Ellen's heart leaps. "You look pale," her mother says. "There's flu going around. Are you eating right?"

A week goes by in which Ellen doesn't see or hear from Marty at all. She misses him, although she tries to squelch the feeling by revving her anger like an engine whenever the blues get too bad. "That bastard," she finds herself muttering in the grocery store between cliffs of cans. "That son of a bitch." Unfortunately even in her anger she finds herself frustrated by the situation; for instance, is it still accurate to call Marty a son of a bitch? "That bitch," she adds just for good measure. But it doesn't feel right.

By the end of the second week, she's given up on her anger. It's worse than a car on a cold day: just gives a tired cough and dies. By now she's missing him—their jokes, his mustache. But what can she do? Apologizing is out of the question. It wasn't her fault. This stage passes, too, and she's thinking reluctantly but seriously about calling him when there's a miracle: she runs into him one rainy Saturday afternoon in the cafeteria of their favorite museum. It's fate, or something better. Even the mob of pint-sized Cub Scouts has been sent by fate or God to set off their reunion like something in a movie, and she fights her way through the turbulent waist-deep blue throng to the table where Marty sits reading the paper, a cup of coffee in front of him.

She reaches him, breathless, and he looks up from his paper. He looks surprised. "Ellen," he says. ". . . Hi."

"Hi," Ellen says. Even though she's forgiven him and everything is going to be okay now, it's still necessary to get through the preliminaries. She smiles at him. He seems dazzled, or maybe dazed. She sits down.

"Hi," he says again. He heaves a big sigh. Ellen looks into his eyes. She's glad his eyes are still the same.

"Hi," she says.

His eyes shift and drop. "Ellen," he says.

But she wants to be the generous one, the one to say it first; she wants to forgive him, not make him crawl. "Marty," she says, "listen, Marty—"

He shifts in his chair and looks up, not at her but over her shoulder, across the room.

He makes a little grimace so eloquent of misery that she turns and looks too. The Cub Scouts have started a jello fight; so what? It's all part of their romantic reunion. Then she sees Dee.

Dee looks terrific. There are raindrops covering her hair in a fine sparkly mist; her cheeks are pink. She's halfway across the cafeteria when she sees Ellen, and the sight makes her falter, but she gives a little shrug and comes ahead anyway. "Hi," she says when she gets to the table. The scouts are making an ungodly racket. Dee pulls out a chair and sits down. Ellen sees the look that passes between her and Marty and suddenly it's too late: she doesn't want to know but she can't stop herself now, can't stop knowing that it's happened the way she knew it would all along. They're having an affair, those stupid bodies of Marty's and hers, wanting each other and nothing else mattering, just the way bodies always are. But she's been left out and it hurts, and she gets up, indignant at finding herself crying, the scouts staring at her. Dee and Marty get up too, both talking at once. "Ellen—" "Listen, Ellen—" and she tries to push past them, but Marty is in her way. Below his unhappy face, arms reach out for her; and her own body, that betrayer, that beloved now lost perhaps forever, wordlessly clasps her close.

◆ ◆

JUDITH HAWKES, who teaches in New York City now, grew up in Memphis and is a graduate of Hollins College. Her *Julian's House* was published by Ticknor and Field in 1989, and Dutton has just published her most recent work.

PHYLLIS GOBBELL

The Tourists

Edie swings a tote bag with "Music City, U.S.A." on it. She is greased with sunscreen, outfitted in green Bermuda shorts and a striped knit top. The new clothes hang except around her stomach, which bulges gently from the last baby, three months old, left back in Birmingham with Edie's mother. She pulls Lela Beth by the hand, and at their heels, Chip, too big to hold anybody's hand, keeps bumping into his dawdling sister.

Glenn, always a few steps out in front, keeps hitching up his polyester pants. He keeps jerking at his red-and-white baseball cap. His Kodak Star bounces, swinging from his neck. His baby-blue knit shirt is snug around a middle that used to be rock-solid.

All the canvas shoes in the family are immaculate, too white to have been worn before their first day of vacation.

They are tourists in Nashville in July. The Watlings have planned for it all year.

Edie and the kids pose in front of a sign: "Tours—Homes of the Country Music Stars." Glenn focuses. "A little bit left. *Left*, Chip!"

Glenn dubbed him "Chip"—a chip off the old block—and it stuck. His name is Glenn Darnell Watling Junior. In kindergarten he learned to print "Chip" but not "Watling." This worries Glenn because Lela Beth, who starts kindergarten in the fall, can already print "Lela Beth Watling." He's been telling Edie she babies Chip too much.

"Smile, everybody!" he calls out, and they all smile big.

"You can still make the tour," a clean-cut student-type fellow shouts to Glenn, over the growl of the bus at the curb. Glenn shakes his head.

"Can we ride the bus?" Chip puts in.

Glenn judges from the way Edie lights up that she's about to say something, and he knows what. He says, "Do you have any idea what it costs to go on a tour like that?" He frowns at Chip, but his scolding is for Edie, too. "It's a rip-off," he tells them all.

Edie rubs her son's prickly crew-cut. "You'd get tired. It's a three-hour ride."

"I'm tired already," Lela Beth whines.

"Lela Beth, you can't be."

"Just shut up that *tired* business," Glenn says, taking off at a fast clip. "What this vacation's costing, everybody better have a good time or bust *acting* like it." He nearly trips over a blind man, sprawled against a storefront, playing a bluesey tune on a guitar.

Chip says, "He don't have hardly anything in his cup, Mama." Glenn hears the clink of a coin. He shoots a distrustful glance over his shoulder.

Edie says, "Hey. Are we having fun yet?"

Glenn comes to a halt. Smiling down at him is a life-size window display of Katie Austelle. "Yeah," he says, smugly, ducking inside the record store.

"Do you know Katie Austelle?" Glenn asks the clerk, a lanky fellow wearing the tightest jeans Glenn ever saw on a man.

"Sure. She's a fine new recording artist. We're promoting her new album."

"Personally, I mean? You ever met her?"

"Nope, but I met Dolly Parton once." He flashes a gap-toothed smile.

"I'm in the union with Katie's brother, in Birmingham. We're electricians."

"You don't say."

Outside, Edie works on Lela Beth's straggly ponytail. Loudspeakers blast a country tune into the street, maybe Ricky Skaggs. Edie's not sure. "Lela Beth, you're about to lose your do-dad," she groans. Hair is big with Edie. She has tried to curl Lela Beth's, but it's too fine, too limp. It's soft as baby-fuzz. She looks bald when it's short. Lela Beth wails. "Be still, honey. Don't pull away. You just make it worse."

"It hurts!"

"Oh come on. It's not that bad. I'm making you pretty." Trying, anyway. Lela Beth's hair is a real disappointment, considering Edie's training, all those months in beauty school that came to nothing, not even to fixing her own daughter up like a little doll.

She had a flair, everybody said so. Then Glenn Watling swept her up in a whirlwind, making her dizzy with all he wanted to do for her. All she had to do back was let him. Be his little woman. She never even got her beautician's license.

"Come on inside," she tells the kids. "It can't be as hot as out here. Or any louder." It looks like a dump to Edie, but so do all the other shops.

"I got me an album," Glenn says. He's in a decent mood now, humming "Never Forget Your Face." Edie knows that one, Glenn's all-time favorite.

Chip presses his finger to the photo on the album. "Katie Austelle," he says.

"Good boy!" Glenn tells him. Edie rolls her eyes.

"Katie's on the Grand Ole Opry tonight," Glenn is telling the clerk. "We've got tickets. Rick—that's her brother, my buddy—he told her we'd be there."

Edie steps up to the counter and lays down a Barbara Mandrell album. "This is for Retha." She gives Glenn a sidelong glance, the kind she uses on the kids, mostly, a *Don't cross me* look. Glenn does not acknowledge it. He wonders why Retha gets a souvenir. It's her daughter who's feeding their cats. But he pays for their records without a word.

"Have a nice stay, folks," the clerk says. "I hope Katie Austelle gives you a real Nashville howdy from the stage."

Glenn laughs, like that's far-fetched. But to Edie he says, "Sometimes the stars do say hello to people in the audience. Rick told her we'd be there."

"Sure, Glenn." She shakes her head, amused, like he's hopeless.

"Broad Street's sure not what I expected." Edie makes a wide sweep with her arm. "Pawn shops, beer joints. Are you sure we're on the right street?"

"Sure I'm sure. And that beer joint, with the purple front, that's Tootsie's Orchid Lounge. It's famous."

"Uh huh."

"It is, I swear. Me and Rick Stanfill were right down here on Broad. We went to that very place, Tootsie's."

"Looks like tee shirts are the best I can do. Come on, kids." While Edie's in the tee-shirt shop, Glenn leans against the brick wall, studying the street.

The weather is fine. Edie says it's too hot but she's hard to please, about everything. Glenn watches a supply truck maneuver into a loading zone in front of a furniture store. He hasn't said so to Edie, since she's already voiced her opinion about Lower Broad, but he can tell they've cleaned it up a whole lot since the time he was here with Rick Stanfill on union business. Glenn's not sure he didn't like it better, a little sleazier. It was like Rick said over their beers at Tootsie's, "You have to come to Lower Broad to feel the pulse of Nashville." Rick knew how to feel the pulse, all right.

Rick was pulling out all the stops, and pulling Glenn along with him. They picked up a couple of girls at Tootsie's, had a few drinks, a few laughs, and then Rick and his girl disappeared. Glenn went on back to the motel room alone. He was already married at the time. Rick was engaged, but not to anybody like Edie, with her principles. "My luck, Edie would find out," he told Rick the next morning. "Nothin' gets past her."

"If I was married, I wouldn't of done it either," Rick said. Glenn didn't believe him, but it was nice of him to say so.

The next night, Rick was set up with the same girl. "Hey, Buddy, my little sister's coming by, expecting me to take her out to eat. How 'bout you taking her, on me?" He pushed some bills into Glenn's hand. "Unless you have something else to do." He didn't.

"Kathy can sing, but she's set her sights way too high. She'll never break in. Tell her she's fooling herself. Tell her to come on home, will you?"

It's a memory Glenn likes to wash through his mind. Somewhere near Broad, in a little smoky-dark cafe with a jukebox, Glenn ate greasy spaghetti and drank cheap wine with Katie Austelle. She laughed, with a careless toss of her dark shimmery hair. "Kathy Stanfill might not make it to the charts, but Katie Austelle will."

"I believe it," Glenn said.

Katie kept the jukebox going. "Stand By Your Man," "The End of the World," and Patsy Cline's "Crazy" a dozen times. Katie loved the standards. Katie loved a jukebox. She loved to dance. There was no dance floor and nobody else dancing, but that didn't stop Katie. Her hair smelled like springtime. They danced till the place was closing.

Katie Austelle winked. "If you weren't married, Glenn—"

"If you weren't my best buddy's little sister—"

"Look for my name up in lights, hon."

Glenn felt her lush lips pressing on his cheek. She left a big red lipstick print.

The supply truck makes it into the tight space, and two stocky black guys climb from the cab. One's gray-haired, the other's a young fellow, and the old guy does all the lifting. It beats all. Glenn likes to watch people. Edie has never liked this craving he has to be part of the big world out there. Glenn doesn't see it as a failing, though. Like Rick said, sometimes a man has to step out of his own tight boots and wiggle his toes.

Down toward the river, a withered old drunk staggers out of a bar and joins a ragged bunch on the curb. Two painted-up women in high heels and halter tops come out of the western wear store carrying boxes that hide their cleavage, but their tight shiny pants show up every curve and cranny. Not much doubt about their occupation. Glenn can't remember what the girls looked like that he and Rick picked up, but he believes they were a nice class.

Farther up the street, a white Cadillac pulls to the curb and a tousled guy gallops into a pawn shop, swinging a guitar case at his side. Lower Broad still has plenty of character, Glenn decides. A few less adult book stores and peep shows. Maybe some of the weirdos wait till night to come out, and maybe several rounds at Tootsie's make you see it in a different light, too.

"Look!" Edie's voice startles Glenn. "Do you think it'll do for Bennie? They didn't have anything smaller than a size two." She holds up a tee-shirt that says "Mamma loves me *beary* much." It has bears hugging on it. Edie is so corny when it comes to her kids.

"I wonder if he's doing all right on the bottle. I hated to wean him so soon. I miss it, too. My arms do. My breasts do."

"Edie!"

"What are you smiling at?" she asks, about the time he takes the shirt and digs out the price tag.

"Ten dollars? Damn! Ten dollars for a doll-size tee-shirt?" Glenn can't believe her sometimes. He just can't believe her.

Lunchtime, at a sandwich shop nestled between a dry cleaners and an auto parts store, Glenn wonders if they're anywhere near that other cafe, his and Katie's place.

It is not a cheap lunch, two ninety-five for a hamburger, but Burger King is several blocks uphill. Glenn is fed up with shopping and everybody is too cranky to hike uphill.

The walls are lined with autographed photos of country music stars. Glenn points to one. "Hey, Chip, who's that?" Chip doesn't recognize Johnny Cash. Glenn can't believe it. "Aw, Chip, sure you know! If you'd just think about it!"

"Leave me alone!"

"Well, don't get sassy! And don't tune up to cry!" It irritates Glenn that a boy of his would cry over such a thing.

Glenn is paying at the cash register when he spots Katie Austelle's picture. She's a beautiful woman, smile as wide as Texas, eyes that sparkle with mischief, just enough. "Look whose picture they got behind the register," he points out.

"You've got Katie Austelle on the brain," says Edie.

"I do not."

"I don't think she's pretty, anyway. She's got big lips. Inflated-looking."

"She's Rick's sister, that's all she is to me." Glenn lets the door swing behind him, leaving Edie to herd the kids along. *Full* lips, he's thinking. He remembers how her lips felt on his cheek.

"You think she's gonna invite you back to her dressing room, Glenn? Maybe she'll call you up on stage. Y'all can do a number. Wouldn't that be cute?"

He's forced to wait for them. The kids just putter along, like it's a common thing for their mother to be goading their daddy on the wide open street. "Will you shut up, Edie? Just give it a rest."

It's the longest day. A splash in a pool would be fine. Glenn wishes he'd splurged for a motel with a pool. Edie smooths it over with the kids but she cuts her eyes at Glenn, and he feels cheap. Finally it's time for the Grand Ole Opry. Katie Austelle comes on stage. She's a knockout, in boots and white Stetson, sequined jacket and pants. She sings her big hit, "Never Forget Your Face." She blows kisses to everybody.

Edie turns to Glenn, bless his heart, all down in the mouth. She'd try to smooth it over, but he gives her a scowl, daring her to say one word.

They pull into the Crown Tourist Court and park in front of their room, not more than half a dozen yards from their door. This is one of the advantages Glenn pointed out when they checked in, when the kids were fussing to go swimming.

"This does make it nice," Edie says, unlocking their room. The kids are crumpled in the back seat like rag dolls. Glenn picks up Chip and hoists him over his shoulder like a sack of flour. Edie gets Lela Beth. She carries her like she's still a baby. It almost seems she is, she's so light, but her legs are getting long.

Glenn locks the car, and Edie covers up the kids. It's still dark in the room except for moonlight falling across the little lumps in the bed. Edie just stands there for a minute, taking it all in, smiling at her babies.

Glenn comes in and flips the switch, and the cheap room lights up, an ugly mustard color. Edie gives a swift tug on the cord at the window. The draperies swish shut.

"I'm gonna find some ice and a Coke," Glenn says.

Edie puts on her nightgown. It's pink and satiny. She bought it last week on sale for twenty-five dollars, marked down from forty. Retha talked her in to it. "Splurge a little, it's for your *trip!*" Retha said naughtily. Edie pointed out that it didn't much matter, with the kids sleeping in the next bed, but Retha said, "Take my word, it *matters*. Take it from somebody who made that same mistake, thinking it didn't."

In her cosmetic case Edie finds several liquor miniatures that Retha gave her for the occasion. There's vodka, gin, Chevis Regal, a handful of bottles, compliments of the airline that screwed up Retha's seating arrangements on her very first flight ever.

Edie thinks maybe a drink will make it finally feel like vacation.

Glenn comes in with a Coke and a Diet Sprite.

"I thought somebody kidnapped you," Edie says.

"I had to go to the other side. The ice machine out here's not working."

Edie is scooping little bottles from her cosmetic case as Glenn says, "There's music in the lounge next door. I could hear it when I went around for the ice."

He stands at the foot of the bed, shifting from one foot to the other, like a schoolboy before a stern teacher who's keeping him in at recess while his friends play ball.

"Well?" Edie says, flatly.

"I thought I might check it out. I wouldn't be long."

Edie is careful not to clink the bottles. She closes her cosmetic case.

At the door he says, "It's not that late, Edie."

She doesn't say a word. She is Glenn Watling's little woman.

It's Katie Austelle all right. Glenn recognized her voice. He just didn't know whether she was there in person or he was hearing a record. But it's Katie Austelle, live, on stage at the Starlight Lounge.

He pays the cover charge and goes into the dim, noisy, crowded room. He stands in the back for a minute, trying to spot an empty table but there's not one. He goes to the bar, claims a stool, and orders a Michelob. "She's good," he tells the bartender.

"Yeah. She's a good kid."

She is a beauty, with a voice like an angel, Glenn thinks. He drinks his beer and asks for another and begins to think about what he might say to her. Hi, remember me, Glenn Watling from Birmingham, Rick's buddy. No good. People don't just go up to a star like that. He's not sure he could get close to her, anyway, the way celebrities are always surrounded by bodyguards.

He is studying the situation when Katie Austelle finishes her set and walks straight over to the bar. "Bud and a Bud Lite, Bill!" she tells the bartender, laughing. She's with somebody from her band. Glenn hasn't paid much attention to her musicians, but the fellow's just a boy, Glenn sees that. His heartbeat pounds in his ears. Here is Katie Austelle seated on a stool at the other end of the bar. Katie Austelle in the flesh.

It's his chance to say, Remember me? He sips on his beer, calming himself down.

A girl comes up and hugs Katie. They squeal a little. "Hey, this is Ace," Katie tells her. "He's my drummer. Well, he's lotsa things." Katie squeezes the fellow's arm. Now that his cowboy hat's off, his hair appears a goshawful carrotty color. He's just a kid.

"Pipe down, Katie," the drummer says, out of the corner of a lopsided grin.

Playful, Katie shushes herself. They all laugh, and Katie begins talking to the girlfriend, confidentially. Glenn can hear the soft music of her voice. Same as he remembers. Look for me up in lights, hon. If you weren't married, Glenn.

It's me, Glenn. A drink for old times, Katie?

Her girlfriend leaves. Ace is having a joke with the bartender.

Katie drains her beer. She gets up, hops off the bar stool.

Now it's his chance to say, Hi Katie. She's a vision. His eyes fasten on her, and he's stuck. His blood races. In his mind he's saying, Remember me Katie? Remember?

Her dazzling eyes sweep past him. He follows the sway of her hips as she goes.

Glenn pays for his drinks. He's thinking he used to have a good time before Edie.

"What in the world are you drinking?"

Edie is outside their room, sitting on the hood of the car. She has a robe over her gown, but it's hanging loose.

"I'm having myself a vodka cola."

"Where the hell did you get vodka?"

Edie laughs. "Are you worried about me, Glenn? You're acting so funny! It's not like

I'm drunk. I'm only on my first drink. So far."

"I didn't expect to see you on the car in your night clothes, that's all."

"I'm just an unpredictable woman, Glenn."

"So where'd you get it?"

She tells him. "Retha don't drink hard liquor," she says.

"You don't either."

"Maybe you don't know. Maybe you don't know as much about me as you think."

"I swear, Edie." Glenn shakes his head. It's all he can do to keep a grin from breaking through.

Finally she says, "Fix one for yourself if you want to. Don't wake the kids."

"It's not the kids I'm worried about. It's the management."

"I'm not worried about a thing."

They don't go inside for a long time. Glenn finds a station on the radio that's playing country and turns it down low. The night cools off after a while. They scoot close together on the hood of the car. Glenn lets his arm slide around Edie's waist, and she leans against him.

"Katie Austelle was kind of pretty, in person," she says out of the blue.

Glenn says, "You got Katie Austelle on the brain or what?"

• •

PHYLLIS GOBBELL, a native Tennessean, is president of the Tennessee Writers Alliance and a member of both the Women's National Book Association and the International Women Writers Guild. She writes for children as well as for adults and is the author of *Like a Promise* and *In Search of a Quiet Place*.

DOROTHY FOLTZ-GRAY

Mothering

I have made a truce with my children.
After throwing them off the earth,
I threw a lasso after
and let them climb, tiny soldiers,
hand over hand, back to me
because I missed them,
their hot cinnamon breath.

I think they are other people's children
here for a visit.
I turn sheets down for them,
piece their faces, puzzles of my ancestry.
When I lean over them,
their night stars glow in the dark
like messages from another life.

I read to them of an island boy
who will get bigger.
I put my embrace on them.
My body says, come and go.
My reading turns steady as a clock.
I try to be their memory,
although I live the scene in fact.

Night Reading

Nine-thirty
and I've not
eaten. I
climb the stairs
to my son's
room, and on
the bed lies
Matthew reading
Alphabetalia.
I lie down
next to him,
pick up on
J where his
father stopped.
Jackal, *Jack*,
Jangle, *Jam*.
Matthew finds
the jar and
joker and
together
we find the
little boy
who hides on
every page.

Or part of
him, Matthew
says, turning
to the front
of the book.
This is the
whole boy, this
is what he
looks like.

NIGHT SWEATS

The I said-he said,
the undone, the undone again,
the nightgown of skin,
here the articulate
middle, the snare in the brain.
Here lies memory,
alive in a night that existed:
my father in silk pajamas
pouring a glass of milk.
Here is the way the body
works, the clock of itself
heading into daylight.

DOROTHY FOLTZ-GRAY's poetry has appeared in numerous publications, including *Mississippi Review*, *Chicago Review*, and *Homewords: A Book of Tennessee Writers*. She is a past recipient of the Tennessee Arts Commission's Individual Artist's Fellowship and the Poetry Society of America's award for narrative poetry. Currently a freelance writer, she lives in Knoxville, Tennessee, with her husband and two sons.

ABRAHAM VERGHESE

FROM *MY OWN COUNTRY*

When I was an orderly in the Battley Nursing Home in New Jersey (during the period when I was between medical schools), being paid by the hour for changing diapers and giving baths, it seemed as if my medical career had ended. That I would never be a doctor. And then, as I crossed each hurdle—getting back into medical school, becoming a doctor, then an internist, then an infectious diseases specialist—I had naively expected that each milestone would transform me, bring me happiness and peace of mind.

But happiness had come in another form: my infant son, Steven, and the way he added a new dimension to my relationship with Rajani. And instead of escalating goals, I wanted nothing more than to settle in one place and be a good physician. Stateless and roaming for so long, I wanted to put down roots. My son was American by virtue of his birth, and his father would become a naturalized citizen that year. I wanted my son to have a permanent home, something I never had.

Johnson City was going to be my town. I felt at peace in this corner of East Tennessee. Finally, this was my own country. . . .

• • •

Essie said that Gordon's temperature had remained normal with only a few spikes ever since his discharge. As soon as they got home, Gordon had wanted to be baptized before anything else was done. He talked of nothing else for that first day. His uncle was a lay preacher. Gordon asked his uncle if he would baptize him. He agreed.

The next morning, the family took Gordon in a borrowed van to the church. The pastor had given Gordon's uncle free reign to use the place. They walked Gordon into the vestry, one of them on either side. He was extremely short of breath, but they helped

Excerpts from *My Own Country: A Doctor's Story of a Town and Its People in the Age of AIDS*, by Abraham Verghese (New York: Simon and Schuster, 1994).

him up the stairs to the baptismal tank and then down the stairs into the water. The process exhausted them all. They had to carry Gordon back to the van and later lift him like a baby into the house. But it was worth it: the expression on his face was priceless; he was at peace and greatly relieved.

The baptism produced opposite effects on Gordon and his father. The father was sure that now Gordon was going to live. The father's denial had taken on new heights. He talked about perhaps starting a business with Gordon. His speech was peppered with "when Gordon gets better. . . ." It was not possible to reason with him about this.

Gordon, on the other hand, Essie reported, was feeling a genuine peace, not the passivity with which he had dealt with his illness thus far. He told Essie he was ready to die, and that his Saviour was waiting for him. The Gordon who returned from Florida may have seemed like an impostor, but the impostor had been exorcised. Gordon was back. His major regret at this point was the burden he felt he was on his family.

At one point Gordon felt well enough to sit out on the porch. When Essie had returned from work, she found Gordon there in his dressing gown. When she stepped out of the car, he put on his Bugs Bunny voice: "Hello, dolling! What say you and I go rashmagooling, just you and me." Essie had laughed till she cried.

Gordon was trying to use the bathroom himself, but his legs were tiring out and sometimes he did not get there in time. They had convinced him to wear diapers at night. He was having frequent accidents, day and night.

I asked Essie how the community was reacting to this. Did anyone know?

"Oh, I think everybody knows."

"How?"

"*I* told them. I don't think we have anything to hide."

Essie had no time to waste on worrying about the reaction of her neighbors. If there was shame in her brother having AIDS, in his being gay, she did not feel it. If anyone else felt it, it was irrelevant. I remembered her saying when I had visited her house that "he was Gordo before he was anything else. Gay was what he did, not who he was."

"And have you had any negative reactions from anyone?"

"Not really. Some women from our church have been coming by, bringing food—not that Gordo eats anything. If there is negative reaction, they sure better not come and say anything to me."

I was sorry I asked. It was as if I was digging for dirt. But it was something I wanted to know. The reactions to AIDS elsewhere in the country had not exactly been kind and understanding.

Essie went on: "I think people are real scared of AIDS, if that's what you mean. One time I was cleaning up Gordo when Jack, my friend from work, walked in. I'll be honest with you: Jack never has married. I have heard tell that he might be gay—which don't matter to me none, cause I love him to death. Well I had Gordo rolled over in bed and you know how skinny he is now. His back is just bones, a line of little marbles running down from his neck to his butt. And his buttocks—he don't have buttocks anymore. His butt is as flat as a pancake. The skin sort of sags there like an old man's. And his anus is one big hole in the middle of all this sagging flesh, bigger than the rest of him. Well, I turned and I seen Jack looking. He was in shock, his mouth open. I don't think it had really hit him till then how bad this disease does you. Well I stopped what

I was doing and just let him see that—I wanted him to see it. Gordo's face was turned to the wall; he didn't know Jack was watching. . . .

• • •

I was amazed by the ease with which medical services were being delivered to Gordon. A local pharmacist was providing the medications I prescribed, which he had in turn acquired from a distributor in Charlotte; the pharmacist knew the diagnosis. The nursing supervisor at the hospital, a friend of Essie's, had loaned her some oxygen equipment. This was a time when, elsewhere in the country, AIDS had generated some ignoble responses from doctors and other medical personnel. But in Blackwood, none of this was in evidence. . . .

• • •

"Well, he went off looking for the key. I was getting more and more nervous. He finally comes back with this big old key—I meant it was *huge*. And he puts it in the lock and opens the casket and sure enough there was Gordon. And he looked so pretty in there with his white suit. They had done him good. I had to give Doochie that. I almost wished that it had been an open casket service so they all could see how beautiful my baby brother was.

"But then I looked at his feet and he didn't have no socks on! I said, 'Doochie, hows'a'come Gordon don't have no socks on?' 'Essie, we don't usually put no socks on,' he says. I said, 'I don't want my brother going to heaven without socks. You *get* some socks for him, right now.' Well he goes off and gets some white socks and he comes back and he's got them big calving gloves on again! Son, I was mad. 'Doochie Jones! What in the world do you think you're going to catch from him now? You done pickled his body; there ain't a bug that's going to survive that.' He says, 'Why, Essie—' And I said, 'Don't you *why Essie* me! You take off those gloves and *put* his socks on right now. Go on. I want to see you do it. Git!' I stood there and made him put those socks on Gordon's feet." . . .

• • •

I told Essie that I would like to see where Gordon was buried. The kids wanted to come with us, but Essie discouraged them.

We drove out of Blackwood to Big Stone Gap and then out of the city limits into the country. Maple and pine trees lined the side of the road, forming a shady canopy. We drove past sea-green pastures with mares and foals grazing freely. Essie pointed out a driveway that sprang on us suddenly; the driveway led to a mansion on top of a knoll. She told me the name of the owner; a doctor from India, who was now also a gentleman farmer.

The road became twisty and I took the curves carefully, staying clear of the median. The traffic coming round the curves in the opposite direction was hidden by the overhanging foliage and the hedges that spilled onto the shoulder. We seemed to be descending, plunging down into a basin.

Suddenly, as we rounded another curve, the trees dropped away and the whole world seemed to open up: I saw ahead of me a breathtaking valley; huge in its expanse, gradually rising on all sides to towering mountains, the shadow of one range thrown onto the other.

Essie guided me to the cemetery entrance, a discreet path off the main road that I barely saw for the splendor around me. I stumbled out of the car when she told me to stop. High up, at the top of the mountain facing me, I could see the faint outline of the bridge that Essie told me was part of the new highway to Norton, a highway that had been under construction when I last visited. That mountain had to be Stone Mountain. And the one to my left was Little Stone Mountain—the town of Big Stone Gap sat right between the two. To my right was Powell Mountain. The cemetery sat at the very center of Powell Valley.

We trudged past neat brass plaques in the grass. When I looked ahead, I saw Sabatha and Joy: they had driven Essie's pickup through the back roads and arrived at Gordon's grave ahead of us. Essie scolded them but without any conviction.

Gordon was right next to his infant brother, Robert Lee, whose epitaph read, "Safe in the arms of Jesus."

◆ ◆

ABRAHAM VERGHESE, professor of medicine at the Department of Internal Medicine, Division of Infectious Diseases, at Texas Tech University Health Sciences Center in El Paso, is a graduate of the Iowa Writers' Workshop. His writing has appeared in such prestigious journals as *Granta*, the *New Yorker*, and *Sports Illustrated*. Dr. Verghese's *My Own Country*, a moving account of his years as a physician among AIDS patients in the mountains of East Tennessee, led the nation to the new sensibility about the disease, about those who suffer from it, and ultimately about those who treat it.

SHARYN McCRUMB

PRECIOUS JEWEL

Dying cost nothing and could be done alone—otherwise, Addie Hemrick might have lived forever. As it was, she grudgingly loosed her spirit from its wizened body, saying no good-byes to the kinfolk duty-bound to her bedside, and leaving nothing to anyone except the obligation to bury her in sufficient style to satisfy the neighbors that the family had "done right by her." Gone, but not forgotten. Legends of her temper and antisociability might outlast the marble slabs in the little mountain graveyard.

She was a McCrory from up around Cade's Cove; one of the Solitary McCrorys, as opposed to the Tinker McCrorys or the Preaching McCrorys. Her clan was known for living in little cabins as far up the mountain as they could get and staying put. They didn't hold with church-going, and folks in the cove said that if a bear-tracker or a drummer headed for their cabin, they hid in the woods until he went away again. Not scared, the McCrorys weren't. It was just in their blood to keep to themselves. A Solitary McCrory could no more make small talk than he could lay an egg.

So it was one notch short of a miracle when Wesley Hemrick, the circuit preacher's sixth boy, let it be known that he was marrying Miss Addie McCrory, of the Solitary McCrorys.

She had spent a few months in the one-room school learning her letters. Probably the meeting took place there; and Wesley Hemrick may have hunted squirrel in her neck of the woods on purpose thereafter. However it came about, she accepted the proposal and became a sullen, gawky bride one Sunday after meeting. Strangers clabbered around her, and she blinked at them. No telling what they meant for her to do, so she stood patiently until they went away.

A few days later they went down the mountain to catch the logging train, and no one saw them off. Wesley had got a job in the machine shop of the Clinchfield Rail-

"Precious Jewel," from *Our Separate Days*, by Sharyn McCrumb (Blacksburg, Va.: Rowan Mountain Press, 1989), 1–9. Reprinted with permission of Rowan Mountain Press.

road in town. They clattered down from the hills, standing in the engineer's cabin, holding everything they owned in two paper sacks. That logging train would someday become Tweetsie, a children's ride in a tourist park. Addie Hemrick's grandchildren would ride squealing through tunnels on Tweetsie; she never went with them.

They rented a little frame house close to the railroad, and set up housekeeping. Addie was a town-dweller now, but she kept to her old ways. Neighbors were nodded at across a privet hedge; she rarely spoke and never visited.

Company did come to call, however, in the form of Wesley's five brothers: M. L., Lewis, Francis, and the twins Tom and Harvey. In the evenings after work they'd appear in the back yard and slip into the smokehouse for their guitars and fiddles. They couldn't keep them up home, because the Reverend John B. Hemrick claimed that stringed instruments were of the devil, and he wouldn't have them on the place. He always contended that the upright piano in the parlor was a percussion instrument. So Wesley's house became the gathering place for the pickers. They'd sit in kitchen chairs beside the smokehouse and sing "Barbry Ellen" and "A Fair Young Maid All in the Garden," while the Mason jar was passed from one free hand to another.

Addie never set foot in the yard when that was going on, but she watched from the kitchen window, feeling as trapped as if she were tied to a chair. One of them might come in for a glass of water or some such excuse, and he'd glance over her kitchen and the little parlor, and, whatever he saw, he'd be talking about it to those people back up the mountain. The house was always clean and neat, with just the two of them, but if they came in, they'd find something to say, and she couldn't bear to be talked about. She imagined their voices in her mind, and it felt like being in a cage poked with sticks.

She stood it for months—until that first baby was on its way, due in the winter—and then one August evening, she charged out of the house with a broom, screaming for them to get off the place. "And take your liquor!" she'd shouted between sobs, "and don't you'uns ever come back!"

They hadn't.

In fifty years, they hadn't. Other factors were in play, of course: Lewis, Tom, and M. L. all went north to Chicago to work in the factories; Francis got a farm near Spruce Pine; and influenza took Harvey in 1920, the year Sam was born.

Sam was followed a year later by Frances Lee, and then came two stillborn babies—both boys—and then no more. The babies were always clean and seen-to, fed amply of whatever there was, but they stayed strangers. Addie peered into their wobbly infant eyes and decided no, she didn't know them at all.

Frances Lee married at sixteen and ran off to Chicago, away from her mother's cold stare. Sam took a little longer, long enough to work his way through a semester of teachers college, and then he let the army take him out of East Tennessee and into Normandy. That war and two others had come and gone, and the family was coming home.

The old frame house was bulging with kinfolk, mostly Wesley's side of the family. The women and their young'uns sat together in the tidy parlor, having put their bowls of beans and potato salad on the dining room table.

"A-lord, I wish Addie could be here," sighed Sally Hemrick, M. L.'s wife.

The others nodded in mournful agreement.

"If she was," thought Frances Lee, "you'd all be going out the window."

Nobody had been allowed in that parlor. Even the sofa, of stiff green fabric laced with metallic threads, was deliberately uncomfortable. If anyone came to call, they sat on the back porch, if they got in at all.

Frances Lee and her second husband Wayne had driven down from Brookfield after Aunt Sally phoned them the news. They had delayed just long enough to drop the boys off at his mother's house, and for Frances Lee to get a Kitty Wells permanent at the Maison de Beaute. In a way, she felt good about going home. Wayne's brassy Chrysler was the biggest car in the driveway, and, thanks to the union, he was doing all right at the factory. They had a four-bedroom ranch house and a camper. Frances Lee thought she must be about the most successful person the family ever had.

"Has anybody heard from Sam?" she asked.

Aunty Sally nodded. "He's flying down from Washington. Tom's oldest boy went to pick him up."

"Well, I guess I'll go see what the menfolk are doing," said Frances Lee.

She found them in lawn chairs in the back yard: Daddy Wesley, Uncle M. L., and Wayne. Lewis had his old Stella guitar, and he was picking out "Precious Jewel."

"May the angels have peace, God rest her in heaven; they've broken my heart and they've left me to roam."

Addie was lying alone in DeHart's Funeral Home, as she would have wished.

Major Sam Hemrick settled back in the front seat of Tommy Ray Hemrick's pickup truck and closed his mind to the blare of the local country station. Things hadn't changed much in the county since he was a kid: same rambling farmhouses gently decaying into green hillsides. The road was better, of course. He remembered when Model-As skirted the ruts in the deep, red clay and the fifteen miles to the city had been an all-day excursion. He glanced at his watch, the silver Omega he'd picked up in Germany. His plane had landed at three, and they'd probably be at the house by four-fifteen.

"Who was there when you left?" he asked his nephew.

"A passel," said Tommy Ray. "Dad, Uncle Lewis, M. L., and Aunt Sally and their young'uns. Frances Lee and Wayne got in last night. They're staying at Mrs. Lane's Boarding House, though. They figured it was easier than driving in from one of the farms every day. Don't know how long they'll be staying, though."

Not long, thought Sam. Frances Lee could get bored with the home place mighty quick. She always did. But she still came back from time to time: maybe the dutiful daughter, maybe just to show off.

Not like him. . . .

It had been more than twenty years since he'd left home, and even after the anger had burned itself out, he hadn't gone back, not even to see Dad.

Sam missed him sometimes, though. In the autumn he'd get to thinking about hunting with Wesley and Uncle Francis in the hills above Cade's Cove. He'd sit in camp surrounded by leaves that always stayed green, and remember the bands of red and gold ridges against a cloudless blue sky back home. And he'd be cleaning an M-16 instead of the Winchester 30-06 he used to have.

He still remembered the smooth feel of the walnut stock of that rifle, and the carving above the trigger that he kept shining with alcohol. It had been a custom job, and the $72 it had cost might as well have been $700 in 1940. It took him nearly a year of working every job he could talk anybody into giving him, but he finally saved up enough to buy it. With a jarful of change from picking blueberries at ten cents an hour, the five-dollar gold piece he'd got for winning the spelling bee, and a stack of dollar bills from a month of Saturdays at the sawmill, he paid the $72 plus tax (donated by Wesley) and bought the gun. Oh, but it was worth it! He used to brag that he could take the wings off a fly on top of the smokehouse, and he almost believed it.

Parting with that rifle was like leaving behind a chunk of himself, but he had decided to go to college, and firearms were not allowed in dormitory rooms. He had tucked it away carefully in the back of his closet, telling himself it was just as well he was leaving it home. After all, somebody might steal it. In a way, somebody did.

He had come home for the first time on the weekend of Thanksgiving. Teachers College was only twenty miles away, but he worked nights and weekends to pay his way, so he missed most of the hunting season. He'd make up for it, he told himself, by spending as much time up in the hills as the folks would allow. When he opened his closet to clean the Winchester his first night home, it was nowhere to be found.

"Mom!" he called. "Where'd you put my gun?"

She had appeared in the doorway, as cold and impassive as ever, and said simply that she had sold it. It was cluttering up her house.

Sam was half Solitary McCrory, and they never were much on arguing. He just put his clothes back in the canvas valise and walked out. The army sent them a form letter when he graduated from boot camp, and a telegram when he was wounded in Normandy. Years later he took to writing a few lines telling them where he was, and about his brief marriage to Mildred, who couldn't understand that the army came first with him. He sent them a cuckoo clock from Germany one Christmas (Mildred's idea), and Wesley had gotten a watch from Japan, but they never wrote him back. Neither one of them was much on writing letters. He wondered if Wesley had aged much. Funny, he always pictured him as he had been all those years ago—just a little over forty.

"Well, we're here!" called Tommy Ray, pumping the horn. "And there's everybody in the yard, a-waiting on us."

"Which one . . . which one is Dad?" asked Sam.

Frances Lee gave her brother time to adjust his memories to the real thing before she tackled him for the talk they had to have. He'd kept calling Lewis' teenage granddaughter "Frances Lee," and he'd had to make war talk with the menfolk in the backyard, and tell the women what things were like overseas. Then they'd all gone off to the funeral home to view the body for the last time before tomorrow's service, but now—finally—the house was quiet. The kinfolk and their covered dishes had disappeared around ten o'clock, leaving them in peace. Wesley was in his room.

She'd settled Wayne in front of the t.v. and gone out to the porch where Sam was reading this week's copy of the *Clinchfield Scout* with a bemused smile.

"Anything interesting?" she asked, curling up on the glider.

He shook his head. "Fred Lanier became a lawyer."

"On his daddy's money," snorted Frances Lee. "If Dad had been a shop foreman making good money, there's no telling what you could'a done."

"I did all right," he said. "Washington is good duty to pull."

"I guess I did all right, too," said Frances Lee. "We got two cars and a camper. Leastways, we both got out of these hills."

Sam smiled. "Like M. L. and Lewis and Tom. The trick is not to come back. But everybody does sooner or later."

"You thinking about coming back?"

"I don't know, Fran. Why?"

"Because we've got to figure out what to do about Dad."

She told him how, after fifty years of marriage, he couldn't even fry an egg and might be too old to learn. The question was: should they try to hire him a housekeeper, look into retirement communities, or arrange for him to come and live with one of them?

"Washington or Chicago," said Sam. "That's a pretty big change for a man his age."

"Well, he might like it," snapped Frances Lee. "Lord knows, anything would have to be an improvement after living with Mama all these years. He can finally start to enjoy himself."

"Okay," said Sam. "Go get him and we'll talk about it."

The straight-backed kitchen chair on the porch was always Welsey's chair. He sat down in it now, feeling a little like a man asking for a bank loan, in front of these two stern-faced adults who were—and weren't—his children. Frances Lee was doing most of the talking, but he couldn't quite make out what they wanted. It was too soon after—the other—for him to think about anything else. It had to do with his future, though.

"Of course, we want you to do whatever will make you happy, Dad," his daughter was saying. Her voice used to be like her mother's, but she had a yankee accent now, and the resemblance was gone.

"Happy . . ." he echoed, catching her phrase.

"We don't want to force you into anything," she smiled, patting his sleeve. "You had enough of being bossed around from Mama. So we want you to feel free as a bluejay. You can finally be happy and do as you please."

Do as he pleased. . . . Her voice faded in his mind and became Addie's voice. They had been courting for a few weeks that fall—mostly just walking in the woods while he called himself hunting. He had done most of the talking—about his knack for machinery, and his plans to make something of himself. She had walked along beside him in silence, sometimes nodding at what he said. She was small, with a broad bony face under a cloud of black hair, and though she never said anything about how she felt, her blue eyes shone when she looked at him. When they were alone. Never at any other time.

"I've got to get down outta these hills," he told her that day. "Makin' a livin's easier in town. I can get a job with the railroad, workin' in the machine shop. But I got to live in town to do it."

"You do as you please," said Addie McCrory.

"But. . . ." He hesitated with the weight of the asking. "I want you to come with me."

He didn't say any more, and she didn't either. No Solitary McCrory had ever been fool enough to leave the hills. They weren't used to town ways, and they couldn't change any more than a chicken hawk could. Kept to themselves and didn't make friends.

"Ain't nothing we want bad enough to go to town for," the McCrorys used to say. He had almost realized even back then what it would be like for her to be set down among people who never would understand. A house in town and all those strangers; it was like asking anybody else to live in a cage, but he had asked because he wanted her with him. He would have gone anyway, but he wanted her with him.

She looked at him for a long time before she finally said: "I'll come."

He reckoned she liked him then, but he hadn't really understood until after she was his, and he learned that McCrory feelings were like a fire in a wood stove: the flames were hid behind iron walls, but inside they burned brighter and longer than any open fire. She had gone with him, and never once in all those years that followed had she mentioned it, or asked to go back. If she had, he would have gone with her.

"Dad?" said Frances Lee a little louder. "What would you like to do?"

"I don't reckon it matters," said Wesley.

◆ ◆

SHARYN MCCRUMB is the author of twelve novels, including the "Ballad Books," published by Scribner's. The Ballad series includes *If Ever I Return, Pretty Peggy-O* and *The Hangman's Beautiful Daughter*, both of them New York Times Notable Books, and *She Walks These Hills*.

STEVE STERN

THE STRAITJACKET CHALLENGE

I was in the audience at the Idle Hour Cinema with my mother and father for my friend Hymie Weiss's Amateur Night debut. This was on North Main Street in the spring of 1927. Of the several acts preceding Hymie, the first was Mr. Dreyfus the jeweler, who'd aspired to be a comedian ever since Mogulesco's touring company had played the Workman's Circle lodge hall. The problem was that Mr. Dreyfus knew only a couple of jokes, which he repeated at each performance, so that everyone already had them by heart. As a consequence the earnest jeweler found himself in the role of straight man to his own shtik of riddles and gags.

His favorite was the one that went, "What hangs on a wall, is green, and whistles?" to which the audience would answer in a chorus so loud that plaster fell from the ceiling, "A herring."

Says Mr. Dreyfus, flapping his baggy pants in case you hadn't noticed: "Since when does a herring hang on the wall?"

Audience: "Who stops you from hanging it?"

Mr. Dreyfus adjusting a rubber nose scarcely larger than his bulbous original: "Is a herring green?"

Audience: "You could paint it."

Mr. Dreyfus: "But who ever heard a herring whistle?"

Audience: "Nu, so it doesn't whistle!"

Mr. Dreyfus does a modest hornpipe to Mr. Elster's organ, exiting to raucous applause.

Next the little Elster girl, done up in blackface like Topsy, commenced a bubble-eyed tapdance, making window-washing gestures with the flat of her hands. Her mama, the resident organist, accompanied her in a medley of Stephen Foster tunes. Wearing a false beard that covered his goiter, Ike Taubenblatt, the shoe repairman, did the "Blow wind, crack your cheeks!" speech from Shakespeare. Mrs. Padauer juggled three rolling pins, and Mannie Blinkman swallowed a light bulb, only to belch it back up again. Cantor Abrams sang his three-handkerchief rendition of "The Czarist Recruit's Farewell" through a megaphone. Then it was Hymie's turn to perform what he'd talked Mr. Forbitz, the theater manager, into announcing as the evening's pièce de résistance.

He came on dressed like the Phantom of the Opera in a getup borrowed from Nussbaum's Drygoods Emporium. With a flourish he doffed the top hat and removed his silk cloak, revealing a sleeveless undershirt that showed off his stringy physique. When he handed the hat and cloak to his assistant, my sister Miriam, there was polite applause, though whether it was for Hymie or Miriam (who was an uncommonly dishy girl) was hard to say. In either case, Hymie had the attention of the house.

Having placed the accessories over a chair, Miriam took up the stiff sailcloth straitjacket trimmed in leather. This while Hymie, running a hand through his upstanding auburn hair, announced gravely, "Ladies and gentlemen, for your express delectation I will attempt Houdini's famous punishment suit release." Then, as Miriam held the straitjacket in front of him, Hymie thrust his hands into the sleeves, which overlapped the ends of the outstretched arms. He gave her the nod and Miriam turned to the tittering crowd.

"Hymagnimummm . . . ," she mumbled to her sandal-shod toes, nervously flouncing the handkerchief points of her skirt. But when some of the onlookers demanded she speak up, she repeated almost defiantly, "Hyman [pronounced High Man] the Magnificent requests volunteers from the audience."

Practically all the young men in the theater, eager to assist Hymie's assistant, rose and stampeded the stage. Miriam glanced sheepishly at Hymie, who maintained his rigid pose but rolled his eyes, as the small stage was overrun by the sons of North Main Street. Conspicuous among them was Bernie Saperstein, the most aggressive of my sister's suitors, looking spruce in his canary blazer and waxed mustache. Shouldering his way to the forefront of the would-be volunteers, he left Miriam no recourse but to choose him to help fasten Hymie's restraints. She also chose, probably to compensate for Bernie's vigor, the consumptive Milton Pinkas.

Exercising somewhat more zeal than was called for, Bernie went to work on the buckles and straps, slapping down Milton's hands whenever he tried to pitch in. With his torso constricted until he'd turned the blue of moldy cheese, Hymie spoke in a voice trapped somewhere in his diaphragm. "The committee will confirm," he managed hoarsely, "that the punishment suit is secure." Bernie tugged at the jacket and smugly grinned his assent. "And now," croaked Hymie, "as I say the mystical word 'Anthropropolygos' [which I mouthed along with him], Miss Rosen, if you please—"

Miriam rolled out a gauze hospital modesty curtain from stage left and folded its panels around Hymie. Then she said what she'd been coached to say, the phrase uttered by Bess Houdini before shutting up her husband in his various cabinets: "Je tire le rideau comme ça!" "It means 'I draw the curtain thus!'" I told my mama next to me, who grunted that I shouldn't be such a wisenheim. Stepping to one side, Miriam made an artistic gesture and smiled unconvincingly, embarrassed as always by her own drop-dead beauty.

Mrs. Elster played an appropriately suspenseful signature on her organ, while I pictured Hymie behind the curtain, drinking in the moment he'd waited for. Mentally I prompted him, reciting under my breath the pertinent passage from *Magical Rope Ties and Escapes*: "The first step necessary in freeing oneself from the jacket is to place an elbow on some solid foundation and by sheer strength. . . ."

The ordinarily boisterous Amateur Night audience were subdued as they listened to the sounds of the struggle behind the curtain. They remained almost reverent, even as the curtain toppled over on its clattering frame, revealing Hymie wrestling furiously with himself. He thrashed around like a cat in a bag, flinging his hampered body here and there, assuming contortions certain to cause him an injury. Against the painted asbestos backdrop, Miriam had begun to chew her braid, her pale cheeks gone intensely crimson. The jaws of the volunteers hung collectively open. Then Bernie Saperstein, always the joker, called out, "Somebody get the rabbi, there's a demon in Hymie Weiss!" and the whole theater split their sides. This was Mrs. Elster's cue to strike up a rollicking tune.

The general hilarity seemed only to encourage Hymie's violent behavior. Puffed with concern, Mr. Forbitz marched out of the wings, shooing everyone from the boards, "All right, Weiss," he blustered, dewlaps swaying, "that's enough already, shoyn genug!" "Stop it, Hymie!" cried Miriam, stomping her foot, but her agitation on his behalf if anything only fueled his abandon.

At length Mr. Forbitz returned to the wings and lowered the movie screen with a dust-raising thud, thus separating the spectators from Hymie's ordeal. He stepped back out again to signal the projectionist, upon which the lights went out, a beam shot over our heads, and the picture began. It was a John Barrymore melodrama entitled *The Beloved Rogue* ("Even torture could not quell the spirit of the vagabond poet," the posters read), for whose credits Mrs. Elster modulated her rollicking organ. The rooftops of medieval Paris, brooded over by Notre Dame, appeared to be caught in a blizzard of blackbirds, so poor was the quality of the film. What's more, as the dauntless vagabond swaggered into the frame, the screen, patched and seamed as an old topsail, began to flutter from the goings-on behind it. The crooked streets rippled as if in an earthquake and the audience howled over the distortions. Then, in the side of a house from whose window a bosomy lady was waving, a fissure opened and Hymie hurtled through. Still in the throes of his desperate struggle, he lurched headlong into the orchestra pit, breaking an arm.

◆ ◆

STEVE STERN, associate professor of English at Skidmore College, was born and grew up in Memphis, Tennessee. His first collection of stories, *Isaac and the Undertaker's Daughter*, received a Pushcart Writer's Choice Award, and the title story of that collection won an O. Henry Prize. His second short story collection, *Lazar Malkin Enters Heaven*, won the Edward Lewis Wallant Award.

JOHN BRIDGES

Chosen One

It had been a long time since anybody had actually heard Marian Anderson sing. There were recordings, of course; but, for the most part, all that was left of her was pictures—a few quiet, black-and-white photographs, all of them silent, none of them capable of even suggesting any sound.

Those photographs are all the news reports showed. There was Marian Anderson, demure even in bias-cut velvet, photographed in a Harlem studio by Carl Van Vechten. There was Marian Anderson on the steps of the Lincoln Memorial, wrapped in sable, facing a crowd of 75,000 people in the middle of a gray Easter Sunday afternoon. There was Marian Anderson, backstage in a dressing room at the Old Metropolitan Opera House, done up in a bad wig and gravely awaiting the stage manager's call.

Her face, in all the photographs, is beautiful. The cheekbones are high, and her skin is smooth and unworried; its color is soft, the way the color of copper softens with the touching of time. The only flash of bravura is the lips, which threaten to flare out, like the sleek, grand bell of a trumpet, even though they are always pressed together in a mild, unsmiling line. Even in Van Vechten's studio, the eyes are filled with terror or simple, lonely sadness. They stare at the camera as if it were an intruder asking unwanted questions, seeing intimate things. In those eyes there is no glimpse of lightness. They are eyes that do not know how to trust.

It is hard to tell from these pictures whether Marian Anderson ever knew a moment of laughter. It is hard to know whether she chose her dignity or came to it by nature, whether it was her simple homage to the Schubert songs she sang or her defense against being asked to peel grapes and scrub floors. She may have honed the sleek, solemn chastity of her singing—which would have made her miserable in opera, even if she had been given a true fighting chance—in humble, sexless service to music. Or it may have been—in a world of white people who would give her standing ovations but would not shake her hand—the only means by which she could survive.

"Chosen One," by John Bridges, appeared in *The Nashville Scene* 11, no. 11 (April 15, 1993): 11. Reprinted with permission of John Bridges and City Press Publishers.

Because the people who write news reports have never heard the sound of her singing, they can only remember the P.R. hoopla of that concert on the steps of the Lincoln Memorial, with Harold Ickes and Mrs. Roosevelt taking the credit and Sol Hurok pulling the strings. They can only talk about her long-overdue Met debut, when she was fifty-seven years old and the voice was growing hollow and phrases were occasionally veering off pitch for shortness of breath. They can only reduce her to a gesture—the first black singer to sing solo on the stage of America's greatest opera house. There seems no reason to mention that she was safely consigned to the role of a voodoo gypsy woman, that there was no need for any white man to touch her, that she appeared only in a single scene.

In her autobiography, Marian Anderson herself chose only to be grateful, noble-minded, and a trifle melancholy. She was no Rosa Parks, changing the world by moving a few rows forward to the front half of a bus. To sing Verdi, Marian Anderson required the cooperation of stagehands and a full orchestra. She was not interested in stirring up anger; when she told her story, she took no pleasure in reliving pain. Her business was not speeches but song.

Black people had sung high-toned music long before Marian Anderson. Vaudeville houses had been trotting out "Black Nightingales" and "Negro Opera Quartets" since Reconstruction; but she chose not to take gimmick billing as "The Colored Contralto." She chose to succeed not on the basis of her strangeness but on the terms laid down by the white people's world. She determined to present herself to audiences accustomed to grandiose singing—if she were to survive, it would only be because she was great. Before her, only the tenor Roland Hayes had come close to succeeding in such an act of hubris. Long before his voice had broken, however, his soul had fallen apart.

It was not Marian Anderson's blackness that made her a wonder. Even if she had not been a black woman, her life would not have been easy—when she returned in triumph from Europe in the late 1930s, singers with threadbare last names like "Anderson" were not offered top billing at the Met. In recompense, she had the concert stage, she had her voice, and she had her craft.

The voice itself was smooth and fathomless like the sheen of mahogany. When she sang, she closed her eyes and stood in the curve of the piano, folding her hands in front of her so that everything she sang became an anthem, every note was part of a prayer. When she closed her eyes and sang, it seems, she managed almost to disappear. The fact that she was a black woman seemed of absolutely no significance. By comparison, the fact that she was from Philadelphia seemed a far greater marvel indeed.

As the war approached, however, European singers sailed home, some for reasons of patriotism, some out of paranoia. The world should have been able to make better use of a Marian Anderson, but the calls did not come. The embarrassment of her greatness was that there still were places where she could not go. The irony of her grandeur was that it did not allow her to make scenes.

She hardly could have been surprised that the D.A.R. denied Hurok's request to book her for a Constitution Hall recital. Surely, Mrs. Roosevelt was already part of the game. Anderson had lied about her age for decades, but she knew that she was already 42; there was little chance the world would change quickly enough to make much difference to her. Still, on that gray-skyed Easter Sunday afternoon, standing behind a bank of microphones, with newsreel cameras whirring on all sides, Marian Anderson consented to become an icon. After that day, her life was frozen in pictures. She was defined—inescapably and by her own volition—by the color of her skin.

The recordings of that afternoon crackle with static and the whip of the wind, but the Anderson voice is there, steady and solemn and seamless as ever, unfurling "My Country 'Tis of Thee" as if it were a bolt of midnight crape. The pictures of that afternoon, however, are different from all the others. On that afternoon, Marian Anderson has folded her hands in front of her, but her huge, frightened eyes are wide open. When she sings, she stares hard out over the heads of her audience, facing straight into the cold Easter Sunday sky.

◆ ◆

JOHN BRIDGES is a senior editor for *The Nashville Scene*. His weekly column, "Keeping Up," is syndicated in independent newsweeklies around the Southeast. A collection of his columns, *Keeping Up: Blue Blazers, Iced Tea and Everything Else Worthwhile in Life*, was published in 1993.

JANE BRADLEY

BARBIE MOURNS THE DEAD

When my mother was a girl she liked to bury her dolls and dig them up to bathe them in a pan of soapy water, wash their clothes, and dry them in the sun on the grass. She rocked her babies, pretended to feed them honeysuckle, and sang to their blue wide-open eyes. Then, compelled, she buried them, using a spoon stolen from the kitchen to scoop the earth up and her palms to slide the dirt over their faces until they were buried from the light.

She wasn't a bad girl, not mean like her grandmother said when she'd whip her with a switch, shouting with each stroke: "One day you'll learn to appreciate things." My mother would run and sit under the pecan tree in the back yard. She would watch the sun move through the delicate lacy pattern of swaying leaves and try not to miss her daddy who was dead and her mother who never seemed to be home. She would sit, sweat mingling with tears on her face until a breeze came and cooled her, as she hoped she could keep the promise and not bury her dolls again.

I never buried my babies. They were too dear and hard to come by. I needed those plastic dimpled arms, round bellies, and soft heads to cuddle under covers through the nights. There was enough real death in the world to keep my dolls alive. My puppies choked on chicken bones; some were hit by cars. I cried, screaming always, teased sometimes for the ugly way my face twisted with my pain. I tried to cry in private, but death is such a public thing, with puppies writhing in the grass while flies and fleas buzz in summer heat. Finally, the tears cried out, I calmly claimed dead puppies, while my sisters, repulsed and angry, always ran away. I wrapped my dead in pillowcases stolen from the closet and carried them to rest in their corner in my woods.

In addition to puppies, I loved and lost my goldfish that always in time bloated and turned belly up, their tiny fish souls swimming off as I went back to Woolworth's and

"Barbie Mourns the Dead," from *Living Doll*, by Jane Bradley (Sag Harbor, N.Y.: Permanent Press, 1995). Used by permission of Permanent Press.

plunked my quarters down. Carrying pair after pair home, sloshing dully in their plastic bags, I dumped them in their bowl and named them the eternal names of Flip and Flap, as if persistent naming could make resurrection true.

There were also turtles, tiny store-bought things with hard and fragile backs, yellow bellies, tiny claws and cool black bead eyes. Without complaint they climbed my dirt piles, swam mud-hole creeks, and lived dull short lives in my turtle bowl with the spiraling ramp that ended at a flat plastic palm tree glued upright at the center like a rigid useless flag. Such lives weren't meant to live, but ever hopeful, I kept buying more turtles so lively green at the start when they crawled across my hand. Then I watched them slowly wither like freshly dying leaves plucked from trees.

The grown dogs, my daddy said he buried. But as I watched him roll them in a plastic sheet and throw them in his truck, I knew he'd toss them in a woods I couldn't walk to, or he'd throw them with our garbage at the county dump.

Some things went beyond my service. But puppies, turtles, goldfish, even beyond death were mine. My private graveyard was for smaller things, a little world of loss. A perfect place, a tiny space where I was too human, giant-sized to fit my thick grief in. So I shrunk the pain down to a smaller scale, set a little stage of death, and reduced my sorrow to the plastic human forms of Barbie and Ken.

My momma's boyfriend, Wally, brought my first Barbie doll. He was a truckdriver and came on days my daddy worked. With Daddy's twenty-four-hour fireman's shifts, my momma took the risk. Wally was a lean man with biceps that bulged like living things breathing in his arms. I couldn't help but stare at his flex, his flashing eyes, his grin. Sometimes he'd let me run my fingertip along the thick veins that curled like snakes under his taut tanned skin. Wally smelled like Old Spice and cigarettes and looked cleaner than my dad. He always tapped the front door, opened it, peeked with a sneaking smile, then let himself come in. He brought us balls and jacks and Bo-Bo paddles, and Little Debbie Snack Cakes he pilfered from his truck. Momma always took the brown paper sack he brought her with a laugh. She'd unwrap the fifth of whiskey, give him his kiss and us a look that meant we had to go. Without complaint we took our snack cakes, toys, and secrets out the door into the yard. We'd play outside under trees knowing what went on inside our mother's house. We'd seen the dirty magazines underneath the bed, had squealed at the mottled skin and hairy crotches, that wild dog look frozen in some stranger's eyes. We knew what Wally came for, but we kept our momma's secret as we kept our minds on the games we played until we saw Wally's truck leave and heard Momma call us in.

I knew that sex was a dirty steaming swamp ahead. My older sister had told me it was awful, that being a girl only got worse each year once you let some boy get in. I clung to my Barbie's perfect grown-up body, its smooth flat crotch, its promise to stay pure. My Barbie was a virgin, even though she came unwrapped and plainly offered from rough truck-driving hands. Wally had pointed to the brown bubble-do hair, big blue eyes like my momma's and said, "She looks like your momma. Why don't you call her Bobby Jo." He squeezed my Barbie in one hand, looked at me and grinned. "No, she's Barbie," I said, reaching. I'd seen my momma naked and knew she was no doll. She had hair and fat and freckles. I'd seen her pee and bleed. My Barbie was a lady. She had money, cars, and boyfriends who only kissed with mouths sealed off from tongues and spit. So I gripped my Barbie in both hands and stared at those sweet blue eyes that could only belong to Barbie. My Barbie, my real Barbie. The name-brand Barbie. I couldn't help but smile. Now I would be like those blonde girls on TV with straight teeth and ponytails with ribbons and nice clean clothes. They all had real Barbies, and their mommas baked them cookies and never locked them out when Wally, the truck-driving boyfriend, came. I looked up at Wally and whispered, "Thank you, thank you, Wally." He beamed down and said, "Take her out and play now." I went happily that time to my place out in the yard. I was reborn then into a purer world of name brand toys, like real girls in that clean bright world beyond making do with what they had. No more cheap pink imitation fashion doll, no more pretending I had a real Barbie with that dime-store fake Babette.

While Barbie was a debutante, Babette was local white trash. With her sluttish black-lined eyes, her lips too red and skin too pale, she looked cheap no matter how she dressed. So Babette died that day I was reborn with Barbie. It was a quiet death in the back corner of my closet, with only my child's blind loyalty preventing her from being thrown away. So she remained my secret low-class self, the doll not good enough to play with Barbie, the girl I kept, but hid.

My momma said she had really looked like Barbie once, before she met my dad. She said she was the kind of girl all Ken doll boys had wanted to go out with, said she was neat and sweet and pretty back then when she was young. My momma cried when my daddy got drunk and swore, "Like Barbie, like hell, you were never nothing but a whore." I wanted to believe she looked like Barbie with her blue eyes and bubble hair-do, but then I'd seen her laughing when Wally grabbed her butt. I'd seen her open mouth, her cheap red lips, her pale pink skin that never tanned. I knew she was no Barbie. Babette was in my blood.

But Barbie was what I could be if I practiced, prayed, and tried. I planned one day to be a Barbie but had to struggle first to make my Barbie look like that bright Barbie who was always fresh and clean and perfect in commercials on TV. That Barbie had a boyfriend, cars, houses, and at least a dozen outfits with tiny shoes that always matched. That Barbie went to California beaches, New York nightclubs, sometimes even Paris, France. But mine never went beyond my woods and the backyard of my house. She couldn't afford those fancy outfits. She made do with homemade clothes.

I swiped my family's socks to do it, cut them down to tube-shaped dresses, shirts and skirts. I snipped armholes, added buttons, rick rack, ribbons, glitter, glue. I used my pink lace-edged Easter socks for her cocktail dress, and loved the girlish ruffle stretched across her rock-hard breasts. The sexy cocktail dress was my most prized creation until I saw Flash Gordon on TV one day and was inspired to higher realms in my design. I ran to my mother's kitchen, swiped a roll of foil and scissors, tape, then hid for hours in my bedroom where in all her flashing crinkling glory, my Space Barbie was born.

First I wrapped her in press-on foil pants, made a halter top, and used scotch tape to secure her flowing cape. I made a mini-skirt and a straight shift dress that glistened above her silver press-on boots. I added foil wrist bangles, and when her hat fell off I stuck it on with a pin rammed in her head.

Space Barbie came from Mars. She knew secrets of the universe and came with wisdom from beyond. Space Barbie flew above the daily trauma of dead pets, secret boyfriends, and my mom and daddy's fights. But she didn't visit often. She had better things to do out there with stars and angels, her visitations holy holidays that couldn't come too often or they'd lose the magic that could lift me from my world. So most days she was plain bubble-do Barbie in her homemade clothes of cut-up socks. She was happy with her shoebox house. My Barbie had a good life, never once got hit or hurt or sick. And she had Ken to talk to when I sealed them up at night in their cozy shoebox home. I never thought to bury them. They'd always be alive above ground where they were a promise of an eternal present without age or loss or pain. They always smiled and never argued with my plans and so became the perfect tools of grief for the mortal living dying ones, my pets.

My graveyard was scaled down to my pets, with paths just wide enough for the dainty steps of Barbie and the flat bare feet of Ken. Mourning clothes always meant the risk of black socks stolen from my Daddy's drawer. I sneaked when my mom was out, pushed through the rolled lumps of socks to finger his heavy silver dollars, dirty playing cards and rubbers wrapped in foil. I held in secret my fascination for the grownup man things he only thought he hid. But I justified my theft, claiming proper death a higher purpose, thinking things couldn't really be stolen from a family since, with a blood connection, lost things weren't really lost. They simply moved around. I knew he'd never miss those socks, and I was safe since mom was too busy with Wally and whiskey on the days my daddy worked to notice what I did.

I hid Barbie's grieving face with a veil cut from the toe of my daddy's sock. She walked the pebble-lined path and was slowly guided to the gravesite with my right hand as Ken followed barefoot in my left. They stood balanced in my grip above the open grave and assumed my role of grief.

A girl finds comfort in her small worlds: shoebox houses, tiny toys, and painted castles in the bottom of fishbowls for indifferent, short-lived fish. A girl needs a small-scale kind of peace in a house where yells and smells and secret things are too thick to grasp. So I reached for what I could hold in my quiet, careful hands. A living doll, they called me for my sweetness, silence, cuteness, my ease at being good. I knew from my baby dolls how to do it, how to smile and eat and drink and sleep and pee on cue. A living doll, they called me, but I knew that underneath the plastic, my blood breathed, heart pounded, belly moved. Just like my puppies, I could cry and choke and bleed. I could die like my dead things, and once buried I would rot.

I knew I was a creature more like my puppies that rotted when they died, that I was nothing like those dolls who only looked alive. I looked to the perfect grownup doll face of my Barbie and knew she'd always live. I thought if I could be like Barbie, no one would tease or hurt. If I could be like Barbie, some larger loving hand would always hold me safe above an open grave. If I could be like Barbie, I would never die.

So I played my graveyard game and kept my private line between the living and the dead, split myself between the smiling sunlight side and the rank decay of graves. I lined my little graveyard paths with bright pebbles taken from a park. I transplanted mosses, violets, and wild strawberries, and I watered, loved, and tried, but they never seemed to grow. In time they always died. I dug neat graves and wrapped my dead in clean bright cloth. Then I offered my pets to the ground like little presents while Barbie and Ken grieved. They carried bouquets of honeysuckle rubber-banded tightly to their stiff and outstretched hands. They stood at the gravesite until I ended the proper time for grief. Then I laid them on the ground with their rigid arms reaching, and eyes staring up at treetops as I scooped the dirt back slowly with my spoon. I held them upright in my hands again and prayed. Then I carefully peeled the wilting clumps of honeysuckle from their hands and let Barbie place the flowers on the grave. Finally I shoved a Popsicle Stick cross for a headstone in the dirt. I knew the first rain would knock it down, but I loved the daily tending of my graveyard the way I'd seen my momma tend her petunias and red pepper plants. My dead pets were my garden. Barbie, Ken, and stolen socks and spoons my tools.

I wanted to be my Barbie. She never cried and made her face twist ugly while others teased and laughed. She seemed happy in her sock clothes, and when my dog chewed her head flat, the face bounced back and smiled. She could stand all day at a graveside, stay pretty, sweet, and upright as long as I could hold her in my sweaty, gripping hands.

Barbie taught me that death was not a sequence, no cycle of darkness and light made by some sad girl's need to dig holes with stolen spoons. I knew my mother's claim was wrong that scooping dirt from a dead doll's mouth meant she was revived. For me death was a dark division made in private shadows of my head and heart, not a cycle as my mom thought but a constantly shifting border like the horizon that stood rolling between the earth and sky.

A mortal girl, I went down and died a little with my puppies, turtles, goldfish. The hurt part stayed buried with my pain and love and hunger, blocked with each little scoop of dirt. But the living doll girl stayed above ground just like Barbie, stiff but smiling with my rigid chest and hollow head. I knew mortal things were too ugly to be left above, too stinking full of blood and bugs and rot, while Barbie, clean and pretty, always smiled above. There was a future with my Barbie, a life that felt no pain with that hollow heart and head. So I lived on, like Barbie, stayed above ground, steady, and forgiving, so sweet and pretty sometimes they would swear I was alive.

• •

JANE BRADLEY, who was born and reared in Chattanooga, is the author of a book of stories, *Power Lines*, which was honored as a *New York Times* Editor's Choice, and a novel, *Living Doll*. A recipient of an NEA fellowship in 1992, Ms. Bradley now teaches creative writing at the University of Toledo.

JEFF CALLAHAN

Pissing in Greenbriar Woods

A dry snow picks at the firs.
The wind is sharp with camp smoke.
We climb past unmarked burial mounds,
cold wrenching steam from our tongues.

Just past Indian Flats
Ethan pleads he's got to go.
Dances about, holds himself
like he's been kicked there.

I lead him to a low stand of asters,
the stalks still sleeved with bits of frost,
and he goes at it.
The thin stream probes the mud, turns

left, coaxes bubbles from sodden leaves.
He cocks his head with a loopy grin
as if listening for Cherokee dead.
Deep pleasure stills his face,

his belly quivers like a baby trout.
Then he sniffs and sheaths his weapon,
pauses briefly as if anticipating
the smell of blood.

Blueberries

Such ripeness in early summer
when beauty doesn't hide beside the fence
and scowl but shows itself openly
like a bride in a see-through gown.

I love to sleep late in June
before midsummer's heat swells
the doorframes and sinuses,
dims the flash in Forsythia's bare bulb.

To wake at ten to an empty house,
stripes of light on the wall and the sound
of sparrows twittering in the attic.
To wear my robe with the fraying collar

and pathetic shrunk sleeves and take
my breakfast on the porch, the tart
early blueberries voluptuous in bluish milk.
I love to watch squirrels chase each other

round the trunk of an old oak
and jump from branch to high branch,
their legs splayed far apart in flight.
I love the solace of jays and tiger lilies,

the slow parade of bees on the lawn
where blue jeans hang still wet from the wash,
and dark as bruise-blue blueberry skins
strung up like dripping flags to meet the sun.

• •

JEFF CALLAHAN teaches English and creative writing at Farragut High School in Knoxville, Tennessee, where he lives with his wife and three children. His poetry has appeared in *Intro*, *Embers*, *Wind/Literary Journal*, the *Asheville Poetry Review*, and the *Denver Quarterly*.

MADISON SMARTT BELL

CHAPTER SIXTEEN FROM *SAVE ME, JOE LOUIS*

Struggling with the worn-out clutch, Lacy drove to the new shopping center, to the new grocery there. They'd widened the road that went by the thing, put in an extra lane each way, to keep the cars running smooth toward Nashville. The fields around were subdivisions now—a bedroom community in formation. . . . Well, it couldn't all have happened since she'd last been back, only that it seemed that way. She parked and entered the brand-spanking-new grocery and glumly pushed a cart up and down the wide empty aisles, under the greenish aquarium-style lighting. The place was oddly empty, though it was midday. Muzak played for nobody but her and a few old ladies who looked dazed and lost, the idle cashiers, and a couple of stockers strolling around in their red aprons.

She shopped like a person with practice being poor, loading the cart with rice and dried beans, carrots and onions, the cheapest cuts of meat, for soup. There was a little nut of money she'd saved in Philadelphia and she meant to stretch it as thin as she could. In the right place, she knew she could make good money as a waitress or a barmaid, probably working only half a week, but she didn't have the stomach for it now. The right kind of place, where she'd have the eyes on her, less frequently the hands on her maybe, dumb jokes and false friendliness and *Honey, when do you get off work?* In the right place you'd get that certain breed of businessman, overfed and overpaid, "getting over" his divorce or just on his way to one, tie undone, breath hot and sweet, sweating alcohol through the Arrow shirt. Yeah, they were big tippers. The money would be good, but right now she didn't want it. Blinking in the unfamiliar outdoor brightness, though it was overcast, she crossed the parking lot with her arms hugged around her bags, admitting sourly to herself that right now she didn't quite know what she wanted.

The car backed out of the parking slot and she wrenched it onto the road again. Not even prayer would hold the clutch much longer, that was sure. She didn't feel like going home—to the house, she should say. Well, she might still be in Philadelphia, with the spring rains washing the garbage over the sidewalks, getting braced for another summer in the ghetto. It wasn't a thought that especially appealed. She turned off between ranks of orangy-striped barrels where another road was being widened, to cut from one highway to the other, farther west. But still between the highways there remained a wedge of land that was all farm or forest. Ahead of her the sun broke through the marbled sky and she reached to the dashboard for her sunglasses. Her mood improved a little. In another mile she was on a dirt road.

On the downside of a hill she stopped and backed the car into a set-back gateway. The gate itself had long fallen down and the gap was freshly fenced across; there'd be no one needing to come through. With her elbows braced on the top strand of new wire, she focused her Leica on the boards of the fallen gate, scattered through the new spring grass and whitening like bones. Finally, she didn't take the picture. She zipped the camera back in the bag and pushed the whole business up under the driver's seat, out of sight, before she locked the car. Better sometimes to go without a camera, use your eyes instead of it, and try to really see.

She climbed the fence, swinging her jeaned leg high over the barbs of the top strand, landing with a soggy thump on the spongy turf on the other side, heels of her cowboy boots digging in. With a toe she flipped up one of the loose boards from the gate. Beneath it the grass was pale and wrinkly, like noodles. Someone had mowed this patch of hillside pasture, though, within the year. At its edge it went back to buckbushes and blackberry bramble, threaded through with animal trails she saw when she got nearer—ground hogs, foxes maybe. Beyond the thicket were old apple trees in rows of an untended orchard, and among them the wild blackberries had grown in hedges higher than her head.

She picked her way around the briar patch. At the far side of it, the hill got sharply steeper. There was a shaley slope she couldn't climb; she circled her way around to an area where the footing was firmer and climbed up, holding on to saplings for support. It half winded her to reach the crown of the hill—because she was smoking again, no doubt. The cigarettes were on the dash of the car, where she had left them. She stood with a hand on the earth-caked roots of a fallen elm and looked to the west. The trees had not yet leafed, so the view was clear between the trunks and spectral lacing of bare branches, all the way across the valley to the other hilltops that rolled around to enclose it. Their wooded flanks were copper and blue, a patina like old bronze. Into them crept a network of new roads, new driveways, spreading like varicose veins or a rash. It was all being eaten away, she thought. On the far side of the valley the windows of new houses winked at her in the spring sunshine, but where she was, she felt gray and ancient, winter still cold in her bones. It occurred to her that if Macrae were there, he wouldn't be thinking such thoughts. He might feel it, but he wouldn't be thinking it so plain. Sometimes there were virtues in obscurity, she thought, sometimes, and felt the corners of her mouth bonding in a dry and slightly bitter smile.

She descended from the hill's round head and struck a trail and followed it. When it petered out, she climbed again to the backbone of the ridge. The circle of linked hills kept leading her north, northwest. Sometimes she saw below her through the naked trees a barn or a house, and once a doll-sized man on a tractor whose engine noise came to her as a distant, staticky crackle. All the while she kept well back in the trees, though at one time or another she'd known all the people who owned this land and she'd have been welcomed to wander if only she'd asked. But she hadn't gone calling, hadn't presented herself. . . . There was something she didn't want to see them wondering—*Did you give it all up and come home this time? Or are you just passing through?*

Maybe it was loneliness, she thought, that made her want to keep away from waitressing right now. She'd only feel it deeper if she had to drift among those packs of drunken people, pretending that there was really something between them, some connection that would last. If her parents had been here it might have made a difference, but they'd sold up and gone to Arizona for her father's emphysema, they were done. She thought of Marvin's cheap cocktail psychology—regression, sure, just show me how.

She didn't know where she was going, maybe, but she did know where she was. Stepping over a jumble of old wire brought her onto Macrae's place, his daddy's, theirs. She kept following the ridge until she overlooked the barn lot and the yard. A small International pickup was pulled alongside a tree halfway between the house and the milk barn. It looked deserted down there, deadly still. She felt her breast pocket for the cigarettes that weren't there, and wondered vaguely where Macrae might be this minute, *just passing through* somewhere, she'd bet.

A sound behind her turned her head, a breath. A few yards up the slope a brindled dog sat on its haunches, panting, watching her from yellow eyes. It sucked in its tongue briefly and assumed a serious expression, then let it hang again and seemed to smile. Lacy snapped her fingers and beckoned. The dog once again became grave, then picked itself up and went off quietly through the trees.

There was a stump and she sat down on it. Flat diamond-shaped stick-tights coated her jeans legs. She began to pick them off and peel them, eating the tiny, hard seeds inside. In the cover of old leaves there was a ticking sound, a small brown rabbit foraging. It raised its folded ears and looked at her with a black bead eye. She was still. The rabbit's attention shifted; it hopped along. Of perversity she reached for a worm-eaten stick and threw it. The rabbit fled in springing bounds that carried it in effortless high arcs, crashing over the dead leaves. Farther downhill the brindled dog reappeared and chased it out of sight.

Lacy stood up, her mind gone agreeably blank at last, and wandered along the inner slope of the hill, into a dense cedar grove. Here it was dim, and cool enough to make her shiver. Underfoot were moss and fragrant dry fronds from the cedars. Crossing a hummock, she came upon a dairy cow who rounded on her with a bellow and a snort. Startled, Lacy took a step back, placed her palm on a shaggy cedar trunk, and froze. The cow watched her a moment more, then dropped her head and went back to licking the spotted calf curled there in a hollow of the moss.

It must have been born just minutes before, Lacy deduced. It was still wet, hair matted in twirls, still a little bloody. The cow's heavy tongue passed over its neck and shoulders. Not far away was a glistening swirl of afterbirth. She watched the calf struggling to get up, hind end first. The skinny legs braced and the forequarters came up shakily. The calf lifted its heavy head, opening its mouth, and tottered toward the bursting bag. Its muzzle brushed the teats but the cow swung away and the calf fell to its front knees. It rested, rose again, and staggered to the cow. A knot of tension came undone in Lacy when she saw it latch on succcssfully. The cow sighed and lowered her head while the calf's kinky tail lifted just enough to wag.

Lacy batted at her hip for the camera bag, which also wasn't there, and reminded herself that this time she'd only come to see. The calf lunged, thrusting at the bag, lost the teat, and recaptured it. Its one eye rolled white with pleasure. Lacy sat down on the moss and wrapped her hands around her knees.

It needs a human eye, she told herself, that's what it takes to see these things. Or show them. So this is what you'll do. You'll go around and see these people, and you'll admit you know them. Take their pictures if they'll let you. . . . And let them think whatever they want. She picked a patch of lichen from a stone and crumbled it between her fingers. That was what her pictures had been lacking, she thought now; they needed people in them.

◆ ◆

MADISON SMARTT BELL, who grew up in and around Nashville, lives now in Baltimore, where he is writer-in-residence at Goucher College. The author of nine novels and story collections, he is married to the poet, Elizabeth Spires.

MICHAEL LEE WEST

SPRING FEVER, IT'S CATCHING, RUN FOR YOUR LIFE

On the first warm Saturday in March, while geese flew north and crawfish filled the bayous, Olive Nepper turned against Jesus. She was sixteen years old, a teenaged Baptist, the only child of Henry and Vangie. Thanks to the delicate nature of her upbringing, the renunciation seemed like the crime of crimes. Ashamed and heartbroken, she stood in her mama's kitchen and swallowed a whole bottle of rose poison. Even though she mixed it with orange Nehi, the taste (not to mention the act itself) was a letdown. She'd already done so much worse.

The poisoning occurred on a sunny morning, seventy-five degrees, not a cloud in the sky. All over the parish, women stood in the backyards, gossiping over crepe myrtle hedges, hanging up cold, dripping-wet linen on clotheslines. High above them kites flapped like pinned butterflies. A yellow kite snapped loose and veered west, over Geranium Street, over the cemetery, toward the First Baptist steeple. It was the tallest landmark in town, taller than the Presbyterians', even. The kite smacked against the steeple, then slid down, following the slope of the roof, bumping along the shingles. It drifted to the front yard, startling a flock of pigeons; they flew up, a dark spill against the flat blue sky.

Below, the church door swung open, banging against the bricks, and Olive Nepper ran out. She clattered down the steps, then jumped over the kite. The minister stepped onto the porch and watched her run across the yard. He was young for a man of God, with long sideburns and a cleft chin, but his eyes were old, small-lidded, and blue. "Olive?" he called out.

From the sidewalk, Olive turned. As she stepped backward, she hooked her ankle into a rusty croquet wicket. She toppled over, skidding against the bumpy concrete. Her dress ripped at the waist, exposing a white cotton slip. *Good*, she thought, lifting one skinned palm. *Maybe I jarred something loose*. She scrambled to her feet and dusted

From *She Flew the Coop*, by Michael Lee West (New York: HarperCollins Publishers, 1994). Reprinted with permission of HarperCollins Publishers.

off her knees. The Reverend lifted one finger as if to call her back; she shook her head, then took off running again.

Two maiden sisters—Mamie and Meredith Marshall—spotted the girl and called out to her. They were staunch Methodists, on their way to the cemetery to say hello to Mother and Daddy, and to set out some fresh lilacs. "Is that Vangie's child?" said Mamie, gripping her sister's arm. "Olive? Olive Nepper?"

The girl whirled around and wiped her eyes. "Yes, ma'am?"

"Well?" Mamie stepped closer. The child was a Baptist, which explained a lot, but *still*, her behavior demanded further explanation so the sisters could savor it later, when they weren't so preoccupied with grave tending. "What's the matter, child?"

"Ask him." Olive pointed to the church. The sisters turned just in time to see the Reverend T. C. Kirby dart inside, the heavy walnut door catching the tail of his jacket. Before he jerked it through the crack, the cloth protruded like a black tongue. The sisters gasped and turned back to Olive, who had taken off again, running down Geranium Street, a speck against the yellow bells and azaleas.

"Reckon what's happened?" they whispered, looking back at the church. The sisters shook their heads. You could never figure what a Baptist would do—always so goodie-good, but seething inside with sin. Yes, indeed. Seething. "One of these days," said Mamie, "this whole town'll see the light and cross over to First Methodist."

"Amen," said her sister. "But we'll need a bigger church." By the time they'd reached the corner of Geranium and Washington, they were castigating the Presbyterians and Lutherans. They'd clean forgotten Olive Nepper, who was a whole two blocks away. The girl turned down Lincoln Avenue, passing through sun, then dappled shade. She moved without thinking—her mind was still with the reverend. All her life she'd read the Bible and recited prayers at her bedside. She'd been raised to believe that prayers were like wishes. If your wants were sincere, the Lord would provide. Reverend Kirby assured Olive that she was a very sincere girl, and he would provide what the Lord did not. Now she felt betrayed by all men. Since Jesus was a man, and probably a Baptist, too, she held him responsible. After all, He'd led her straight to the Baptist Church and Reverend Kirby.

She wiped her eyes on her sleeve, then lifted her skirt. Her knees were smeared with dried blood, and her hands were still stinging. She uncurled her palm and stared down at her lifeline. The bottom half was rubbed raw. That, too, seemed like Jesus' fault. She darted toward her house, flung open the screen door, and stepped into the kitchen. Light streamed through the windows. Breakfast dishes were stacked in the plastic drainer, beads of water still clinging to juice glasses and coffee cups. "Mama?" she called out, then held her breath.

Silence. Just the drippy faucet and whirring icebox. She sat down at the table and cradled her head. Today was Saturday, market day—nothing more than an excuse to gossip. She wouldn't be home for hours. Olive sighed. No one knew the truth—she was polite and prissy on the outside, man-crazy underneath (and there were precious few to choose from in Limoges). Last year she'd advertised in *Pen Pals of the South*, and every morning when the mailman dropped letters in the box, she ran outside to snatch them. One day the mail arrived when she was frying bacon—she took the letters straight to her bedroom, forgetting the smoky skillet on the burner. She spread the envelopes on her bed and looked at the postmarks—Atlanta, Charleston, Mobile, Clearwater, Lake Charles, Meridian. She smelled smoke, remembered the skillet, and raced into the kitchen, screaming *fire fire fire*! While her mama ran next door, screaming for help, flames leaped to the curtains. After the neighbors doused the fire with salt, Vangie turned on her daughter. "How did you let this happen?" she cried. "Don't you know your daddy will kill us both?"

Olive had been afraid of that. She walked outside, straight into the lake, and tried to drown herself. When the cute undertaker pulled her out of the water, she bit his hand. That's how much she didn't want to face her daddy. Home disasters could really provoke Henry Nepper. Small wonder that she couldn't face him now. She marched straight to the sink and opened all the cabinets. She hunkered down, knocking over bottles, and grabbed a can of rose poison. She took out a funnel, sifted the powder into an orange Nehi, and shook the bottle, using her thumb as a cork. Then she began to drink. With every swallow, she imagined her mama's nasal voice, instructing in fundamentals of gardening: herbicides worked from the taproot, strangling the plant, but insecticides killed the pest that fed on the leaves. These potions, she knew, must be measured with care; too little would have no effect, too much would sink to the marrow and kill.

First thing, she had discarded the notion of telling her mama. Olive had gotten herself into this trouble; she'd trusted the wrong man, believed his every word. And it was a sorry day when you couldn't trust a preacher. Her mama wouldn't understand about young girls getting into fixes. She'd said plenty of times that no man bought the cow if he got the milk free. And the Reverend had enough to open his own dairy.

Olive had lost her virginity (it was dangling by a hair anyway) on a youth choir trip to Lookout Mountain, Tennessee. Reverend Kirby had driven the bus, with no other adults; he had insisted. "These kids are good as gold. I won't have a bit of trouble." Olive had chosen a seat directly behind him and spent the whole trip gazing at his ears, admiring how the sun turned them pink and transparent. It was the first time she'd been away from her mama and daddy, the first time she'd seen mountains. Shortly after they crossed Signal Mountain, the reverend turned and smiled. "How we doing back there, Sister Nepper?" he asked. Thrilled that he'd singled her out in front of the others, she blushed all the way to Chattanooga. Like a fool. He was probably laughing at her right now (he'd threatened to write a sermon about her).

Now she wished she'd stayed home. Not fifteen minutes ago, when she'd told Reverend Kirby about her condition, he'd raised his eyebrows and said, "Well, I'm sorry, just real sorry, but it's your word against mine. And God's." He riffled through his night table and took out a comic book, *Victims of Vonnatur*!

"What about those afternoons at the parsonage? And that one time in the belfry?" Her eyes filled. "You said you'd marry me."

"Did I?" He turned a page. "Why, I don't have a recollection of that."

"You took advantage of me!"

"But I never penetrated," he said fiercely. "At least, not much."

"Then how'd I get your baby inside me?" She pointed to her stomach.

"You're sure it's mine?"

"No, it's a *Victim of Vonnatur*!" She slapped the comic book from his hands. "Of course it's yours!"

"Does it have my name written on it?" A vein pulsed in his neck. "Do you have a witness? Somebody who saw us together?"

When she didn't answer, he raised his eyebrows. "I'm not the only man in Limoges. You could've laid with anybody."

"I just laid with you and you know it. A preacher should own up to his actions."

"But I don't have to own up to yours."

"I'm telling my daddy!"

"You go right ahead, Sister Nepper. Just the other day he told me how proud he was of you. What a good girl you are, and how much he loves you. How he's counting on you to go to college and be a teacher. It'll break his heart."

"He'll make you marry me!"

"Not if I leave town, he can't. Anyway, Sister Nepper, my name's clean as a whistle."

She fled from the church, but his voice was trapped inside her skull. He wasn't going to marry her. Even if her daddy believed her, she'd still be disgraced. No college would accept a woman who carried a baby on her hip. Certainly *no man* would want her. (And that's all she really wanted out of life—a man, a baby, and a color-coordinated kitchen.) She looked around the room for something to throw—the pink canisters? Mixmaster? can of poison?—but decided it would make too much noise.

"Sister Nepper, my foot," she cried and kicked a chrome step-stool, stubbing her toe. She limped out of the kitchen, and picked up a snow dome from the TV set. She turned into the hall, limping over the rose-strewn carpet. As she walked, she shook the dome. It was a souvenir from Lookout Mountain, and it showed two miniature people standing on Lover's Leap, a lip of bone that slanted into a gorge. Reverend Kirby called it a cleft, but the word hadn't meant anything to Olive. "It makes me think of wedding nights," he confessed, but she still didn't get it. She'd bought the dome with babysitting money, thinking it would look pretty in the rectory, when she was Mrs. Kirby (he'd promised), a bonafide Baptist wife.

"Even if he marries me," she thought, "I'll still be disgraced." She supposed they could move—a church in Texas or Georgia would be nice. The congregation wouldn't count months—they would accept her baby as full term, legitimate.

She knew exactly when she'd conceived this child—not on the trip to Chattanooga and not in the rectory, but in the tall, white steeple of First Baptist. It was late January, too cold to undress. Freezing air blew through the arched windows. She remembered how heavy he felt and how the wood floor squeaked beneath her. She looked over his shoulder, into the narrow, pitched roof where the bell hung above them. Pigeons flew in circles, disturbed by the lovemaking. When Olive squinted, they looked just like angels. Later, when Reverend Kirby stood up and turned, she saw that the back of his sweater was splattered, white commas against the red wool. She didn't have the heart to tell him—how could she word it? "Pardon me, Reverend, but you might want to change your sweater?"

"Why?" he'd say, looking down at his spotless front.

"Well, a bird has shit all over you." (There was no other way to say it—"dookie" and "pooped" just didn't have the same ring.) She had to admit the whole thing had weird symmetry. While the Reverend deposited one thing, the pigeons deposited something else. Except for the birds, everybody got a souvenir.

No matter how hard she shook the snow dome, the people never jumped. She turned it upside-down, and the couple stood on their heads, fine grains of rice collecting in the curve of plastic. She flopped down on her bed, causing the box springs to creak, and held up the dome. The walls looked distorted through the plastic. It was her childhood room, pale, 14 x 15, with a ceiling of hand-painted clouds. She imagined a warm October afternoon, with light falling like strained pear juice, the cypress turning red along the lake. She'd wheel the newborn baby down the sidewalk, with all the neighbors looking on. They'd lean together and whisper. The child, Olive was certain, would resemble a miniature reverend, clutching a Bible rattler.

Gossip would be ferocious—like a meal served to starving people, they'd lap up everything. She pictured her body stretched out like a kite, her skinny legs trailing down. She wasn't the first girl to have a child out of wedlock, but she probably would be the last. Women in Limoges would set her up as an example. "It ruined her," they'd say. "Poor Olive Nepper. No decent man will touch her with a ten-foot pole."

She blinked at the gauzy blue ceiling. Poisonings were delicate things. Life, death, sex—even conception—it was all in the timing. Waiting to die, she reasoned, couldn't be too different from waiting your turn in the doctor's office. Waiting for the snow to settle in the gorge. She guessed the baby was the size of a jelly bean, a grasshopper on a rose leaf, a tiny figure in a snow dome.

All the bedroom windows stood open, blowing in coolish air, ruffling her Venetians. The back of her mouth tasted bitter. From outside, voices move through wind and sun, weaving through trees and telephone wires. She heard a dog bark, children running down the sidewalk, music rising up from a scratchy record player. Tomorrow was Sunday. If she woke up, she'd walk to the Catholic church on Sparrow Street. She was drawn to the idea of veils and holy water and pretty black beads with crucifixes. Also, the Catholic Jesus seemed different—a little less handsome than the Baptist version, but serious and noble.

The noise fell away, and she saw herself rising into the clouds, high above the back yard. She could see far into the future. Her mama would stand next to her rose beds, turning her face up to the sky. The baby would fall through Olive and land into Vangie's outstretched hands, slippery and red, its mouth opening like a bud. All around her the wind blew and blew, sending spring across the Delta, and she drifted between clouds, waiting for the voices to sing her back to sleep.

• •

MICHAEL LEE WEST, a native of Louisiana, grew up in Cookeville, Tennessee, roller-skating up and down the aisles of her father's dimestore. The author of two novels, *Crazy Ladies* and *She Flew the Coop*, West holds a B.S. in nursing from East Tennessee State University and now lives in Lebanon, Tennessee, with her physician husband and their two sons.

DOUG GRAY

THE DROWNED BOY

I made it to the river by midmorning, a tin can of night crawlers and a sack of Granny's sausages and biscuits in the basket of my bike. Strapped across the handlebars was my cane pole with the float secured tightly to the line. After two miles of bumps, ruts, and weeds, I dropped the bike in a patch of cottonweeds and picked my way down the steep, muddy bank. I was settled within the thick, snaking roots of a sycamore, when I noticed a hundred yards upstream Mr. Norton's boat making its way down the river. That Mr. Norton could trotline by himself was amazing, a trial for a sturdy man. As a skinny, curious twelve-year-old, a dynamite cap had taken his right hand. So watching him maneuver the old green fishing boat was a study, pulling the lines from the water, removing the fish, and rebaiting the hooks—all with one hand. Serving him well were his chin, his chest, and the crook of his right arm.

"Yoo hoo," he called when he spotted me on the bank.

"Yoo hoo," I answered, my soprano voice embarrassing me with its echo.

I caught some nice bluegill and hooked them to my stringer, each time easing it up from the shallow water at my feet with care, an eye out for water moccasins. Most of the time I just sat contentedly, mesmerized by the deceptive benignity of the water below me.

Minutes later, I was pulled from my reverie by the loud, hollow thumps of Mr. Norton knocking around in his boat. I was surprised because I was certain that the old man knew the most basic tenet of fishing: no noise. I shaded my eyes in his direction to see him stumbling as he yanked at a stubborn trotline. It appeared to be caught on something, although the river was a good twenty feet deep along there. My heart jumped with the idea that he had hooked one big granddaddy of a catfish, a Mississippi Blue, and I knew that this possibility was not lost on Mr. Norton either.

"What you got?" I called, jabbing my pole firmly into the damp bank. The bobber rode quietly on tiny ripples.

"Don't know," he grunted, tugging away with his hand and running the excess line under his right armpit. "Might just be hung up on a log or something."

"Looks like it's giving, though," I said. With my eyes locked on his line, I began to edge in his direction.

A flash of white teased the dark surface of the river a few feet from his boat, about a dozen hooks down the line. If Mr. Norton noticed, he didn't react.

"I think I saw it." My heart skittered. "I think you've got a whopper there."

"Tell what it was?" His voice shook from strain and anticipation.

I slipped down the bank toward him, glued to the struggle, tripping over rocks and roots. I could see where the calloused skin on Mr. Norton's hand had split from the cord's friction. Blood ran down his wrist and dripped over the edge of the boat into the water.

Mr. Norton gave a mighty yank.

"Oh my Lord."

He released the line and sat down hard in the boat. His Co-op cap was twisted sideways, and a few sprigs of greyish brown hair were plastered against his forehead. Small, troubled eyes peered from under the brim.

"It ain't no fish."

"What?"

"It ain't no fish," he repeated. "It's a boy."

I was confused. Uttered under the harsh, white sky, the words didn't fit. There couldn't be a boy on Mr. Norton's trotline. My father and Uncle Joe had hooked bats and snakes and gars, but no boys.

Using his teeth, Mr. Norton cinched a rag around his bleeding hand. He looked down into the river and then back at me.

"Reckon you could help me with him?"

The flesh pimpled over my shivering bones. His words formed a picture; and, as eerie as it was, it rang real. The hair on the back of my neck bristled. Instead of trusting my voice, I kicked off my Keds and snatched my Barlow and two quarters from my pocket, dropping them at my feet. Under no circumstance was I ever to go swimming in the river, but this thing, this happening, transcended trivial circumstance. I jumped off the bank and swam to the boat. Mr. Norton's hand grabbed me under my shoulder and pulled me up. I smelled bait. During the struggle with the line, a minnow bucket was sent flying, and it now lay on its side, the contents in various stages of death in the killing air. The baby fish squirmed and flashed like new nickels in the sun.

I fought for patches of the hot July air through chattering teeth, realizing I had just swam half across a river twenty feet deep, climbed into a boat with a careless one-handed man, and stood within reach of a dead boy hung up on a trotline.

It was almost too much, and I regretted my need to fish that day.

"You're going to have to help me pull him in," Mr. Norton said, kicking aside oars and the empty bucket.

One of the minnows swam in a splash of water at my feet. When Mr. Norton moved to the right, the water shifted, leaving it high and dry. I reached down and nabbed it by its tail and threw it into the river, giving it a fighting chance.

"Come on, son, get over here and help me pull."

I knelt beside Mr. Norton and leaned over as he did, grabbing the line just where it disappeared over the side of the boat and almost straight down into the water. Having never been this close to his stub before, I was amazed at how smooth it looked—round and pink and soft—like a baby's leg. Quickly, I reached into the water and grabbed the taut line and pulled with Mr. Norton. My marginal strength suddenly made a difference. The line sang smoothly against the lip of the boat.

We hesitated just before the boy broke the surface. I tried to look away but couldn't. Mr. Norton mumbled a short prayer for the poor little fellow, remembering to bless the two of us at the end.

The truth was the boy wasn't really little, not by my standards anyway. He was awfully white and fat; he looked to be wider than the boat. One final tug brought him out of the water with his bloated body bumping and bobbing off the side.

He looked like an inflated doll, not really hooked, just tangled in the main cord and the hook lines. His arms were blown straight out to his sides. His thick, stiff legs angled out from his hips. Except for a belt pinching his waist, the boy was naked. I sniffed the air for death and found none. Part of my brain studied a pair of piggy-backed snake doctors, as they skipped and buzzed along the top of the water.

"Let's get him out of there."

That was the first time I realized that I was going to have to touch the dead boy. My greasy breakfast rose to the top of my throat. Looking was one thing, but touching was something else entirely. I didn't see why we just couldn't tie him off behind the boat and pull him the short distance to shore. I shared that with Mr. Norton. His head pivoted on his thin, leathery neck and fixed me with a perplexed stare. He started to speak but instead he turned back and began to prepare a place for the body. Suddenly, like an acorn hitting me on the head, I realized that the dead were due a respect that we had to show but few of the living. No matter what a man did or didn't do in his lifetime, our gentle treatment of his remains forgave all shortcomings. Eventually, Mr. Norton squinted at me and saw I had it figured out.

"Let's do 'er," he said.

We leaned over at the same time and grabbed whatever was closest. I caught the boy under his arm much the way Mr. Norton had grabbed me earlier. His skin was river water cold and slippery like the belly of a catfish. We were as gentle as we could be, but we had to wrestle the body in. We landed him on his stomach, and I saw that his entire backside was black. I jerked and Mr. Norton said, "Blood. His blood's all settled there." I figured he knew what he was talking about. We turned him on his back and maneuvered him to the rear of the boat, where you usually toss the fish you catch. Now that I had a better understanding of respecting the dead, I decided to sit in the back with him. Balanced at the bow, Mr. Norton rowed.

It was so strange. I don't believe the river had ever been more beautiful. The sound of Mr. Norton's oar slicing the water, on the left, and then the right, over and over, was percussion to the woodwind of the July flies' hum and the raspy rattle of katydids. The river was a band of milk chocolate stretched between the healthy, humid green of the banks. Weeping willow tendrils draped gracefully into the water at the foot of the near bank, the current streaming on each side of the fuzzy fingers. The air I breathed through my nose was fresh and minty.

Mr. Norton glanced back at us from time to time. I think he was proud of me. He was rowing us to Mr. Freely's farm, because that was where he had left his pickup when he put into the river. Everybody did. Mr. Freely didn't mind just as long as you closed the gate back so his cows didn't get out. I knew that cows tended to walk right off bluffs and plummet into rivers, given half the chance.

I studied the drowned boy. His missing eyeballs left deep, dark sockets that defied my stare. Most of the skin on his fingers and toes had fed the river life. Something had gotten to his penis, too. I peeled off my wet tee-shirt and covered him. His hair was drying blonde and shaggy, odd in the days when fifty cents got you a good shearing. I realized he was poor. His hair and the fact that he had drowned in the river spoke to a certain level of society. Kids seldom drowned in rivers. Swimming pools and lakes, maybe, but not in rivers and certainly not left to get tangled in some old, one-handed fisherman's trotline.

I couldn't tell if he was handsome or not, being swollen up the way he was, or even his age, though I felt he was about mine. His mouth was opened to an O, and his teeth needed work. The sun was warming him up and I got whiffs of rot, but that wasn't the boy's fault. I figured if he could stand the drowning, I could stand the smell.

There was a man and his son fishing off to our left. We passed by and they saw the dead boy in the boat.

"What happened?" the man shouted. His son was frozen in a wide-eyed stare, his jaw hanging down to his chest.

"Drowning," Mr. Norton answered, staring straight ahead, mind on his job.

Looking back moments later, I saw the two of them scrambling up the bank, lines swinging free and tackle boxes bouncing against their legs. Shortly after they disappeared, a car started and pulled off, rattling and creaking up the dirt road that ran from the river to the highway.

I remembered my discarded tennis shoes and my knife and money and wondered how I was going to get back for them. I hoped that somebody didn't steal my bike. I looked down and saw that my foot was touching the drowned boy's ribs. I left it there.

"You okay back there, son?" Mr. Norton had pulled the oar up and was resting while the current carried us along. To row he had to use the crook of his bad arm as a brace. I knew he was tired.

"You want me to come up there and row awhile?" I asked, figuring he could watch the boy for a while.

"Nah. I got 'er here. We'll just keep at it till we got 'er done."

Fifteen minutes later—the boy still heating up—we rounded the bend at the river bridge. Cars and trucks and a tractor lined the steel-framed span. The drivers and passengers, a fair mix of age and sex, my fellow citizens, were lined along the rusty railing, peering in our direction. Someone said, "Here they come," and the line straightened and quieted as one. Again, Mr. Norton stopped rowing and let the current take us along. I didn't look directly at the sightseers, but I could see them staring down at me and the dead boy. I was proud of my place and my duty. Another acorn fell and told me that every time this story was repeated, over the next few days and on through the years, I would be a part of the telling and my conduct at this very moment would add a certain seasoning. Several possibilities loomed. I could have stared stoically ahead, seemingly oblivious to the attention of the crowd. I could have looked up and smiled and waved to a familiar face. I could even have leaned back and lounged casually like a young tough who runs across dead boys every day.

But what I did was reach down and grab the boy's hand and hold it in both of my hands. I have no idea why, other than I believed that this is what I would have wanted had the positions been reversed. So we glided below the river bridge in silence, Mr. Norton at the helm with the oar resting across his thighs, and me at the stern, holding the hand of a drowned stranger. As we went under the belly of the bridge and out the other side, the crowd shifted for a longer view. Finally, one engine after another kicked in and the cars and trucks carried their passengers off in all directions to tell the story. I never looked back and didn't let go of the boy's hand until we got to Mr. Freely's farm. The black Cadillac ambulance from Simmons' Funeral Home was waiting. Several men came down to the boat and lifted the boy out, wrapped him in a sheet, and carried him up the bank. Sadness struck me like a wave of nausea, and I ran behind a stand of trees and sobbed.

My granny came and drove me to get my bicycle. I never did find my knife or the quarters. Not that day anyway. Not the quarters ever.

We heard that the boy was a runaway from the orphanage in Pulaski. They didn't say who his people were or where they buried him. I never even knew his name. My parents never mentioned the incident to me. I had the feeling that they were ashamed that I was involved in such a thing or mad because they knew that I had swum in the river. Later I realized that it was just too much for them to acknowledge, much less talk about.

I keep promising myself to stop in at the nursing home some Sunday and see Mr. Norton. They dammed the river to make a lake, and the only trotlining he does now is in his head. Same with me. But every so often, when I lean back to rest my eyes, I take a moment to run my lines, snapping off the sludge and debris, and always rebaiting with the hope that there will be time for at least one more run. And every once in a while, among the throwbacks and empty hooks, I come upon a keeper, a real granddaddy of a Mississippi Blue. Yeah. A real, sweet catch.

• •

DOUG GRAY, a graduate of the University of Tennessee at Chattanooga, received first prize for short stories in the school's literary magazine in his senior year. Several years later, he began to write again, was published in *Oasis*, took second place in the Tennessee Writers Alliance short story competition, and attended the Sewanee Writers' Conference.

BOB ARMISTEAD

WARRIOR FORREST

The General's appointment was for eleven o'clock, sharp. He had never been in Richmond before. Prior to the war, he had only once traveled east of Nashville, to Chattanooga on slave-trading business. The small but bustling cities, Nashville and Chattanooga, were nothing like the capital of the newly created Confederate States of America. . . .

When Nathan Bedford Forrest stepped from the train, for the first time in his life he felt awkward and out of place. He was a westerner, like the cities he frequented, rough and tumbling, not refined by any standards. But Richmond was a horse of a different color. The center of the Confederate war effort was literally busting at the seams with commerce, industry, and all conceivable activities associated with a nation at war. . . .

The following morning, Forrest and Duckworth were at the executive offices, the center of Confederate political power, at precisely 10:45. It was Tuesday, February 15, 1863, a cold, overcast Tidewater day, typical of Richmond in the middle of winter. As they waited in the foyer outside the president's office, not a few high-ranking general officers, whom—with the exception of Lt. Gen. William J. Hardee, corps commander from the Army of Tennessee—they could not identify, preceded them into the executive suites. Hardee was most cordial and pleasant, as he always was, and seemed as surprised to see Forrest as Forrest was to see him. Plainly, General Forrest was not the only person who did not know why he had been summoned to the high-level conference. As Hardee left the foyer to enter the inner confines of the Confederate high command, Forrest raised his bushy right eyebrow toward his aide, as if to say, "Mus' gonna be one hell of a meetin'!" . . .

Stepping into the crowded office, the General immediately recognized several faces familiar from the western theater of the war, as well as many more men whose likenesses he had seen but whom he had never dreamed he would actually meet. Being six feet, two inches tall and standing as straight as a fence post, ole Bedford could easily

Excerpt from *Warrior Forrest*, a forthcoming novel by Bob Armistead.

see everyone in the room. As greetings were initiated and in some cases renewed, Forrest could not help thinking that he was in a place where history was being made. Just the type of meeting that N. B. Forrest liked to be a part of. . . .

To be sure, Forrest felt the privilege of being at this gathering, as all the rest were equally awed by his presence. Warm welcomes and congratulations were offered from all sides, as the conversations ran toward the general's most recent accomplishments of the past November. He had virtually destroyed Union General U. S. Grant's lines of supply and communication through Tennessee as he tried to close in on Vicksburg. For the time being, Grant had had to back away from the Confederate Mississippi River city, bringing great relief to its garrison and inhabitants. Elsewhere, Lee had soundly and convincingly whipped Ambrose Burnside and the Federal Army of the Potomac at Fredericksburg in December; while the Army of Tennessee had obtained a tactical draw with the Union Army of the Cumberland at Murfreesboro, Tennessee, in a three-day battle ending January 2. Earl Van Dorn had destroyed Grant's base of supply at Holly Springs, Mississippi. Joe Johnston vigorously had repulsed Bill Sherman's invasion of the interior of Mississippi; and, in his West Tennessee sortie, Forrest had severely punished two Yankee forces at Parker's Crossroads by "chargin' both ways," as the general put it when he discovered he had been attacked in both front and rear. The infant nation had thoroughly whipped one of the most powerful countries in the world on the field of battle. Though most of Tennessee and the Mississippi River were in Federal hands and many southern ports were effectively blockaded, if not captured, the Confederacy was alive politically and fighting the North to a standstill militarily. . . .

Still, the Yankee General U. S. Grant had proven himself to be a bulldog. Although his line of supply and communication had been cut and he had met with defeat in every effort to take Vicksburg, he kept at his job undaunted. Able effectively to supply his army of seventy thousand off the Mississippi farming country with impunity, Grant continued to move ever closer to the last major river port on the "father of waters" remaining in Confederate hands. Very simply, Vicksburg could not be allowed to fall! It was the last great link between the Confederate East and its ever-growing demand and the Confederate West and its abundant supply. The potential for a "situation" at Vicksburg had precipitated the meeting. . . .

The Confederacy was blessed to be led by a man of vision in Jefferson Davis. As president of the new nation, he had resisted the efforts of many in the legislature and beyond to persuade him to pursue a departmental strategy in prosecuting the war. From the beginning, he had recognized the greater needs of the country as a whole and been willing to shift resources throughout the South so as to meet the most acute and critical demand and reap the greatest benefits. He also had had the good sense to let his generals be generals. The government, with his guidance, set war policy, which was implemented by the generals. . . .

Robert E. Lee surpassed even Jefferson Davis as the man most revered in the Confederacy. There were many who clamored for him to replace Davis as president. Lee, however, had no such aspirations. Both Davis and Lee felt completely secure in their respective positions, each possessing the unfailing respect and support of the other. Theirs was a relationship which bred only confidence, never dissent. Standing an erect five feet, ten inches in height and immaculately dressed in his best Confederate gray,

Lee confidently addressed the group: "Gentlemen, the plan as submitted by General Pemberton, I feel, is both bold in concept and tactically possible. My only reservation is that the size of the force may not be adequate to ensure success. Grant's total strength, which would surely be increased if he were to become hard pressed, would remain at least sightly higher than our combined forces. To overcome his numerical superiority would require us to achieve pinpoint coordination and timing, something that you all know is nearly impossible to achieve in the real world of war. Accordingly, the president and I have taken the plan to yet another level. What we are proposing is to augment General Pemberton's concept of uniting Taylor, Forrest, and Johnston. A new force of all arms created by transferring regiments of cavalry and infantry and a battalion of artillery from existing commands should be added. We feel that the best man to lead this new army is General Forrest." . . .

Forrest could hardly believe his ears. After two hard years of recruiting, training, and outfitting his legions at considerable expense to himself, he was being offered meaningful numbers of battle-hardened veterans to lead in conflict that could prove to be the most important of the war to date. . . .

After several minutes of discussion within the gathering, Lee raised his hand for silence and continued on. "If he accepts the command, General Forrest will build his force around his existing 1,100-man cavalry brigade. The additions will be supplied by one regiment from each of the following commands: Generals Stuart, Wheeler, Cleburne, R. H. Anderson, Hood, Cheatham, Ewell, A. P. Hill, and S. D. Lee's battalion of artillery. All will assemble in Chattanooga by the fifteenth day of next month. The six units from my army will travel by rail from here to Chattanooga with General Forrest, while the three from the Army of Tennessee, which are already near Chattanooga, will converge there under the leadership of General Cleburne. Then General Forrest will assume command of the force and when ready, hopefully by April fifteenth, will march to a junction of his command and those of Generals Johnston and Taylor somewhere east of Vicksburg. It is hoped that General Forrest's army will gather many new recruits as it moves west. The ultimate goal of this strategy is the defeat of Grant's army and relief of Vicksburg, but there is more." . . .

Again, speaking for himself and his president, Lee addressed his underling, "Well, General, I feel we surprised you. At least, you looked so when we first announced our plan. What do you think?" . . .

As Forrest began to rise from his chair, his complexion began to take on a crimson tint and his dark eyes began to close, both only slightly, but enough for Lee and Davis to notice, causing them to instinctively glance at each other and begin to smile. It had been spoken often of Forrest that when he went into battle his whole countenance changed, controlled by some internal and instinctive force that conflict aroused. Lee believed that he was undoubtedly seeing a part of that side of the renowned warrior coming to the surface in his presence. . . .

Standing squarely in front of the president's desk, Forrest answered: "It sits real good, real good. Mr. Davis, General Lee, I've known all along we could whip 'em. All we have ta do is make the right moves by puttin' the most men in the right place at the right time 'n' fight. With the right leaders in the field we kin whip every damn one of 'em. They have a good general in Grant. He'll be hard ta beat, but I accept the assignment 'n' opportunity ta do just that. I was, indeed, surprised when you first announced your plan. I came here figurin' I would have ta plead for more men 'n' material. For so long I have had ta subsist on the Yankees only. But now I know that I have not only your confidence but also the cooperation of other leaders in my department. With that we can return Tennessee and Mississippi ta their people 'n' the Confederacy. I'm sure that many men of the region will flock ta my banner as we drive for Vicksburg. I'm equally sure that Rosecrans' Yankees can be destroyed if General Bragg will cooperate 'n' can be prodded ta act. I can only assume that you know of my stated feelin's about 'im." . . .

Davis winced as Forrest uttered his last few words concerning his old friend, Braxton Bragg, under whom Forrest had stated publicly that he would never serve again. Painfully, but in complete understanding of the situation, the president responded to Forrest's query. "Yes, General we know. General Bragg will cooperate with you or be replaced. He will know that explicitly, and that your orders are final in this campaign. We are taking a gamble here that you continue to achieve the kind of successes that you have previously, only on a much larger scale. We are also gambling that you can handle an army of 30,000 to 40,000 troops as well as you have one of 10,000. There is a great deal of difference between the two." . . .

Forrest answered, "I have the greatest confidence that I can. I have twice gone into West Tennessee with no more than a skeletal force, recruited several thousand men, 'n' fought my way out with ample munitions 'n' supplies, all right under the noses of Yankees many times my own number. Of course I can't see into the future or in any way predict how this expedition will turn out, but I can tell you that we'll fight 'em whenever we find 'em 'n' kill a mess of 'em. Now gentlemen, if you feel satisfied with me 'n' I may be so bold, I would like ta discuss the who's 'n' how's. What outfits will I have 'n' what about transportation?" . . .

Without rising or even shifting in his seat, General Lee thanked the president and addressed Forrest: "We have selected several renowned fighting units to form the nucleus of your command. Not only large in number, they also possess great spirit and experience. They have shown themselves to be the cream of both armies. More are coming from my army than the Army of Tennessee, simply because there are more to give. To weaken the Army of Tennessee more would, we believe, court disaster. . . .

"Accordingly, from the Army of Northern Virginia we are sending six units, as previously mentioned. From General Stuart's cavalry corps, the 9th Virginia from my nephew Fitz Lee's brigade will go. Also as stated, I will be sending Stephen Lee's artillery battalion of six batteries. The infantry from my army will be the 53rd Virginia from "Lo" Armistead's brigade of R. H. Anderson's division, the 4th Texas from Hood's Texas brigade, the 14th Tennessee from Archer's brigade of A. P. Hill's division, and the 31st Georgia from Lawton's brigade of Dick Ewell's division. From the Army of Tennessee, we are adding the 4th Tennessee cavalry from General Wheeler's command and the 1st and 27th consolidated infantry regiment from George Maney's brigade of Ben Cheatham's division; and from General Cleburne's division we are including the 15th Mississippi Battalion of Sharpshooters. . . .

"Consistent with your past, we assume that you will mount every man that you can. And we certainly approve of the tactic. From a practical standpoint, however, most if not all of the infantry cannot be mounted, simply because of a lack of horses and the time needed for training to convert infantry to cavalry. Therefore, we want Pat Cleburne to be your second-in-command, not only because he is as bold and audacious as yourself, but also because he has valuable experience as a leader of infantry. He is a man you already know well, having fought with him on many fields. If something were to happen to you, we would be comfortable with his succeeding you. Finally, as we had to know first whether or not you would accept the assignment, we have not yet put anything into motion besides alerting the regimental commanders here to cook several day's rations and be prepared to move at a moment's notice. Adjutant General Cooper is standing by to put the orders in writing to have the men and material in the city within two days. Are you ready, sir?". . . .

Undaunted, Forrest retorted, "I will plan ta leave Richmond by midnight on Friday, ready for a scrap!"

◆ ◆

Bob Armistead, who grew up in Franklin, Tennessee, and graduated from Vanderbilt University, is a Civil War authority who owns and operates Southern Historical Showcase, a southern military art gallery and bookstore in Nashville. His publications include the volume *Never to Quit! Historical Fiction of the Civil War Era* (Egeman Publishing).

LINDA PARSONS

LOSING A BREAST: PRAYER BEFORE SURGERY

For Libba Moore Gray

In another time and place
I would show your hand the way
under this bloom shimmering like a hunter's moon
just below the skyline. I would lead you
to drink at this paper-white fountain,
roots now severed at body and soul.

Valium, howl through me.
Surgeon, bless and keep me.
I am young, so young.

There's still time to remember the lilacs
I used to sell on Russell Street.
They always ripened in the rain.
Am I anything like that purple time,
those buds down on Russell?
Am I lovely today as you take up the knife?

Lights, burn above me.
Birches, dance round me.
I am so young
to empty out my time.

"Losing a Breast: Prayer Before Surgery," by Linda Parsons, appeared in *Iowa Review* 20, no. 3 (1990): 125. Reprinted by permission of Linda Parsons Burggraf.

Here is the pulse of my children.
Will you silence it? Will you toss it aside?
How can you know the years pounding
like my baby's heart in the soft cleft of bone?
Her head the wide world, my milk its tides,
our nights bearing down in constant song.
How can you know the long, the beautiful hunger?

I am so young
to be in your hands.

THE LIFE YOU SAVE

For Rachel

The day your friends jumped into the pickup truck,
boys hell-bent for whatever came along, I whispered
in your ear. Remember the summer you were born?
We slipped into a warm, white lake, young branches
rocking you downstream all June, July, long past fall.
You broke into bloom whenever I lifted my blouse.
We had never known such hunger.

The day that truck, with four in the bed and two
in the cab, took the exit ramp too fast some say
(or maybe the steering was faulty), I introduced you
to the trees. We pressed our bodies to birch and sycamore,
yellow and mottled, learning their lanky talk,
peeling down to the heartwood. We had never heard
the hawk sound so lonely. I had never seen
the man-in-the-moon like this.

The day your friends landed in the median
on the concrete, one dead, the others broken,
I took you back to the water. We swam like music,
dove for pennies and came up breathing.
You found someone you knew from school, let him

"The Life You Save," by Linda Parsons, appeared in *Wind*, no. 73 (1994): 19. Reprinted with permission of *Wind*.

hold you under, pretending to struggle.
We had forgotten that day how hot summer can be.
I had forgotten how good the air tastes
when we think it's our last breath.

Companion Pieces

I.

You come to the summit alone,
paths of stone and briar clearly yours
to untangle, the May-apples budding,
the day's climb a lone echo.
You dip your cup in a mountain pool,
your beard the only reflection.

In the break of your step, the bough
at your back, you remember the one
who waits all day at first light,
warming the last bed of night.

II.

Bee balm lifts its red skirt,
haze rests its hand in the cove,
cypress stand kneehigh in water,
lotus turn their cheeks to the sun.

Without her mate, the pale hummer
stirs the leaves, the mountain pools.
Alone at the summit, he dips his long cup,
her wings budding all day in his bright heart.

"Companion Pieces," by Linda Parsons, appeared in *Purple Monkey* 2, no. 2 (Fall, 1994): 2. Used by permission of the author.

LINDA PARSONS is poetry editor of *Now & Then*, published by East Tennessee State University. She is also a poetry teacher and an editor at the University of Tennessee at Knoxville. Her poetry has appeared in numerous journals and anthologies, including *Georgia Review*, *Iowa Review*, *Wind*, and *Sow's Ear*. In 1991, her musical *Lambarene* received a staged reading at Paper Mill Playhouse, New Jersey.

MARGERY WEBER BENSEY

THE WINTER OF BLACKBERRY CORNER

It was Christmas week. The air was gray and cold with winter, and yellow leaves stuck to the bricks on the walkway around the side of the house. Dusk was falling and the houses along White Avenue loomed in darkness broken by an occasional square of yellow light in a window where someone was starting supper. The neighborhood was silent, as though waiting for slumber. Down the street a door slammed; a dog barked; then silence came over the street once more.

My house receded colorlessly into the twilight, except for the bright ribbons on the wreath we had hung on the door of my garret apartment. In the back yard, Michael was riding his bicycle, bumping up the muddy bank from the alley. Arrietty scurried after him in the wet leaves. When they saw me, Michael careened up and dismounted, and Arrietty skittered up a tree. Our voices echoed in the chilly twilight, our noses dark shapes on our winter-red faces. We jumped and shivered with anticipation and with cold, our embrace thick with woolen sleeves and gloves, then raced up the back steps to the garret under the eaves. Pine needles brushed our faces as we pushed open the heavy door. Behind us, Arrietty waited a moment, poised in the boughs of the tree, then raced down the trunk, up the steps, and through the door into the warmth of the attic.

We pushed the door closed behind us, leaning against it, shutting out the darkness of the longest night of the year, laughing as we let our heavy coats fall away, our mufflers trailing on the floor, joyful in the lamplight, because this was the day we had found Blackberry Corner. We bundled the coats away into the closet and went through the apartment turning on more lights, turning on music. Light filled the rooms, illuminating the sloped ceilings and gables and corners, and Gabrieli's antiphonals resounded, triumphant horns and brass announcing the holidays—and the good news that we had found a house!

In a corner of the garret, the good smells of supper came from the oven and coffee bubbled in the little pot. Just outside the door, footsteps thumped on the steps. We threw open the door and were met with beaming faces—Rose and Charles, with little Christie, and behind them, Aunt Eugenia and Uncle Donald, arms full of Christmas presents and good food to add to our dinner. They came in with a flurry of wool and red cheeks and rustling paper, followed by drafts of cold and scents of pine from outdoors. Then we were a babble of ideas and excitement as we crowded into the little kitchen, while Christie followed Arrietty through the attic apartment.

The attic was hung with garlands of pine, with a plump white pine in one corner, draped in pearls and paper snowflakes. Christie wanted to wear the pearls. We were gathered there for our annual small family dinner, to open presents and share Christmas cheer before holiday travels began. Aunt Eugenia and Uncle Donald were spending the night on their way to winter in Florida. "I can't wait to see your house," said Aunt Eugenia. "It's wonderful that you've found a house so soon. You'll have such fun making plans now." Michael and Uncle Donald came in the door laden with overnight bags. "It's good that we'll get to see the house before we leave for Florida, or we'd have to wait all winter."

After dinner, Rose, Charles, Michael, and I all went skating, pulling on extra layers of wool socks and sweaters before heading for the rink set up on the Market Square under the wintry night sky. Stars were out now, glimmering faintly beyond the city lights. We took Christie with us, bumping her about on the rough ice, our mittened hands in hers. Charles skated quickly and smoothly; Michael wobbled a bit and then cut a daring figure; we all laughed. The stars rose and the night grew longer. We bought hot chocolate and sipped it, burning our tongues, and watched the skaters go around and around on the frozen pond.

We had found Blackberry Corner on the first day of winter. The morning had been silvery cold, the sky filled with white clouds and gray-white air, as though it were going to snow, the trees tall brushes against the sky. Inside the garret, below slanted ceilings, we had read the morning paper, sitting cross-legged on the creamy carpet, our coffee mugs beside us. Michael circled an advertisement for *Renaissance Realty Company* in blue pencil, and we were off to look at a house.

It was an ordinary tall white two-story house, somewhat in need of paint, with a row of white columns along the curve of the veranda, sitting on a muddy bank up over the street amid a cluster of bare plum trees. In the back yard was a small pond filled with black water and sodden dark leaves. We looked at each other and smiled.

"I wonder how deep it is," I said.

"At least it holds water," said Michael. Then he said, "You know, this is just what we wanted. Now we won't have to build a pond ourselves."

I was already bending to peer down into the dark waters. My hand brushed the leaves at the edge of the concrete. "Look, here's an inscription," I said, "November 14, 1944. That's when the people who lived here built the pond."

That would be the Etters, said the realtor, Martha. The Lanes, who lived there next, had filled in the pond with earth and planted a rose garden in it. But the Stallmans had dug it back out so that it was a lily pond again and had kept it stocked with goldfish. We stood over the pond, imagining its past and its possibilities, picturing waterlilies in summertime. And then Martha unlocked the back door and took us inside the house.

The house had been built in 1909, on a double lot in Elmwood Park. There had been eight fireplaces that burned coal. The chimneys had since toppled, tall and narrow, made of brown brick and eroding mortar, like the chimneys on the Creamers' house down the street, and the bricks had been hauled away. Inside the back door, the kitchen floor slanted from the weight of the brick chimney that had stood between the two windows. The floor had linoleum on it that was coming off in places. I wondered, if we took it up, would there be wooden floorboards underneath? The kitchen wainscoting ran all the way around the room from the floor to the sills of the windows. It was painted blue. Under the paint it was oak, shining dark through the chipped places.

The house, with its old-fashioned kitchen, had been built by the Blacks. There had been Mr. Black and Mrs. Black and their children. Mr. Black had been a conductor on the Southern Railroad. Every night he would have come in through the kitchen door. Every day Mrs. Black would have gone to the market, or sent Claude, unless she had an icebox. Then the ice man would have come to put ice in it. There was a refrigerator now where the icebox would have stood, with rounded corners, and on the opposite wall a large white enamel double sink. Both of them looked old enough to have belonged to the Etters, or even the Blacks.

We next walked into the dining room and gazed around us. The dining room looked medieval. There was a tall china cupboard with glass doors and a heavy linen chest with curlicues carved on the front, both of the same dark wood, coated in layers and layers of blackened varnish. Both were built into the walls. The linen chest had six drawers, two feet wide and three feet deep, which fit under the foyer stairs. They smelled musty inside. The china cabinet stood as high as the ceiling. I opened the doors and looked inside at the wavery glass panes and the shelves for plates and dishes. The backs of the doors were unvarnished wood, a dark reddish-golden oak, shimmering with the patina of eighty years. I smoothed the wood with my hand, in reverence, and left the doors open. Across the room, Michael was examining the walls in the wintry light from the tall windows. Under the layers of wallpaper the plaster was painted deep cranberry red.

In the foyer, the woodwork was splendid. Shining oak wainscoting paneled the walls, and French doors opened onto a little parlor with an ornate corner mantelpiece. Beside a massive front door set with thick beveled glass rose the curving dark bannisters and rails of the stairway. The Blacks' daughter Annie had been married at home; she had come sweeping down the stairs on her wedding day, and had moved into the little gabled house next door. Which was Annie's room? Was it there at the top of the stairs? The stairway walls loomed in light and shadow, rising twenty feet to the ceiling above. As I climbed the stairs to the second story, looking down at the tremendous woodwork below, I thought, *This house has been waiting for me to live in it and preserve it*. I was ready to buy the house.

I stood on the veranda with Aunt Eugenia in the early light of the following morning. The old floorboards sprang lightly under our footsteps, the six Doric columns reaching high overhead to follow the curve of the Queen Anne roof. Above our heads loomed the second story; below our feet twenty steps ran down to the street. Through the tops of the plum trees, I could see the city, the mountains, and the sky. I was going to live here!

"Well, you can't call this Blackberry Cottage," said Aunt Eugenia. "This house certainly isn't a cottage."

We had expected to buy a bungalow, covered in vines, awash with hedges and flowers. We had planned names we could give it and colors we could paint it: *Periwinkle Cottage*, *Raspberry Cottage*, *Blackberry Cottage*. We could plant periwinkles or raspberries or blackberries if there weren't any already growing in the garden. But now, instead of a bungalow, we had a high house on a corner overlooking all of Knoxville. I surveyed the front yard with its muddy banks covered in ivy and what looked like a profusion of mimosa and mulberries on the corner where the two streets met. I said, "We'll call it Blackberry Corner."

We lost no time in meeting our neighbors and finding out more about who had lived in our house and in our neighborhood. Aunt Eugenia wanted to know how we were going to manage, living in a cavernous ten-room house with peeling wallpaper, drafty doorways, and a twenty-foot hallway down the center of each floor. We wanted to know who had lived there before, what they were like, and what the neighborhood had been like. I was sure that Annie had had the room at the top of the stairs above the parlor, with its mirrored corner fireplace and flowered wallpaper. I chose it for my own sitting room and not long afterward began stripping the eight layers of old wallpaper down to the pinkish-brownish flowers that would have been Annie's when the house was new. Michael chose the sunny back room overlooking the lily pond. I could tell that he was blissful, planning for waterlilies and goldfish.

I went back to the library time after time that first week to research the history of the house. Hunching over thick books until my shoulders ached, I yearned for a way to go back in time and see Blackberry Corner eighty winters before, with its eight little coal grates lit for the winter, its inhabitants moving through the shadowy rooms. If only I could find old brown photographs of the Black family and Blackberry Corner.

In the library's special collections were fire insurance maps, the earliest one from 1917. On it were diagrams of all the houses in the Elmwood Park neighborhood. I was excited, taking the map with eager hands and peering at the tiny inked outlines of houses, porches, walkways, outbuildings. I found Blackberry Corner on the corner of East Fifth Avenue and Holly Street, and behind the house, outlines of what the librarian said were probably an outhouse and a stable. So there had been an outhouse, where the apple tree stood now, and a stable along the alley, "a one-and-a-half-story wooden building with a composition roof." The old cement foundation of the stable was still there at Blackberry Corner; we had seen it: two raised garden beds with cement edging and a driveway in between, where the places for two horses and a carriage had been.

Neighboring houses and outbuildings were inked in delicate black lines as well. In 1917, East Fifth Avenue and Magnolia Avenue were scattered with occasional houses amid the woods and meadows. Volumes of the old city directory supplied more details about Elmwood Park around the turn of the century. Down East Fifth Avenue from Blackberry Corner was the Creamers' tall, narrow house with stained-glass windows, built in 1892. Mr. Creamer had been a manager for the Western Union Telegraph Company. His house had a porch across the front, a shed in the back yard, and a fifty-foot chicken coop along the alley. The Creamers' house was still standing, and inhabited, but the chicken coop was long gone, and the shed was a heap of toppling boards.

Across Holly Street from Blackberry Corner, the Rosses' house had been built in

1894, a huge structure with wings and turrets, according to the fire insurance map, and a circular porch. The Rosses had a lumber company on Willow Avenue in Park City and a business in Knoxville, Ross and McMillan Box Manufacturers, where the whole family worked, even Mrs. Ross, who kept the books. Mrs. Ross lived in the magnificent house the rest of her life. After Mr. Ross died, she took in boarders. After Mrs. Ross died, the house stood empty and was torn down in 1958. The Rosses' stone wall was still there, and their stone steps, and their shade trees, but Michael and I were moving to Elmwood Park years too late to live near the magnificent old turreted house. I felt disappointed at having missed it. How sad it was that so much of our history and culture was being deleted from the surface of our city.

Outside the library window, dark was falling. I had spent Saturday afternoon leaning over the volumes, following names through years of time. My shoulders were stiff and my eyes saw spots. It was dinnertime and the library was closing. I pulled my wraps around me and made my way up the hill in the blustery evening to the gray house where Michael lived on Highland Avenue. There we would celebrate the New Year.

The well-lit house welcomed me as I reached the top of the hill. In one window was a Norway spruce hung with strings of cranberries, a silver star at the top. In another window was Thomasina, silhouetted against the light in the hallway behind her, observing the comings and goings of the neighborhood. The freezing air seared my lungs. I wrapped my muffler about my face and breathed through the cold wool and ran up on the porch.

The downstairs was full of housemates and friends. I went in and stood in the kitchen while Michael dipped hot cider into my mug. Sitting at the big kitchen table with our cider mugs in front of us, we drew the rooms of our house on a napkin, trying to remember the nooks and closets and how the halls narrowed and jogged at the back of the house. We had made an offer on the house and it had been accepted; we were beginning to refinish the wood, paint the walls, and plan the gardens.

It was the new year and a time for new beginnings, but we were going back in time. It was 1989, but we would live in a 1909 house, read about life in 1909, and learn more about the family who lived in our house in 1909. Those were our inspirations and our resolutions as we looked forward to planning our wedding, moving into our house, and raising our children. And, we vowed, if we could, we would live to be a hundred, keep the house in the family, and keep our own history alive at Blackberry Corner.

◆ ◆

MARGERY WEBER BENSEY is a writer at the University of Tennessee at Knoxville, where she is managing editor of two biweekly campus publications and teaches writing and word processing to university employees.

CATHIE PELLETIER

MATHILDA WATCHES THE WALL: PURPLE TRAINS IN NORTHERN MAINE

In the long, sleepless watches of the night,
A gentle face—the face of one long dead—
Looks at me from the wall, where round its head
The night-lamp casts a halo of pale light.

—*Henry Wadsworth Longfellow, "The Crosses of Snow"*

When you want to remember only childhood, only the sweet things, you can't do it. It's as if something pulls you forward, like you're on some old wagon you got no control over, and it just rolls wherever it wants to. Memory's driving that wagon, and when you're as old as I am, you just kind of hang on tight and try your best to enjoy the ride.

I was fourteen when I married Foster Fennelson, and fifteen when Walter was born. After that, there was a lot of kids. Some of them I hardly remember. You can say that ain't motherly, but it's true. They was just kids, like everyone else's kids, nothing to make them stand out. But there's some of them children I won't ever forget. Some stood out real good. I remember Mary a lot, maybe because she was my first girl. She was born second, right after Walter. Maybe I like to remember her because I was still young myself, and things still meant something to me. After a lot of years of life go by, you get kind of like an old badger. You get a shell-like heart, and you back your way into a corner and show everyone your teeth. But Mary—no, I hadn't shut any doors to my heart until Mary died.

She was born in 1899, and didn't hurt me none at all, not like Walter. She was a girl, and tiny, and she didn't hurt me. All I remember about her birth was my water breaking, and then her crying—that's how fast and simple it was. Water, and then Mary, like they belonged together. And she was like a little sprite, all pranks and strange giggles, or silent and staring off across the river as if she could see something no one else could. And you can tell you got a special child when that happens. You can just tell.

It was right in the heart of autumn and, oh, them days around Mattagash Brook in the fall, well, there ain't another place on the earth like them. They turn over before your eyes all red and yellow and orange, and over your head, and under your feet. Some days it seemed like you could trip on the colors. Some days it seemed like the colors was bees all buzzing around your head. And then there was the land, pulsing, getting itself ready, the birds packing up, the squirrels filling their cupboards with hazelnuts. It was in the fall, and that's the saddest time of year, you know, the fall. Everything's harder then. Longer.

She'd gone out on the front steps, had been out there with her little book, hers and Walter's book, the one the schoolteach give them. It was a real little book with hard covers and pictures of trains. There was all kinds of locomotives, panting and puffing across the pages. It was a wonderful gift back then to give a child, especially a child living and growing up so far from the rest of the world, but with a big wide curiosity about that world. When Mary looked at the pages of that little book, it was good as magic before her eyes. So there she was, out on them steps, the leaves on fire all around her, just looking at pictures and sucking her thumb. At least I thought it was her thumb. She'd had that habit, and I meant to break her of it, but she was still only four. And it was all color that day, God in every leaf, in every bird that flew. You don't see that anymore. There's no real color left these days. Maybe in heaven you will, but you don't see color here no more. So I let her be, let her sit out there on the steps, humming her little tune and sucking her thumb. Only it wasn't her thumb. It was my sulfur matches, the *sulfur* on my matches! When I saw what she had, well, I dropped everything and ran to take them from her. But she had already eaten too much. "You won't even eat potatoes!" I remember I yelled that at her. "You won't eat potatoes, yet you eat my sulfur matches!" She was such a fussy eater, who would have ever dreamed? Walter, on the other hand, ate anything. He ate bark, so help me, and many's the time I caught him eating *dirt*. There was a doctor at St. Leonard in them days, and he told me Walter needed potassium was why he did it. Can you imagine that? Medicine for the body just laying there in the ground.

When it hit, her forehead caught on fire, like she'd been lit up. And her little hands curled into balls. I bundled her up like she was kindling, light as a wish, and we took her in the canoe. We had twenty miles of river before a doctor. It was night and only moonlight. Well, you got to see it to know. You can travel by the moon, just like you can the sun, so we knew our route. We knew, I suppose, our destiny even, and it all lay downriver. Sam Gifford, the old half-Indian with cat's eyes, he took us. He steered us by the moon. And them rapids looked like silver, like you could spend them if you had the time, all froth rearing up at us, like fish spawning. I closed my eyes, but I could see right through my lids, could *feel* how it was all moving around me. Real fast rapids. And I was moving too, like trying to get out of a bad dream, me and little Mary, pulled by the moon. She began clutching at my breast, like she wanted to nurse, but she'd been weaned by then. I give it to her anyway, but she couldn't keep her mouth on it. Then she tried to sit up, as if she was well, and remember all them rapids beating against the canoe. Foster and Sam Gifford was just outlines to us, one sitting, the other standing straight up in the night. And night birds cried out from all along the shores, sounds you'll never hear again in this life, on this earth. They was real wild sounds, to match the way things was back then. And then Mary said—and it was like all the sound died away when she said this, like only *her* sound was important. Or was it because I could hear nothing else but the words of my sick child? Her little mouth made an O in the moonlight, like she was a little fish washed up on shore, and she said, "Trains, Mama. Purple trains, and tracks." And then the fit came upon her. I held her down. What would you do? What could anyone do? I held her down like you hold a kid you're gonna whip and they squirm to get away. That's just how it was. And white, spitty foam came out of her mouth, like the kind you see along the river near the bank. Frog spit, the kids call it. I could see her mouth full of it in the moonlight, like the white rapids all around us, like a little river was in her mouth. I dug it out with a finger so she wouldn't choke, but her whole body shook. It looked like she was going under the power, if you believe in that kind of thing. Or better yet, she shook like a little sheet out on the clothesline, a pillowcase maybe, flapping with no control. When I saw that light at St. Leonard Point, the lantern they kept hanging all night on the ferryboat, it was as bright as the star in the east. We could have been three wise men, that's how bright that light was. But we wasn't very wise, and the only gift we brought was little Mary, not ready but willing to go to God. Still, autumn ain't a good time for things like that. That's what I kept telling myself. I'd want a little more of earth when it's autumn.

The doctor had to be stirred up from his bed, and he seemed to want no part of a sick child in the night. I heard his wife, her voice coming down from upstairs, like she was some kind of god. "Tell them to come back tomorrow," the doctor's wife said. "But she's sick right now," Foster said, in one of them voices the poor use. I used it too back then. And like all the others, I hunkered down in clothes I was ashamed of. And like all the others who ain't doctors, or schoolteaches, or store owners, I suppose I thought I didn't have as much right to breathe the same air as them folks. Maybe I thought the doctor's wife owned the air. "Please," I remember Foster said. "She's sick *tonight*." So the doctor give her a red medicine, for growing pains. "But she sucked all the sulfur off them matches," I said to him in a quiet little voice, the voice of a mouse. It was then that Mary sat right up and looked at the doctor. She looked him right in the eye and said, "Trains!" It was like she was accusing him of something. And when I put my arms around her, a shiver shot up both of them. I can still feel it when I remember. It was like I'd been hit by lighting. It was like I'd got the shock of my life. It was her soul passing through me, is what it was. Mary's sweet little soul. And I knew then that she'd gone off to where little children go. "She won't suffer no more growing pains." I told the doctor.

Foster and I sat up with her all night. We watched dawn come in through the downstairs curtains of the doctor's house, listened to him and his wife snoring upstairs. Foster put a few dollars on the table. He said we didn't owe anybody for Mary's birth, and we wasn't gonna owe any son of a bitch for her death. And we was glad, then, that she'd be going to a place where money don't matter to anyone. Then we put on our coats and left, left them nice snores rattling like Mary's little trains up in that warm bed, up in that place where little children are made.

My sister Laddie lived in St. Leonard, before that Spanish grippe come through in 1912 and took her and a parcel of her children with it. I went over to Laddie's house and woke her up and said, "Mary's gone. We lost Mary." That was about all I could say. We didn't have a long time to dwell on things back then. We always had other kids. We always had things that needed doing. You don't stop for it, but you carry it in your heart forever. You carry it around, silent, like a germ. We didn't make no graveclothes for her. We left her in the little calico dress I'd made down from an old one of mine. But I had to take her coat and boots, and, oh, how I wanted her to have them. Mary's little blue coat. She wore it all winter like it was a piece of sky. But I had three little children back at Mattagash Brook, one barely walking. Them other babies, them babies waiting for me at home, they could still feel the cold. And all them babies still in me not born, they'd need something to keep them warm until the little coat wore itself out. Until the little boots scuffed themselves to death. So I took them off her, think about that. I pulled them stiff little arms out of that sky-blue coat. Then I took them tiny feet out of them boots. I did this just like a grave robber. It's a difficult thing to get folks nowadays to understand how hard times was back then. Nature weren't always your friend. Sometimes it seemed that nature was out strictly to get you.

Sam Gifford had spent the night making up a coffin. He's good at work like that. It's the Indian in him. He makes baskets, too, the old way. He goes off into the mountains before dawn to find the right ash tree, and then the right cherry, and from the cherry he makes a stick to beat the ash. But the sun has to come up just so on them trees or Sam won't do it. Ain't that something? The sun just so on the cherry tree or he'll turn right around and come back home. But that ash beats out so fine it's like yarn. He makes good snowshoes, too, and I was glad he made the coffin, because I think he put a little bit of his heart into it, the Indian way. He was all drawn inward building it, like his heart was pulling him inside his chest, so there must have been a lot of Indian went into that coffin.

We took Mary to the graveyard at St. Leonard, up on the high pretty bank where you can see the river. I wanted to bring her back to Mattagash Brook, bury her on the edge of the blueberry patch. But Foster said it didn't matter which part of the earth took her. What mattered is that she was gone. And he was right. So we buried her next to Albion, my sister Laddie's oldest child, who built a snow tunnel and it fell on him. He was always building something, Albion was. Anything his hands touched, he made something out of it. I often wondered if Albion would've gone off to the city one day and built some of them tall skinny buildings that seem to scratch the sky. The weight of the snow suffocated him. Laddie said she looked out and saw a red arm sticking out of the snowbank, just one red sleeve, like it was blood seeping out. We buried Mary next to Albion, aged nine. Maybe with Albion there beside her, she could go on dreaming her train dreams. Maybe Albion could build her some little snowy tracks. And I remembered how she had looked that doctor right in the eye, not one little bit afraid of him. Maybe death gives you some courage, allows you that extra edge. I know it taught me a big lesson. I started looking at everyone real different after that.

We poled back up the river, back up to Mattagash Brook, back up to where you could fall off the edge of the world if you wasn't careful. I sat in the middle of the canoe, holding that little blue coat and them boots. I could still smell her in them. I could *smell* her, like she was a spruce. Like her soul was all fresh pine. Foster sat in front of me, in the bow, with his head down. Once in a while I'd see a shudder run through him, a little memory, I suppose. "Cough syrup," he kept muttering. "That weren't nothing but cherry cough syrup he give her." And we went on upriver like that, with me holding that coat and them boots, me sitting up like the prow of some old ship.

And there was a door slammed shut that day. I heard it, above the rapids and the birds—I heard it. And everything went quiet for it to be heard, like it did the night before, when Mary sat up in the moonlight and said, "Trains, Mama." There was a real banging noise. I looked at Foster, to see if he heard it, but he was far off, turning that bottle of syrup in his hands like it was blood. It stayed on a shelf in the cupboard, that bottle. I never used it, but I couldn't throw it out. It's still back at my house, and think of that, having a house and knowing where things are in it, and not being able to go there. Someone will when I'm dead. They'll go in like crows to throw things out, to keep what's shiny and interesting to their eyes. That bottle's so dusty and sticky you can't even read it, so they'll toss it out. No one will remember that cold autumn night, October 1, 1903. No one will remember the softness of a sick child against my breast, her head full of angry trains and empty tracks running nowhere. I think that's why I never liked Winnie, the way she always sported that little coat like it was nothing. After Ester got too big for it, I put it away for a few years, for Winnie. How many times did I see her take it off and throw it down, like it was just a *coat*. And for years I'd come fast awake, out of a dark sleep, and ask, "Are you cold, Mary?" I'd ask this so soft that no one ever heard me. But all I could hear her say back was, "Trains, Mama. Purple trains." So I'd lay back and try to sleep, until dawn came in the window, until I heard the first kid put a foot out of bed and onto the floor above me. And I got to be honest with you. For a lot of years there I didn't care which kid it was.

◆ ◆

CATHIE PELLETIER, a resident of the Nashville area for several years, has written five highly-acclaimed novels, the most recent being *A Marriage Made in Woodstock* (New York: Crown, 1994). Her poetry has appeared in numerous literary and academic magazines, and her book reviews have appeared in the *New York Times Book Review*, the *Philadelphia Inquirer*, and the *Atlanta Journal-Constitution*.

LEIGH WILSON

FROM "MASSÉ"

"OK, little lady," said the one named George, winking and grinning to his friends, "Let's see how you deliver." He could not contain himself. "Did you hear that? Did you hear what I just said? I said, I asked her, 'Let's see how you deliver.'"

They all snorted, stamping their cues on the end of their boots, and I regretted not changing out of my uniform. It was a bad sign because I'd never worn it to the bars before, just one result of hurrying trouble. You never knew when somebody might take a wild hair and try to mess up your job, somebody with a poor attitude toward losing and a bad disposition and a need for spreading chaos. I felt dizzy for a minute, as though I'd been submerged in water and couldn't make the transition.

"Winners break," George said. Now he was all business, ready to get the game over with so he could play with his friends. He strutted around, flexing his workshirt. Most nights, when I had the break, I would try to sink a couple, then leave the cue ball in a safe position, ducking my chin and smirking shamefacedly, as though I'd miscalculated. The point is, never let the guys waiting in line see that your game in no way depends on luck; it scares them if you do, shrinks their pockets like a cold shower, so to speak. But that night I was crazy, must have been. George went into an elaborate explanation of how he had to go to the bathroom but would be back before his turn, how I'd never even know he was gone. I said, "Five bucks." He rolled his eyes comically, performing for his friends, then said it was all right by him. "You're the boss, Chuck," he said. I don't know what got into me. Before George was out of sight, I broke and sank two stripes. Then I hammered in the rest of them, taking maybe three seconds between each shot. By the time old George could zip up his pants, I'd cleared the table.

"Fucking-A," said one of George's friends.

"Whoa," another one said. "Holy whoa."

It was a dream, that whole game was a dream. I had read somewhere that a sure sign

Excerpt from "Massé," in *Wind Stories*, by Leigh Wilson (New York: William Morrow and Company, 1989), 31-36.

of madness was when life took on a dreamlike quality, when you started manipulating what you saw as easily as you manipulate dreams. Those pins and needles came back into my feet, prickly as icicles. George came back, too. I figured the night was over. They would all get pissed off and quit playing and begin to attend to their beers. But—surprise—they ate it up, practically started a brawl over who was up next. It wasn't anything you could have predicted. I guess it pumped them up with adrenaline, or else with a kind of competitive meanness, because for the rest of the night they banged the balls with a vengeance. They were none too polite, and that's a fact. Whatever happened during those games happened in a dream. A wad of five-dollar bills began to show through the back pocket of my uniform trousers. The guys in blue workshirts were like a buzzing of hornets around me, their faces getting drunker and redder every hour.

Near closing time, around two in the morning, George came back for a last game, I'd been watching him play on the other table, and even with the handicap of a dozen beers he could run five or six balls at a time, which is not embarrassing for bar pool. But there was real hatred on George's face, sitting there like a signpost. All those beers had loosened his features until his eyebrows met in a single straight-edged line, the kind of eyebrows the Devil would have if he had eyebrows. Some men just can't get drunk without getting evil, too. I suggested we call it a day, but George would have none of it. He swaggered around, foulmouthed, until I said all right just to shut him up.

"Fucking dyke," he said, loud enough for me to hear. I kept racking the balls. He was the one who was supposed to rack them, but now I didn't trust him to rack them tightly.

"I said," he said, a little louder, "fucking dyke in a uniform." He was drunk—and I should have known better—though, as I've said, that day was the beginning of trouble. One rule of pool is never get emotional. You get emotional and first thing you know, your angles are off, your game is a highly unclear business.

"Asshole," I told him. "Fucking *asshole* in a uniform." My hands shook so much I gripped my cue as if it were George's neck. I am not a grisly or violent person, but there you go.

"Just play, for God's sake," said one of his friends. They were all grouped around the table, their faces as alike and featureless as the balls in front of them. I imagined that their eyes were the tips of cues, blue, sharp, nothing you wanted pointed in your direction.

"Radiation mutant," I said. "Rockfish." Then I broke. Sure enough, emotion had its effect. None of the balls fell.

"Fifty bucks, you pervert," George said, rippling those eyebrows at me. "No, make it a hundred." All that beer was working up some weird, purplish coloration into his cheeks.

They say that during important moments time goes by more slowly, elongates somehow just when you need it most. It is a falsehood. Time goes slowly when you're utterly miserable, or when you might be about to die, and both are situations any sane person would want to go by quickly. When you really need it, time isn't there for you. I wanted to study the table for a while, get myself under control and ready. I wanted to go outside and have somebody point out the constellations, show me the difference between Taurus and Arcturus. I wanted somebody to give me a fish that didn't die in the tank. I wanted somebody, anybody, to tell me that I was living a good life, that my habits were excellent, that I was going places.

"This is all she wrote, Chuck," George said, leaning over the table like a surgeon. It looked grim, not because the spread was all in George's favor—which it was—but because I had gotten emotional. Nothing was clear anymore, not the angles, not the spin, nothing. My cue stick might just as well have been a smokestack.

"Shit!" George cried and he slammed a beefy hand against his beefy thigh.

He'd run the table except for the eight ball, leaving me with some tricky shots—stop signs all over the table. By now everyone in The Office stood around the table, watching, belching, not saying a word. I thought about what Minnesota Fats would do, how Fats would handle the situation, but all I saw was that corner of the poster, unstuck and curled ominously over Fats's head. I wondered what would happen if I picked up each of my balls and placed them gently in the pockets, like eggs into Easter baskets. Crazy, I must have been crazy.

The first couple of shots were easy, then it got harder. I banked one ball the length of the table, a miraculous shot, though it left the cue ball in an iffy position. I made the next one anyway. After each shot I had to heft the stick in my hand, get the feel of it all over again, as if I were in George's league, an amateur on a hot streak. Finally the game came down to one shot. I had one ball left, tucked about an inch and a half up the rail from the corner pocket, an easy kiss except that the eight ball rested directly in the line of the shot. There was no way I could bank the cue ball and make it.

"All she wrote," George said, "all she by God *wrote*!"

I hefted my cue stick for a massé, the only thing left to do.

"Oh, no," cried George. "No, you don't. You might get away with that shit in lesbo pool, but not here. You're not doing it here. No, sir. No way."

"Who says?" I asked him, standing up from the table. I was sweating a lot, I could feel it on my ribs. "Anything goes is my feeling."

"Bar rules." George appealed to his friends. "Right? No massé in bar rules. Right? Am I right?"

"Phineas!" somebody called. "Phineas! No massé on the tables, right?"

Phineas came out around the bar, rubbing his hands on an apron that covered him from the neck to the knees. He had short, black, curly hair and wore round wire-rimmed glasses, the kind of glasses that make people look liberal and intelligent somehow. He looked clean and trim in his white apron, surrounded by all those sweaty blue workshirts. For a minute he just stood there, rubbing his hands, sizing up the table.

"What's the stake?" he asked philosophically.

"Hundred!" George said. He was practically screaming.

Phineas puckered his mouth.

"Well," he said, drawing the sound out. Maybe he was buying time. Maybe he was leading them on. Or maybe he was a bartender who didn't like crowds and didn't like crowds asking for his opinion—which is exactly what he is. "Anything goes," he said. "Anything goes for a hundred bucks is my opinion."

"I'll remember this," George said, snarling, his purple face shaded to green. "You prick, I'll remember this."

"Fine," said Phineas, almost jovially. He folded his arms across that white apron and looked at me. He might have winked, but more likely he was just squinting, sizing me up.

"Massé on the ten into the corner," I said stiffly, formally, the way Bernie would have done. Anybody will tell you, a massé is ridiculous. You have no real cue ball control, no real control, period. You have to bring your stick into an almost vertical position, then come down solidly on one side of the cue ball, which then—if you do it right—arcs around the obstacle ball and heads for the place you have in mind. It is an emotional shot, no control, mostly luck. And anytime you get yourself into the position of taking an emotional shot, all is pretty much lost. I hefted the cue stick again, hiked it up like an Apache spearing fish. Then I let it rip. The cue ball arced beautifully, went around the eight ball with a lot of backspin, then did just what it was supposed to do—kissed the ten on the rail. The trouble was, it didn't kiss the ten hard enough. The ball whimpered along the rail about an inch, then stopped short of the pocket. A breath would have knocked it in, but apparently nobody was breathing.

◆ ◆

LEIGH WILSON lives now in Oswego, New York, where she writes and teaches at the State University of New York. Her stories have appeared in numerous magazines, and her first book, *From the Bottom Up*, won the coveted Flannery O'Connor Award. *Wind Stories*, her second collection from William Morrow, also is available in Penguin paperback.

KIERNAN DAVIS

Soul Snag

A truly wicked man boarded the train in Mobile, a Yankee, who done himself some business with this fella in Alabama. He gonna cut across the South on iron wheels, riding high to keep hisself clean. Got him a spanky suit and fingers in his lap. That old cracked leather seat make him sick. Look out the window, see that dust go by. Mind him of southern sweat; lots of it, with nothing solid ever gonna come of it.

Now, brothers and sisters, this here man was brought to my attention having cheated that fella I was speaking of. And I knew what that Yankee was thinking, and I knew what that Yankee was feeling, because it come to me. And that bad soul of his made a squealing sound like one of them big warehouse rats, soon as he got on that train, heading north.

He ain't never gonna see no cold blue northern sky, because the heat's gonna bring him down, and the trees and the dirt and the heavy air gonna drag him under. And I sent me a soul snag to see that it was done.

She follows him onto the train in Mobile, an old woman in big shoes. A sweet faced, honey-bun of a woman with a hook for a heart. My pride and my beauty and my soothing lambie, and she sits across from him for one whole day and tries to lull that wicked man to sleep. She does her the crosswords and hums a little under her breath, keeping her eyes polite. And that train rocks and rocks. But he never will fall to sleep so's she can get close enough to suck the breath out of him.

At a stop the next day she changes herself, and she comes back on the train as a young woman, good and trashy. She got a full bosom and liquid sugar for lips. She sits herself down across from him and long dark hair tumbles round her chin, practically pointing for a kiss. For two days he ignores her and he hates her. She talks on and on, about everything, and laughs by herself. Her words have flesh on them and roll on her tongue like they are alive, and it scares him. He thinks there's a different kind of language down here. And he thinks maybe she sweats in the bed and got something dirty on her somewheres that don't wash off. No way that girl gonna get near his mouth.

Another stop and the border's getting close. The land is changing and laying flat and the trees are disappearing and the girl is losing her curve and her words are losing their meat in all this lowdown flatness.

She's got to hurry and get away from him and it comes to her to go to his bed that night.

He draws back the curtain. And there she is, laying on the pillow, and all that's left of her is this little bitty baby. And he looks, and looks, and wonders who left it, and how does he get rid of it.

It be a scary, wild eyed, concentrated soul sucking infant. And it whispers to him. Like this, just a breath of a whisper.

And he leans over. What that baby say?

And I gets him.

Mouth just close enough to snatch his air, and that child's lips part and swoosh, it hooks on and sucks hard and tears that man's soul right out of his body. The spanky man struggles a little over the fold-down bed, then falls to the ground an empty husk.

My old woman in the big shoes gets off that train with a full mouth, just in time. She's tired and needs her rest and walks up slow to the ticket master, and says, real soft and kind of mumbly:

"Mobile."

◆ ◆

KIERNAN DAVIS, who earned her M.F.A. in creative writing at Vermont College in 1989 and lived for some time at Signal Mountain, has twice been nominated for a Pushcart Prize. A recent winner of the Short Fiction Award from the Associated Writing Program and the First Prize for Fiction from the Tennessee Writers Association, she is currently finishing a work of nonfiction.

DON KECK DUPREE

Love Letter

This last storm broke fescue-blazing heat and
Hove our maples at the house like bats or big
Brothers playing at vampires to scare by night.
I ate alone and went to bed with a dog
And cat for friends, candle or two for a read

Before sleep. Then dark. Odd how candles smudged
To night recall Dan's stone saw and Kelvin
Goggle-eyed, piecing the new chimney to meet
Your design. Do you sleep yet tonight where you
Are? All those stones are rejected scrap the builder

Refused. I think of a garden wall I'd like
To raise before you return, to use those block
For something, at least. Remember the newspapers
We found under the kitchen floor? We read
Old times for hours, never stripped the first board.

I read sandstone this afternoon, never
Stacked the first block. One angle holds a moon
And galaxy swept beyond God. What on past
Its edge unknown; I can't find that rock. Another
Stone holds terror of trouble sands constellated

Toward a cleft where angles play; dark crevices
Threaten each one the mason cast aside.
Do you sleep yet where you are? I'm not
One to notice it's night but mind this dark
Without you. Angles sweep; edges cleave; shadows

Feed on blood surprised by storm and dark.
Stones sheer against paleolithic faults; won't
Quarry clean. So we are, crevice and cleft,
Stones the builder rejected. Come home; we'll
Sediment corners, mortar sure, and layer
Stone for readers, long, long, away.

Faith and Works

Nascence, his, draws no drag through water,
Tadpoling this pool with others. Fathers
Score an air; they track the target of their
Delight. These share an innocence of bathers
Caught in daguerreotypes; we're men of years
To whom a guiltless Saturday matters.
Croup the chlorine, invidious across the water.

Mine won't take this meet, not now, never;
Water's not his element. He'll receive
Wide and carry another team but that's
Years away. Now it's zippers and sleeves,
Warm-ups, welterweight cheeseburgers; that's
For our minds. Suburban assurance, I'll wager.
But, I'll wager. Smile sweet over water.

His milk-skimmed lip predicts no razor,
Quavering above drinks he carries to men—
Their sons all boothed at Wendy's. We're Nashville's
Best—out-game all comers.

Mine's a friend,
Sure, but he's a hard play to call—
Does Saturdays for points with me, never
Quits about football, says I'm not for water.

He swam for Vandy, nearly made an Olympic
Squad too. He's a shipper now, river barges
To sea then boats. We used to take kids down
To blow whistles but not any more. His barn's
His thing today—out back, six miles from
Town. We moved last year; he'll groom a winner.

Horses are fun but guys can't ride his winner.
We're stuck with a glue-pot nag bought for kids,
And he's big among dads for it. They'd all
Like to be one to saddle every last kid
A horse, woods, and yes, hoops for ball.
My guys like to ride his boats and water.

• •

DON KECK DUPREE, who now lives and works at Sewanee, has had recent poems in the *Missouri Review*, *Grand Street*, *Southern Review*, and other publications. A graduate of Vanderbilt and Bread Loaf, he is a finalist for the Roath Prize.

L. LEE WILSON

Birds of a Feather

Her name was Edna and she was as unassuming and plain as her name, the sort of woman whose ripeness at thirty turns, through hard work, into muscle and sinew at forty. She was big and long-boned, with broad shoulders and the lean flanks and arms of a farmhand. Her square jaw, not yet softened by the jowling of middle age, was saved from severity by the frame of her heavy waving brown hair, caught in a knot at the nape of her neck.

Her hands were big and so rough that on Sundays she covered them with an old pair of white cotton gloves before she put on her stockings, but she handled the African violets she was watering as lightly as if she had the little, soft hands of a pampered girl. She worked quickly, carefully and methodically picking off the dead pink and blue blooms before returning the delicate plants to the wide-silled white window over the kitchen sink. Except for the side window in the parlor, the kitchen window gave the only view in the house of the rough, green farmhouse lawn that sloped under the oak trees down to the fenced pastures. She like to watch the sun come up in it every morning as she made breakfast.

She looked at the clock on the stove, pulled a thick marble slab from its place under the linoleum-covered counter, and, after dusting the slab deftly with flour, began to roll out a pie crust with short, sure strokes. Today she took special care in crimping the rim of the crust. She knew the pie would be scrutinized by her husband's mother, who was expected for dinner and an afternoon visit.

Her sister-in-law Zadie Pearl was coming, too. Her ready-made clothes and slender legs made Edna feel clumsy. Zadie Pearl's husband Oscar never came; he was a bootlegger, and Amos wouldn't have him in the house. His money kept Zadie Pearl in flashy dresses and smart hats and allowed her to dress their five-year-old daughter Jeweldine in delicate lawn dresses that each cost more than any garment Edna had ever owned. Edna thought the dresses only emphasized the little girl's chinless face and squinting little brown eyes.

The three females always unnerved Edna, but they were Amos' closest women kin, so she tolerated their painful visits, ignoring Zadie Pearl's sneering comments and her mother-in-law's obvious preference for Jeweldine over Edna's three round, blond boys. Still, she wished they would stay in town, where the old lady lived with Zadie Pearl, and leave her in peace.

She heard Zadie Pearl's car in the driveway as she closed the oven door on her pie. Hurriedly, she took off her apron, smoothed the skirt of the new blue seersucker dress she wore and viewed the buttonholes on the dress front with consternation. The thread had lumped at the ends and, in spite of her care in marking the fabric, one buttonhole was a full quarter-inch closer to its neighbor than the pattern called for. She told herself it was still a nice dress, but she knew her sister-in-law would notice its failings.

She looked up and saw Zadie Pearl and Jeweldine walk into the kitchen, followed by Mother Blackwell. They never knocked, but their proprietary air in her house always surprised her.

"For God's sake, Edna, don't you ever leave this kitchen?" Zadie Pearl said as she blotted the pancake makeup over her painted-on eyebrows with a little lace handkerchief. "It's hot as Hades in here!"

Edna moved toward the counter by the sink, reaching it just in time to stop Jeweldine from pulling the last pot of violets to the floor. She set it on the sill with the others and took the squirming little girl firmly by the hand.

Old Mother Blackwell, who had been standing sullenly behind her daughter, advanced and angrily took Jeweldine's hand out of Edna's grasp, leading the little girl toward the parlor.

The room, seldom used, was slightly musty. Mother Blackwell raised an eyebrow and looked significantly over her shoulder at her daughter, who was sniffing the air. The old lady stationed herself in the corner in a big maroon and grey armchair. Her short sticklike legs missed the floor by several inches, but she wiggled her round body like a nesting hen until she was comfortable. She then took a can of Bruton snuff from her immense black leather handbag and positioned a pinch of the ground tobacco between her furrowed upper lip and her nearly toothless gum.

"What's Granny gonna spit in? Where's her spit can?" Jeweldine, now standing on the sofa, screeched at Edna. Without a word Edna got up and went to a closet in the hall to fetch a gallon fruit can with one end cut out and the label scrubbed off. She set it by the old lady's chair and sat again in her straight-backed chair by the door to the kitchen. Zadie Pearl powdered her beak of a nose and pretended not to see. "That new lamp's nice, Edna," she said as she snapped her compact shut. "Mavis Allen got one just like it with green stamps. I told Mavis I bet you got yours with stamps, too, but Mavis says to me, 'No, she couldn't have got it with stamps because the grocer don't give you stamps for trading eggs.'

"Butler Brothers? I didn't know they had anything like it. Oh, you ordered it special! Well. I certainly didn't know they ever special ordered just one piece. I mean, my whole living room suit was special ordered, but I didn't know they ever ordered special for just one piece.

"Edna, I hope you didn't forget that Mother can't eat pork. Beef is all right, but the doctor says her colon can't take pork. I think pork is dirty, anyway. I never let Jeweldine eat pork. It's not good for her figger. One of the reasons my figger is still so good is because I never eat pork."

"Pork is pigs, ain't it, Momma?"

"Yes, Jeweldine, and pigs live in the mud."

"Pork is pigs and pigs live in the mud! Pork is pigs and pigs live in the mu-ud!"

Edna got up to check on her pie and put the rolls in. The kitchen was like an oven, and sweat ran down her neck into her deep bosom in little glistening trails. Her hair drooped over her brow. Zadie Pearl's marcelled waves never fell out, she thought.

Amos and the boys were hot and dirty when they came in. They had been topping tobacco, cutting the big, sticky pink bloom spikes off the tops of the stalks so that the tobacco leaves could grow larger. It was messy, disagreeable, stifling work. Lewis, the oldest boy, had cut his thumb with the tobacco knife.

Amos helped her put the leaf in the kitchen table. The boys, grateful to be out of the airless tobacco patch for awhile, washed up at the sink outside the kitchen door and sat on the back porch steps in the breeze.

Suddenly Jeweldine stood in the kitchen doorway with her hands on her hips. "Momma says ain't it ready yet and Granny says she's gonna leave if she cain't eat soon," she chirped, obviously delighted at the prospect of conflict.

Edna set the last dish on the table and motioned to her niece to call the women. The marshmallows topping the whipped sweet potatoes had gotten a little too brown in the oven, and the round cake of cornbread was slightly lopsided when she turned it out of the skillet onto the plate, but everything else looked, she reckoned, all right.

The meal went quickly. There was only room for seven chairs at the table, so Edna helped a plate for herself and sat in a chair by the stove to eat. Jeweldine refused to sit by the boys but was quieted when put between her mother and grandmother. Zadie Pearl took Edna's accustomed place at the corner of the table next to Amos and, it seemed to Edna, made over him even more than usual. She didn't like the cloying tone Zadie Pearl used when she called him "Brother" or the way she punctuated her sentences by touching his shoulder with her pale hand with the painted nails.

Amos and the boys, who had been at work since six, ate rapidly and silently. Edna was hard put to keep their tea glasses filled. The beef roast apparently suited Mother Blackwell. She ate as big a portion as any of the men and belched unabashedly when she had finished.

The old lady never got a chance to criticise the pie. Zadie Pearl objected to it first.

"Really, Edna, cherry pie? You know mother cain't abide cherries in anything and Jeweldine is allergic to them. I never eat pie because of my figger. We'll just go set in the shade."

Amos and the boys split the pie into four big pieces and wolfed it down. While Edna cleared the table and washed the dishes, they sat on the back porch long enough to let their dinner settle. After a few minutes, they filled water jugs from the pump at the wellhouse and traipsed back into the hot afternoon, leaving the social duties of the day to Edna.

When Edna walked outside, she found Zadie Pearl and her mother in the backyard between the wellhouse and the garden, fanning themselves on a big settee placed at an angle under the big oak tree. Zadie Pearl had a little Japanese paper fan that folded like an accordion. Oscar had brought it to her last year from Nashville. Mother Blackwell's more effective fan was a cardboard one from McDaniel's Funeral Home. It had a four-color Jesus on one side and a calendar on the other. Jeweldine, her sheer bodice sticking to her scrawny torso, was pulling the tail of Edna's favorite cat, a half-grown girl cat with russet-colored fur and a flat face.

"Edna, why will you wear those awful sunbonnets? That one must be years old and you can tell they're all homemade, even if you do starch them like that. Not another woman I know would be caught in one and, besides, your face has been brown for years, anyway. Mother thinks so, too, don't you, Mother?" Zadie Pearl asked.

The old lady had dropped her cardboard fan on the settee beside her and was sitting with her legs agape, waving her long skirt up and down between them to cool herself. She aimed a long stream of ambeer at the ground beside her, looked at Zadie Pearl, squinted at Edna, and frowned. Edna untied the long, limp blue strings of her bonnet and stuck it in her apron pocket.

The afternoon settled over the women like a warm, wet blanket. Only occasionally would a breeze cool their damp skin. Mother Blackwell dozed. Jeweldine sporadically tormented the cat. Edna sat shelling butterbeans into a big tin dishpan in her lap. Zadie Pearl speculated about the minister's wife and the town piano teacher, a man Edna considered exemplary.

Edna listened with half an ear, watching Zadie Pearl's bright pink mouth pout with pleasure as she talked. "And so I told Mavis, 'What does a woman her age want with piano lessons, anyway?' And Mavis said she heard she's going twice a week now. And to his house, mind you! Says the church piano is out of tune. If you ask me. . . ."

Edna stood up abruptly, dropping her pan of shelled and unshelled beans with a rattle. Zadie Pearl was startled. The old lady woke up and stared at her. Jeweldine, standing by her mother, choking the breath out of the poor cat, whimpered. Edna strode over to Jeweldine and wrested the cat away from her. She walked under the clothesline, knelt at the garden fence and put the cat gently through an opening. Then, tying on her bonnet as she went, she walked to the chicken house and captured three fryers with a swift, practiced aim.

She carried the hapless chickens back to the clothesline in one hand, fingers looped around their legs, her arm swinging with her stride.

The three under the oak tree watched in amazement as she grabbed one of the flapping, squawking birds by the head and swung its body in a broad arc around its skinny neck. The neck broke, the flesh and feathers tore and the headless chicken flopped and quivered on the ground at her feet, spattering the green summer grass for several feet with shimmering drops of blood.

Edna tossed the chicken head, its dead eyes rolled back and the ugly, almost vestigial, tongue lolling out of the yellow beak, over the fence into the tomatoes. Never taking her eyes off the three staring females for a moment, she repeated the process twice more, wringing the weak necks easily with her strong right arm.

She then picked up the headless fryers and turned to hang them by their scaly feet on the clothesline so that all the blood could run out of the still-twitching bodies.

When she looked again, Zadie Pearl, the old woman, and the howling little girl were marching toward Zadie Pearl's bottle-green sedan. The sun, now low in the sky, lit the trio from behind and gave them feathers around their edges.

The car coughed, backed up with a jerk, and roared down the hill toward the highway, destroying a rosebush in the process.

Edna wiped her bloody hands on her apron, picked up the dishpan, and sat on the settee in the hazy afternoon, shelling butterbeans to go with the chicken she would fry for supper.

◆ ◆

L. LEE WILSON, who is an attorney specializing in intellectual property law, lives in Pleasant View. Active in the state's literary arts, she is currently at work on a mystery novel and an anthology of Tennessee women writers.

DON WILLIAMS

OLD CHRISTMAS EVE

We three kids came home from school and caught Mama smashing out the window panes of the front door with a high heel shoe. She froze when she heard the screech of the school bus, braking to let us off. Then she just stood there, anguished and lopsided in her other shoe. The bus driver stared straight ahead, but our friends looked out from all the bus windows.

Her face was black around the eyes, so that at first I thought Daddy had hit her there, but he hadn't. It was just the way her makeup had smeared.

"You all go play," I told Jake, who was only eight years old, and Iris, just six. Then I went up on the porch and looked in through the broken glass. I saw Daddy's whiskered face dodge back too late for me not to see him standing there with his bottle. I reached in and straight down my arm a shard of glass drew a red line that beaded up, then ran warm between my fingers. The blood dripped onto the floor as I turned the knob, and the door swung open.

"Good God, son," Daddy said and set the whiskey on the coffee table. He took my hand and stood staring at the blood. I was lucky, though. It wasn't as bad as it looked, and the sight of it ended the fighting.

I didn't ask what they were fighting about, or why Mama was trying to beat her way into the house. They fought too regularly for that. You may as well worry why frost gathers on the grass or why the birds fly south. The fighting would pass. We all knew that, just like we knew it would come again. I only hoped we could make it through Christmas first.

The door had been fixed by the next day when we got home from school. Mama and Daddy were sitting on the couch like lovers you see in the movies.

Daddy had shaved. His black hair was combed back and his new sports shirt was open at the neck. He was holding Mama's hand. She was made up like a movie star, wearing stockings and high heels, and her red hair was piled up on her head. She

"Old Christmas Eve," by Don Williams, appeared first in *Christmas Blues: Behind the Holiday Mask—An Anthology* (Albuquerque, N.M.: Amador Publishers, 1995). Used with permission of the author.

smelled like a flower, and I thought of when I was small enough to sit on her lap all those years ago and play with her earrings. She looked up at Daddy like she was grateful for something.

Me and Jake and Iris stood looking at them, glad the fighting had stopped. Mama and Daddy smiled back like nothing had happened. Nothing at all.

Daddy said, "We're going to go out to eat, maybe do a little shopping. Ronnie, I want you to stay and watch after the kids," he told me. That was my chance to say something, but I didn't ask any questions. "By the way," he said, "what do you all want Santa Claus to bring you?"

"A sled," Jake said. "I want a Speedaway sled," and he began describing one he had seen at Wal-Mart. Then Iris told them about the twin dolls and double stroller she had seen on T.V. I asked for the Daisy pump-action BB gun just like my friend Danny Logan's. I had coveted it ever since I first shot it. It had felt smooth and natural in my hands, and as soon as I aimed, I knew I was a better shot than Danny was. I knew how to squeeze the trigger. Easy, like Clint Eastwood in the movies.

About a week later, Daddy came outside where we were playing and called to us. He wore old clothes. His left hand held a pair of work gloves and his right held the axe.

"Pick your coats up off the ground," he said. We looked around nervously, breathless from our playing. "We're going down to John's Bottom," Daddy added. That was where we always got our Christmas tree, down where the evergreens grew thick along John Sutton's good bottom land by the creek. We followed Daddy down Bent Lane. Our shoes scraped icy gravel as we walked, past dried weeds hanging with faded seed pods, past fields of dark cedars that you could smell.

Naked oaks cast a web of shadows across the road.

At the big curve, Daddy left the lane and stood by the rusted barbed-wire fence that Mr. Sutton had strung years before. He stepped on the bottom strand and picked up the next one, and we three hunkered down and went through. Daddy stepped over the fence, straddling it carefully, and we walked into the field.

A flock of blackbirds feeding there lifted like a new-made cloud and I pretended to catch a bird in the sights of a gun and fire at it with imaginary bullets.

Jake remembered an old family joke. "We're going down to cut a whisker offa John's bottom," he said, and we laughed. We passed Mr. Sutton's herd of cattle, brindled black and dingy white. Daddy nudged me with his elbow.

"Watch out for old Jeremiah," he said as we walked past the big bull with the black face. "Don't look in his eyes. He'll think you're challenging him."

"Ruthie's big," Iris said, pointing. We looked at the calf that had been born in the fall, standing there against her mother's protective flank, then looked away as Jeremiah shifted his weight and took a half-step our way.

Jake pointed to a tree up ahead and ran to it. It tapered into the air like a steeple. Iris danced around it in the weakening sunlight.

"Its perfect, Daddy," Jake said.

"Yeah, perfect," Iris echoed. She had a finger in her mouth worrying a hang-nail as she waited for Daddy's verdict. I pulled her hand down and picked her up, so that my nose was in her red hair. It smelled fresh and clean. My hair is black like Daddy's and so is Jake's.

"Don't you think it's kind of big?" I said.

"We could take the roof off the house," Daddy said, "but then where would Santa land?" Jake laughed and ran off to look for another tree. We found it at the crown of a small knob. It looked too little when Jake first spotted it, but when we got there we saw that it was seven feet high at least.

"Stand back," Daddy said, and his axe struck white chips from it. They flew after each fierce stroke. "Here, try it out." He handed me the axe. I took it, avoiding his eyes. It felt heavy and solid in my hands. I felled the tree, so that it lay hanging by a strip of bark. Daddy made me give the axe over to Jake. He heaved two strokes and the tree rolled over at our feet.

We all looked at it, and in the sudden silence I heard the dull thudding of hooves, followed by a snorting sound. Mr. Sutton's cattle had gathered at the base of the hill. They stood in the pocked field watching with gentle eyes, all of them facing our way, and I wondered what it would be like to be so big and yet that quiet.

"Watch out for Jeremiah," Daddy warned again. He motioned for us to follow him down the back side of the hill, then over the fence. On the road, we passed the cattle again and they regarded us silently through the fence.

Daddy said, "Grandma used to tell it that if you went over to the barn there after sundown on what folks called Old Christmas Eve you'd see the cattle kneeling, a-worshipping the baby Jesus."

"Really?" Iris asked. Her green eyes were big with the wonder of it.

"That's what Grandma used to say."

That was something I would like to see.

Daddy brought the tree into the yard and stood it up. Mama came to the door. She let out a sigh and nodded. She looked pretty standing there in the doorway.

"It's real nice," she said.

"I chopped it down," Jake bragged, smiling big. He had lost a tooth and his tongue came up to fill the empty space.

"Get a bucket," Daddy said, and I began gathering pebbles in a pail by the garage.

In the living room, Mama had spread out the decorations. Daddy draped a tangled vine of lights and a shiny yellow rope on the tree, and we began to hang the ornaments. Mama hung the ones that had survived from a time before I was born.

We watched with solemn eyes as she took the tissue from a wine-colored globe that had "Silent Night, Holy Night" written in white on it. She cradled it in her hands.

"This is the first one we ever bought," she said. "Remember, Tommy?" Daddy nodded, then she hung it on a sturdy branch above the reach of children. We stood looking at it. It was from another time when none of us were in the world.

The days dragged by. At night after the others were in bed, I would look at the growing pile of presents under the tree, searching for the gun, even though I knew Mama and Daddy would put the big gifts out last.

I liked being the only one in the quiet room. Tinsel icicles glistened. The smell of cedar was on the air. The manger scene Mama had crafted from cardboard, paste, and figurines was on the coffee table. Three kings brought gifts. A sheep, a cow, and a donkey knelt beside miniature shepherds amid bits of brown grass.

On Christmas Eve we sang carols, my mother's rich alto filling the room. I kept waiting for Daddy's sturdy bass to join in on "Joy to the World," and so I sang louder to make up for its absence. We sang "Away in a Manger" slow and gentle, then made our voices deep and strong for "We Three Kings." Mama read from the Bible about the shepherds keeping watch over their flocks by night. At bedtime she set out a slice of fruitcake and coffee for Santa.

Daddy took down a glass and poured whiskey in it.

"This is what I would want if I was to fly in on a cold night like tonight," he said, and Mama looked at him. I saw her mouth go tight, then she stood up and led us down the hallway to tuck us into bed in the room we shared on cold nights. She lingered over us, sniffing something back, patting us to show us everything was all right, patting us with her hands white and light as doves' wings.

After she left we lay awake, restless in our eagerness to possess the presents that would come. At last Jake and Iris settled into their familiar easy breathing, but I couldn't sleep. My mind drifted, and I remembered what Daddy had said about Mr. Sutton's cattle kneeling in the darkened barn to honor Jesus on Old Christmas Eve.

I got up and pulled on my bluejeans, my flannel shirt, the black and white vinyl jacket with fringe down the sleeves, cowboy boots, and gloves. I raised the window beside the bed and stepped through, into the night's cold breath.

I walked down Bent Lane beneath a three-quarters moon. Its reflection shivered fragmented in the creek. I stopped once and looked back the way I had come. The house was small and far away, so that it fit with the rest of the neighborhood. I saw the lights of our living room come on. I knew Mama and Daddy would be laying out the main presents. I pulled my coat tight around me and walked along the shoulder of the road. "Please God," I said.

I saw Mr. Sutton's barn and started to cross the fence to it, then I heard a sound down by the creek, and I saw that the cattle had gathered there by a mound of hay. Their heads were inclined towards me. I watched them for a long time, hoping for the miracle, not knowing then that the Old Christmas Eve that Grandma talked about came later and not on Christmas Eve like we have it.

Had I known, I wouldn't have stood there until midnight before I walked away.

As I came close to the house, I could see the yellow window panes of the living room and the silhouettes of my parents. I walked into the yard and heard their voices, and I knew they were way too loud. I trembled as I went to the front door and looked through the new panes of glass.

I saw that the tree was down sideways on the floor, its lights still flashing red, blue, yellow, and green. Mama was sitting on the living room rug in her nightgown. Daddy was standing over her, and I could hear the rage in his voice as he shook a new red-checkered shirt in front of her face, tore off a piece of green paper that fluttered to the floor, then grasped the shirt on either side of a seam and began ripping it apart until he held two flannel rags in his fists. Mama covered her face in her hands, and I saw the redness on her shoulder where he had hit her.

My legs began to shake and a tightness came into my chest. When he looked up toward the window, I ran, around the house to the window of my room. I raised it, then climbed in. I kicked off my boots and pulled off the jacket and somehow I got into bed without waking Jake. I heard Daddy's voice rising and falling with his rage, even though the sound was muffled by doors on either end of the hallway that separated us. My breath was coming hard, and I realized I had been holding it ever since I looked in the house. By the time I was able to quiet my own breathing, the house had gone silent again.

Then it was daylight and Iris was patting my face and saying, "Guess what, Ronnie, Santa Claus came. Guess what, Santa Claus came. Come see. Come see." I pulled on my bluejeans and followed her into the living room. The tree was upright again, its decorations restored. Only the "Silent Night" globe was gone. Mama and Daddy sat in their housecoats. Jake had already taken the ribbon off his sled and had it propped against the couch, pretending to ride it down a hill. Mama and Daddy smiled, despite their bleary eyes, as Iris unwrapped her dolls and put them into their double stroller and pushed them through the house.

Daddy handed me the package that held my gun, and I opened it slowly, then sat looking at it. It was a Daisy pump-action, just like I had asked for.

"What's the matter?" Daddy asked. "Don't you like it?"

I cocked it and thumped it once into the air. "I'm going off to try it out," I said. I went to my room and put my boots and coat back on. At the door, Mama stuffed Christmas cookies into my jacket pocket. She knelt there before me and, as she zipped up my coat, her eyes searched mine to see if I had heard their fighting, but I didn't let on.

"Be back in time for dinner, boy," Daddy said as I went out the door. It was a strange thing to say. Christmas dinner would be in the afternoon, and that seemed like a long time away.

The creek in the pasture was glazed with ice. It flashed in the sunlight as I walked. Above, the whisper of a thousand blackbird wings took my thoughts traveling south.

I pulled the gun off my shoulder and bit two fingers of a glove to pull my hand from it. Then I tore open the little pack of coppery pellets. I cupped my hand to form a funnel and directed the BBs into the bore where they rattled and slid to the bottom. Propping the stock of the gun against the side of my boot, I slid the compression pump up and down the barrel until my arm ached and the pump was taut.

I paused on a plank bridge and looked at the cattle scraping around among the scattered straw across a fence built to match the contours of creek and field and hills. A dried seed pod from a mimosa tree floated down the stream and I took a shot at it, breaking it cleanly in two. Then I looked around for another target. A stray blackbird had fallen behind the flock. I followed its low trajectory, gave it some lead time and fired, then chased its ragged course down the sky, through the limbs of a big sycamore. I walked beside it as it fluttered along, one wing grabbing at the ground. I turned it over with the toe of my boot and pinned its good wing in the dirt. I put the bore of the BB gun to its breast, closed my finger, and pumped it full of death.

I walked toward home then. I thought of the steaming kitchen and felt sick at the thought of us all together around the table. I stopped beside Mr. Sutton's herd of cattle where they stood among the scattered hay. They stared at me with mild and empty eyes. I swung the gun towards the black face of Jeremiah, standing out front.

I cocked the gun and knelt in the gravel. The big bull turned his head away. Then, when he swung it back, I homed in on the white of an eye, steadied my hands and squeezed the trigger. The eye closed, and one knee crumpled as if it had been slammed by a two-by-four. Gratified by this response, I fired again. It took two shots to Jeremiah's black face before his other leg gave out so that he pitched forward, uttering a high, broken cry as he went down on both knees in the hay.

"There," I said.

I lowered the gun and looked around to see if anyone had seen me do it. I saw the glitter of ice on the creek, dark cedars on the horizon, the ascending sun. When I looked back at Jeremiah, the parts of his left eye were like bits of candy that had melted and run together and threatened to drip down his face.

I turned my back on him and walked quickly up the gravel road toward home. I held the gun before me. It felt solid in my hands, as if with it, some way, I could change things around.

◆ ◆

Don Williams, a columnist and feature writer for the *Knoxville News-Sentinel*, also publishes in literary journals like *Poets & Writers* and the *Chattahoochee Review*. A 1991 recipient of a Michigan Journalism Fellowship from the University of Michigan, he is a founding member of the Knoxville Writers Guild.

DIANN BLAKELY SHOAF

THE CEMETERY BOOK OF CAROLINE MCGAVOCK

—Carnton House, Franklin, Tennessee

Gathered like rumors, clouds hung close
to the ground, whitened each dawn with frost.
When the battle started, she thought she heard
thunder then remembered the season and three years
of war, scouts she'd let sleep on her rugs.
A prayer to the God of Calvin

her forebears brought with them from Ulster
came next; she knew will was damnation
and all things predestined, and yet protested
as she had her firstborn's last fever,
his sister's choking on phlegm, the cousin and brother
who'd limped home that month, one missing a leg,

the other three toes to frostbite, also an eye.
By afternoon, more than two thousand lay dead,
twice that wounded, five generals shrouded
on her porch. The children huddled downcellar
with the few house servants who had claimed
they were too old for freedom, hoping to die

where they'd lived, raised young ones
their own. They trusted in prayer, having prayed
for years not to be sold from their families.
When the surgeon cried for more hands

than she had, she brought Gabriel and Susie upstairs.
The nursery they'd tended that morning was a riot

of bodies, strewn toys soaked from the blood
that spurted with each scalpel-cut
through sinew and tendon, severing shattered arms
and legs, the hands or feet of the luckier.
The walls themselves seemed to bleed; the horror
of splintered bone protruding from a length of flesh

she couldn't name as the surgeon reached out
the window and dropped it two stories below.
I stand at a glass case, examining pages
yellowed and speckled as the linens spread
without wrinkle on the four-posters upstairs.
Mass graves were the norm then; too many to dig

separate holes for, not enough men left to dig them.
And they had a hurry: the ground, though warmed
by puddles of blood, would harden with frost
at nightfall. After the final surrender,
what kind of help did she have, reclaiming bodies
from Tennessee soil, checking their pockets

for letters or inscribed photographs, anything
to tell her those names? Each was reburied alone,
a limestone slab etched with a cross
stating all she'd learned. At night, both children
beside her, she knelt on this floor,
still dark with stain over a hundred years later.

DIANN BLAKELY SHOAF was educated at Sewanee, Vanderbilt, NYU, Harvard, Boston University, and Vermont College. She has been awarded a Pushcart Prize, fellowships to the Bread Loaf and Sewanee Writers' conferences, and a citation from the University of Chicago for excellence in teaching. Currently she is an instructor at the Harpeth Hall School in Nashville.

ELAINE FOWLER PALENCIA

THE LESSON

At night when Lena put her son to bed upstairs in the slanted room under the roof, he would ask her questions. He was five and named Irish. Lena was twenty.

When are we going home?

We are home. This our home now.

Then where is Granny Ulvie?

You remember Granny Ulvie lives in town.

Will we ever see her again?

Of course we will. Someday.

Tell me about my daddy.

Your daddy was a rich man.

How rich?

He had his own truck. A big, black truck named Widowmaker. Once he drove clear to California in it.

Why don't he ever come to see us?

He drove over the edge of the world. Hush now, go to sleep. Caleb is your daddy now.

Then the boy would put the pillow over his head, so he couldn't hear the hoot owls in the woods. Living in the country scared him. It was too quiet everywhere, like something was waiting to get him. But the pillow was nice. Granny Ulvie's scalp showed through her hair. It was pink and her hair was yellowish white. Her hands were rough and knobby and she wore flowered dresses that were faded almost white and were dirty in two circles over her big bosoms. Once out in the yard she got down on her knees and showed him how to whistle the doodlebugs out of their holes. All day long he and Granny Ulvie would be together. Then a car would stop and his mother would light down and it would be suppertime. On some nights a rusty red truck would pull up and his mother would leave again. When they came here he found out the truck belonged

"The Lesson," from *Small Caucasian Woman*, by Elaine Fowler Palencia (Columbia: University of Missouri Press, 1993), 132–40. Reprinted with permission of University of Missouri Press.

to Caleb Wooten, who was his daddy now. At Granny Ulvie's there was a little black-and-white TV but here the TV was busted.

Sometimes after the boy was in bed, Lena would sit on the davenport and look at the blank television screen, imagining what would be on now. Caleb was gone a lot at night with his dog Buster. If he took the lantern it meant he was gone coon hunting. But most of the time she knew he went down to the Pit Stop at the crossroads. Sometimes he would eat dinner first and sometimes he would want it when he came in. The first meal she cooked for him, he threw on the floor because it wasn't fixed like he was used to.

Lena knew how to cook but Granny Ulvie had done most of the cooking, while Lena had gathered aluminum cans to sell to the recycler and later worked at the shirt factory. When she started they paid her below minimum wage because she was underage and the first week she stitched her hand. She thought she would live and die a factory girl until Caleb.

Tell my about my daddy.

Your daddy was the smartest man in the world.

How smart is that?

He had the dictionary memorized. And he had books.

How many books?

More books than anybody in the world. Maybe a hundred.

Why can't he come to see us?

He's busy learning things. He lives in a library, up in the attic.

Can I feel your stomach?

Here. Touch here. Feel that bump?

It moved.

That was its leg.

Who is it?

I don't know yet. It will be your brother or sister.

It feels like a puppy.

Caleb was gone all day. If he was working for himself, down in the field called the round bottom, he took Buster. If he was working for Mr. Pritchard, Buster stayed home. The farm was called the old Forrester place. If they got behind on the rent, a man named Charlie Carruthers came to see about it. Old man Forrester had dropped dead on Charlie Carruther's porch. The rent went to the daughter, a McDonald woman, in Ohio.

Besides the cooking and cleaning and washing, Lena was supposed to take care of the chickens and the garden. She was glad that Caleb's first wife had put in the garden before she died. The fresh vegetables would make a healthy baby. Granny Ulvie didn't have a garden, but she knew where to find wild mustard greens and dewberries and watercress in the woods beyond the railroad tracks.

Weeds had taken over since the first wife's death. One early morning Lena was untangling bindweed from the tomatoes when something peeped under her left hand, causing her to jump straight backwards from a crouch and land standing up. The chick had little blood dots on her head, like she'd been pecked by the mother hen. Lena figured it was because Nettie, as she came to be called, had a toe missing on one foot, which made her hop funny. Lena knew about the crowd shunning the different one. Every time she went to live with a new family and they put her in another school, it had happened to her. She took Nettie up to the house, washed off the blood and dried her dew-soaked fuzz. Then she and Irish wrapped her in a dish towel and put her in a cardboard box on the back porch. After that, Nettie didn't want to go back to the henhouse. She hung around the back steps all day, pecking for bugs and taking dirt baths. Whenever Irish or Lena went to the outhouse or down to the creek, she hopped along behind. By the time she got her feathers, she would eat corn out of Irish's hand and would ride on his shoulder all the way around the yard.

Tell me about how you came to live with Granny Ulvie.

This woman I was staying with, we were driving to Louisa and she stopped at the East Side Grocery there in Blue Valley to get lunch. She got us two cans of Vi-eenies and crackers and two Nehi grape pops. And I asked for a banana.

Did she buy you one?

No, she said I wasn't grateful and shoved me out of the car. Then she drove away.

And Granny Ulvie—?

She saw me crying on the grocery steps that day. That night I slept across the street on the porch of an empty house. The next morning Granny Ulvie came back to the store to get some milk and some peppermint drops. She had an upset stomach. I was setting on the steps again, so she asked me to carry the sack for her. When we got to her house, she fixed me breakfast and asked me about myself. Then she let me stay.

What if we had to sleep on somebody's porch?

Why would we do that?

What if Caleb gets mad like that woman and makes us leave?

Hush that. We'll be all right. We got a real home now and we won't do nothing to lose it, will we?

But when she was by herself she feared they might make a misstep at any time. In the bedroom, hers and Caleb's, the chiffarobe still held the first wife's clothes. Caleb would not let Lena empty a drawer for herself. When she asked him about it, he said he would see. She kept her things in two boxes against the wall and coveted a pair of black leather pumps in the bottom drawer of the chiffarobe, the first wife's church shoes. Under the nightgowns she found four photographs: posed portraits of three young families and a picture of a young woman with a long nose and close-set eyes, wearing a nurse's uniform. These pictures were all that remained in the house of Caleb's four grown daughters. Caleb said they were mean as snakes and he had gotten rid of them. They did not look mean to Lena and she wondered where they lived. Sometimes at night when Caleb and Buster were gone and the wind moaned and the house creaked, she wished some of them lived just down the road and would drop in of an evening. The nurse looked about her age. But she couldn't complain. Caleb had kept the promise he made because of the baby and married her two weeks after the first wife's funeral. They were married by a Holiness preacher over in Elf King, where his mother was buried. After the short wedding ceremony, he told Lena to get in the truck. Then he went into the graveyard beside the church and stood in front of his mother's grave and his shoulders shook.

One day when she and Irish were looking for stray eggs in the shackly old barn, they found something interesting. Or rather, as Irish pointed out later, Nettie found it by fluttering into a stall, where he went after her.

It was a toy, a simple little metal wagon, a box on four wheels with a shaft in front. Lena cleaned and oiled it. After lunch she made a little cloth harness from strips of feedsack, and by suppertime they had taught Nettie to pull the wagon a few feet. Practicing to show Caleb, Irish said, "Then he will like us for sure, won't he, Mama?"

At first Caleb did like the trick. Grinning and nodding he said, "Hey. That's all right. That's okay." But then he frowned and jabbed a finger at Irish. "A chicken is the stupidest animal there is. It'll drown trying to drink the rain. Stands with its head throwed back and beak open, catching rain till it chokes."

But Nettie was smarter than any other chicken, Irish thought as he petted her tiny skull. They were teaching Nettie another trick that Irish had thought of himself. She was going to be his alarm clock when he started school. By putting a trail of corn kernels up the stairs, they were trying to teach Nettie to go up to Irish's room of a morning. Nettie still slept on the back porch. They didn't have to worry about a varmint getting her because of Buster sleeping in the yard. While Caleb was down at the barn milking, his mother could let her in. Someday she would just need to open the door and Nettie would hurry straight up to Irish's room, not even needing the trail of corn. But for now, Mama had to carry her to the stairs and set her on the bottom steps and tap her finger on the step above, to show Nettie the way, and Irish had to sit on the top step and to call her.

Mama, when the baby comes, will Nettie still be my pet? Just mine?

Sure she will. We'll get the baby something else. What do you think he'd like?

I think he'd like a lizard. I could let him play *with Nettie. But she'll still be mine, won't she?*

Forever and ever.

How long do chickens live?

I don't know, honey. But Nettie will live a long time.

I love Nettie, Mama.

I do too.

As Lena got heavier, the air around the farm got lighter and cooler. Pumpkins swelled in the garden. One morning when she came down to the kitchen and looked out, frost silvered the grass. She placed both hands on the small of her back and pressed herself into an arch. A dull ache throbbed deep under her palms. Soon, she thought. Soon.

Nettie waited at the door. Bending gingerly, Lena scooped her up and carried her through the house.

At the stairs she called softly, "Irish? I'm sending her up."

Irish took the pillow off his head, rolled over, and sat up. Today was the day they were going to try Nettie at coming up the stairs without the corn.

"Nettie. Nettie," he called, and listened. After a long time, he heard it faintly: scratch flutter   flutter flutter scratch

"Oh, boy. Come on, Nettie."

scratch   flutter tap tap

"Up here, Nettie." He took the ear of corn from the nightstand and shelled a few kernels onto the quilt.

Downstairs, the kitchen door opened and shut.

Caleb set the pail of milk by the sink, washed his hands, and sat down at the table. "Where's the boy?"

"He'll be along." Lena put a plate of biscuits and a platter of side meat in front of him. She poured coffee in his cup and in hers and sat down opposite him.

Caleb split three biscuits and spooned gravy over them. "He ought to help you more. Sissified little town boy."

"He's only five."

"He don't need to be babying that chicken, either."

"You're right fond of Buster," said Lena.

"A dog's different. A dog does its job. I won't feed an animal that don't."

"But Irish is just a child."

"He ought to get started on being a man. Time I was twelve, I was doing a man's work. I was strong as a by God ox." He laughed through a mouthful of food and held out his arm, bending and unbending the elbow to flex his muscles. "You don't know how strong I am. Don't have any idea."

"Oh, I know," said Lena, reaching for the fried apples.

Caleb's hand shot out and clamped her wrist.

"Hey," said Lena.

He laughed again. "Try to get away."

Lena tried to pull her arm back. His fingers pressed into her flesh like steel hooks.

"Quit. You're hurting me. Be nice," she said.

"Be nice," Caleb mocked her. "Be nice. Is that what you're teaching Irish? I want him on time for breakfast. You'll make a damn woman out of him, letting him sleep away the morning."

"He's awake."

"Then why ain't he down here?"

Lena looked away but it was too late. He'd read something in her eyes.

He let go of her arm and pushed his chair back. "I reckon I'll just see what's going on."

Upstairs, Irish hung over the foot of the bed, peering down the dark well of the stairs.

With a last flutter, Nettie hit the landing.

Irish scampered to pick her up. Nuzzling her neck, he brought her back to the bed. While she pecked at the corn, he lay on his side and stroked her feathers.

"Man, Nettie, you could be in a circus," he said.

The landing creaked and he looked up. A sickening wave of weakness swept over him.

Caleb stood there, tall as a tree.

When they passed through the kitchen, Lena watched them from where she stood against the sink, holding her belly with both hands. Irish walked in front, barefoot and shirtless in a pair of cutoff jeans, his body so small and thin and white that Lena suddenly felt she had not been a good mother to him. His lips were tinged blue, as if he had been swimming on a cold day. He did not look at her, did not seem to know she was there. Caleb carried Nettie, and he did not look at her either.

Lena stepped to the door and watched them march out to the woodshed. Caleb put Nettie on the chopping block and held her down with a foot on her head. He gave instructions which Lena could not hear. Irish shook his head. Caleb cuffed him so hard that he fell backwards and sat down. When he got to his feet, Caleb gave the instructions again and Irish shook his head and Caleb knocked him down again. The second time Irish got up, Caleb grabbed him by the shoulder and pulled him over to the chopping block. He showed Irish how, while Nettie's head was pressed under Caleb's foot, to pull her body up sharply and break her neck. He placed Irish's hands on Nettie and held them there.

Rolling away from the door, Lena braced herself on the edge of the sink and vomited into it. She vomited until the dull ache in the small of her back turned to a blazing knot. While she was rinsing her mouth and splashing water on her face, Caleb came in and dropped Nettie's body on the drainboard.

Her voice came out a ragged whisper. "Where's Irish?"

"Run off." Caleb went back outside, got in his truck, and drove away.

Lena sank to her knees. Holding her stomach, she rocked slowly forward and backward.

Irish stayed in the apple tree in the back yard all morning. Straddling a fork high up in the leaves where nobody could see him, he laid his cheek against a smooth-rough limb and closed his eyes. After a while, he thought of something to do. First he made the ground around the base of the tree go away. Then the yard went away, then the house, and the outbuildings, and finally the fields and woods. The apple tree hung in blue sky. There was pure blue sky above him, around him, and under him. He sat in the apple tree and there wasn't anything else. He would live on apples forever. But that meant he would never see his mother again. He started to cry.

The back screen door opened and shut.

Irish caught his breath and hiccuped.

His mother stood on the back porch, shading her eyes and looking across the ravine that dropped off below the house. She was looking into the woods on the other side. Buster lay on the porch. When he saw she was carrying Caleb's twenty-two, he thumped his tail and got to his feet.

Lena looked down at Buster. "Good dog," she said, and slapped her leg several times, so that Buster followed her off the porch. Underneath the apple tree she stopped. Without looking up, she said, "Don't you go out of the yard while I'm gone." Then she and Buster went down the bank and across the creek, Lena picking her way clumsily from stone to stone.

When they had disappeared into the trees, Irish climbed down and went in the house. Upstairs he crawled under his bed where it was cool and dark and the friendly dust bunnies lived. Soon he yawned. Crying always made him yawn.

The next thing he knew, his mother was coming up the stairs calling his name. In the center of the room the light on the floor had turned a deep gold; he must have slept into afternoon.

"Irish? Are you up here?"

He stirred, scattering the dust bunnies, and sneezed.

The bed springs squealed as his mother sat down. Her feet were right in front of his face, the shoes caked with mud.

Tell me about my daddy.

Your daddy was a strong man.

How strong?

He could lift me over his head with one hand.

Stronger than Caleb Wooten?

I found something for you on my walk. Persimmons. Granny Ulvie showed me what they are.

Stronger than Caleb Wooten?

Don't get biggety with me. And get out from under the bed. You're not a baby.

When Caleb came home from Mr. Pritchard's, Irish was on the back porch, hiding outside the screen door.

Caleb sat down and unlaced his shoes. "Where's Irish?"

"He's around," Lena said from the stove.

"I want him eating dinner. That's part of the lesson," Caleb said.

Lena's voice hardened. "Irish! Get in here!"

Irish sidled inside and stood with his back to the wall, making himself as small as possible.

Caleb said to Lena, "Where in the hell's Buster? He didn't come out to meet me. I whistled and whistled for that sucker."

Lena turned the pone of cornbread onto a blue flowered plate and brought it to the table. She looked back toward the door and as her eyes swept around they caught Irish's eyes and held them just a moment; and in that moment, Irish knew.

"I haven't seen Buster since this morning," she said, and went back to frying the chicken.

◆ ◆

ELAINE FOWLER PALENCIA, whose poetry has appeared in such journals as *Sou'wester* and *Spoon River Anthology*, has published three mass-market novels under the name Laurel Blake. A graduate of Vanderbilt, where she studied with Allen Tate, she is also the author of a critically-acclaimed short story collection, *Small Caucasian Woman*.

DEBORAH ADAMS

HAGSEED

Years of mulch and compost had softened the upper layer of soil. Norea Greene, who knew nothing of gardening, had been seduced into believing that the earth would continue to give easily beneath her shovel, but the loose black dirt had soon given way to rock and hard red clay.

The cool night breeze was full of peppermint, throwing its scent in outrage at the way she trampled on the rampant growth. If anyone had walked across the open pasture behind the house, they would have seen only the shadow of a woman gardening by moonlight, and might have concluded that Sarah's ghost haunted her beloved land, standing guard over the ramshackle house and sprawling gardens, armed with her favorite black-handled knife and a steady faith in her own omnipotence.

Norea had inherited everything, even though she wanted nothing more of her mother's than genetics had already forced upon her. "Damn you," she muttered to the stubborn soil, out of breath and sweating. But she wouldn't stop until the last hairy root and rhizome had been eradicated and her mother's herb garden demolished. It would be a good idea, she told herself, to cover it over with concrete.

Sarah Greene had wanted to be close to her daughter, but she'd never been able to communicate with a flesh-and-blood child, tuned as she was to communication with the spirit world. For as long as Norea could remember, she'd been uncomfortable in her mother's presence, Sarah never having learned when not to talk of angels and demons. It was her father whom Norea had adored, a man of vision and rational thinking, who read to her at night not the tale of princesses and witches that her mother lived, but the words of philosophers and scientists, who faced the world and asked, *What is?*

"Sarah, we've gone round about this for the last time! It's a job to kill for, in a college town. Norea would have the benefit of the city! I'll be damned if your unnatural attachment to this farm is going to spoil it for me this time. We'll sell the house and take a lease on something in Denver. I've already looked into—"

"Damn your itchy feet! And your job, and all your notions about the great wide world!" Sarah's voice, usually kept soft in a deliberate attempt to mimic the astral voices she claimed to hear, seemed especially shrill and threatening.

Upstairs young Norea had covered her head with the blanket and tried to fall into a deep, dreamless sleep so the night would end sooner. She prayed her father would win the argument this time.

The shouting had gone on and on, until Norea heard the screen door slam twice, signaling her father's exit and her mother's frantic chase after him. The next morning when Norea went downstairs for breakfast, her father was gone, and her mother served up hot biscuits with honey, humming an eerie tune and smiling placidly.

Norea felt the loss for the rest of her life, while her mother continued as if all she would ever need could be found right there on the farm. Cowan Greene had been his daughter's hero and protector, her only hope for escape from her mother's world, and Norea knew he was gone forever. For years she prayed he'd return in the darkness, prop a ladder against the house beneath her window, and rescue her from the evil witch-mother who'd imprisoned her. But no prayer could bring him back, and Norea clung to the belief that he was kept away by one of her mother's spells. It was necessary, just that once, to believe in the power her mother claimed to possess, because the only other explanation was that her father had deserted her.

Driven by anger and desperation, Norea charted out her escape. She excelled in the subjects her mother scorned—math and science—and chose a university far away from the farm. She held a single-minded determination to do whatever was required to escape the dusty, lifeless town and the dull-eyed girls and slack-jawed boys around her who wanted nothing more than to get on at the mill, set up housekeeping in a double-wide trailer with cinderblock steps, and breed a herd of snotty kids to carry on the decline.

She met Larry at work. Falling in love was, for Norea, akin to torture. Her normally organized mind suddenly turned itself loose, shooting out thoughts and images that were neither logical nor productive, that came unbidden and always at the worst possible moment. The simplest daily tasks were excruciatingly difficult, because color and light and space had changed and if it was only her perception that was askew, that did not alter the fact that she was unable to function at maximum efficiency.

Norea pointed out the advantages of a brief courtship, building her case on the strength of common sense. Marriage, she reminded him, rewards its players with tax breaks, eliminates the expense of two apartments, and so forth. Being a man of logic himself, Larry agreed. They married quietly and quickly in a judge's barren office and went home to his efficiency apartment to await the return of normalcy.

It was only practical that she give up her job to follow Larry when he was transferred to Detroit. With the move came a promotion and a raise in pay, and Norea, with her qualifications and outstanding recommendations, expected to land a position right away, but the country was in a highly illogical recession, and the business world was caught in a panic of stagnation. This didn't bother Norea as much as it should have, for recently it had occurred to her that the time had come to have a child.

She spent weeks drafting an argument to present to her husband that would not expose the truth. She gave him a desperately contrived list of sensible reasons to procreate, and never, ever let on that her sole reason for wanting a baby was simply that her arms craved the soft flesh of a being who would belong eternally to her. She also did not tell him that she'd failed to use any method of birth control the last several times they'd made love.

Larry was easily persuaded. He latched onto the idea immediately and began coming home once or twice a week with baby rattles or teething rings, occasionally calling her Mommy. Norea was relieved that they'd come to an agreement but felt vaguely disappointed, although she couldn't say why.

There was no point in applying for a job once the doctor confirmed her self-diagnosis. In a haze of euphoria, drunk with the power of her own body to create life and nourish it, she decorated the nursery and learned to knit small items of clothing. After the child was washed from her womb in a torrent of blood, she cried too much and too often to seek employment. She clung to her sense of loss and half-believed the dark voice that whispered, *Mother's curse*.

Maybe it was the weight she'd gained and never lost, or the melancholy expression she saw in the mirror that caused Larry to stop looking at her. Most evenings and weekends he'd work late or attend a sporting event. If he stayed home, it was only to sit in front of the television, idly flipping from channel to channel, watching nothing.

By the time her mother's cancer reached its final stage, Norea knew that she was losing her husband and was frightened enough to have tried every suggestion she'd found in the women's magazines. Nothing had worked, and the emptiness in her abdomen expanded to fill her heart and soul.

"Go to your mother. She needs you," Larry had said one night.

Nonchalantly, as if his words hadn't shot terror through her, Norea said, "She doesn't need me. She needs professional medical care. If I don't go, she'll have to stay in the hospital where she belongs."

Larry, stretched on the couch, remotely wandering from sitcom to sitcom, debated with little fire but great practice: "There's nothing a doctor can do for her that you can't. At least if you're there, she can die at home. I know you aren't close, Norea, but give her that much. It's your last chance, for chrissake. Don't you have any compassion?"

It was the way he tossed the remote control away, as if he'd like to toss her away with the same disgust, that spurred her decision to go home. Larry must see in her all the warmth and tenderness that a man could ask for in a woman. Otherwise, she knew, there was no hope of keeping him. Now she wondered, had the child deserted her because it sensed something missing? A lack of kindness or mercy?

For two weeks she tended her mother, feeding her, bathing her, changing the soiled sheet protectors, and listening to Sarah's soft moans of discomfort when it was almost, but not quite, time for another injection of painkiller. Sometimes her mother whispered in a rambling voice, "You can't take my land, you can't take my land away from me."

She couldn't sit still in the cluttered house, watching her mother's bony chest rise and fall endlessly, so Norea busied herself with the tasks that would need doing eventually. She cleared the drawers and closets of clothing her mother wouldn't need again. Pots and pans and the black-handled knife were washed and stacked, ready for packing. The refrigerator was almost bare, except for the smell of rotting fruit that mingled with the odor of her mother's decaying flesh and spirit. In the cupboard, amid the boxes and cans of convenience food, there were Mason jars full of dried herbs and the special blends her mother concocted. In this one area, her mother had been organized. Every jar was labeled, not only with the name of the herbs it contained, but with clear instructions for use.

Valerian, Peppermint, Passion Flower, steeped for tea to calm the nerves and aid sleep.

Oak bark, Saffron, Witchwood, Ash, to aid divination and psychic power.

She pulled the jars out two at a time, setting them on the counter to be emptied into the fireplace. She'd hauled out a dozen or more when her left hand halted, as if stopped by some unseen force, above the jar labeled *Attraction*. *Apple peel, Birch bark, Vervain* the label said, and there were directions for preparation. She followed them to the letter.

Larry arrived two days later, just as the late spring sun dropped behind the hills, and barely an hour before Sarah Greene gasped, smiled, and died. Norea offered him coffee and food, but he refused both, sitting on the edge of a kitchen chair, nervously plucking at the hair that had grown too far over his ears.

"There's no reason to drag this out," he'd said. "We both know it's just not working, Nor. I'm not going to stiff you. You can have everything you want. All I really need is my freedom."

There'd been no hysterical pleading. That would have been useless, Norea knew, because she had seen the expression on his face so many times before. It meant he'd weighed the consequences and come to an irrevocable decision. She had no choice. Her mother's black-handled knife, waiting on the counter to be packed away, was the end to the argument.

If Norea had been satisfied with a shallower pit, her shovel would not have struck the tiny piece of metal. As it was, the first glint of moonlight on gold nearly escaped her. Flat on her stomach, head dangling down into the grave, she stretched out an arm to retrieve the ring. Drunk on adrenalin and bereavement, Norea accepted without question that it was her father's wedding band, and the yellowed bones were undoubtedly all that remained of Cowan Greene outside her own vivid memory.

Sliding the ring onto her thumb, Norea rolled her husband's body into her father's grave and covered it over with soil. In a day or two, she would plant her own herb garden on the spot.

• •

DEBORAH ADAMS, a seventh-generation Tennessean, was nominated for the coveted Agatha Award for her first book in the Jesus Creek mystery series. She lives on the banks of the Tennessee River near Waverly, Tennessee.

MARGARET RENKL

The Gift

"Marian Butcher, 37, was in the ninth grade when she met Ella Faulkner, 45. Little did she know she would one day become a kidney donor to the teacher who helped her battle her way through science. On July 23 in Memphis, Faulkner became the city's first transplant patient to receive a kidney donated by a friend instead of by relatives, spouses, or brain-dead donors."

—*Nashville Tennessean*, Oct. 11, 1993

In Memoriam: Ann West Granberry, 1943-1980

1. Nashville, 1993: At the Girls' School

Monday morning: I know I need a test, a project,
to startle them awake. I'm sluggish, too—
a cold I can't seem to shake—until they stumble in,
remind me again that half of being a teacher
is paying attention, the way they come into my room
or open their books can sometimes tell more
about what matters than test answers and themes.
This morning they bend, earnest, over essays
as I walk among the rows to see their pencils
clutched too tightly, their hair gleaming,
even under buzzing fluorescence, and brushing
their flushed cheeks. Still, quite, utterly
self contained, they're like sleeping children—
so perfect I can't be sure they breathe.
Kathleen sighs, and Courtney looks up in sympathy;
Abigail shifts in her chair. Across the room I grip
my hands to keep from reaching out to touch
a lock of hair, to brush it from a burning cheek.

2. Memphis, 1970: Ella

Her long brown hair's parted in the middle, falls
halfway down her back though it's clean and brushed:
she's no hippie but the new teacher, just out
of Southwestern, barely twenty-two. In the cafeteria
she doesn't know to skip ahead in line and waits
her turn among some seniors, boys who elbow each other
in the ribs and grin. Holding her tray she pauses
in the doorway, looks at the hunched shoulders,
the beehives at the teachers' table, then moves
toward a seat at the end. A colleague asks for salt.

3. Birmingham, 1978: Ann

A fight with a boyfriend, and I've cut my hair
to spite him who loved it swinging in his face
as he lay on the sofa in my parents' living room.
In English, first period, everyone is teasing,
wondering what the next spat will lead to:
Amputation? Castration? Excommunication?
Mrs. Granberry turns, distracted, from her notes
on Donne, calls the class to order, asks for our thoughts
on the epigraph to Meditation 17: *Nunc*
lento sonitu discunt, Morieris. A boy in back snorts
at *dicunt*, scribbles something in the margin.
She walks past me to have a look, ever so
slightly brushing a finger across the top of my head.

4. Nashville, 1993: Kathleen

End of the term, the worst of the year—time
for a pause, a breath, a brief celebration:

donuts and juice to surprise them, always
so hungry, complaining about the long wait till lunch.
This class is my favorite, and maybe they know it;
I wouldn't admit I have pets even among them.
Kathleen (who sits at the edge and misses no turn
in the poem, no twist in the plot) declines all
but the juice; the others descend like the toddlers
in my son's play group at snack time. I offer
seconds, but Kathleen still shakes her head.
"Let her nibble the boxes," Mary suggests.
"She won't eat anything unless it's fat-free,"
Courtney explains. Then the others start up,
remind me they aren't always the darlings
I like to imagine: they're offering Kathleen
leaves from the windowsill violets, a handful
of mulch from the bushes outside. I watch her
grin in good humor, and though I know she's not
in immediate danger—her athlete's muscles
are solid, her eyes bright, her hair gleaming—
still, I've seen girls wasted to bones in the past.
I'm at my desk when she comes looking, as usual,
for a calm place to study before practice begins.
She nods when I ask if she's dieting despite
her spare frame, admits she's all muscle and bone:
it's been six months since she bled. "I'm being
careful, I promise, but I just can't help wishing
I were pretty somehow." She turns back to her notes.
I look down at my book for a moment—where
to begin? Suddenly I can't trust my voice.

5. Memphis, 1970: Marian

Fourteen, Marian's new to everything: this town,
this school, this body. Holding her books close
into her chest, she sidles into Biology,
takes the only place left, up front, farthest
from the door. From the podium Ella waits,
then begins: "To learn about science," she says
in a voice so human to Marian's ear—a voice as young,
as hopeful as her own—"you must believe that even
the smallest things, the most silent, can change
everything in the world and should not be ignored."
On the front row Marian looks up from her notebook,
meets Ella's eyes. "The trick is to wake up.
Keep your eyes open. Miss nothing."

6. Birmingham, 1979: Ann

"I've been through this before—cancer runs
in our family. It's a tumor, just like the one
I found at sixteen, and the other at twenty.
I plan to beat this one, too, so don't start
thinking you'll get out of the final." She smiles,
but the class is still silent; no one looks up.
Her voice is steady, explaining; "I'll miss some days.
I'll leave lessons, but you're too old to need
a substitute teacher who just sits while you work.
I'll trust you to be good when I'm gone."
We look at each other, startled to be left alone,
frightened of what that must mean. She swallows.
"In time I'll need to wear a wig; you'll feel strange
at first, but we'll all get used to such differences.

Besides, the real work won't change—" Milton
and Wordsworth and Shelley and Hopkins:
Summer ends now; now, barbarous in beauty.

7. Memphis, 1970: Marian

"I hang around outside her room, inventing reasons
to stay—a question about the lab, advice
on how to manage my mother or talk to a boy.
She remembers so well what such things feel like,
I imagine she must feel them still, just as I do;
it's a relief to know I'm not strange. I wish
I could do something to help her, somehow,
to be useful, but I'm too old for clapping erasers
and emptying trash. Perhaps for Christmas
I'll write a note on her card, something to tell her
how thankful I am. Or maybe just wait."

8. Nashville, 1993: Kathleen

From the top bleacher her hair is ringed with that halo
gym lights bestow on blondes, and its wavering
is what I watch instead of the ball. I can cheer
with the others, rise at the right times, and still
not know the score, or even who's winning. I've come
because half the team takes my third-period class,
and they're all too intense; I want them to see
I know there's more to their lives than essays
and books. I worry for Kathleen, especially—
Kathleen, who could earn As hardly trying
but who even so takes down each word in her notes,
studies too hard for each test and polishes draft

after draft on the simplest assignment.
Let her hear me cheer, instead, what comes as much
from luck as hard work: height and strength,
the instinct to guess where the ball will go next.
In school I was clumsy and wooden, nothing
like this—after roll call in gym class I hid
under the bleachers to study—but I've learned
since then the wonder of bodies—the worth
of labor and sweat, the comforting grip of a hand—
and I know now to cheer while I can. No use
to tell Kathleen of all those nights I woke
over and over, afraid my child wasn't breathing,
too aware of how quickly flesh changes to dust.
She slams the ball over the net one more time.
What's to be said of such grace?
Only marvel, try to sustain it, and pray.

9. Birmingham, 1980: Ann

Her husband has dressed her in white, though I won't
go forward to look for myself. He and the boys are also
in white; the organist plays, to my fury, Beethoven's
"Ode to Joy" though no day in my life has seemed
less joyful than this. I've never been to a funeral
before, have no idea, yet, that the message of hope
is just one of the things that seem wrong this time.
To this church full of children, all of them stunned
at the price of mortality, "eternal life" is nothing
but talk. What matters are those boys, seven and five,
standing up at the altar next to their father,
each looking too much like Isaac at the altar of God.

10. Nashville, 1993: At the Girl's School

They wander in, not looking at me, comparing notes
on the history test they're all sure they failed.
I stand at the window and watch the leaves fall
on one more autumn she's missed, the season
she came to love best because of its courage.
"Margaret, are you grieving?" she would tease
after school—before she got sick—amid the red
dogwoods and gold maples where I'd waited to ask
one last thing before she went home. And even now
I am, I am. It's not just the leaves that remind me—
or the news full of that medical milestone,
a teacher's life saved by her student—or the Donne
we'll read today, when all the bells toll to recall
the lesson everyone finally learns. Whatever
I wanted, whatever I still curse or regret,
I could not save her life. Yet I've spent the last
thirteen years trying—hoping—to give someone back
what she gave to me, though nothing's enough:
grief has its own ways and won't be forgotten.
For now I turn from the window, open my book;
back in the corner, Kathleen raises her hand.

MARGARET RENKL is an Alabama native who now lives in Nashville and teaches at the Harpeth Hall School, a preparatory school for girls. Her poems recently have appeared in the *Southern Review*, *Manhattan Poetry Review*, *Poetry Northwest*, the *Texas Review*, *Painted Bride Quarterly*, and *Southern Humanities Review*, among others.

ANN PATCHETT

ELIZABETH GROWN

On the bus home I try to remember Elizabeth's face. I want to get a fix on her, to look out the window and imagine I see her, but every time I get close she moves just beyond my sight. I look around the dinner table, and I see all the kids and Mama and Pop. Everything is the same as I remember it, the side board on the far wall that holds the few pieces of my mother's wedding china that haven't been broken, the smell of biscuits mixing with the smell of the wisteria that grows around the casements of the windows. I can scan by Elizabeth's face, see it for a second, but when I turn to her, she slips beneath the tablecloth. She crawls around under the table, kissing us on the knees, tying our shoelaces together. She plays kid games, Peekaboo and I Spy. Now that she knows I want to see her face she's in heaven, laughing and clapping and running off, coming back with a napkin over her head. She knows she's got me and she won't let up. I spin in my chair, grabbing at her from the back, but she's gone, out the door and down the steps. From the window I see her dart by in a passel of girlfriends, through the yellow grass and out toward the creekbed. The grass is so tall and they are so small that they have to leap to get through it, and from here it looks like the leaping is the point of the game. All of them smile back towards the house, bare-headed, open, but I can't tell which one is her.

Out the window of this bus, I see the thick twists of trees are full of children. It's almost like they've grown there, and I wonder if the world has always been this way, full of children I have never seen before. When we go by, they rush the edges of the road and wave to us. When I wave back, they holler Hey! Hey there! For a minute I wonder if they want us to stop and take them on, even though they'd have no way of knowing where we're headed. I look to see if any of them look like Elizabeth, my sister. There are plenty of girls her size, but I can't tell for sure.

When I left home five years ago to look for work on the dams in Tennessee, I was

"Elizabeth Grown," by Ann Patchett, first appeared in *Epoch* 39, no. 3 (Summer, 1990): 225–32. Reprinted with permission from *Epoch*, Cornell University, Ithaca, N.Y.

seventeen and Elizabeth was seven. There were eight children between us and another one that came after her. I don't remember the day she was born or if the midwife came in time. I don't remember if there was one special doll she played with or who she liked or if she could swim. What I do remember is coming home one day and finding her in the front yard wearing my good shoes. They were fine shoes, spectators made out of white and brown calf leather. I bought them because I thought they were the kind of shoes a gangster would wear, a shoe that called attention to itself, a shoe that meant business. I had saved for them for more than a year without ever once thinking I'd have no place to wear them. I put shoe trees in them and kept them wrapped in tissue paper in the box they came in. When I took them out I would put the hall mirror on the floor of the bedroom and stand in them, stock still, so as not to bend them. From time to time I would let my brothers and sisters come in to watch the shoes with me. We were as quiet and respectful in front of them as we were in church, watching their bright colors against the faded carpet. Elizabeth, I guess, took more than her share of liking to them, because when I was gone one day, she took them out and walked them outside. They were so big they were slapping around on her little feet and she was laughing, and when I saw her I hauled off and hit her, whaled her one because those shoes meant the world to me. It had rained the night before and the ground wasn't exactly muddy, but soft. To see the dirt caked behind the heel and grass against their sides made me crazy. It's the only memory I have of her, just by herself, separate from all the other kids. I remember how I hit her and I remember how she cried. But even crying I can't quite see her, she puts her face in her hands and turns away from me.

It was just after that I got on with the WPA and left Alabama for Tennessee. My Pop had a bad leg that kept him from working most days, and no one needs to be told that these were hard times for money. I was such a big man, going off to work, sending every penny home to my family. When I left, my mama cried and turned away from me. "All grown up, this boy," she said.

I worked a lot of different crews in those years, but this last one was the hardest. Our boss at the site was a heavy man called Lovejoy who I imagine turned mean from all the fights he got into over his name. He had a thousand ways to ride us, always looking to start something so he could fire you. He knew how bad we all needed the work, and that we would take more than we ever thought possible so as to hold onto our jobs. Some weeks our pay would come in low, and he'd say, "I saw you sleeping out there." And not a damn thing you could do about it but work harder right in front of him. It was like he didn't think we deserved to have the jobs in the first place. And if you didn't like it, where were you gonna go? "Straight to hell," Lovejoy used to say.

For all the big things he did, it was the thing that would seem small to most folks that cut into us the most. He held up our mail. We were all a long way from home and so a letter was the only way we knew how we were doing, if our sweethearts still loved us, if our brothers had left home. Not everybody got to go to school like me, lots of folks went right into the fields alongside their parents as soon as they were able and never learned to write more than their names. So when the time came, the ones that didn't know how to write went to the ones who did and said their words slowly aloud, while the other one copied them down. *I am working very hard. The food is bad and I remember your sweet potato pie. I miss you.* The men here who didn't know how to read took their letters to the ones they trusted most and had them say the words over and over again. *When you coming home, now? I keep your picture close to me. I love you. I love you. Goodbye.* Lovejoy knew how we waited to hear from the world and so he kept the world from us. He'd tell you while you were working that you had a letter, and you'd squint up from the ditch at his big shape in front of the sun. Then at the end of the day he'd say, not good enough, and there'd be nothing for you that night. I think a lot of times a guy never had a letter at all, he just said it to make them work harder.

These letters made me feel like a great man. I would lie in my cot at the end of the day, my arms so sore I couldn't pull the shirt off over my head, and read them again and again. My Mama could write pretty good, and she would tell me where the money went, who got a new pair of shoes and how they were eating fine. She would tell me about the family, *Price has met a good girl. Lou tends the garden like it was her own child. Elizabeth is so smart, brought home all As and the teacher says she could be a teacher herself some day.* Then she would tell me about the people in town, the ones who were not as lucky as us. *The poor Averys down the way don't have a son as good as you. He went off and they never hear a word. Now they're getting old and I wonder, what will become of them this winter?* After awhile I stopped being so lonesome, because it was like I was more there than not. I felt the weight of all of them on me, and it kept me warm at night.

Lovejoy'd been riding me three days. "Groundwater, you got something smells sweet," and he'd pull an envelope out of his pocket and wave it in the air, then he'd hold it up to the light. "Baby, I miss you so bad," he'd say. "Groundwater, what you getting at home?" I kept my head down and threw the dirt straight over my shoulder, acting like I didn't care. I found with him the less you seemed to care, the more likely you were to get what was yours. After a couple of days of him not giving it to me, I figured it wasn't really mine. He was just pulling my chain. But he kept after me so hard I started to wonder, what if it is? What all could be inside? So the next day I worked like the devil and brought up twice the dirt of any man. That night it was there beside my plate and when I opened it up I found my sister dying.

"Come home," the letter said.

It is a sin that I thought first of Lovejoy and not of Elizabeth. I turned my direction toward him, the letter in my hand like a knife.

It was as hot that night as it had been all day, like the only difference between day and night was the light going away. He was sitting on the porch, rolling a cigarette with one hand.

"Hank, you come out here to share that love letter, or don't you know how to read? Give it here and I'll read it to you." He held out his hand to me.

I asked him how long he'd had the letter.

"You look all hot, son. I guess you found somebody to read it already. What did it say? That she's coming here to visit? Did she say she was coming here tonight?"

I asked how long.

He smiled and turned his head away from me. "Now normally I wouldn't remember such a thing, but a letter as hot as that one can be accounted for. It's been eight days now. Yes, came last Tuesday, a sizzler. Who could forget it?"

I wished it was a knife. I wanted the letter to turn hard and sharp. I wanted to cut his throat with the paper my mama wrote on. I looked at him in the little light thrown out by his dying fire and I thought, What kind of man would keep a fire going on a night like this? "Yes, Mr. Lovejoy," I held out my hand to him. "you read this to me. Tell me what the words say."

Oh, he was pleased. He puffed himself up like a preening bird and tapped his fingertips together. We didn't let him near our letters once he gave them to us, for fear he'd ride us into the ground over whatever little thing they said.

"Let me see about this," he said, starting out in a big voice. "My Dear Hank." He turns to me with a grin so big it eats up his face. "It breaks my heart to tell you Elizabeth has taken scarlet fever and we are all past hope she will survive."

He stopped there and read the rest to himself, going over every word twice, then he read it over from the beginning. You would think he didn't know much how to read, the way he struggled with something so simple. He used his clean hand to smooth it out against his leg and gave it back to me. I was hopping a little bit, up and down, waiting for him to stand up so I could kill him for killing my sister, since that's how I saw it then.

He didn't say anything for a long time and I kept waiting for him to get on his feet like a man. But he looked straight ahead, toward the place where we'd torn up the earth.

"I can give you money," he said. "You can get a bus out of here tonight."

And I knew what he was saying, because for a man like Lovejoy money would be all there was to offer. I looked down at the crown of his head, at the thin yellow hair that he wore slicked back. I thought, twenty years ago it would have been thick and the color of ragweed. He looked up at me. "My sister," he began but then stopped. I let him give me five dollars because I was sorry for him and then hated him all the more for making me sorry.

I thought she would be dead and buried and I would never see her face. I thought she would have died thinking her brother had not cared enough to make the bus trip home. So I decided to buy her something pretty, something that she would have liked waiting around for. When the bus pulled in I went to Cain Sloan's to spend Lovejoy's money. I bought Elizabeth a doll with glass eyes that clicked shut when you leaned her back. It cost more than he had given me.

"Is this for your little girl?" the sales girl asks me while she slips the doll into the sack.

I give a little start at the thought that I could have a daughter. "No, Ma'am, it's for my sister."

"Well, isn't she a lucky girl, having a big brother like you."

It's just past noon when I come up to our house. It looks smaller than I remember it, kinda turned down around the edges, but still it is the place I know best of all. I carry the doll up the road in the crook of my arm like a baby asleep. A baby asleep in a bag.

"Hank?" my brother says and stands up on the porch. He puts his hand over his eyes and peers out at me, like you would imagine a man on the bow of a ship doing, the guy whose job it was to spot dry land.

As he comes towards me I see that he is as big as me and I'm thinking, Price? Is that you?

Then suddenly they're all out there, my Mama and Pop and all these children. Each of them looks bigger than the last, tall and thin, all the roundness of them gone away. And

I keep thinking, didn't they get enough? Did I not send them enough? They kiss me and hold onto my arm and I think, these five years I've been gone, not a soul has touched me, not pulled at my neck or put my hand to their face, and I had never known to miss it.

"She's been waiting on you," my mother says when I finally get inside. She is wearing a dress I remember, a blue dress with a red chinaberry pattern. "Every day you didn't come I thought, this is another day she'll last. She's so tired now, Hank. This thing has her worn bare."

Because I had not thought of Elizabeth in the last five years, I cannot imagine she has thought of me.

"All the time she talks about her brother in Tennessee who sends his money to the family. The way she goes on, folks think you're a movie star. She was so happy when I told her I'd written for you to come. Didn't think about what that meant, only that you were coming back to see her. But these last few days she's lost her mind. It's burned her up, she won't remember now." My mother lowers her voice, like a girl telling secrets. "She talks all the time now, but you can't make heads or tales of anything. The things she goes on about. Poor baby doesn't know the words in her mouth."

When she first fell sick with the fever, they moved her from her bedroom upstairs to the pantry off the kitchen, where it seemed a little cooler in August. Only the doctor and my mother were allowed in to see her. My mother thought we would all take sick and die.

"I'll go in, too," I say. My brothers and sisters stay mostly out on the porch, as my mother had told them. They watch us from the kitchen window. I take Lovejoy's doll from the sack and lay her on the table. My mother picks it up and smiles at it like she's a girl, a girl who has never seen a doll before.

"She'll know you're here," my mother says, and smooths back the doll's hair. "She understands as best she can."

"But I want to see her, that's why I've come home." I look in my coffee cup and see part of my own face. I can't tell her the truth. I can't ask for a picture or a description the way I want to. What kind of man doesn't remember his sister's face?

"You'll do what I say," she says quietly.

From time to time my brothers and sisters forget and call out to their friends who live across the street. They laugh. Price has a girl who comes round, and he tries hard to stay sorry for Elizabeth when she's there, but a smile comes over him just the same. It's in their happiness I try the hardest to see her, but I can't be sure. What had she looked like on Christmas morning? What was the color of the dress she wore? In my mind she is always stepping away. I know that I have seen her a thousand times, running down the stairs, asleep in my mother's lap. I know I must have kissed her and put her on my shoulders. I promise myself that.

That night when everyone has gone to sleep I go to the kitchen and lay beside the door of the pantry. The tile floor feels cool and I lay my head against my arm. I can smell the wisteria, even though it's months past its time to bloom. It's as if it's been there so long that it's blown in through the windows and attached itself forever against the walls. Sometime later I hear a voice say, Portugal. I had fallen asleep outside her door and dreamed of Lovejoy's sister.

"Brazil," she says through the door.

"What?" I whisper, confused by the darkness and this new voice. "Elizabeth?"

"The valley of the river Nile."

When I stand up I feel the height of my body, it's like I'd grown in my sleep. Gone to sleep a child in my parent's house and woken up a man of twenty-three. When I step into the pantry, the heat of her comes to me. The room is completely dark for the safety of her eyes. The doctor had said that even the smallest of lights could blind her now. I feel my way to the edge of her bed, touching the jars of preserves and blanched beans for direction. I take her hand. It's large and heavy, and I press it into my own.

"Istanbul, Tokyo, Newfoundland."

Her voice is thick, as if her tongue had grown to fill her mouth. Her breath makes a labored roar like water through a broken dam.

"Do you need something? Is there something you want?"

"Tibet," she tells me. "The Cape of Good Hope."

I wonder where she heard of so many places. Who had told a child about the world? Had she meant to go everywhere?

"The Shetlands or the Isle of Skye?" She says the names slowly, as if she is asking me to choose between the two.

I think about it carefully, though neither is a name I'd heard before. It feels like it's all come down to me, that if I make the wrong choice everything will be lost.

"Skye," I say.

"Skye," she says to me and squeezes my hand.

She talks about places I've never heard of, listing their names as if she had seen each one. Some she likes better than others, she says their names twice and laughs like she's remembering a friend. I think of how well she must have done in school to know so much.

"Kilimanjaro, Mount Everest, Mount Blanc."

She talks for most of the night about exotic places, places I had never thought about, but after awhile I can tell she's pulling back, agreeing to settle for a little less. As the hours pass, she finds places that are easier to visit, places that with work she might have seen.

"Texas," she whispers to me, "Wyoming, New York City."

Now and then I add one to her list, a place I had thought of as a child. I had wanted to see Chicago and the gangsters. I had thought of California. She agrees with me. "California, Hollywood." I had forgotten what it was to be a young man, to wonder about the world and dream of other places.

I have half fallen asleep when she says Point Clear. It's Point Clear, Alabama, she means, not two hundred miles from Birmingham. She had gone everywhere and was headed back towards home. I'd been to Point Clear with my friends when I was fifteen. We had run away from home and hitched a train. With the boxcar door flung open, we would watch the things we knew rush up and then fall away, so fast that if you turned your head for a second you would miss your life. We thought we were men of the world.

"Yes," I say, and slip onto my knees beside her bed. "That's on the Gulf of Mexico."

"Mexico," she repeats.

"It's a part of the ocean, a corner of it. You can walk on the beach and sleep in the sand. You can swim and eat fried fish. I can take you there. I know how to go."

And then I know that's what I should have told her all along, that I will take her everywhere, that I have been everywhere.

She finally drifts into sleep. When I get up and open the door, it's morning and a pale light falls into the room. I see her there for the first time against the white sheets.

She isn't the person I was trying to remember. This girl is nearly thirteen and she's long in the bed, I would say nearly five and a half feet, taller than most full-grown women I've known. I'd forgotten that she would have grown. I'd thought all along that she would still be seven, just as I'd left her, as if my leaving would have frozen her life. The fever had made her hair fall out in clumps, and my mother had cut the rest short, in some attempt to keep things regular, but it is still the same hair we all have and without even thinking about it, I raise my hand to my head. Her face is thin and tired, but pretty in a way that makes me think how pretty she must have been a month before. The fever has made her darker, like she's been sleeping in the sun, like it was a hot day and she was swimming in the lake and then laid down in the grass and fell asleep. Beneath her sweaty nightdress are the makings of breasts. It's something I had never accounted for, that like the rest of the world Elizabeth had grown. Beside her on the bed is the doll I bought for her. It looks silly in her arm, small and young. Not a thing she would have chosen for herself. My sister is a pretty girl, old enough to have boys wait to walk her home, I hope, old enough for kisses.

I wonder how I could have missed an entire life. The life of my sister who loved me and who I loved. It's as if I had overlooked it while going through a huge stack of things. In this house with seven sisters and three brothers and parents who looked to me as a man, I had missed one life completely. By the fall of that night, Elizabeth is gone.

It isn't long after that I leave, too, heading back toward Tennessee, but with a feeling I won't be staying there. Price is older now, older than I had been when I first left home, and he would be there to help if I should fail. I had started to think of what else I must be missing in this world.

There is a tombstone in Birmingham, Alabama, with her name on it, Elizabeth Ann Groundwater, born nineteen hundred and twenty six, died nineteen hundred and thirty-eight. Much loved daughter and sister, it says. In the cemetery there are angels carved into stone. They are crying over names, their torches turned down. But for Elizabeth there are two wings pushing out from the top of the stone so we can believe she just flew away.

• •

ANN PATCHETT is the author of two novels, *The Patron Saint of Liars* and *Taft*, both published by Houghton Mifflin Company. She was a Bunting Institute Fellow at Radcliffe College in 1993-94.

STEVE WOMACK

LIFE'S LITTLE MURDER MANUAL

Chapter One—from a work in progress

I'd heard of the book. I mean, who hadn't? It had been on the *New York Times* bestseller list for over a year. *60 Minutes* did a feature segment on the author. Every woman celebrity anchor and interviewer from Diane Sawyer to Oprah to Sally Jesse to half-a-dozen others I'd never heard of had fawned over him on-camera. I opened up the Sunday paper a month or so ago, and there he was in the special slick magazine section: Robert Jefferson Reed surrounded by his beaming wife and three fresh-faced teenaged children, looking like they'd just come in from an afternoon on the slopes. His book was everywhere; you couldn't swing a dead cat in the Wal-Mart without hitting a copy.

But who would have ever guessed that a book called *Life's Little Maintenance Manual* would have been such a runaway smash hit? Or that the author would be from Nashville, Tennessee?

C'mon, give me a break—it's not even really a book. I picked it up at the Inglewood Kroger about six months ago while I waited in line—my Budget Gourmets dripping through the basket—behind some wild-eyed lady who was raving at the cashier. Something about the price of bacon or her food stamps being late or some such crap. I tried not to listen. You know how it is, when something really unpleasant is happening in a public place and you don't even want to watch, but you're stuck there, so you do anything to divert your attention, right?

Anyway, here I am with this lady screaming in front of me, so I reach down on the rack and pick this $9.95 paperback up and flip through it. It's oversized, ornate, but very thin and divided into four parts, each devoted to keeping one area of your life in tip-top shape. Part One tells you how to keep the physical side of your life humming. I opened to the first page of that part, and there in bold type about a half-inch tall was the admonition:

EAT YOUR VEGETABLES.

And that's it. That's the only thing on the page. There's a cute border around the edge, and a couple of swashes of color, but that's it. Eat your vegetables.

So I turn the page:

Drink Plenty of Water.

Jesus, I'm thinking, a tree had to die for this? So I flip to the second part, which is all about how to keep your marriage perking along.

Never Let a Day Go by Without Telling Your Spouse You Love Him (Her).

Now mind you, I'm not even Jewish, but expressions like *oivey* are beginning to run through my head. Meanwhile, the old lady in front of me in the checkout line breaks into a continuous stream of obscenities, like a Subic Bay sailor having a psychotic break in the middle of shore leave.

I open to page two of the section on marriage:

Never Go to Bed Angry.

I look up just as the screaming old lady slams down a carton of eggs on the conveyor belt.

Or at least not without your lithium, I thought. The cashier picks up the white courtesy phone by her register and calls for help, then starts wiping up yellow slime as the old lady rants on.

Part Three was on the care and feeding of children. I turn the page:

Patience Will Carry You through Anything.

The guy who wrote that sewage ought to be standing in this freaking checkout line.

Part Four covered the maintenance schedule for one's career.

Give a Little Extra Each Day

it advised.

Oh, puh-leeze, I'm thinking, somebody get me some insulin.

By this time, a security guard is trying to escort the old lady out as quickly and quietly as possible, only now she's pretending to have a heart attack. She screams and clutches at her chest, then paws at the security guard's face as she slumps to the floor. The manager comes over; apparently he's been through this with the old lady before.

I flip through *Life's Little Maintenance Manual* one last time. On the last page of the part about keeping your body in one piece is the exhortation:

Treat Yourself to Dinner Out Every Once in a While.

I take this as divine guidance. I set my by now flaccid frozen food boxes on the conveyor belt and step around the scrum of people hovering over the old lady. Then I got back in my car, eased out of the parking lot, and headed to Mrs. Lee's for Szechuan Chicken. That was the last I thought of Robert Jefferson Reed, his well-scrubbed family, and his thin little bestseller.

That is, of course, until the day his wife knocked on my office door.

◆ ◆

STEVE WOMACK, who is an adjunct professor of English at Nashville State Technical Institute, where he teaches screenwriting, is a widely acclaimed mystery and crime writer. His five novels include *Dead Folks' Blues*, which won the 1994 Edgar Allan Poe Award for Best Original Paperback Novel of the Year, and *Murphy's Fault*, which was a *New York Times* Notable Book of 1990.

SUSAN UNDERWOOD

I Sleep With My Grandmother

The house is pregnant
with cousins.

I wake with her old breath
drawing in and out
of my open mouth:
slow wind of supper onions.

She tarries over air.

I assemble attention
on her whistling mouth;
all my listening powers squint,
preparing for her sudden stillness.

Slowly, slowly I am a cup
for all her dwelling breath.

I curl, a sleepy ear
away from her

to face cold
wallpaper primroses,
their arc and twine

cast into dimness,
resembling hillsides
with shadows of mountains
beyond them.

Far below this hill
we house on,
the river surges through darkness
between swells of earth,
weaves under mist,
becoming my dream
as I bridge toward sleep.

She tucks her knees
up under mine
as we swim through this night,
warm fetuses of twin sleep
under dark
and churning quilts.

Light and Sound

Come with mornings in their mouths,
a league of fleet-footed farmboys,
wise with the whereabouts of wide meadows, gathered
from the Sugarhollow to herald the first of summer with softball.

Seven or so of them, whistling and hooting, stomped
to hustle the herd of angus heifers
and their black, bawling calves from the broad base
of the sprawling steep hillside where I spied.

Only wind arced my way,
rousing the ridge to a tousle as they readied,
mapping out indistinct boundaries of a diamond,
traipsing the trampled, nubbed-down timothy.

The towering two pines I took a place underneath
hovered far from homebase, and I hugged my knees to chest,
curious for their careful game,
hungry to hear their high voices
carried on air,
delicate as dandelion down-seed, as tender hearts of daisies.

Time and again it never varied:
their narrow voices vaulting sweet, and the vision

of the ball arched bold into azure, already
falling ground-ward or toward a gloved palm
before the close cracking call;
the spinning sight chased by the snap-whipped sound,
as thunder trembles after lightning,
as the blow of an ax breaks the air
seconds after the distant splitting stroke.

I waited for the chant, the welter and whack
after the wooden bat met the white-seamed ball,
the pitch of sound scattering.

Still, I was more eager for the mere sight of each stride,
each head of hair
blazing in sun, and the one boy running,
shirttail flying behind in shadow,
his feet bare, a bloom of light bursting
through sweet grasses, swinging swiftly for home.

SUSAN UNDERWOOD, whose work includes both poetry and fiction, is a professor in the English Department of Carson-Newman College. Currently she is writing her doctoral dissertation on the works of Fred Chappell.

LUCINDA HODGE

THANKFUL MEMORY

It's Thanksgiving, at my grandmother's house in South Knoxville. The weather is bright, clear. Only a few clouds powder the periwinkle sky. Accommodating.

He sits on the front porch, bathed in golden light, red paint peeling beneath him.

I stand beside him, memorizing. Every moment, every expression, every crease and crinkle. His eyes are listless, fixated on the lime green pond in the distance. His lips are thin, pressed together in unwavering silence. I try desperately to read the thoughts plowing through his mind.

He swallows and takes a few deep breaths. They are gasps. Already, I want to breathe for him.

He is the sun, orange and glowing, bright and brave. I sit down beside him, leaning closer to his sagging shoulder. His hands are clasped tightly together. His fingers gently tap the back of his calloused hand.

"It's a nice day," I say. "Weatherwise."

He nods weakly. "It's beautiful."

I try to think of something to be thankful about. It's strange, but I know he is thankful for everything. For my mother, whom he adores. For the years they had together. For life, and the good times he has had. The adventures, the dreams that came true, the ones that didn't.

It's his last Thanksgiving Day, and we both know it.

We should still have hope. After all, the doctors haven't said there is nothing that can be done for him.

But we know that tomorrow that news will come. That there won't be any way to save him from the cancer racking his body. We have faith, but no hope. He will die, and already we are accepting that fact.

I lean closer to him. His jacket is pulled tight around his frail shoulders. He shivers beneath it. The sun is not warm.

I sit quietly, savoring his presence. Next year I won't have it. Next year, I will sit on the same porch without him and remember this moment, this precious, precious moment, frozen forever in my mind.

If I could see the future, I would tell him how miserable the next six months will be. I would tell him how many nights I will cry myself to sleep. I would tell him how many times I will stop by the door of the living room, peering into the darkness, to make sure his chest still rises and falls.

I would tell him how guilty my mother and I will feel when we eat out, or when we eat in, or when we eat. He won't be able to, and it doesn't seem fair that we can. I would tell him how we will watch helplessly as he struggles to swallow, as he sleeps restlessly and shrinks daily. I would tell him how I will pray for him to die when I see those precious hands clutching his head, screaming in pain, asking my mother what he has ever done to deserve these headaches, this pain.

I would tell him how proud I will be of his courage. How I will resent many of our church members for not coming to see him. I will watch him stare out the window, up the road, longing for company, for reassurance that he hasn't done anything wrong, and I will hate them for their absence.

But he will hold no grudges. He has made that discovery, found that fortunate wisdom. Time is too precious to waste with that. He would tell me that, if he could see.

And if I could see, I would tell him that he is my hero, that I love him and appreciate all he has done for me, that I will carry him forever in my heart.

But we can't see, and we say nothing.

The air is thick. Birds are singing. He loves listening to them. When he is gone, I wonder if they will ever sing again.

"Where is everyone?" he asks.

"Inside arguing politics," I say.

He grins. "I'm glad we're out here."

I smile. In the midst of it all, I know his humor will endure. I know that someday I will walk down the street, and his "corner of walk and don't walk" joke or "Life is too short to be in a hurry" advice will filter through my mind, a melodious echo of times past. I know we will have other precious days in the months to come, days when we search for my mother's Valentine's Day gift, or when he eats his last onion ring or when I sit quietly and watch him sleep.

But for now, we stare into the sunlight, into its promise of eternity, each of us lost in our own thoughts, thoughts each of us will never share with the other.

He shivers.

I clutch his arm. "Do you want to go back inside now, Daddy?"

He nods.

I sigh. This precious moment must end. We must return to the business of living.

For as long as we can.

• •

LUCINDA MICHELLE "MISSY" HODGE is a 1991 English-Journalism graduate of Tennessee Technological University in Cookeville. Currently a legal secretary in Knoxville, she has had several articles and feature stories published in various newspapers.

JEFF HARDIN

Pickwick Lake

"Pickwick was never the wind. . . ."
—Charles Wright

It's now fifteen years
since I started school in Savannah,
river town lodged in a bend of the Tennessee,
town so obsessed with the river
its boys fresh from high school
give themselves to it as their lives'
first occupation, first testing ground.
It is the brown flow and monotoned drawl
their lives have always known. Behind
Pitt's store, above the rock bluffs,
they pitch tents and build fires
to sit all night and talk their dreams,
to listen to the river, to the story it tells
about their fathers and uncles,
their grandfathers: *I am the woman*
you love beyond words.

From the beginning there was the river
and then there was Pickwick, magical sound
in all our childhood ears. At school
I could never sit still knowing my brother,
younger, was there with our aunts,
swimming in the lake, his skin turning
brownish gold in the sun. Pickwick

was the sun we carried with us,
which we thought our lives would become.
Even now, sometimes, I still do.

The last time I was home in that county
my grandfathers made, I drove the new-paved
roads off 69, followed them past where we camped
on Porter branch, past Gordon's One-Stop
to the Bruton side of the lake.
From the boat dock I watched the lake
open wide and spread downriver
toward the dam and bridge, where at night
the lights from that bridge
are enormous from any shore.

My shore is the afterwards, the long look back
at the past, all I really have and more.
Those lights still hold me as they did
those years ago through the car's back window
when Pop turned us toward home and said
school will come early in the morning.
How those lights flashed in my closed eyes
when I couldn't sleep, thinking of sandbars,
of speedboats, of the barges with their
waving men. In his bed, already, my brother
was adrift in his boat, his breathing the waves.

There are days the soul of waves is inescapable.
I feel my life forgetting what could save it.
Those long days, the Pickwick inside me rises,

burns away the fog, the way it does
on any weak-kneed morning above that lake
in southeast Hardin County,
south of Savannah, south of home,
though, oddly enough, upriver.

My Father Cuts Wood in the Rain

Hat tilted, coughing hoarsely, he climbs
the leaf-slick hill from the hollow,
gets back in the cab to wait out
the storm's stiff face and feel his own,
to warm the white-shocked hands
flaked as bark I'll watch until they're mine.
The tailgate is open, the truckbed cleared.
I've no idea how long he'll sit.
Against his legs he rubs the hands,
front then back, back and forth,
but the bark-scratch soul won't fade.
His hands are too worn for this work,
and I am twelve. He'd tell me no
if I touched the saw. Water films
the windshield, and he coughs
and shakes his head. The boat's
called him back and the back porch is empty.
Winter will come before he's home again.
He's waited too late, but he doesn't yet
say so, and tomorrow he leaves for the river's
thin, twisting channel, the slow unraveling
of two more cold-wheelhouse, radio-staticked months.
Pop, I want to ask, because he's silent,
because I know the wood will not be cut today,

exactly how lonely is your life out there?
But I don't dare. He would never tell.
He's found the blood back in his hands,
looks hard through the windshield
for a break in the clouds. I stare
down that hollow for what answer I know.

• •

JEFF HARDIN, born in Savannah, Tennessee, in 1968, is the eighth generation of his family to date from the founder of Hardin County. In 1990, he was a fellow at Bucknell University's Stadler Semester for Younger Poets. Twice nominated for the Pushcart Prize, he also twice has received an Academy of American Poets Award (1992 and 1993). Currently he teaches at Columbia State Community College in Columbia, Tennessee.

CANDANCE J. WEAVER

FOR H. B.

I remember long, blond strands of angel hair
with a scent I couldn't name
but wanted to infuse the air.
Scissors were forbidden
unless in my hands,
and then you trembled.

You turned the tables on me
in the front seat of your car
with your tongue in my ear
and the tiny silver chain
that I tried to put on wrong
around my neck,
but you slipped it
gently
around my waist,
with fingers calloused
and bleeding.

I still have it,
tarnished,
in a box.

I made you angry
when I
would not make love with you
because I found another one
who didn't scare me,
threaten to eat me alive with
passion.

Now it is I
that hungers
again
for a scent
I cannot name
and your tongue
and your music,

But they tell me
you have consumed
yourself.

Firedog

Firedog,
you cradled my burning body
until it fell away to
ash.

Your metal
stood the heat
and hammering heart.

You are
stronger
than I am
hot,
immune to smithing.

Correspondence

You are the clean, white vellum,
the vast empty page
where I tried to write my name,
my poem,
my story,
your edges sharp,
like shattered milkglass,
where I cut my fingers,
my pencil slipping
off the page.

I am the rice paper
thin
and uneven,
where you pressed too hard
to inscribe your
agenda,
fractions,
formulas.

My corners curled and creased.
Holes appeared
in the center
from the weight of your instrument,
the names of our unborn children falling through.

◆ ◆

CANDANCE J. WEAVER began writing poetry as a child and now is assistant professor of English at Pellissippi State Technical Community College. A member of the Knoxville Writer's Guild, she appeared in their 1994 publication *Voices from the Valley*, and she recently was awarded second place in the Tennessee Writers Alliance poetry competition.

BETH WALKER

WHY MY MOTHER SAYS I DREAM OF STAIRS

First, two steps and out the door, then down two more:
that's how, mother told, I got from the drive to the road.
Too late, she heard the door creak, pitiful and weak
like my throat when I have the Strep.

Clutching at her blouse, not even buttoned to the waist,
she ran—though she doesn't recall screaming:
"STOP!" "BETH!" "MY BABY!" or some such;
though now we're both sure she must,

as certain as I am of the way her breasts
full from their year's store of maternity,
must have fallen, forgotten, before the man
who stopped his car, stepped out, and did not let me cross.

"Why My Mother Says I Dream of Stairs," by Beth Walker, appeared in *Widener Review* 10 (Fall, 1993): 85. Reprinted by permission of *Widener Review*.

ARROWHEADS

near the Obion River, November 1990

My breath hangs cold, thick as loam,

as I look for arrowheads flushed
into the bottomland in flood seasons,
now drained, frozen, slabbed like winter meat,

silt gritting under my feet
like the hunter's bone-worn teeth
just before bow-strike.

This is the first winter I know
without water here, this place
Chickasaw said leaked too much to stay.

Now their spirits stale, linger for rain,
their tribal whoop a gasp,
cracked, split like ice-packed soil.

I come for atlatl and clovis points,
piercing the leathered layers
like half-exposed last secrets

of medicine men, warrior princes.
Instead of stamping back the cold,
my steps echo the flick and spark

of arrow-stone on grinder's stone,
echo the blood-spurt in animal flesh.
Numb, I seek the still-sharp edge

against satisfied Indian thumb.

◆ ◆

BETH WALKER is a native and resident of Rutherford, Tennessee, whose poetry has been widely published. An adjunct instructor in English at the University of Tennessee at Martin, she is currently completing a master's degree in English and creative writing at the University of Tennessee at Knoxville.

JEROME WILSON

The Witness Tree

The sun ain't up when I wake this morning, but I still don't hear Big Ma in the kitchen. I don't even smell bacon tickling my nose. I get up and put my clothes on, then I peep over the hanging quilt to see if Thomas is still sleeping in his bed. But he not there.

I go to the kitchen, but they're not there, everything looking the same way as it was yesterday.

I go to Big Ma room—it's sort of dark in here 'cause the sun steady trying to come up—and I see her sleeping in her bed. And there's Thomas, looking like a graveyard ghost, sitting on her bed, shaking her real hard even though she not move. I just stand in the doorway and look. Thomas steady shaking and don't stop until he see me, then he get off the bed and run and grab hold of me.

We go to her bed and I bend down and shake her, just like Thomas did. But when she don't wake, I put my head down next to her arm and start crying. I'm crying so hard that it look like it's raining in Big Ma bedroom. Thomas—he start pulling all over me like he don't know why I'm crying. "Big Ma dead," I tell him. But I don't know why I say this, being since he stone deaf and can't hear what I just said. "Big Ma dead," I say again, just in case he can hear. He put his head down next to mine and he cry, too.

I go get Thomas ready and we start walking down the road. Not too long before we see Trish's house and see her sitting on the porch. I holler her name.

Trish look up, see it's me, and start smiling. She put down her bowl of peas and holler my name back: "Jessie Leigh!" Thomas already run up in the yard and hugging her. I start crying when Trish look at me. She start running at me, but then she forget about the baby and go back and pick him up, then she come out here to me.

"Big Ma dead," I say. "She didn't wake up when I shake her this morning. I didn't

"The Witness Tree," by Jerome Wilson, appeared in *The Final Word* (University of Memphis) 1, no. 1 (1994). Reprinted with permission of *The Final Word*.

hear her in the kitchen. Big Ma dead," I say again just in case she didn't hear me the first time. We hug each other, our baby in the middle. Trish—she my best friend.

We go inside—Thomas already in here playing with Mr. Curtis. Mr. Curtis is Trish husband. He real old; I don't know how much, but his hair is starting to turn white.

"Hi, there, Jessie Leigh."

"Hi," I say, and that's all I say 'cause I'm steady wanting to cry some more.

"Miss Mabel just passed," Trish tell him.

"Oh," he say.

Me and Thomas stay up at Trish house all day today. Later on, Mr. Curtis gone up to the square—to drink probably, which is something he always doing when he ain't sleep. He took Thomas with him 'cause he like Thomas and Thomas like him.

We sitting in her kitchen sewing Big Ma's passing gown. Trish main one talking—talking about getting Big Ma ready for her wake. "I'll get Curtis to build Miss Mabel a nice box," she say. But I still say nothing.

When we finish up Big Ma's gown, they come home—Mr. Curtis as drunk as he want to be, just like Trish said. "Hi, y'all," Mr. Curtis say, tipping a hat off his head like he never been inside his own house before.

"Fool." That's Trish.

But here come Thomas, and he wobbling, too.

Trish jump up out of her seat. "Curtis, has Thomas been drinking?"

"No."

Trish grab Thomas and smell his breath. "He has! What kind of fool do you think I am, Curtis?"

"I don't know, baby," Mr. Curtis say. "What kind you want to be?"

"Don't you mock me, Curtis Brownlee Taylor. I'll scratch your damn eyes out."

He laugh some more, then grab and hug her.

"Don't you touch me!" But she laughing, too.

I look at them and I smile; but then I look over at Thomas and get sick cause he just threw up on the floor.

"Lord." That's what Trish say.

Later on, Trish make popcorn for us to eat and after that we go to bed. I lay awake listening to the night, then I think about how Big Ma doing. The last thing I hear tonight is Mr. Curtis making a heap of noise—as drunk as he still is—steady hammering away on Big Ma's box.

This morning, me and Trish and Thomas get ready to go up to our house to get Big Ma ready. Before we leave, she try to get in touch with my daddy who's living in Memphis, but she can't find him.

Trish go behind her house and get that rusty—it used to be red, but it's old now—that rusty wagon that we used to ride each other in long time ago. We put the box across it and head on down the road. Thomas pulling the wagon 'cause that's something he like doing. Me and Trish hold the box at each end so it won't fall off, being since this road is real bumpy.

Before we can get up in the yard good, here come Dudley out from under the house and get to barking. But when he see who it is, he come out here with us. Thomas let go of the wagon and run off with Dudley. So, I got to pull and guide the wagon the rest of the way home almost all by myself being since Trish really can't help too good 'cause she steady holding the baby.

Inside, me and Trish stand around Big Ma's bed. I'm scared to look so I cover up my face. But when Trish pull back the cover I have to look. She don't look scary; she look like she sleeping.

"Go get some hot soapy water and a towel so I can wash up Miss Mabel."

I go make the water. When I get back, Trish got Big Ma naked. I stand and look. She look like a monkey with no hair. I look so hard 'til Trish say, "Hurry up, baby."

While Trish washing Big Ma, I go get Thomas and we go bring the box in the house and set it on the kitchen table.

"Go find a nice clean sheet and line up the box," Trish say.

I go outside and get the bedspread that Big Ma hung day before yesterday.

Thomas come over here by me and both of us carry the bedspread back inside the house, holding it up real high so it won't get dirty.

We put the spread in the box. I'm doing the spreading 'cause Thomas just run outside.

I go back in the bedroom and Trish already got Big Ma in her gown—Trish got Big Ma hair made up real good; her face cleaned up real good, too, so the light hit it nicely and make this pretty shine being since Big Ma always had good skin anyway.

"Big Ma look pretty," I say.

"She sure does." That's Trish. "Where's the box?"

"Kitchen table," I say.

"Okay, help me get Miss Mabel in there. Here, grab her legs."

I do, even though I don't want to, but I do anyway. She feel funny; she feel cold. Not cold cold. But just cold. She so little that I could have, or Trish could have picked her up all by ourselves, not weighing no more than a big basket of peaches.

We in the kitchen now and then we lift her up and try putting her over into the box. She don't fit this way, so we turn her this way. But she don't fit this way either. We keep moving her in and out of the box until Big Ma hair come undone. Finally, we find out that Big Ma won't fit in her box at all. So Trish holler out: "That damn Curtis Taylor made this box too damn narrow!"

I start crying and run to my room. I hear Trish bring Big Ma back to her bed, but I'm steady crying.

"I'll be back, Jessie Leigh," Trish say real mean-like, so Mr. Curtis is going to have the devil to deal with when she get home. She get the baby, who Thomas been having all this time outside, and she go. There she go, walking—marching down the road like there's a real war somewhere.

I might been sleeping for a long time 'cause I wake up at Thomas shaking me; and when I open my eyes, I see him looking at me real scared, but when he see me see him, he gets real happy and hug me.

Later on this afternoon, I go outside and get the wagon and start pulling it down the road, Thomas walking with me. Then Dudley see us walking and he come running out here, barking and jumping around 'cause he real happy.

And I here I go walking—Thomas and Dudley just jumped in the wagon and I'm pulling them. Town ain't far, so it ain't long before we get on the main road that will take us where we going.

This road mighty bumpy; the wagon jumping everywhere every time it hit a rock or go down off in a hole, making Thomas and Dudley jiggle around inside the wagon—but we steady go on and not stop.

I hear a car or truck coming up behind us. I don't turn around though. I will wait 'til it get up next to us. Dudley barking up a fine storm now, which making Thomas looking at whoever it is. I look over and see Mrs. Massey—this nice white lady Big Ma use to work for.

"Jessie Leigh," she say, "I just came from your house yesterday. Where's your grandmother? Is she sick?"

"No, ma'am," I say. "She ain't sick."

"Then why hasn't she been to work?"

"She dead. She didn't wake up and I didn't smell no bacon in the kitchen and then—hush up dog!—and then we got ready and went up to Trish house."

"Who is Trish?"

"Trish—she my best friend."

"Where is she now?"

"She gone home to cuss Mr. Curtis out."

"No, Jessie Leigh. I mean your grandmother. Where is your grandmother?"

I say, "She on her bed now."

"*Now?* Where was she at first?"

"On the table," I say.

She look at me for a long time, then she look at Dudley, lying down in the wagon breathing real hard from all that barking; then she look at Thomas, who steady sticking his tongue out and making faces at Mrs. Massey. She breathed out real hard then she say: "Jessie Leigh, why was your grandmother on the table?"

"We was trying to put her in her box but Mr. Curtis made the box too little 'cause he been drinking too much. Now Trish gone to cuss him out. She say she be back though."

For a long time she don't say nothing again. Then: "I got to go over in Madison County, but I'll be back late this evening to see Miss Mabel. Hear?"

"Yes, ma'm," I say, and that's all I say, 'cause I'm tired of talking and ready to get into town.

"Bye," she say, then she drive off bringing up all this dust off the road, making Dudley bark all over again, making me and Thomas squint and rub our eyes.

For a moment we blind, the dust so thick; but then the dust start cleaning up and we can see, so we steady tread on.

I leave the wagon in the sidewalk and go in the General, walking through the door they got for us in the back, leaving Dudley in the wagon nodding, Thomas holding my hand 'cause he not too sure about this place.

This place—Harper's General Merchandising Store—smell good. It smell like Christmas: candy and apples and oranges and a heap of spices, foods and stuff.

"May I help y'all? My shelves full of peaches if you coming to sell me some more." This here Mr. Harper. He own this store. He used to buy my Big Ma's jarred peaches.

"No, sir. I ain't selling no peaches."

"Then what you want?"

"A box."

"A big box," I say.

"What you going to put in your big box?"

"My grandmama," I say, getting tired of him asking me all these questions.

"Your grandmama? Who? Mabel?"

"Yes, sir," I say. "She didn't wake up instead of cooking breakfast, then I got ready and went and got Trish so she could . . . but Mr. Curtis box he made was too little and Trish say. . . ." I'm about to cry, so I get quiet; I cover up my face with one of my hands, so he won't see me cry; my other hand I'm steady holding onto Thomas.

For a long time he don't say nothing, then he go: "You go outside out back, by that big pile of wood. There's two crates I just put out there yesterday that Mr. and Mrs. Campbell's coffee tables came in. You get yourself one of those and—is that your old rusty wagon out there where that dog is?"

"Yes, sir," I say, steady trying to hide my face.

"Okay, you get yourself one of them crates and put it across that wagon and you put Mabel in that. Hear?"

"Yes, sir." I don't move, but steady standing there hiding my face and holding Thomas hand.

"Go on and do like I say. Mabel ain't getting no fresher."

Me and Thomas hurry on out the store.

We back on the road with the crate on our wagon. I'm pulling, Thomas holding the crate. We ain't on this bumpy road a long time when one of the wheels pop off and the wagon turn over. I try putting it back on, but it keep popping off, so I leave it in the road. Now, me and Thomas got to switch up: he doing the pulling, and I'm bending over holding up the wagon where the wheel used to be and we bring Big Ma's new box on home with us.

I clean it out real good, then I line it up with the same bedspread. I go get her and put her in her box. She fit real good.

"Jessie Leigh! Where you at?"

"I'm in the kitchen," I holler back at Trish. I'm standing beside Big Ma so I can see how happy Trish going to get when she see that Big Ma got a new box.

I hear Trish coming, she already talking even though she not in here yet. "I still can't get hold of your daddy and Curtis is going to make another box and folks are going to be coming to Miss Mabel's waking so we need to clean this place up before. . . ." She stop when she get to the kitchen, looking at me, then looking at Big Ma. She look like she might cry, even though there's nothing to cry about. Finally, Trish say, "Miss Mabel's new box looks just fine. Just fine."

I'm happy.

Our house packed. Folks from everywhere here. There's Mrs. Fannie Taylor and her twin sister Miss Frances. Mis Annabelle, Mr. Cook, and his wife Mrs. Cook. Mr. Ford and his oldest, Eva. Mr. and Mrs. Williams—that's Sonny Buck's mama and daddy, Terry's mama and daddy—Terry here, too, with his bad self—Miss Linda, Miss Teresa Jackson, and a heap of other folks I don't know.

They brung food. It's so much food in Big Ma's room 'til every time I go back there to peep at it I get dizzy. So I quit doing that.

In the kitchen, the older folks sitting around Big Ma talking every now and then, 'til somebody get to singing church songs, even though Big Ma wasn't the churching kind, but they sing anyway.

Me and Trish—we got the kitchen looking real nice—plenty of candles everywhere so it look real holy like.

Miss Frances walk in the kitchen—she wearing this real loud purple dress—she walk in the kitchen and look over in Big Ma's face. She look like she might cry, she looking so sad. Then she step back and read what's on the side of Big Ma's box: THIS END UP. "This end up? Hell, don't y'all know which way this woman suppose to go in the ground?"

I start crying. Trish tell me to be quiet; she tell Miss Frances to shut up.

"I didn't mean nothing by that," she tell everybody. "You know, I buried my Reggie several years back. Dead folks don't mind you having a little fun."

"Now, how do you know?" This Mrs. Taylor, Miss Frances sister.

"'Cause Reggie told me."

"Frances, quit your lying."

"I ain't lying, girl. I talk to Reggie all the time. He used to scare me, but I'm used to him now. He's a damn good spook. That's 'cause I gave him a good waking. We sang, we danced—hell, we had a ball. That's how you make good with the folks on the other side."

"Ah, Frances," say her sister, "you talking foolishness. Hush up and sit down somewhere, now."

"No, I ain't talking crazy either. Remember Sam Davis? That crazy fellow in Madison County with that funny walk?"

"Yea," everybody say.

"Well, how y'all think he got to walking like that?"

Mr. Ford say, "He fell out of a tree 'cause he been drinking."

"Nope," Miss Frances shaking her head, making sure nobody say different. "That's what he tell everybody to keep from telling the truth. You remember Raymond Brown? that big black nigger that used to live up there on old man Rabbit's place?"

Everybody say yea.

"Well, Sam Davis owed him some money and he never did get around to paying Raymond. And when Raymond died of pneumonia, Sam said now he don't have to pay Raymond that money back. Well, about two years later, you can just imagine who came knocking on Sam Davis door one night just as bold as he want to be."

"Who?" I holler out.

"Raymond Brown," Miss Frances holler back.

"Frances, you lying!"

"No, I ain't," her eyes getting bigger. "He told Sam to give him his money he owe him. Course, Sam as scared as he want to be, but he tell Raymond that he ain't about to give good money to a man who been dead for two years."

"Then what happened?" I ask.

"What you think happened? Sam Davis got his ass smacked by a damn spook. Smack his head so hard 'til his head is tilted to one side to this day. That's why he walk so funny, he thinks the ground is crooked and not his head."

"Hush up, Frances," her sister say again, "you not doing nothing but talking crazy."

"Well, believe me if you want to," and that's all Miss Frances say about that.

We sit for a long time helping Big Ma pass on through. Tonight we bury her. Mr. Curtis already dug a grave—Trish already been out checking to see if it's big enough—out there under the biggest peach tree in our front yard.

It ain't a big tree, but it got a whole big field by itself. It look like it is looking at us, like it's trying to figure out what in the world we doing, digging a big hole where it is standing and dropping stuff off in there—probably on its feet—then we standing around it doing nothing but looking down at the thing we just put in the ground. Or, this tree remember me and my brother Thomas and my Big Ma picking peaches off its branches every day, every summer—and now it's real sad, too. It look real sad; even though it is dark out here (some folks got flashlights, holding it for Mr. Curtis, who steady packing the dirt on Big Ma) you can see the branches and they drooping over like they weeping. Yes, it's sad, too. Mrs. Massey drive up and she come stand out here by the grave with us, everybody looking at her real hard, 'cause she's the only one who ain't black, like it's her fault.

The preacher man say a few words, I can't remember what 'cause I'm now crying. Trish and Miss Frances try to hush me up, but I'm steady crying. Thomas holding my hand and he crying, too.

After awhile, we come on back up to the house. Now everybody start eating, but I go to my room and look out the window where Big Ma at now. The tree look like it is watching the grave, then it look like it is looking at me, too—real sad like. I look at this tree for a long time, then I lay down on my bed 'cause I'm real tired and real sleepy. Later on tonight, I feel somebody trying to get me up and make me eat, but I don't get up. Before falling off to sleep again, I think about Big Ma, but I'm figuring she's being watched over now.

◆ ◆

JEROME WILSON's stories have appeared in *Ploughshares* and *The Final Word*; and his work is anthologized in *You Have Got To Read This: Contemporary American Writers Introduce Stories That Held Them in Awe*, edited by Ron Hansen and Jim Shepard (New York: Harper Collins, 1994). Wilson is a native of Memphis and is employed at the University of Tennessee Health Sciences Library there.

WILMER HASTINGS MILLS

A Dirge for Leaving

The Plow-man homeward plods his weary Way,
And leaves the World to Darkness, and to me.
—Thomas Gray

I.

In Tennessee the first light snows will soon
Begin to fall, filling the spider webs
Like chalices of ice above the ground,
Above the garden there I've kept since June,
And where, tomorrow, when the daylight ebbs,
I'll be again, inside the screen door's sound,
Far from my family's home.

Bed rows turned
In the tiller's wake, sod of family plots,
They draw me here, steam in the compost heap,
Flat lands full of water, running churned
And turgid where old things erode and rot.

Home for the living. Home for the dead, laid deep.

II.

Wind motion bends the heart of living wood.
Brown water winds in the roots of graveyard trees
Where we have spent the morning, small price to pay
For old respect, for long-misunderstood,
Dead secrets in the soil of cemeteries—
This place where twenty years ago, they say

Great uncles disinterred a Spanish man
Whose glass-front coffin left him perfectly
Preserved, his eighteenth-century coat, his hair,
The features of his face—a long death span
Cut short.
                    But in the air his body instantly
Caved in like angel food against a baker's prayer.

III.

The day has passed. Our pressed white shirts
Have wrinkled in the arms.
                                        I can't protect
Myself from death this way. The barns are full
Of hay. Last summer's fences have been checked
Around the lot where heifers pawed the dirt's
Weak hold from posts and wire, learning the pull
Of thirst for milk and teat.
                                        Their muddy tracks
Will dry and crumble when the harrow spreads
Them smooth and ready for the winter rye.

Cow skulls dissolve in the tree line's shade. Rib racks
Collapse around the scattered spines and shreds
Of hide and hair, deaf to the heifer's cry.

IV.

Inside the house, I watch the darkened wall
At sundown where the kitchen window's light
Falls into blocks and lines across the floor.

Bright filaments of dust well up, then fall
Below the shadowed sill, until twilight
Consumes the room like water on a shore.

All afternoon the hay barn's poisoned rats
Crawled from the loft in search of water, thirst
For the ditch bank mud, for wet sewer lines,
Their black eyes beading like blood drops to burst
Into the blind, diurnal dreams of cats
Before they died beneath blackberry vines.

V.

Coyotes find the rats. They freeze and stare
Into our flashlight beams. Hunger. Death's bait.

The house falls still around me, teaching
Silence, grief in the eyes, a sweet despair
Like vigils when the old lie cold and straight.

I've felt the chill that stiffens them. Dying,
My great grandmother's breath in the master bed
Blew weak where I was told to kiss her lips
Before they whitened, her eyes dimmed for palls.

I see them in nightmares, the eyes, like heads
On fishing lures caught staring blind.

Love slips,
Tightens on the weakened test, then fails.

My Mother's Loom

I used to watch her wrapping yards of thread
Around my sister's arms, my mother's hands,
Turning over and over themselves like somersaults.
Her harnessed loom held webs of unmade cloth
That opened when she pressed the weaving pedals
And closed when the shuttle slid from end to end.

I often sat beside the dangling ends
And ran my fingers over the tightened threads
Like strumming a silent harp whose pedals
Only kept a foot-tap rhythm with my hands.
My mother watched me while she rolled her cloth
In front of her, sweat from her hands salting

The shuttle wood while I did somersaults
Around her loom, played with the tangled ends,
And poked my face in the raveled gauze of cloth.
I remember the cardiac clatter of harnessed thread.
I remember going to sleep and waking up, her hands
Still throwing the shuttle, her feet still on the pedals.

But that was years ago when I heard pedals
Crushing through cloth like the sound of ice cream salt.
My mother does not weave anymore. Her hands

Don't have to mend her work's unraveled ends.
So when she sees me now she cuts loose threads
From my shirts and I can't help but think of cloth

She used to weave as if she thought to clothe
Her children with fabric soft as flower petals.
It's like a childhood dream, a frazzled thread
Of memory, learning the trick of somersaults
Where all I did was turn end over end
Beneath the sound of curious hands

Being pressed against the movement of my hands.
It seems so far away, my mother's cloth,
My boyhood games beneath her hanging ends,
When today I see her loom in the house, its pedals
And harnesses, suffering the slow assault
Of dust, its shuttle empty of thread.

I put my feet to the pedals, my hands on the frame
And I can almost smell the salt in the cloth,
Feel the ends of thread on my face.

• •

WILMER HASTINGS MILLS is a graduate of the University of the South and, in 1990, received a Bucknell University fellowship for advanced study. He has served for several years on the staff of the Sewanee Writers' Conference.

REGINA WILKINS

WHERE IS WHEN

When light drinks darkness we get
a sun. In Bohinj, Slovenia, Lucian
pulls me with six year old hands
to the waterfall. When water drowns the sun
we get darkness. He smiles rabbits and sneakers
and bright candles. When darkness
shatters the sun we get stars. Robert's
treehouse is high above the fears flapping
on the clothesline. Water is a cognate
in seven languages. Robert is nine
and wants to fly like Batman.
The ice of a comet is thirst flying fast.
There are silk fish suspended from the mall ceiling.
Robert says, "From above they're floating
but from below they're flying."
Rain on a tin roof in Georgia could be
sniper fire in Karlovac, Croatia.
Lucian asks me if I have seen his mother in America.
When a charred house is touched by rain it hisses.
The water at Bohinj falls straighter than
the bombs sixty miles away. When a soul picks stars

like blueberries its fingertips get burned.
On his bike, Robert follows darkness into the mouth of the sun.
When Lucian says water he is speaking to me.

Today, You Ask

If I had known you would ask
about today, I would have scooped
a pint of Arkansas sky into a jar
and opened it against your neck.
I would have photographed the hitcher
on the side of the road, the blackbirds
of his hair scattering up, then
settling to his head again as trucks
passed. I would have saved the sketch
of my sister and me he drew
from the back seat, sparing myself
the guilt of not feeling guilty
when I tossed it into the wake of
the car's exhaust. I would have put
a handful of dirt into the pocket
of my black dress, dirt turned today
for my grandfather. I would have
brought it for you, this tired soil
of my long ago home, and rubbed its smell
across your lips. And though I am no more
prepared to describe tonight, I could
try to tell you anyway, how the occasional
headlights of another car whiten
my sister's hands on the steering wheel.

I could tell you about the coolness
of glass against my face, and about
the pale ghostbirds swooping in, then
out of the billboard light. Now I
will show you the dance of a rusty
chain as it dangles from some pickup,
and I will hold your hands against
the white heat of the sparks
that light the silent highway.

◆ ◆

REGINA WILKINS, a native of Memphis who has been actively involved in Bosnian peace efforts, has published poems in such journals as *Prairie Schooner* and *Poetry Miscellany*. She has taught at the Chattanooga Riverquest program for high school students, is on the staff of *Mala Revija*, and is editing a chapbook by the Slovene poet Istok Osojnik.